Wilmington, North Carolina, to 1861

Wilmington, North Carolina, to 1861

by ALAN D. WATSON

McFarland & Company, Inc., Publishers
Jefferson, North Carolina, and London

Library of Congress Cataloguing-in-Publication Data

Watson, Alan D., 1942–
    Wilmington, North Carolina, to 1861 / by Alan D. Watson.
       p.   cm.
    Includes bibliographical references and index.

    ISBN 0-7864-1427-8 (softcover : 50# alkaline paper) ∞

    1. Wilmington (N.C.) — History — 18th century.
    2. Wilmington (N.C.) — History — 19th century.   I. Title.
F264.W7 W38   2003
975.6'2702 — dc21   2002151780

British Library cataloguing data are available

©2003 Alan D. Watson. All rights reserved

No part of this book may be reproduced or transmitted in any form or by any means, electronic or mechanical, including photocopying or recording, or by any information storage and retrieval system, without permission in writing from the publisher.

Manufactured in the United States of America

On the cover: Engraving of the port of Wilmington, circa 1860 (courtesy North Carolina Office of Archives and History, Raleigh)

McFarland & Company, Inc., Publishers
  Box 611, Jefferson, North Carolina 28640
  www.mcfarlandpub.com

Acknowledgments

Over the years the historian accumulates a myriad of professional debts—to archivists, editors, research librarians, and academic associates, among others—and it would be impossible to mention all. In this present effort I would like to thank Chris Fonvielle for his sound advice, frequently shared knowledge, and always pleasant and informative conversation. I extend especial gratitude to Beverly Tetterton, director, Local History Room, New Hanover County Public Library, Wilmington, who read the entire manuscript and provided indispensable aid in locating illustrations. Indeed, through the years she has helped this author incalculably in many ways in his attempt to understand the history of the southeastern region of North Carolina. Of course, any errors of omission and commission, and all opinions expressed in this work, remain the sole responsibility of the author.

The author would also like to extend his gratitude to the following for permission to use previously published material: University of South Carolina Press for excerpts from *Wilmington: Port of North Carolina* (Columbia, S.C., 1992); Office of Archives and History, Department of Cultural Resources, Raleigh, North Carolina, for excerpts from Alan D. Watson, "The Committees of Safety and the Coming of the American Revolution, 1774–1776," *North Carolina Historical Review* 73 (1996): 131–155; Lower Cape Fear Historical Society for excerpts from Alan D. Watson, "The Town Fathers of Early Wilmington, 1743–1775," Lower Cape Fear Historical Society *Bulletin* 24 (October 1980); "Wilmington: A Town Born of Conflict, Confusion, and Collusion," Lower Cape Fear Historical Society *Bulletin* 31 (February, May 1988); Nancy Beeler and Rush Beeler, for excerpts from *Wilmington Town Minutes, 1847–1855* (Wilmington, 1997). The author also acknowledges his appreciation to the Office of Archives and the New Hanover County Public Library for permission to use various illustrations.

Contents

Acknowledgments	v
Preface	1

I. The Formative Years, to 1789

1. The Emergence of a Town	5
2. Early American Life	28
3. A Developing Economy	51
4. Colonial Politics	71

II. The Maturing Years, 1789–1861

5. The Growth of a Town	101
6. The African American Experience	125
7. Fellowship, Fraternity, Association	142
8. Education, Enlightenment, and Culture	162
9. Urban Government	185
10. An Expanding Economy	199
11. Antebellum Politics	227

Epilogue	245
Notes	249
Bibliography	283
Index	293

Preface

A decade ago, with *Wilmington: Port of North Carolina* (Columbia, S.C.: University of South Carolina Press, 1992), I sought to trace the economic history of North Carolina's principal port over its more than two-hundred-and fifty-year lifetime. In the process the richness of the town's past seemed to demand a more thorough investigation of its history. Encouraged by my own interest in early American history, including that of Wilmington and the Lower Cape Fear region of North Carolina, and also by the observation of Professor Chris Fonvielle, Jr., my colleague in the Department of History, University of North Carolina at Wilmington, that Wilmington lacked an adequate history, I decided to attempt a more comprehensive study of Wilmington, at least from its inception to the Civil War.

Wilmington, North Carolina, to 1861 presents an account of the founding and development of North Carolina's largest town and principal seaport on the eve of the Civil War. Part I traces Wilmington's history from the incorporation of the town in 1739–40 to 1789, when North Carolina joined the newly-formed United States of America. That section focuses on the confused and disputed origin of Wilmington, life in a colonial urban setting, the growing importance of the port, and town governance. Part II expands upon the preceding topics for the years from 1789 to 1861. In addition to pursuing the economic development of the port and the difficulties of governing an ever-growing community, emphasis has been placed on the large African American population, a wide variety of social and cultural activities in the town, and politics and political parties in Wilmington.

Wilmington, North Carolina, to 1861 makes no claim to comprehensiveness. Rather, it tries to examine some of the more salient aspects of Wilmington's past, occasionally in some detail, in hopes of providing an overview of the history of North Carolina's largest urban area and port before the Civil War. In a state in which the urban population was minuscule and maritime commerce severely limited, Wilmington proved exceptional. And it was the water, more particularly the Cape Fear River, that accounted for its appearance and its prominence. Shipping was the mainstay of the local economy with the port a window to the world that reflected a diverse and ever-changing populace. Wilmington indeed was a singular place in colonial and antebellum North Carolina.

I.
The Formative Years, to 1789

1

The Emergence of a Town

Two and a half centuries ago the English American colonies on the North Atlantic coast presented a rural, almost idyllic scene. Still, from the outset urbanization began to intrude on the pastoral landscape. The large northern centers of Philadelphia, New York, Boston, Newport, and, in the south, Charles Town, South Carolina, all boasted ten thousand or more residents by the beginning of the American Revolution. Providence, Rhode Island; Norwich, New London, and New Haven, Connecticut; Baltimore, Maryland; and Norfolk, Virginia, constituted a second tier of urban communities containing four to eight thousand inhabitants. And countless smaller towns and villages, including Wilmington, North Carolina, appeared throughout the provinces. As governmental, economic, and cultural centers, the urban entities exercised an inordinate influence upon the development of early America.[1]

Of the thirteen colonies, North Carolina was one of the most rural. Granted by Charles II of England in 1663 to eight English gentlemen, the Lords Proprietors, the area that became North Carolina was one of the few provinces that was not settled about a town. From Jamestown, Virginia, and Charles Town, South Carolina, to Plymouth, Providence, New Haven, and others in the north, the English colonies radiated from urban areas. North Carolina, on the other hand, simply appeared as an extension of the southeastern frontier of Virginia in the late 1650s. Residents in the Albemarle, much like Virginia from whence they came, had little need of towns, given the excellent sound and riverine systems along which they settled.

However, the first English attempt to settle the Lower Cape Fear, a joint venture by New Englanders and Barbadians in 1664, revolved about the village of Charles Town, the first of that name in the Carolinas. Located on the west bank of the Cape Fear River at the junction of Town Creek, about twenty miles upstream from the Atlantic Ocean, Charles Town was meant to serve as a trade center for those who lived in the homes scattered some sixty miles along the banks of the river. But the effort proved futile. Division among the whites, opposition by Indians, inadequate support by the Proprietors, and lack of supplies doomed the Cape Fear settlement, which was abandoned in 1667.[2]

The Proprietors nonetheless acutely felt the need for towns in their overseas landholdings, which included present South Carolina. Charles Town, South Carolina, provided the nucleus for the settlement of that colony in 1670. And in 1676 the Proprietors informed the Albemarle inhabitants in North Carolina of the need to establish commercial entrepôts. In addition to fostering trade, the Proprietors deemed towns desirable for promoting defense (mainly against Indians and Spanish at that time), and for contributing to the cultural advancement of the settlers.[3]

Nevertheless, the first town in North Carolina did not appear until the beginning of the eighteenth century. Bath Town was incorporated in 1705–6, almost fifty years after the permanent settlement of North Carolina. It was followed by New Bern, sponsored by Baron Christoph von Graffenried in 1710. Desolated by the Tuscarora War, New Bern began a halting revival in the 1720s. Edenton and Beaufort, incorporated in 1722 and 1723 respectively, but settled several years before those dates, comprised the remaining towns that were established during the first quarter of the eighteenth century.[4]

While urbanization gained a tardy and tenuous foothold in the Albemarle, Pamlico, and Neuse regions of North Carolina, the permanent settlement of the Lower Cape Fear, like the earlier effort in the 1660s, witnessed the immediate appearance of a trade center—Brunswick Town. Peopling the Lower Cape Fear proceeded principally from the efforts of Maurice Moore and George Burrington. Moore, a South Carolinian who came into North Carolina during the Tuscarora Indian War, remained in the northern province after the conflict. He became active in North Carolina politics and by marriage allied himself with prominent Albemarle families. Doubtlessly he turned Burrington's attention to the southeast.[5]

Burrington, the proprietary governor of North Carolina in 1724–1725, and later the first royal governor after the English crown purchased the Carolinas from the Proprietors in 1729, sought to expand the trade and enhance the prosperity of his colony by opening the Cape Fear. In so doing he defied both the Proprietors and the government of South Carolina. The former had previously proscribed any land grants by the governor; the latter claimed the land to the west bank of the Cape Fear River. Burrington paid no heed to South Carolina. The governor made several

1—The Emergence of a Town

trips to the Cape Fear and spent the winter of 1724–5 in the area. He described his efforts to the Board of Trade in 1725:

> Perfecting the settlement on Cape Fear River cost me a great sum of money, and infinite trouble. I endured the first winter I went there, all the hardships could happen to a man destitute of a house to live in, that was above a hundred miles from a Neighbour in a pathless Country and was obliged to have all Provisions brought by sea at great charges.... I discovered, and made known ... the Channells of Cape Fear River ... before unused and unknown ... and never obtained any other reward or gratification, but the thanks of two Assemblys in this Country.

Before he left office in July 1725, replaced by Sir Richard Everard, Burrington issued land patents (an intermediate step in the land grant process) for land in the Cape Fear to several individuals, including Maurice Moore, his brother Roger Moore of South Carolina, and North Carolinians Eleazar Allen and John Porter, relatives of the Moores by marriage.[6]

The permanent settlement of the Lower Cape Fear occurred in 1726–1727 when North and South Carolinians began to filter into the area. Burrington and Maurice Moore spearheaded the North Carolina movement. From the south, Roger Moore, a resident of St. James Goose Creek Parish, led the South Carolina exodus. Many of those who followed Roger Moore to the Cape Fear were leading citizens of Prince George Winyaw Parish seeking sanctuary from political turmoil and economic distress. Together, the Moores and Burrington, who had rewarded himself for his endeavors by means of land grants, claimed more than twenty thousand acres of land in the region.[7]

Richard Everard, who succeeded Burrington as proprietory governor, continued to make land grants in the Cape Fear through so-called "blank patents," which were grants of questionable validity. Before he left office, Everard had disposed of more than a hundred thousand acres to a small group of individuals related by blood or marriage. Hence the grantees became known as the "Family." In addition to Maurice and Roger Moore, Allen, and Porter, Edward Moseley, John Baptista Ashe, Samuel and John Swann, Jehu Davis, John Grange, Edward Hyrne, Thomas Jones, Edward Smith, and Mosely Vail were the principal beneficiaries of the governor's largesse.[8]

The earliest known resident of the Lower Cape Fear was Maurice Moore, whose aid was enlisted by the South Carolina legislature in April 1726 to recover some stolen property from a band of Tuscarora Indians thought to be passing through the area. Presumably Moore was not alone. Two months later he sold the first lot in Brunswick Town to Cornelius Harnett the Elder, father of the famous Revolutionary War patriot of the same name. Harnett, along with Burrington, had fled to the Cape Fear to escape arrest in the Albemarle where they had been indicted for riotous assault. The following year sufficient traffic developed in the Brunswick Town area to justify a ferry operated by Harnett from the village across the Cape Fear River. And in December 1728 the Reverend John Lapierre described the settlement as a "dispersed multitude of People residing up and down Cape Fear."[9]

As the population of the Lower Cape Fear increased, the General Assembly responded by erecting New Hanover Precinct (later called County) in 1729 and designating Brunswick Town as the seat of the precinct. The statute required all precinct elections to be held in the town, and directed the justices of the peace of the precinct, sitting as the precinct court, to levy a tax to build a courthouse and jail in Brunswick Town. Still, the town developed slowly. A visitor in 1731 described it as a "poor, hungry, unprovided Place, consisting of not above 10 or 12 scattering mean Houses, hardly worth the name of a Village." He did admit, however, that it was "likely to be a Place of [substantial] Trade." About the same time, John Brickell predicted that Brunswick Town "no doubt will be very considerable in a short time...."[10]

Boding ill for the future of Brunswick Town, however, was the return of George Burrington in 1731 as the first royal governor of North Carolina. The quarrelsome and almost paranoid executive turned upon his former associates, the Family. Particular objects of Burrington's wrath were Ashe, Moseley, Porter, and Samuel Swann, whom the governor felt had either mismanaged his estate or embezzled his property while Burrington had been in England. The result was factionalized politics in the Cape Fear. Burrington, his friends, and the royal prerogative were pitted against the Family, with their immense prestige, power, and property holdings.[11]

The rift between Burrington and the Family produced the first suggestion for the town later called Wilmington. The governor and his opponents quarreled over the "blank patents" or excessive (and perhaps illegal) land grants that Burrington thought retarded the development of the Lower Cape Fear. They also differed over the payment of quitrents or royal land taxes. Not only did the governor quickly challenge the hegemony of the Family on those issues, but in the first session of the General Assembly following his arrival in 1731 he called for legislation to create a town along the Cape Fear River. The response from the General Assembly was a message, signed by Edward Moseley, speaker of the lower house, stating that, "there is a Town already Established on the Cape Fear River called Brunswick."[12]

Replacing Burrington as royal governor was Gabriel Johnston, who

1—The Emergence of a Town

arrived in North Carolina late in 1734. He immediately found himself at loggerheads with the Family. Land and land taxes were the crux of their differences, for land, as the principal economic asset of the times, was always a critical (and divisive) issue for both the crown and the colonists. Eschewing the Family and their Brunswick Town environs, Johnston bought land adjoining a proposed new community close to the forks of Cape Fear River, as well as lots within the development. The stage was set for a contest of wills over the future urban center of the Cape Fear.[13]

Despite the rebuff to Burrington, the incipient town of Wilmington emerged in 1733 from land owned by John Watson. He, with James Wimble, Michael Higgins, and Joshua Grainger, Sr., planned a town on the east bank of the Cape Fear River just below the confluence of the Northeast and Northwest branches. Watson received a royal warrant for 640 acres at that site, and his name appeared at that point on a map drawn by Edward Moseley and dated 1733. However, on April 16 of that year, James Wimble, who had acquired three hundred acres of the Watson tract, produced another map of North Carolina which substituted "New Carthage town" for that of "Watson."[14]

Wimble, an enterprising Englishman, no doubt was the prime instigator of the new town. Born in Sussex in 1696 and trained as a mariner, Wimble embarked on a career in New World commerce in 1718 when he sailed to the Bahamas. Three years later he was trading with North Carolina and soon purchased land along the Albemarle Sound. During the mid–1720s he had established a home, family, and business in Boston, Massachusetts, but found the West Indies trade difficult to conduct from that northern port. In 1731 Wimble turned his attention to the Cape Fear. As a seaman he recognized the need for a more adequate mapping of North Carolina's southerly coast; as an entrepreneur he saw the potential of the expanding Cape Fear region.[15]

Joining Watson and Wimble in the enterprise were Michael Higgins and Joshua Grainger, Sr. Soon after Wimble's purchase, Watson sold fifty acres north of and adjoining Wimble's land to Higgins, listed as a merchant and tavernkeeper, and to Grainger, a merchant. In 1733 William Gray surveyed the "intended town." From 1734 to 1736 it was called "New Liverpool" in the county deeds, though by March 1735, in legislation and in gubernatorial directives, it was referred to as "New Town" or "Newton." During 1736, as early as May, "Newton" began to replace "New Liverpool" in the local records; by the final months (October–December) of that year, "Newton" was used almost exclusively. That term received general approbation in 1737 from a new plan "of the town of Newton formerly called New Liverpoole," which was prepared from a survey by Matthew Higginbotham that superseded the work of Gray in 1733.[16]

The Newton site encompassed some three hundred acres, extending from present Campbell Street on the north to Wooster Street on the south, and from the river eastward to a line parallel to and 198 feet, or 12 poles, west of present Fifth Street. The 198-foot strip was unmarked; the remainder of the town was divided into blocks separated by streets. The blocks were subdivided into half-acre lots, 66 feet (or four poles) wide and 360 feet deep, except for the riverfront property, which lots were 66 feet wide and extended from Front Street to the low water mark of the river. Each block contained from five to six lots. Market Street, running east from the river, was the principal thoroughfare of the town. It, like Third Street, which crossed Market at right angles, was 99 feet (or six poles) wide. All other streets, which ran parallel either to Market or to Third, were 66 feet, or four poles, wide.[17]

In its design, Newton, the forefunner of Wilmington, greatly resembled Philadelphia, the capital town of Pennsylvania. Both the placement and the names of the streets in Newton and Philadelphia bore similarity. Numbered streets, beginning with Front and continuing with Second, ran in one direction and were intersected by cross streets such as Walnut, Chestnut, Dock, and Market that were common to both towns. In fact, a visitor to Wilmington in 1757 observed that, "the Regularity of the Streets … [is] Equal to those of Philadelphia."[18]

Although a traveler who stopped at the town in 1734 could find no better accommodations than a "small hut," New Liverpool, or Newton, quickly developed into a thriving little trading community. To encourage the growth of the town and prevent the engrossment of land, a few of the original deeds for the sale of lots required the purchasers to build a "habitable" house, at least 12 by 16 feet in size, within a year in order to secure title to their property. Numerous sales of lots, either for permanent residents or for speculation, attested to the promise of the town. By 1737 Newton had expanded to the point that the New Hanover County court appointed a constable for the town. The growing population also necessitated a public ferry across the river at Newton.[19]

The inhabitants of Newton (New Liverpool) and its vicinity in 1735 requested that the governor and council formally recognize the town, but the executive order to that effect was never realized. At the time, the lower house of the General Assembly contested the right of the executive to create precincts (counties) solely by the royal prerogative. By inference, the House of Commons opposed exclusive executive control over the erection of towns as well. Thus the House of Commons ignored the gubernatorial order when it next met, and considered instead legislation to establish "a Town in New Hanover Precinct by the name of Wilmington at a place now called Newton." Final action was not forthcoming, however, for the governor prorogued the legislature in a dispute over a quitrent bill, and the Wilmington legislation received only a first reading. The erection of Wilmington had become enmeshed in the ongoing political controversy between the governor and the House of Commons.[20]

Despite the delayed incorporation of Newton as Wilmington, the legislature and governor showed their support for the village. Quitrent bills considered by the legislature in 1736 and 1739 required payments to be made at Newton, as opposed to Brunswick Town. Governor Johnston likewise advanced the fortunes of Newton, to the detriment of Brunswick Town, by showering the newer village with executive favors. In March 1735, Johnston announced that his council would meet in Newton, where it continued to hold its sessions regularly through 1739. At the same time, Johnston decided to conduct a court of exchequer and a court of oyer and terminer in Newton as well. In 1736 and 1738, the governor held additional courts of oyer and terminer in Newton, and on February 14, 1739/40 ordered biannual meetings of the provincial court of chancery to meet in the town.[21]

A bitter rivalry developed between Newton and Brunswick Town. Although James Murray, the Scot merchant who arrived in the Cape Fear in 1735, determined not to become involved, he could not avoid the complications. He first rented a house from Roger Moore, but "intimacy with some gentlemen [in Newton] was so disagreeable that [Moore] told me to turn out...," wrote Murray. Within a year Murray had bought a house in Newton and became one of the chief proponents of the village, believing that Newton would soon become the principal town on the river, if not the "metropolis of the province...." Exacerbating the rivalry and threatening the foundation of Brunswick Town's existence, its maritime commerce, was Johnston's decision in 1739 to move the collector of customs and deputy naval officer of Port Brunswick from Brunswick Town to Newton. Those who supported Brunswick Town, of course, adamantly objected to Johnston's action.[22]

In its opposition, the Brunswick faction legally and logically had the better of the argument. Not only had Johnston acted arbitrarily in abrogating the decision of the Commissioners of Customs in England to make Brunswick Town the seat of Port Brunswick, but Brunswick Town was the more appropriate location for shipping affairs on the river. Large vessels were impeded in their upriver travel by the "Flats," shoals in the Cape Fear at the mouth of Town Creek about equidistant between Brunswick Town and Newton (Wilmington). Stationing the customs officers in Newton imposed a hardship on captains of deep draft vessels who might not choose to trade in Newton and yet had to go to the town to enter and clear their ships. When Roger Moore called upon James Murray, who had been appointed deputy naval officer by Johnston, to come to Brunswick Town to clear a vessel, Murray firmly refused. He advised Moore to present his case to the Treasury Board in London if he thought that "his Majesties Revenue or the interest of the country is injured" by having the naval officer reside in Newton.[23]

James Murray (1713–1781), plantation owner, merchant, royal officeholder, early resident of Newton, later Wilmington, and developer of the Lower Cape Fear region. Courtesy of the New Hanover County Public Library, Wilmington.

At this juncture Johnston felt more independent of the Family than at any time since his accession to the governorship. He had just secured approval by the General Assembly of quitrent legislation (later annulled by the King in Privy Council) that seemed to settle a longstanding problem of the payment of those taxes and guaranteed the executive an income independent of the provincial legislature. Operating with greater freedom and confidence, Johnston directed his attention to developing a deep water port and "metropolis" at the branches of the Cape Fear. This in turn meant the transformation of Newton into Wilmington.[24]

Having the most immediate impact upon the success of Johnston's scheme, however, was legislation in 1739 that altered the conception of North Carolina's court of oyer and terminer. Before the arrival of Johnston, that court had not met in the southern part of the province. In order to provide relief for the people south of the Neuse region, the General Assembly converted the court of oyer and terminer into a circuit agency of judicature which would convene in the various sections of the colony. The law directed that biannual sessions for the southern district, comprising New Hanover, Onslow, and Bladen counties, would be held in Newton.[25]

Residents of Newton, no doubt with the approval of Johnston, if not at his instigation, began to collect private subscriptions to build a courthouse in their town. At the time, the justices of the New Hanover County court had never acted upon the legislation of 1729 that made Brunswick Town the seat of the county and authorized them to tax the county residents to build a courthouse and jail in the town. After the people of Newton had taken the initiative to construct a courthouse, the county magistrates met in December 1739 to levy a tax for a courthouse-jail complex in Brunswick Town. The four justices sitting on the court—Roger Moore, Nathaniel Rice, William Dry, and Jehu Davis—lived in or near Brunswick Town and opposed the development of Newton.[26]

When the next session of the General Assembly gathered at New Bern in February 1739/40, it received a petition that requested the erection of Newton as the town of Wilmington and the seat of New Hanover County. Drafted by the grand jury of the court of oyer and terminer that had met at Newton in December 1739, the document contained 108 signatures. The petitioners condemned the location of the current county seat (Brunswick Town) as "remote[,] and the River, difficult[,] broad, & dangerous of Access for the Greatest part of the Inhabitants of ... [the] County." Newton, they felt, was more accessible and a more logical choice as a county seat, particularly since the legislature had just decided to hold circuit courts for New Hanover, Bladen, and Onslow counties at that town. Moreover, a courthouse had been built, and the county could be spared the expense of a second structure if the county seat were moved to Newton.[27]

Responding to the petition, the lower house of the General Assembly initiated the legislative proceedings. On February 20, John Montgomery, a representative from Tyrrell County, successfully moved for permission to produce a bill to incorporate Newton as Wilmington. The bill easily moved through the House of Commons, receiving its third and last reading on February 23. While some dissension to the Wilmington bill may have existed in the House of Commons, adamant opposition appeared in the Upper House from the four councillors representing the Family and the economic interest of Brunswick Town—Roger Moore, Eleazar Allen, Nathaniel Rice, and Edward Moseley. (The council, or governor's advisory body, sat as the Upper House of the General Assembly during legislative sessions.)[28]

Johnston, of course, anticipated the opposition and prepared accordingly. Since he could count on the support of only three councillors— William Smith, Robert Halton, and Matthew Rowan—Johnston availed himself of his royal instructions to fill a vacancy on the board. The councillor appointment went to James Murray, close friend, deputy naval officer for Port Brunswick, and Newton merchant. Still, that left Johnston with an evenly divided council, or Upper House, when the council sat as the upper chamber of the legislature. To secure a majority vote on the Wilmington bill, Johnston and the four pro–Wilmington councillors decided that William Smith, the eldest on the council, should be denominated "President" of that group and accorded a second, tie-breaking ballot in case of an even split.[29]

The Johnston faction of the Upper House successfully tested their dubious legislative ploy on February 20, when Smith insisted on a second vote to break a tie over a bill to appoint county treasurers in order to approve that measure. A protest from the Brunswick group followed. They asserted that Smith, the "first Councellor," did not, and should not have the power to cast two votes in the Upper House. It was a practice for which there was no precedent in the American colonies, and one that was "destructive of the rights of the Upper House...."[30]

The same sequence followed the Wilmington bill through its three readings in the Upper House. After the third reading in both legislative chambers on February 23, the measure was sent to the governor, who assented to the bill on February 25, 1739/40. Two days later Johnston prorogued the General Assembly, but not before the Brunswick faction had entered another protest upon the records of the Upper House. They felt that after Brunswick Town had been made the seat of New Hanover County, many people in good faith had purchased lots and improved their property. To divest the town of its privileges seemed unfair. The Wilmington opposition also questioned the propriety of creating a town on private property, a circumstance that obviously redounded to the benefit of a few individuals. The councillors again objected to moving the customs offices and, of course, protested the means by which the Wilmington legislation had been passed—by allowing one councilor to cast two votes.[31]

Wilmington was named for Spencer Compton, earl of Wilmington and Johnston's political patron in England. At age 25, Compton represented the borough of Eye in Parliament, deserting the Tory principles of his family, obtaining the favor of the Whigs, and serving as Speaker of the House of Commons in the 1720s. A favorite of George II upon that monarch's accession to the British throne in 1727, Compton enjoyed numerous royal favors and offices. Wilmington succeeded the illustrious Sir Robert Walpole in 1742 as prime minister of England but died the following year.[32]

Although only four laws had been passed in that rather unproductive legislative session of 1739/40, Johnston had realized a long-standing goal—the incorporation of Wilmington. And the governor envisioned a bright future for the town. In a year or two he hoped to have all public business conducted in Wilmington, though he noted cautiously, "this must be done by Degrees." Eventually Johnston wanted to locate the provincial capital in the town. Meanwhile, the legislature designated Wilmington as the seat of New Hanover County, replacing Brunswick Town. Taxes imposed the preceding December by the New Hanover County court to build a courthouse and jail in Brunswick Town were to be applied toward the construction of those buildings in Wilmington. All county elections, including those for assemblymen and ves-

Spencer Compton, earl of Wilmington (1673?–1743), the political patron of Governor Gabriel Johnston of North Carolina and the second prime minister of England. Courtesy of the North Carolina Office of Archives and History, Raleigh.

trymen, were to be held in Wilmington. In the county court session of June 1740, the New Hanover magistrates decided to use the money already collected to build a jail in Wilmington, and directed the town commissioners to pick a site and erect the structure. Interestingly, six of the justices (Samuel Woodward, John Walker, James Murray, William Faris, Richard Eagles, and John Porter) were Wilmington commissioners, and another, Thomas Clark, was a prominent Wilmington merchant.[33]

In reporting to the Board of Trade in England on the legislative session of February 1739/40, Governor Johnston at first did not mention the conflict over the incorporation of Wilmington, though later he adverted to the "great opposition" to the measure. In any event, the executive of the province justified the incorporation because Wilmington constituted a convenient center for trade and provided a safe harbor for most ships. Furthermore, the town would not only contribute to the improvement of trade in the province but also to "the polishing [of] its Inhabitants."[34]

While Johnston minimized the flap over Wilmington, the Brunswick group did not allow the matter to rest. At a May 1740 council meeting, ironically in Wilmington, the opponents of the Wilmington incorporation formally presented their case to the governor. In a lengthy memorial, Moore, Allen, Rice, and Moseley objected to Johnston's presence in the Upper House during its debates, claiming that the governor inhibited discussion. They contended that Smith, though the eldest councilor, was not entitled to the appellation "President," and certainly was not entitled to cast two votes on the same bill. This was deemed "the greatest Innovation and Infringement that were ever made upon the privileges of all the rest of the Members of His Majestys Council...." The dissident councillors opined that the Wilmington legislation was injurious to the province's trade and contrary to Johnston's instructions from the crown.[35]

The four councillors who favored the establishment of Wilmington responded in vitriolic fashion. Believing that the opposition to Wilmington was designed "to gratify the little spleen [malice] and private Interest of a few people in the neighborhood of Brunswick," Smith, Halton, Rowan, and Murray steadfastly defended the governor without ever meeting directly the arguments of the Brunswick faction. They did correctly note that Wilmington was better located to tap the inland trade. It was a salubrious location, unlike Brunswick Town, where three customs collectors had died since 1734 in what was known to be "the most sickly unhealthy place in the whole Province[.]" The proponents also questioned the right of four men to obstruct the will of the province. Altogether, the pro–Wilmington faction was willing to trust their behavior to the people and to the home government. In fact, the Brunswick councillors appealed their case to England, but to no avail.[36]

The contention and confusion surrounding the incorporation of Wilmington prompted the next session of the General Assembly to reaffirm its previous action. According to legislation passed in August 1740, "several Disputes have arisen about the validity" of the earlier law which "have raised Doubts, and much perplexed the minds of the Inhabitants" of New Hanover County. Thus, the legislature confirmed the incorporation of Newton as Wilmington and sanctioned all actions taken in the interim by the commissioners of Wilmington, by the county court, and by the churchwardens and vestry of St. James Parish. The law reiterated Wilmington's right to borough representation and decreed that county offices, plus those of collector of customs and naval officer for Port Brunswick, should be located in Wilmington. At last Wilmington emerged on a firm legal foundation.[37]

Governing the town of Wilmington were seven commissioners appointed by the Assembly in the incorporating statute. But in the second law in 1740, the legislature introduced a measure of self-government into the proceedings by allowing the residents of Wilmington to meet annually on the first Tuesday in April to elect five men from whom the governor would choose three to serve as commissioners for the following year. The involvement of the governor was unique in the history of North Carolina towns. In no other instance of urban establishment or regulation was the executive of the province granted any voice in the determination of commissioners or their replacements.[38]

Five years after the Assembly incorporated Wilmington, it instituted a radical reform in the determination of the town's leaders by allowing the townspeople to choose their commissioners. Legislation in 1745 authorized the people to meet annually on January 1 to elect five commissioners who would serve during the following year. In case of the refusal of a duly elected commissioner to serve, the remaining commissioners would choose a substitute, but in the case of death or departure from the province, a special election had to be held to determine a successor. By 1754, replacements for any reason were determined solely by the remaining commissioners.[39]

The Assembly in 1745 also determined the qualifications for voting for town commissioners and the eligibility requirements for holding the office of commissioner. For both purposes, the legislature applied the strictures governing the election of a representative from the town to the Assembly. From 1740 to 1745 that had meant that any "tenant of a Brick, Stone, or frame habitable House, of the Length of Twenty Feet, and Sixteen Feet Broad, within the Bounds" of the town who had resided in the house for at least three months prior to the election was eligible to vote and represent the town. After 1745, however, only freeholders who met the above residence qualifications were deemed eligible voters and officeholders, and by 1756 the homes were required to have one or more brick or stone chimneys.[40]

Wilmington was the first, and one of only three towns, in North Carolina in which the people chose their commissioners. Throughout the four decades preceding the Revolution, Wilmingtonians liberally bestowed the office of commissioner upon inhabitants of the town. Fifty-seven individuals were chosen commissioners from 1743 to 1775. Those who held office averaged 2.8 terms. One-third served only one term; nine, five or more terms. Fredrick Gregg and Cornelius Harnett undertook the position seven and nine times respectively between 1750 and 1771.[41]

Election, however, did not automatically mean service. Eleven of the 57 refused office upon election, including John Lyon, who twice renounced the post. Nevertheless, six had previously held office, and three others later were elected and acted as commissioners. The commissioners, as expected, played an active role in local, provincial government. In addition to his duties as commissioner, Daniel Dunbibin was night watchman, clerk, and treasurer of the town. Henry Toomer served as town scavenger and supervised the digging of public wells. William Campbell, Richard Hellier, and Richard Player cared for the town's fire engine. Thomas Finney was a town constable. Altogether, at least one-third of the town fathers held some additional town office before, during, or after their tenure as commissioners.

The commissioners were also prominent in county and provincial affairs. At least 21, or 37 percent, were justices of the peace. Four were sheriffs of New Hanover County, three were coroners and one, James Smallwood, was register and clerk of court. Others served as inspectors of commodities, overseers or commissioners of the roads, and constables. At the provincial level of government, Wilmington commissioners were also conspicuous. Rufus Marsden represented New Hanover County in the General Assembly from 1746 to 1752, and all five of the Wilmington town representatives to the Assembly from 1740 to 1775 were commissioners, including Harnett, who acted in that capacity for more than twenty years prior to the Revolution. John Burgwin, Lewis DeRosset, James Murray, and John Rutherfurd sat on the provincial council, a body of twelve men appointed by the king to advise the governor and act as the upper house of legislature.

In addition to service in the Assembly and Council, Wilmington commissioners occupied other important provincial offices. James Smallwood was the naval officer of Port Brunswick; Burgwin, clerk of the council and clerk of the superior court of the province; Murray, deputy naval officer for the port of Brunswick, clerk of the crown, and secretary of the province; and Rutherfurd, receiver general of the quitrents. Clearly the commissioners comprised an outstanding group of public-spirited, politically-minded, ambitious men.

As would be expected in an urban environment, particularly in a seaport, the majority of the Wilmington commissioners were merchants by profession. Of the 48 commissioners for whom information is available, 29, or 60 percent, styled themselves merchants, a ratio that compared favorably with other eastern seacoast towns in which as many as two-thirds of the town directors engaged in mercantile business. Some in Wilmington (for example, Lewis Henry DeRosset, John Rutherfurd, Robert Schaw, and Cornelius Harnett) were merchant-planters, deriving a substantial part of their income from the soil. Harnett and William Wilkinson, another merchant commissioner, were also partners in a distillery operation in Wilmington.

Another quarter of the commissioners were artisans or craftsmen at one time in their careers. Two tanners, two shipwrights, two carpenters, two coopers, two tailors, and a blacksmith served as town fathers on occasion. As in the case of merchants, it is sometimes difficult to determine their principal occupation. Alexander Ross was both a tailor and merchant; Thomas Cunningham, cooper and planter; and Caleb Mason, carpenter and planter. Thomas James, often referred to as a tailor, owned several plantations and lived at Halton Lodge. Joshua Toomer had been a tanner in St. Andrew's Parish in South Carolina before coming to Wilmington about 1747, operating a tavern, and serving in various civic capacities.

Approximately one-tenth of the Wilmington commissioners were professional men, a slightly higher figure than found in the more northerly towns. Archibald Maclaine represented the bar. Armand John DeRosset, Sr., and his son Moses John, James Mortimer, and Samuel Green were characterized as "Doctor of Physick," "Practioner of Physics," and "Surgeon." Green had begun his practice as an "Apothecary," but later assumed the more prestigious title "Doctor of Physick." Unlike Europe, however, there was little distinction in America between apothecaries, physicians, and surgeons. A man of medicine was a general practitioner in the broadest sense, making his own curatives and treating all illnesses, including those of animals as well as men.

If the commissioners professed religious sentiments, most were at least nominally Anglican in their church affiliation. Twenty-one, or over a third, became vestrymen for St. James Parish; and upon the completion of St. James Church in Wilmington, as many as thirty-seven commissioners, their families, or their estates owned pews in the church. At his death, William Faris left part of his estate to finish the construction of the building. Alexander Duncan bequeathed £400 "toward Adorning [the] Wilmington [St. James] Church...."[42] Evidence indicates that others were Anglican as well. Dr. Samuel Green, neither a vestryman nor a pew owner, was buried in St. James churchyard.

A shared trait more common than their Anglican affiliation was the failure of the commissioners to abide by the ordinances that they had enacted for the benefit of the town. Three-fourths of the town fathers defaulted on their obligation to work on the streets of Wilmington. Lewis Henry DeRosset, Thomas Newton, and Robert Wells failed to pay their taxes; John Ancrum was cited for littering; William Wilkinson was fined "for immoderate riding within the ... Town...." In 1774, upon indictment by the county court, a jury found the town commissioners guilty of "Neglect of duty," probably for their remissness in repairing the courthouse.⁴³ As in the case of most towns in America, Wilmington was not an autonomous enclave, and was subject to the jurisdiction of county as well as provincial authority.

Colonial Americans often patterned municipal governance on the English model, the corporation or borough chartered by the crown, which proved useful for New York, Philadelphia, and Norfolk, among other towns. North Carolina, however, adopted the commission form of governance for its towns, with the exception of a brief interlude before the Revolution. When Governor Arthur Dobbs mistakenly believed that counties and towns could not file for writs of election for members to the General Assembly without corporate charters, in 1760 he proceeded to issue municipal charters to the various counties and to the towns of Wilmington, Edenton, New Bern, and Halifax. New Bern organized and maintained an active borough government for several years. Halifax may have utilized its charter as well, but Edenton probably never implemented its corporate charter.⁴⁴

Wilmington's borough charter of 1760 (supplanted by a second charter in 1763, which made no substantive changes) provided for a government consisting of eleven aldermen, a mayor chosen from the board of aldermen, and a recorder. The freeholders of the town comprised a common council, which made the bylaws of the borough. Aldermen held office during good behavior; from its members the common council filled vacancies on the board of aldermen. The charter conveyed the traditional privileges of an English borough, including the right to hold markets (two weekly), fairs (three annually), a mayor's court, and a court of pie powder. The bounds of the borough included Eagles Island in the Cape Fear River west of Wilmington, and the area within two and a half miles of the courthouse in every other direction. The borough charter conferred upon the corporation a limited power to impose fines and levy taxes.⁴⁵

Wilmingtonians instituted borough government in March 1760, but it ran concurrently with the commission for four years, and evidenced little activity until the conferral of the second charter in 1763. At that point an energized mayor, aldermen, recorder, and common council adopted procedures for their meetings and passed a number of borough ordinances that dealt extensively with the regulation of the market, particularly the sale of meat and the assize of bread. The ordinances also addressed the threat of fire, the activity of slaves, and the threat of roaming livestock, all of which were matters that had been considered by the commissioners. Borough government continued at least through 1766, and gave way altogether to a renewed commission by 1768.⁴⁶

Yet the townspeople of Wilmington only formally surrendered their charter to Governor Josiah Martin in 1773, when they voiced their hope that "His Majesty may grant us another Charter of Incorporation free from the defects and inconveniences" of the present document. The principal objections to the charter included vague borough boundaries, an inordinately large number of aldermen relative to the number of town residents, and the requirement that all town residents meet periodically as a common council to enact ordinances and bylaws, which inconvenienced "industrious Tradesmen." The petitioners suggested delineating the bounds of the borough more carefully, reducing the number of aldermen, and electing a common council annually so that the people could "take the Burthen [of governing] alternately." Wilmington's citizens apparently favored a borough government that included features of the commission.[47]

Together with the borough authorities, the Wilmington town commissioners faced myriad responsibilities in attempting to govern their small but growing municipality. As the seat of New Hanover County, Wilmington was the site of the county courthouse and jail, but the jurisdiction of that complex fell to the New Hanover County court, comprised of the justices of the peace or magistrates. A temporary courthouse had been erected in New Town by 1736, a factor explaining the decision of the legislature to relocate the county seat in Wilmington in 1739–40 when erecting the town of Wilmington. The incorporating statute provided for the imposition of a tax to complete the courthouse. Finished by June 1740, and located at the intersection of Front and Market streets, the courthouse was utilized for meetings of the county court, public gatherings, and the imprisonment of lawbreakers until the construction of a jail. In 1764 the county court ordered the courthouse placed on brick pillars, and directed the construction of a belfry in which to place the town bell, work that apparently was finished by 1768.[48]

Although land for a jail was purchased in 1744, the first prison was not finished until 1749. Sited on Market near the corner of Third Street, it was eventually accompanied by stocks, pillory, and whipping post. The county employed a jailer in 1764 "to prevent the escaping of prisoners lately happening too often." Four years later the New Hanover County court ordered the sheriff to enclose the jail lot with a fence "for a Garden for the benefit of the prisoners." After the jail "had been set on fire and greatly impair'd, and thereby render'd insufficient for the detention of Felons" in 1772, a temporary structure was built, but many years elapsed before a permanent replacement was erected. Despite legislation calling for the erection of a brick or stone jail and jailer's house, as late as 1788 the town lacked a prison, an encouragement to lawbreakers, who "commit their crimes with greater assurance, from a knowledge, that, should they be apprehended, they will have a better opportunity to make their escape from a guard, than from the confines of a prison."[49]

Among the public structures for which the commissioners assumed jurisdiction were the town market and wharf. The area beneath the courthouse originally served for the purchase and sale of meats and produce. During the 1740s the commissioners apparently erected a separate market building on Market Street between the courthouse and the river. However, in 1763 meats again were sold under the courthouse. A tax was imposed in that year to underwrite the construction of a market house, but as late as 1768 the courthouse still served for marketing. By the late 1780s the commissioners either had made extensive repairs to an existing market house or had ordered the construction of a new one, for in 1788 they numbered and rented the stalls in the market house, and appointed a clerk of the market to receive the rents and enforce market regulations.[50]

The town commissioners encouraged waterborne trade by means of a public dock. In 1749 they ordered the construction of a 26-foot-wide wharf from the river to Front Street at Dock, and three years later another wharf had been built at the foot of Market Street. The commissioners periodically ordered the repair of the structures and the removal of naval stores, lumber, and other materials that obstructed the use of the wharves. They also forbade any "Sea Vessel" and decked ship from using the town wharves, reserving those facilities for small boats, canoes, and rafts, and prohibited even those craft from remaining at the wharves for more than twenty-four hours. Additionally, the commissioners directed the construction of boat slips at the market wharves.[51]

Although Wilmington's incorporation envisioned a carefully designed and platted town, and the "Regularity of the streets" impressed a visitor in 1757, adhering to the plan proved difficult. Three consecutive surveys—the last by Jeremiah Vail in 1743, which was accepted as the official plan of the town in 1745 and 1754, and which (with alterations and allowances for increased size) remains the official plan of the present city of Wilmington—provided a basis for the layout of the town. Creating new streets that were not on the original plat of the town required the approval of the General Assembly, which in 1785 authorized the opening of Surry Street along the river. However, order gave way to irregularity as Wilmingtonians built piazzas, chimneys, cellars, platforms, and other obtrusions that extended into the streets. When the General Assembly authorized the town commissioners to assess ground rents on structures that encroached more than seven feet into the street, no less than 58 structures were subject to penalties, including George Moore's stable, poultry houses, and yard on Chestnut Street; John Burgwin's tar shed in Orange Street; and Mrs. Ann

Jones' platform and steps which, with the house, extended 16 feet into the street.[52]

Wilmington's streets, like those of all but the very largest towns (such as Boston, Philadelphia, and New York), remained unpaved for many years. A visitor in 1775 risked her fine silk shoes as she walked through the streets to a dance. But clearing and maintaining the streets and bridges was not an enviable task in a hilly, sandy area through which several streams passed. However, all taxable male residents of the town might be summoned twice a year (for a total of twelve days) under the direction of overseers appointed by the commissioners to repair the streets—or face a fine of 2s 8d per day for their delinquency. Many, in fact, were negligent in complying with what amounted to forced taxation. In 1754 the town constable collected £12.18.8 in fines from defaulters, though three were excused for the imposition: one had moved from town, another was in jail, and a third had died. In 1769, 63 households or businesses were cited for failing to comply with the work obligation. Often among the defaulters were town commissioners. Given the widespread and growing opposition to working on the streets, the General Assembly in 1771 permitted the commissioners to abandon the work imposition in favor of a tax assessment whose proceeds would be used to hire workers to repair the streets. The following year the commissioners instituted the new approach to street maintenance.[53]

At the same, time the commissioners sought to resolve the problem of the many streams that flowed through the town, interrupting traffic and sometimes posing health hazards by contributing to stagnant pools of water. Wilmingtonians early recognized the need to try to improve drainage. When Richard Hellier deeded a lot on the northeast corner of Front and Dock streets in 1749 to Caleb Mason, Hellier reserved the right "to build a Drain Sink or Gutter under ground with Brick into the Run of Water that runs through the ... Lot...." Generally the commissioners resorted to bridging the watercourses, but in 1772 they decided to substitute arches for the bridges. The arches were brick and timber structures, some measuring two feet wide and six feet high, that were constructed over the streams but below ground level to direct the flow of water to the river. The town hired slaves to undertake much of the work. Construction in downtown Wilmington two centuries later occasionally unearthed the remains of some of those subterranean passages, and their apertures at the river's edge may still be seen.[54]

The regulatory authority of the town commissioners embraced the public market, trash disposal, livestock, and fire prevention. The market often occupied the attention of the commissioners. To avoid forestalling, the commissioners required venders of meat, poultry products, and other fresh provisions to display their produce first in the market place for one or two hours, or until 10:00 A.M., before hawking their goods. To prevent price gouging, the authorities imposed price ceilings on beef and provided for the assize of bread that limited the bakers' profits to 12 percent above the cost of flour. To protect the public health, the commissioners prohibited the sale of "unwholesome or stale Victuals," "Blown meat, Bulls flesh, Murrain Beef, Ram Mutton, or Leprous Swine," and to prevent fraud they assized bread and banned the sale of diluted milk.[55]

Clustering large numbers of people together in a small area contributed to the aggregation of trash and the need for rubbish removal. Not only was the trash an impediment to travel, but it contributed to fire and health hazards. Ordinances compelling residents to remove such encumbrances under threat of fines proved unavailing. Thus, in 1774 the commissioners advertised for a scavenger, or trash collector, a position long used by the larger towns to the north. Henry Toomer accepted the position, followed by William Maxwell, though individuals remained subject to fines for "laying nuisances" on the streets.[56]

The presence of livestock in Wilmington not only served as a reminder of the rural nature of early American towns but also represented a public annoyance and sometimes a physical danger. Goats and hogs often wandered freely through the town, playing havoc with the yards and gardens. Unruly horses posed a threat, as did riders who charged through the streets "immoderately or uncommonly fast." Dogs, the most ubiquitous of the animals, could be bothersome and sometimes deadly. Rabid dogs appeared in the town in 1752, causing the commissioners to order all canines to be penned for a month and to allow anyone to kill any dog running loose in the streets. Although legislation permitted the commissioners to enact ordinances to control livestock and to fine violators, few levies were imposed, and the strictures had little effect.[57]

Among the manifold concerns confronting the commissioners, arguably the most threatening was the prospect of fire in the town. Houses, mostly frame with daub and wooden chimneys, were clustered close together, almost an invitation to devastation, and winds whipping along the waterfront made the situation more precarious. The Great Fire in London was a horror long remembered. More recent was a huge conflagration in Charleston, South Carolina, in 1740 that destroyed 334 shops and warehouses, incurring damages estimated at £200,000 to £250,000. Wilmington experienced a small fire in 1756, and two serious blazes in 1771 and 1786. In January 1771 a fire broke out at Capt. Oldfield's store along the dock. It destroyed fifteen houses in the surrounding block and consumed the sails and rigging of two Rhode Island schooners that were tied up in port. An easterly wind and brick buildings blocking the path of the fire saved the town from more extensive damage. The effect of the blaze of 1786 was more devastating, for a traveler recorded in his diary: "The late fire has entirely destroyed the beauty of Wilmington, if it ever possessed any."[58]

When the town commissioners first undertook to protect Wilmington from the threat of fire, they concentrated on chimneys. Low chimneys constituted a danger because sparks could more easily fall on roofs. In 1749 the town commissioners required all residents to raise their chimneys to a height at least three feet above the ridges of their roofs. Five years later the General Assembly permitted the commissioners to order residents to elevate chimneys to a height of four feet above the pitch of the roof. Inasmuch as most fires in colonial towns resulted from sooty chimneys, the commissioners in 1752 passed an ordinance which placed a fine on every person whose chimney caught fire. Most offenders meekly accepted their punishments. James Arlow, constable and tavern keeper, even reported that his own chimney had blazed. Perhaps he represented the public-spirited citizen; or perhaps he cunningly reduced his fine because half of the money went to the town and half went to the informer. Since clogged chimneys were the most common cause of fires, the commissioners in 1754 ordered residents to sweep their chimneys every fourteen days. A chimney sweep would have proved beneficial, but an attempt by the town to hire a sweep was unsuccessful.[59]

Fire prevention was not sufficient, however. Positive efforts were needed, for even the best preventative measures could not ensure civic safety. Wilmington instituted its fire-fighting program in 1750 when a town tax was levied to raise money to purchase fire ladders and buckets. Too often residents used the ladders for private purposes. (They also used the town's wheelbarrows with the same disregard for public property.) Eventually, ordinances commanded every homeowner to furnish one or two leather fire buckets, depending upon the number of chimneys in the house. The buckets were marked with the names or initials of the owners in order that they could be returned to the proper person after a fire. The ordinances were often reiterated, for Wilmingtonians showed a reluctance to comply with the law. An obvious deterrent to the acquisition of fire buckets was their expense, probably 12s to 14s, a considerable sum of money, perhaps equal to a year's county and provincial taxes.[60]

The premier instrument in Wilmington's fire-fighting arsenal was the water engine or fire engine. Wilmington was the first town in the province to acquire an engine. Legislation in 1745 permitted the commissioners to levy a tax for that purpose but it was not until 1754 that the General Assembly mandated an ad valorem property tax on houses in Wilmington to raise the funds needed to buy an engine. Benjamin Heron, who had served in the British navy before settling in North Carolina, agreed to purchase the engine in London, which was shipped to Charleston, South Carolina, and then to Wilmington. Legislation by the General Assembly in 1767 noted that the engine was in a state of disrepair, and directed the town commissioners to see that it was mended and operated monthly. The law also ordered the commissioners to sink two wells near the courthouse in order that water might be readily obtained in case of a fire. Within a year the wells were dug. In 1772 the commissioners decided to purchase a second engine, this time in America (probably Philadelphia), as American engines by that time could rival the expensive English machines in quality. Throughout the 1770s and 1780s Wilmingtonians maintained their fire engines, but they proved unable to combat the periodic conflagrations that beset the town, particularly the ones in 1771 and 1786.[61]

Enforcing the numerous local ordinances, as well as confronting exigencies such as fires and contending with the seafaring population that frequented the port, presented the town commissioners with the constant challenge of law enforcement. Provincial legislation authorized the commissioners to appoint guards or watches "to be ready on all Occasions of Riot and Disturbance," and the town fathers utilized that power in 1756 to prevent looting after a fire. The commissioners relied principally upon constables appointed for the town by the New Hanover County court to apprehend violators of town ordinances. Statutes particularly enjoined constables to walk the streets on Sunday during church hours to prevent disturbances to worshippers. Transgressions of the ordinances or laws usually incurred fines (and whippings for slaves); the jail, if available, was undependable, and labor was too valuable to lose for extended periods of time. However, the county maintained stocks, pillory, and whipping post in the vicinity of the jail, and in 1774 the town commissioners ordered the construction of a ducking stool, designed usually for the punishment of unruly women.[62]

Not until 1745 did the General Assembly confer the power to tax upon the commissioners, and such impositions required the approval of the majority of the town residents (later the majority of those present at the meeting at which taxes were determined). In 1756 the legislature entrusted the commissioners solely with the right of taxation. Taxes, imposed on white males 16 years of age and older, and blacks 12 years of age and older, rose steadily, from £0.1.6 in 1750 to £0.13.4 in 1772. Much of the money underwrote the purchase of fire-fighting equipment, though funds were needed to pay people to clean the courthouse and to ring the market and fire bell, to obtain a standard of weights and measures, and to meet other contingencies. Fines for violating various orders of the commissioners supplemented tax revenues. Taxes and fines were collected by the town constable. On occasion, the temptation was too great for the constables; they sometimes absconded with the public funds.[63]

Although municipal government in Wilmington differed from the pattern followed by larger early American towns—Boston, Newport, Rhode Island, New York, Philadelphia, and Charleston, South Carolina— the function and purpose of governance were similar. Maintenance of public structures, facilitation of trade, regulation of the public market, control of consumer products, maintenance of streets, prevention of fire, and promotion of the general welfare were hallmarks of urban governments everywhere. North Carolina, for the most part, rejected the corporation form of government that was popular in other colonies, but under Wilmington's borough or corporate government of 1760 to 1766 occurred some of the most impressive achievements of regulation and consumer protection in the town in the eighteenth century.[64] Other than the brief anomaly of borough supervision, colonial and state legislation determined the framework of Wilmington's municipal government, and legislators often prodded the town commissioners into action.

2

Early American Life

Originating as a port along the Cape Fear River, and quickly becoming a center of commerce, Newton, subsequently Wilmington, attracted a diverse population. Some came from the Albemarle and Pamlico regions of North Carolina. Others arrived from neighboring Virginia and Charleston, South Carolina. Most immigrated from the northern colonies, the West Indies, and the British Isles. They represented Boston, New York, and Philadelphia; Jamaica, Antigua, Barbados, and St. Croix; London, Liverpool, Somersetshire, Sussex, and Yorkshire; lowland Scotland; Dublin and Ulster. Most, like James Murray of Scotland, sought economic advancement. Some, perhaps, like Joshua Toomer of South Carolina, attempted to escape legal obligations. Whatever their motives, the early immigrants and those who followed made Wilmington the most cosmopolitan town in North Carolina.[1]

At the outset, however, Wilmington and the Lower Cape Fear represented a frontier region in which men predominated. In early American society, Judeo-Christian tradition was reinforced by the institutionalization of English common law, which considered husband and wife as one. And marriage was the expectation of both sexes, though William Hooper remarked of Thomas Hooper when he wed Mary Heron, "he quitted his liberty," but it was "some comfort to have company ... even in the rope." Still, men were not altogether restrained by marital vows. Cornelius Harnett fathered an illegitimate child whose mother in her will beseeched the executors of Harnett's estate to "do justice and be friendly to my unfortunate daughter, as well for her fathers, as her own sake." And some slave owners visited or forced their attentions upon bonded women, the result of which were illegitimate mulatto offspring. Not only were such liaisons reputedly common, but gentlemen in company talked openly of them, and fathers present with their children seemed unperturbed.[2]

Married women often enjoyed little personal freedom, exhibiting "a monastic seclusion and a submission to their husbands," and devoting "themselves completely to the care of home and family," according to one observer. Some prospective wives tried to avoid their impending subservient status by concluding prenuptial agreements to protect their property. Mary DeRosset, with the approval of her future husband, Adam Boyd, transferred certain property to trustees "For the securing and settling [of] a competent maintenance for the said Adam Boyd and Mary DeRosset...." Of course, women hoped for a loving and supportive spouse, but clearly that was not always possible. Since divorce required approval by a statute passed by the colonial legislature, partings were usually less formal. Catherine and Henry McLorinan of Wilmington recorded their separation before the New Hanover County court. Less amicable was the departure of Priscilla Johnson from her husband, Matthew Johnson of Wilmington, who advertised in the local newspaper that she had "absented herself from her ... husband's lawful commands," and informed the public that he abjured legal responsibility for her actions in the future.[3]

Many women, in fact, lived single lives for varying periods of time, usually as widows. Over thirty (whose names appeared in the public records) resided in Wilmington before the Revolution. When the town commissioners levied a tax on houses in 1755 to raise money to purchase a fire engine, eight of the 58 reported structures were owned by women. A petition to the governor in 1773 seeking a new corporate charter for Wilmington contained the signatures of four females. At the approach of the Revolution, the Wilmington women were not unmindful of the momentous struggle that faced the Americans. While the Edenton Tea Party of 1774 is well known, a visitor to Wilmington in 1775 described a protest in which the "Ladies have burnt their tea in solemn procession."[4]

Single women supported themselves variously. Elizabeth Catherine Bridgen DeRosset, widow of wealthy Dr. Armand John DeRosset, Sr., lived independently, owning both a town house and a plantation north of Wilmington, Chinese Temple. Lacking such means, many women were forced to work. Several kept taverns, continuing the occupation of their deceased husbands. Among them was Bridget Arlow, who maintained a public house from the death of her husband James Arlow, probably in 1758, until her death in 1766. A Mrs. Bethelly briefly operated the ferry from Wilmington to Negro Head Point in 1759. The town commissioners employed Margaret Clay from 1750 to 1762 to sweep the courthouse, close the windows and doors, and ring the bell on "necessary occasions." Some women, while married, sought a measure of economic independence. Mary Harnett, wife of the revolutionary Cornelius Harnett, sold minced pies, cheesecakes, and biscuits in Wilmington, and supplied the townspeople with vegetables and melons.[5]

Supplementing the free population of Wilmington were indentured servants and slaves. The institution of indentured servitude encompassed sundry forms of bonded service, but principally consisted of European immigrants who sold their labor by contract or indenture for a stipulated number of years to defray their transportation expenses to America. Most entered into contracts in Europe; some, called redemptioners, in America. The contract or indenture contained the number of years of service for which the servant was obligated. In return for control of the servant's labor, the master or purchaser of the contract agreed to furnish his charge adequate food, clothing, and lodging. At the end of the indenture the master owed "freedom dues" to his servant to assist in the transition to a new life.

The few scattered references to indentured servants in Wilmington indicate a local preference for slavery as the principal form of bonded labor in the town. Among the servants was George Thomas, aged 19 and a native of Wales, whose contract was owned by Harold Blackmore, a sea captain turned merchant. Mary Kelly, a young Irish woman 18 to 20 years of age, helped George Barnes at his tavern. Merchant William Campbell had the misfortune to lose seven servants, who were imported via the brig *Roger* in 1773 but ran away. Their trades included those of whitesmith, tailor, cabinet maker, bricklayer, and farmer. All were in their twenties. The Wilmington servants exemplified those throughout North Carolina. They came from all parts of the British Isles. Most were young, and men predominated. And many sought their freedom before the expiration of their indentures.[6]

Far more numerous in North Carolina and Wilmington than servants were bonded Africans. Given the increasing cost of obtaining and supporting servants, the propensity of servants to gain early freedom by absconding, and the hardening attitudes toward humans engendered by this form of restricted servitude, colonials and North Carolinians turned increasingly to slavery. The appearance of slavery in the Lower Cape Fear coincided with the permanent settlement of the area in the mid–1720s. Several wealthy South Carolinians brought bondsmen with them as they established plantations along the Cape Fear River. Indeed, demographically and otherwise, the Lower Cape Fear resembled more Lowcountry South Carolina than the rest of North Carolina.

The Lower Cape Fear experienced a rapid rise in the number of slaves, which proceeded perhaps equally from their natural increase and from forced immigration, the latter facilitated by the port of Wilmington. Few arrived from Africa directly; most entered the Cape Fear by way of the West Indies or South Carolina. Several Wilmington merchants participated in the slave trade. In 1773 Robert Thresal proposed to sell twenty "seasoned slaves" imported from Grenada, and Dugald Thompson imported "a parcel of choice negroes" from Jamaica. The following year Alexander Hostler & Co. advertised eighteen "prime Negroes" from Jamaica for sale.[7]

Slavery both reflected and contributed to the enormous wealth of the Lower Cape Fear. The region exhibited a pattern of slave ownership that differed remarkably from the rest of the province, both in terms of numbers and density. Slaves constituted approximately 20 to 25 percent of the population in North Carolina in 1767, but over 62 percent in the Lower Cape Fear. Moreover, the 2.49 bondsmen per square mile was the highest of any region in the colony, in which .94 per square mile was the average. According to Lieutenant Governor William Tryon in 1765, "When a man marries his Daughters[,] he never talks of the fortune in Money[,] but 20[,] 30[,] or 40 slaves is her Portion...."[8]

Slaves congregated in the eastern towns along the Atlantic coast, and comprised perhaps as much as half of Wilmington's population. Governmental authorities exerted increasingly strenuous efforts to define a subordinate status for slaves and relegate bondsmen to that position. For Wilmington, numerous laws and town ordinances supplemented the slave code of the colony, represented principally by statutes in 1715 and 1741 in which whites attempted to minimize the independence and mobility of slaves, discourage commercial and social relations between slaves and whites, and reduce the possibility of slave violence.[9]

However, in the towns, and certainly in Wilmington, bondsmen seemed to enjoy considerable freedom. They gathered in the streets, alleys, and vacant lots or houses, often disturbing whites, and in 1772 they may have contributed inadvertently to the outbreak of a small fire. Blacks (and whites) rode horses recklessly through the town and sometimes conducted races in the streets. After dark, slaves often moved almost unnoticed, posing the threat of theft or physical violence along unlighted streets. As a result, Wilmington town commissioners imposed a curfew on bondsmen, exempting only those who possessed passes from their masters, and those who carried candles or lanterns; but such action was largely ineffective.[10]

The ability of slaves to rent houses and tenements, or to obtain lodging in Wilmington, also evidenced their independence. While some slaves utilized the buildings of their masters who might have been away on business or residing in their country houses, other bondsmen possessed sufficient funds to rent dwellings. Town commissioners continually enacted

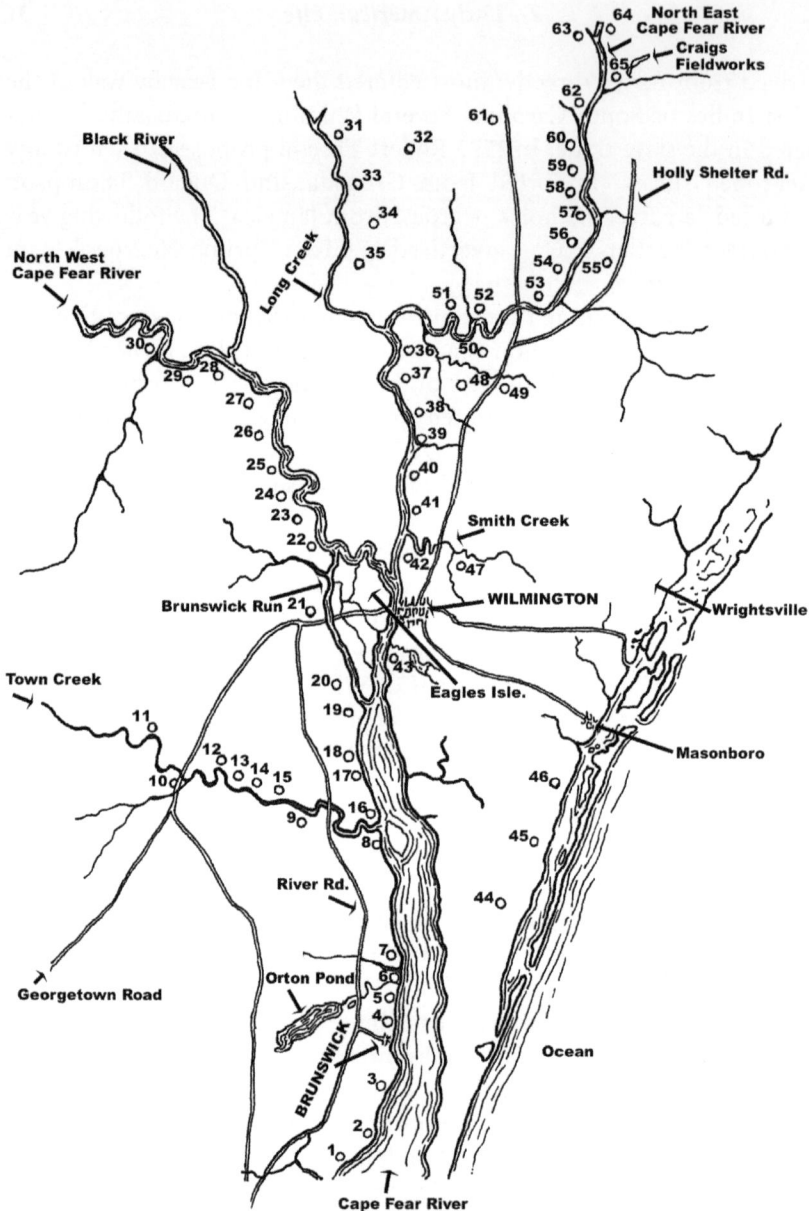

1. Governor's Pt. 2. Norrie's Pt. 3. York 4. Russellboro 5. Orton 6. Kendal 7. Lilliput 8. Pleasant Oaks 9. Dalrymple 10. Rice's 11. Davis 12. Spring Garden 13. Dobbs 14. Watters 15. Hullfields 16. Old Town 17. Clarendon 18. The Fork 19. Buchoi 20. Belville 21. Belvidere 22. Gabourel's Bluff 23. Cobham 24. Schanfields 25. Prospect 26. Mulberry 27. Dallison 28. Auburn 29. Magnolia 30. Point Repose 31. Mt. Gallant 32. Hyrneham 33. Pleasant Hall 34. Spring Garden 35. Bloom Hill 36. Pt. Pleasant 37. Rose Hill 38. Rook Hill 39. Nesoe's Creek 40. Fairfields 41. Sans Souci 42. Hilton 43. Greenfields 44. Sedgely Abbey 45. Hasell 46. Grainger 47. Halton Lodge 48. Rocky Run 49. The Hermitage 50. Castle Haynes 51. Swan's Pond 52. The Oak 53. Heron's Bridge 54. Strawberry 55. Lillington Hall 56. Springfields 57. Vats 58. Clayton Hill 59. Green Hall 60. Mosely Hall 61. Moorefields 62. The Neck 63. Stag Park 64. Bear Garden 65. Rutherfords Mills

ordinances to prevent slaves from renting quarters in the town, which tended "greatly to promote Idleness, Revelling and disturbance, Thieving and Stealing and many other crimes...." Few substantive changes followed those directives, however. Whites continued to let their buildings, and slaves continued to live by themselves.[11]

The independent income of slaves manifested a surprising freedom of action. Bondsmen engaged in sundry trades and hired themselves out, either with the approval of masters or in their spare time. Slaves bought, sold, and bartered firewood, provisions, and various types of merchandise, not only among themselves but with whites, all contrary to law unless the slaves had permission from their masters. Neither provincial legislation nor town ordinances greatly discouraged the "pernicious practice of dealing with Negroes." An exasperated William Hooper threatened to prosecute those in Wilmington who purchased "from my Negroes whatever they pillage from my House in town or Plantation below," and town commissioners imposed fines on several white residents for selling rum to slaves and otherwise "dealing" illicitly with bondsmen.[12]

After the Revolution, the General Assembly in 1785 again addressed the dilemma of urban slavery. It repeated the earlier strictures applied to slaves in Wilmington, claiming that as a result of allowing bondsmen to reside in town and to work for themselves, "robberies and frauds frequently happen, servants are corrupted, and the poor white inhabitants are deprived of the means of earning their subsistence by labour." Thus the legislature required slaves who worked in the town to provide written permission of such intention from their masters to the town clerk, wear a badge, and pay a tax. Moreover, slaves seen entering or leaving any store or house with vendible articles would be deemed guilty of theft unless they wore badges or could provide written permission from masters.[13]

The fragments of evidence concerning the condition of slaves in North Carolina reveal a pattern of life that differed little from that of slaves in other southern colonies, though Josiah Quincy, Jr., a visitor to Wilmington in 1773, opined that bondsmen were better treated in North Carolina "and are of consequence better servants." Nonetheless, the lot of the slave was not an easy one, for masters often paid little attention to appropriate food and wearing apparel. Worse still was the inescapable fact that slaves remained chattel property. Elkanah Watson attended a slave auction in Wilmington in 1778, in which a "poor wench clung to a little

Opposite: Locations of the principal plantations of the Lower Cape Fear region, 1725–1760, the area of the greatest concentration of slaveholdings and wealth in early North Carolina.

daughter, and implored, with the most agonizing supplication, that they must not be separated." But they were. A few years later, Johann David Schoepf found a father and fifteen-year-old son on the auction block. The father declared, "Who buys me must buy my son too." In that instance the two remained together. [14]

Slaves responded to their bondage in ways that ranged from a quest for greater autonomy within the bounds of slavery to running away and insurrection. Bondsmen in Wilmington were whipped for various breaches of the town ordinances, and in 1767 the justices of the New Hanover County Court ordered the construction of a special "Cage" in Wilmington for "the Confinement of Negroes ... the dimensions to be ten feet by ten." But slaves were rarely imprisoned for lengthy periods of time, for incarceration resulted in a loss of labor to slave owners or an opportunity for the slaves to escape. Such considerations provided the rationale for holding special courts for trying slaves accused of capital crimes. At the trial of Quamino in Wilmington in 1768, who was accused of robbery, the court pronounced the slave guilty, sentenced him to be hanged, and ordered that his head be severed and "affixed up upon the Point [Point Peter, also called Negro Head Point] near Wilmington."[15]

Unable to endure their bondage, many slaves fled their masters. Boston left the service of merchant George Parker in 1765; Charles ran away from Dr. James Geekie in 1788, though Geekie suspected that his slave had been kidnapped by a Captain Barnes, whose ship was bound for Jamaica. Runaways on occasion joined together for mutual protection and support. When informed that "upwards of Twenty run away Slaves in abody Arm'd" were in the county, New Hanover justices ordered the sheriff to raise a posse of at least thirty men which was empowered "to Shoot Kill & destroy all ... the ... run away Slaves as shall not Surrender themselves."[16]

Ultimately, the most threatening form of slave discontent was insurrection. An attempted rebellion in 1752 or early 1753 prompted the General Assembly in 1753 to institute the search, or patrol, system. Justices of the county courts might appoint searchers or patrollers to examine black habitations at least four times a year for guns, swords, and other weapons. Most counties in the eastern and central sections of North Carolina availed themselves of the patrol system. The New Hanover justices in 1766 designated three patrollers for Wilmington and ordered "that they walk and Search about the Town at least three times a week."[17]

The onset of the American Revolution raised the possibility of a slave insurrection in the colony. North Carolinians in 1775 suspected that royal governor Josiah Martin might try to emulate the example of Virginia Governor Lord Dunmore, who offered freedom to slaves who would help to quell the incipient rebellion in that colony. Martin denied the allegations, but whites in several eastern counties claimed to have found evidence of an organized plot by slaves to gain their freedom. Wilmingtonians also thought an insurrection was imminent. Reportedly, a number of blacks were found in the woods near the town, and most had weapons. The local committee of safety ordered that all blacks be disarmed. Whites patrolled the town day and night, regularly searching black dwellings. Slaves who arrived from the countryside were sequestered until they were ready to return.[18]

Although the putative insurrection in 1775 never materialized, many slaves gained their freedom during the ensuing war for American independence. The British invasion of the southern states from 1778 through 1781, and their occupation of Wilmington during 1781, provided the opportunity for liberation. Many slaves fled their masters; the British seized others. Blacks served as guides, foragers, and laborers for the British army. Some slaves left with the British upon their evacuation of Wilmington, but others remained by choice with their masters. William Hooper noted that he had lost three men to the British, but that John, his house slave, remained loyal, though he was "offered clothes, money, freedom — every thing that could captivate a youthful mind." John feigned his support for the British but stole away during the night to join Mrs. Hooper, who had been forced to leave the town.[19]

After the Revolution, slaves remained a threat to white society, continuing to run away and live in organized bands or communities, not unlike the maroon societies in the West Indies. After blacks robbed the cellar of Thomas Maclaine in Wilmington in late June 1788, and carried off in boats a hogshead of tobacco, a hogshead of molasses, and two barrels of beef, an investigation traced the stolen goods to a place along Barnett's Creek that "appeared to have been long a camp or asylum for runaway negroes" and probably the repository for property taken in a string of recent thefts in town. About six weeks later, Peter, who had been absent from his master for nine months, was apprehended after a robbery. He was linked with a "gang of which Qua has been principal, who have had the audacity to carry fire-arms, and are continually committing depredations upon the property of the inhabitants…," according to the local newspaper. As a result, the court that tried Peter found him guilty and sentenced him to death.[20]

Augmenting the slave population was a small but growing number of free blacks, mulattoes, and persons of mixed blood. The presence of free blacks, the product of runaways, liberated slaves, and unions of blacks and whites, alarmed whites, for they offered a dangerous alternative role model for slaves and ultimately might undermine the South's economic and social system. Their numbers were few in Wilmington and New Hanover county before the Revolution. Solomon Cumbo owned a residence in the town in the late 1760s and, like many, constantly neglected his obligation to work on the streets. One Thomas lived with Dr. James Geekie in 1774. As their numbers increased, the General Assembly in 1785 required free blacks in Wilmington to register with the town clerk and wear a cloth badge on which was written in "legible capital letters the word FREE" in order to distinguish them from slaves. Still, in the federal census of 1790, free blacks only numbered 67 in New Hanover County, constituting less than 2 percent of the non-white population and less than one percent of the total population.[21]

Another essential, though impermanent, segment of the local population consisted of sailors who frequented the port or called Wilmington home. Mariners often evoked a negative reaction, for they were seen as a rough, boisterous, unruly element—a threat to domestic tranquillity. In legislation in 1784 the General Assembly regretted the absence of a prison in Wilmington "for restraining riotous seamen and slaves...." Complaints about assaults and the destruction of property after dark led the town commissioners in 1789 to recommend to ship captains in the harbor to curfew their sailors in the evening. A month later, after the captain of the brig *George* refused to pay his wages, a sailor gathered some friends and hauled the ship's longboat through the streets of Wilmington. When the captain appealed to town authorities for assistance, a general melee followed. Several sailors were jailed. Subsequently, some of their comrades threatened to set Wilmington on fire, which necessitated calling out a detachment of militia to protect the town.[22]

Nonetheless, seamen played a more positive role in colonial affairs. They appeared in the mob that intimidated Dr. William Houston in 1765 during the political turmoil over the Stamp Act. Ten years later, while white and black Wilmingtonians stood by, some mariners rushed to extinguish a fire that could have devastated the town. Mariners, of course, were critical to Wilmington's shipping economy, which led the legislature to forbid Wilmingtonians from extending credit beyond a minimal amount to sailors or from keeping sailors on private premises for more than six hours without the permission of their captains. In 1768 the tavern licenses of two Wilmington ladies, Mrs. Lettice Blackmore and Mrs. Elizabeth Saunders, were suspended because they "harbour[ed] & detain[ed] Common Sailors, to the great Injury of the Merchants & Masters of Vessels trading to the river of Cape Fear." The women were threatened with prosecution if in the future they allowed "any Sailors or other disorderly person or persons to tipple any Liquors in either of their houses."[23]

Residents of Wilmington occupied a town situated on a hillside on the east bank of the Cape Fear River, an exceedingly sandy site that was crisscrossed by several streams flowing to the river, and bounded by hills to the east and south. It grew quickly and evoked widely different reactions from visitors over the years. On a trip in 1740, Quaker William Logan found a hospitable reception in the town, and the best food and lodging that he had received since he had left Pennsylvania. British postal inspector Hugh Finlay in 1774 referred to Wilmington "as the most flourishing town in the Province." But three years later, Ebenezer Hazard was not impressed by "small Town situated in a sandy Hollow surrounded with Sand Hills...." Even less enthusiastic was a traveler in 1786 who observed, "Wilmington without exception is the most disagreeable, sandy, barren town I have visited on the continent," and added that he was "extremely happy" that he was soon departing.[24]

Although Wilmington's inhabited area in the eighteenth century encompassed only a small portion of its legal bounds, the town's population increased steadily to the point that Wilmington was one of the most populous towns in North Carolina by the Revolutionary era, rivaled only by Edenton and New Bern, and later by Fayetteville (the product of the merger of Cross Creek and Cambellton, incorporated in 1783). Within a decade of its founding, Wilmington was deemed a "metropolis" and in the mid–1750s contained 58 houses or taxable structures and 125 taxables, or approximately 350 people. The famed Joseph Sautier Map of 1769 shows most of the habitations and buildings clustered between present Dock and Chestnut streets, and ranging from the river to Third Street. A few more buildings were scattered north and south along the river front; others lay beyond Third Street on the road leading to New Bern. Immediately after the Revolution, in 1784, Johann David Schoepf estimated that there were 150 houses in Wilmington, though that number was substantially reduced by fire within two years.[25]

Houses in Wilmington were often framed structures, though some were brick, for in 1735 the governor's council required at least six brick buildings be erected before it would formally recognize the town of Newton. Peter DuBois, a visitor in Wilmington in the mid–1750s, found "the Buildings in General very Good. Many of Brick two & three stor[i]es High with double Piazas w[hi]ch Make a good appeara[nce]." Later observers usually echoed the sentiments of Janet Schaw, who found "some very good houses" (wherein resided "almost all my acquaintances") in Wilmington. The Latin American patriot Francisco de Miranda deemed the homes

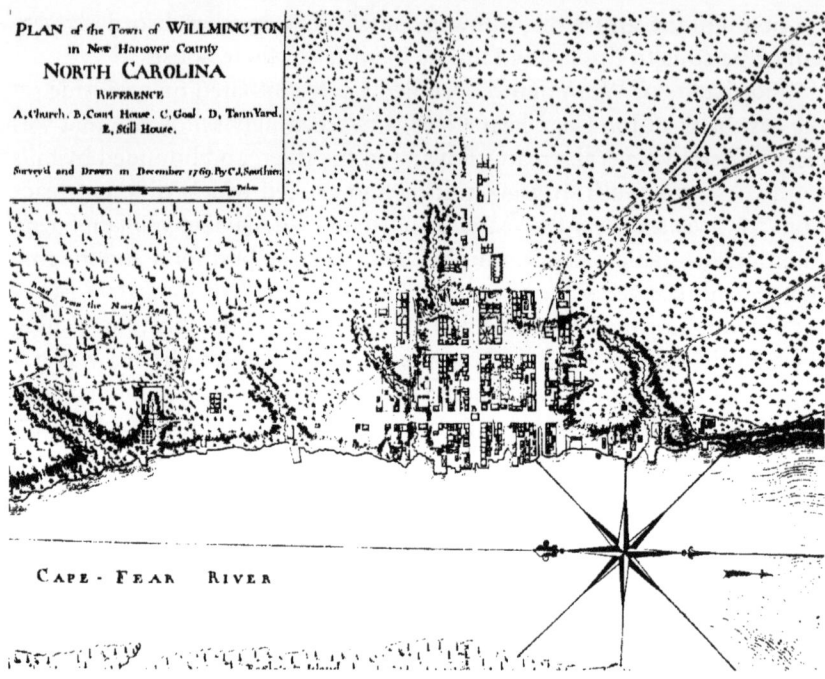

A "Plan of the Town of Wilmington," drawn by C.J. Sauthier in 1769, showing the location of St. James Church, courthouse, gaol (jail), tanyard, and still house (distillery). Courtesy of the New Hanover County Public Library, Wilmington.

"comfortable, clean, and generally better than those in Newbern," some ninety miles to the north and the colony's colonial capital.[26]

Among the early frame dwellings were those belonging to James Murray and James Wimble. Murray, a merchant, described his home as consisting of "a large Room 22 by 16 feet, the most airy of any in the Country, two tolerable lodging rooms & a Closet up stairs & Garrets above, a Cellar below divided into a Kitchen with an oven and a Store for Liquors, provisions, etc.," and that comprised the west end of the house. The other half included the cellar for his mercantile business, the store and counting house on the first floor, and four unfinished rooms above. Perhaps the most imposing building in town was "Wimbleton Castele," the name given to a turreted structure drawn on James Wimble's map of 1733. Located on lot No. 132, the third lot south from the corner of Nun and Front streets, the building commanded a site on a high bluff overlooking the Cape Fear River. Perhaps Wimble fortified his home with cannon to thwart incursions by the Spanish or other enemies. In 1769, the map drawn by Sauthier showed a large home, accompanied by several outbuildings and a garden plot, which was located on Wimble's former lot and which was probably occupied by Captain William Wimble, son of James Wimble.²⁷

Frequent fires erased much of Wilmington's early construction. Among the few extant homes of the prerevolutionary era is the Smith-Anderson House (c. 1740), which stands at the corner of Dock and Front streets and bears the influence of Charleston, South Carolina, urban architecture and craftsmanship. With its two-story piazza in the rear; tall second-story windows on the front and side opening onto balconies; and center hall with two rooms on the east, and one room and a porch (now filled in) room on the west, the Smith-Anderson House probably typified first-generation brick townhouses in Wilmington. The Burgwin-Wright House (c. 1770), located at the corner of Third and Market streets, is the largest and most pretentious of the Georgian-style houses that remain in Wilmington. Built for wealthy merchant, planter, and royal placeman John Burgwin, the frame dwelling stands on the site of the original town jail. A multiplaned gable roof covers its front and rear double piazzas. Within, a broad central hall is flanked by a parlor on one side and two smaller rooms on the other. Representative of stylish urban dwellings of the era, the principal room—a fully paneled, finely embellished drawing room—is located on the second floor. Outbuildings and an ornamental garden accompanied the town house.²⁸

John Burgwin (1731–1803), Wilmington merchant, town commissioner, plantation owner, and royal officeholder, whose imposing town house (1771) stands at the corner of Market and Third streets. Courtesy of the New Hanover County Public Library, Wilmington.

Burgwin represented a number of wealthy Wilmingtonians who maintained landed estates in the surrounding countryside, in addition to their town houses. Born in England, and employed as a merchant in Charleston, South Carolina, at mid-eighteenth century, Burgwin moved to the Cape Fear region, where in 1753 he married Margaret Haynes. From the marriage Burgwin acquired Castle Haynes Plantation just north of

Wilmington, and the adjoining Hermitage Plantation. Burgwin became a successful merchant in Wilmington and occupied numerous local and provincial government positions, including town commissioner of Wilmington, justice of the peace, member of the General Assembly, clerk of the Wilmington district superior court, and clerk of the North Carolina court of chancery. On the eve of the Revolution, Burgwin left the colony for England to seek medical attention for a broken leg suffered from a fall in a game of blind man's bluff at Castle Haynes Plantation. When his property was threatened with confiscation, Burgwin returned to Wilmington by way of New York to prevent its loss, but with the British occupation of Wilmington in 1781, he left again for England. Although suspected of British sympathies (and rightly so), Burgwin returned to Wilmington in 1784 to reclaim his property and resume his successful mercantile enterprises in Wilmington, Fayetteville, and Charleston.[29]

Friends, neighbors, and travelers met a genuine welcome in North Carolina country homes and town houses. After visiting South Carolina, Josiah Quincy, Jr., of Massachusetts spent some time in North Carolina, where he encountered "real hospitality, less of what is called politeness and good-breeding...." Indeed, Quincy found that "Men of genius, learning, and true wit, humour, and mirth" were more numerous in the northern colony. Another voiced similar sentiments when he wrote that Wilmington merchants and outlying planters were "polite, humane, and hospitable; ... nor is this mere pageantry and shew, their behaviour at home is consistent with their appearance abroad." After spending time in New Bern, Francisco de Miranda traveled to Wilmington, where he thought the residents were "more sociable, more generous, and better dressed" than those in the former capital.[30]

Given Wilmington's commercial orientation, most of its residents were absorbed in the pursuit of material possessions, and few initially had time for social amenities. Peter DuBois in 1757 lamented, "I Cannot yet find a Social Co. who will Drink Claret & Smoke Tobacco till four in the morning. I Hope However to Make some proselytes soon." Disappointed, a month later DuBois wrote, "I Live Very much Retired for want of a Social Set ... and pass my hours Chiefly at Home with my Pipe and some agreeable author." A decade and a half later DuBois would have found a more hospitable environment, for merchants in town, as well as planters in the country, were "beginning to have a taste for living." Elegant houses and bountiful tables betokened a sociable and neighborly people who enjoyed one another's company.[31]

As Wilmington developed a more leisured society, the genteel enjoyed visitations and dances, both public and private. Public affairs usually occurred at one of the taverns in town. Janet Schaw in 1775 attended a ball in Wilmington "where [there] were dresses, dancing and ceremonies laughable enough...." While picturesque to pretentious visitors like Schaw, these affairs greatly appealed to Wilmingtonians, who must have been chastened when the local safety committee in 1774 banned public, and then private, dances as unbecoming to patriots seeking their liberty from England. However, when independence was finalized in 1783, "a very grand ball" was held in Wilmington. A warm night and small room "very much abated the pleasure" for the "remarkably numerous" company, according to Edenton lawyer James Iredell, who enjoyed but two dances the entire evening because only a limited number of couples could take the floor at any one time.[32]

Wilmingtonians also gathered beyond the home to celebrate auspicious occasions. Scots in town remembered St. Andrews's Day, November 30, 1788, partaking of a dinner at Dorsey's Tavern and Coffee House, and toasting (among others) the memory of St. Andrew, Old Ricky (Auld Reekie or Edinburgh), and the British royal family. As early as 1789, "a number of the principal gentlemen" of Wilmington recognized the anniversary of the birth of George Washington. They met on February 11 in Dorsey's Tavern, where they spent the day in the "usual conviviality which ever distinguish[es] the sons of Columbia." It signaled the beginning of many such commemorations, though subsequently the date was altered to February 22.[33]

All classes mingled in such popular diversions as cockfights and horse races. When possible, Carolinians obtained their cocks from Great Britain; otherwise, they perforce raised their own. Matches were well advertised. At those events, the genteel and the lowly rubbed shoulders as they shouted, cursed, drank, and bet their money. Likewise engrossing the attention of all strata of society were horse races, where competition was keen and the stakes were high. While gentlemen bet large sums on the outcome, the less affluent, white and black, wagered a shilling or two, a quart of rum, or a drink of grog.[34] As in the instance of dancing, the onset of the Revolution temporarily put a quietus on cockfighting and horse racing. One of the first actions of the Wilmington safety committee after its organization in 1774 was to inform several gentlemen who "intended to start horses, which they have had some time in keeping, for the Wilmington subscription-purse," that racing contravened the directives of the Continental Congress. Noted the committee:

> We shall only add that nothing will so effectually tend to convince the british Parliament that we are in earnest in our opposition to their mea-

sures, as a voluntary relinquishment of our favorite amusements.... Many will cheerfully give a part of their property to secure the remainder. He only is the determined patriot who willingly sacrifices his pleasures on the Alter of freedom.[35]

Carolinians not only wagered on cockfights and horse races, but began to develop a taste for lotteries. Before the Revolution, individuals resorted to private raffles to sell property, but the General Assembly authorized only two lotteries. The first, in 1759, attempted to raise money to finish the Anglican churches at Wilmington and Brunswick Town, but the results were disappointing. Indeed, if the lottery was held, the proceeds failed to hasten greatly the completion of the churches. But that did not dampen interest in lotteries. Thirty years later, after St. James Church in Wilmington had been built, a correspondent to the *Wilmington Chronicle* suggested that a lottery might be used to improve the "ruinous state of the church, and the exposed condition of the public burying-grounds...." Although that proposal never materialized, and the state legislature approved only three lotteries in the 1780s, the number of lotteries mushroomed in subsequent years.[36]

Wilmingtonians tempered their baser pecuniary instincts by developing an interest in the arts. According to one twentieth century historian, "Preoccupation with the theatre and the drama is an index and criterion of civilization." Theatrical productions in the American colonies originated at least as early as 1665 in Virginia. Itinerant actors appeared in Charleston as early as 1703, and Williamsburg, Virginia, boasted the first American playhouse in 1716. Southerners proved more receptive to the theater than colonials to the North, where Puritanism and Quakerism inhibited interest. North Carolina lagged behind other English colonies, due in part to a lack of wealth and in part to the dearth of urban centers. Still, Wilmington's location on the principal highway along the coast between Williamsburg and Charleston rendered the appearance of the theater inevitable.[37]

The advance of "civilization" reached Wilmington at least by 1760, when Thomas Godfrey, Jr., finished *The Prince of Parthia*, a five-act tragedy in blank verse that became the first production in this country of a work by an American-born playwright. Born in Pennsylvania in 1736, Godfrey moved to Wilmington in 1759 as a factor or commercial agent. While in Wilmington, or at least during many visits to Masonboro Sound, Godfrey wrote a number of poems, including "Masonborough's Grove," in which he describes Edenic days along the water, and he finished *The Prince of Parthia*. Godfrey died in Wilmington in the summer of 1763, and was interred in the graveyard of St. James Church. Two years later Nathaniel

Evans published twenty-two of Godfrey's poems posthumously as *Juvenile Poems on Various Subjects with The Prince of Parthia*. Before his death, Godfrey had sent a copy of *The Prince of Parthia* to his friend David Douglass in Philadelphia. Douglass' acting company performed the play on April 24, 1767. It was unsuccessful, however, and withdrawn after one night, never to be presented commercially again.[38]

By the 1760s, strolling players and theatrical activity toured North Carolina. One group, probably the Virginia Company of Comedians, played in the Cape Fear region in 1768, no doubt in Wilmington, when one of their number asked Governor William Tryon to commend him to the Bishop of London for orders of ordination. The advent of the American Revolution briefly scotched interest in recreational diversions, which were deemed unpatriotic, and for several years theatrical activity in America was dormant.[39]

After a long hiatus, traveling companies of performers again played to North Carolina audiences, and inspired the formation of local companies of thespians. In 1787 the American Company of Comedians, which had opened a theater in Charleston two years earlier, toured the principal towns of North Carolina, and the manager of the company announced that he fitted out an "elegant theatre" in Wilmington where the company intended to remain for a month. The following year the Kenna Company of Comedians and the American Company visited Wilmington. In the wake of the strolling companies appeared organizations of local amateurs, among which was the Thalian Association of Wilmington, one of the most active and long lived in North Carolina.[40]

Supplementing the traveling companies and the local Thalians were other forms of public entertainment. A waxwork exhibit appeared in town in October 1788, containing figures of George Washington, the king and queen of England, African Americans, Native Americans, and "the much admired Piece, called Robinson Crusoe," as well as various kinds of fruit. Apparently the exhibition met a popular reception, for it returned for a brief engagement in December. Not long thereafter a Mrs. Robinson presented "Lectures on Hearts," a series of talks "calculated for the edification as well as amusement of every person," according to one who attended and deemed his money well spent.[41]

In addition to organized forms of public entertainment Wilmington men congregated in local taverns. More frequently called ordinaries in early North Carolina, and sometimes public houses (of entertainment), taverns not only offered respite for the traveler and comfort for those in its immediate environs, but also furnished a medium for auctions and slave sales, served as repositories for the public mails, and provided a center for political deliberations. Although found throughout the colony, taverns tended to cluster in urban areas, particularly port towns, which offered obvious advantages of a larger and more dependable clientele. Wilmington contained at least ten such establishments in 1768. Taverns doubtlessly represented the best example in early America of a government-regulated business, for county courts licensed the ordinaries, and controlled the prices of food, drink, and lodging. The General Assembly tried to curb gambling and excessive drinking in ordinaries, and in Wilmington specifically forbade tavern keepers to allow anyone to drink during church hours or become intoxicated on Sunday.[42]

Beyond the taverns, free adult males from Wilmington and New Hanover County gathered quarterly for militia musters. The English colonials quickly transplanted the institution of local trainbands or militia from the mother country to the colonies. Theoretically, militia service was a serious civic obligation, but too often musters degenerated into drinking sprees and brawls. Still, the New Hanover militia apparently comported themselves well when welcoming William Tryon to Wilmington in 1765 for the formal announcement of his commission as governor of the colony. Moreover, the militia ably assisted the governor in quelling the Regulators in 1771, suppressed loyalist sentiment at the outset of the Revolution, prevented a possible slave uprising at that time, and protected Wilmington on occasion from depredations by unruly sailors. In addition to the New Hanover regiment, Wilmington organized an artillery company, the captaincy of which in 1789 rested with John Huske, Wilmington merchant and New Hanover County legislator.[43]

A select number of Wilmington men enjoyed the camaraderie of the Freemasonry. The Masonic Order in North Carolina originated in Wilmington in the 1750s, though legend contends that the colony's first Masonic lodge, "Solomon's Lodge," appeared in 1735 in the vicinity of Masonboro Inlet, and was succeeded a quarter century later by "Hanover Lodge." The historical record, however, recognizes the appearance of organized Masonry in North Carolina when St. John's Lodge, chartered by the Grand Lodge in England in 1754, formed in Wilmington, probably in early 1755. In his will in 1761, Joshua Toomer of Wilmington requested that his "Brethren the Freemasons" attend his funeral "with their jewels and aprons." Cornelius Harnett, the Revolutionary patriot, was the Worshipful Master of the lodge in the mid–1760s and in 1772 became the Deputy Grand Master of Freemasons in North Carolina. Although the Revolution occasioned an interruption of the activity of St. John's, in the later 1780s the lodge reorganized. At a meeting on December 27, 1788, interested Masons met in Brother Lawrence Dorsey's tavern and coffee house in Wilmington to observe St. John's Day and revive St. John's Lodge. Among the seventeen members present was William Campbell, who was chosen Master.[44]

Religious observances offered Wilmingtonians an opportunity to gather on a regular basis. At the beginning of the eighteenth century the General Assembly established the Church of England, or Anglican Church, in North Carolina. Although few in number in North Carolina before the Revolution, Anglican ministers were resident in the Lower Cape Fear from the beginning of the permanent settlement of the region. The Reverend James Moir arrived in the area in 1740, his appearance coinciding with the erection of Wilmington. Moir established his residence in Wilmington and agreed to serve as minister of St. James Parish. The rivalry between Wilmington and Brunswick Town intruded upon his duties. Wilmingtonians resented his officiating on occasion in Brunswick Town, and, in 1742, a year after the creation of St. Philips Parish (which included Brunswick Town), Moir accepted a position in St. Philips Parish. The minister returned to St. James Parish in 1746, but, unable to persuade the vestry to provide him a house and glebe, he left the next year for Edgecombe County. The Reverend John McDowell officiated in St. James Parish from 1754 to 1758, followed by the Reverend Michael Smith for three to four years before his disgraceful past in South Carolina was revealed.[45]

Meanwhile, Wilmingtonians and residents of St. James Parish attempted to construct an Anglican church in Wilmington—St. James Church. In his will, dated 1737, William Flavell, a local merchant, left a bequest for erecting "an English Church" in Newton. The legislation incorporating Wilmington in 1739/40 authorized the building of the church in town. Michael Higgins offered a lot on the south side of Market Street, extending from Third to Fourth, as a site for the church. No further action was taken until 1751, when the legislature authorized a tax to raise money to augment the personal gifts, such as those made by Flavell and Higgins. The statute appointed commissioners to plan and build the church, as well as to acquire additional property for the edifice.[46]

Construction on St. James began in 1753, but, like other Anglican Churches in North Carolina, the work stretched out over many years. New commissioners were appointed in 1757. Additional funding came from the wreck of a Spanish ship which had sunk in 1748 in an attack on Brunswick Town (traditionally said to be the source of the painting *Ecce Homo*, currently owned by St. James Episcopal Church), and a lottery. However, little money was derived from either source. Nonetheless, gifts by town residents, including that of William Faris, plus funds raised by subscriptions helped to defray costs. The Wilmington commissioners in 1763 ordered the town treasurer to purchase "as much fine Cloth & fringe as will be Sufficient to make a Slip & Cussian for the Pulpit." As late as 1765, Anglican services still were held in the courthouse, but in 1770 St. James Church was consecrated. Even though the legislature in 1771 appointed commissioners to finish the church, doubtlessly the church was in use by that time.[47]

From the outset, religious dissenters, non–Anglicans who opposed the establishment of the church, were numerous, amounting to half of the whites in New Hanover County in 1742, according to the Reverend James Moir. A Quaker cemetery in Newton indicated the presence of the Society of Friends as early as 1738. Presbyterian minister Hugh McAden in 1756 preached to "a large and splendid audience" in Wilmington, which doubtlessly included many Scots and Scotch-Irish who had settled in the area. New Light Baptists added to the religious diversity in St. James Parish by 1760; and in 1773, the Reverend Joseph Pilmore introduced Methodism to Wilmington, preaching in the courthouse "to a large congregation of genteel people." And Deism was not overlooked in the eighteenth century age of enlightenment. Though a vestryman at St. James, and interred in the churchyard, Cornelius Harnett wanted to be remembered by an epitaph that read, "Slave to no sect. No private path he trod; but looked through nature, up to nature's God."[48]

Several sectaries in North Carolina, principally the Anglicans, Presbyterians, and, in the west, Moravians, took the lead in fostering education, though in Wilmington schooling was a laic as well as a religious function. The Reverend James Tate, a Presbyterian from Ireland who arrived in Wilmington in 1760, established the first classical school or academy in North Carolina, though the duration of that institution is indeterminate. At the time of the Revolution, William Hooper worried about his fifteen-year-old son Tom, who from "want of employment ... [was] falling into habits of idleness which e'er long ... he will not be able to shake off." But, Hooper lamented, "We have no school in this town, and there is none in the neighbourhood to which I could send him with the expectation of his laying up a stock of knowledge that may be useful to him...." Thus Hooper sought a position for his son as clerk in a mercantile firm.[49]

The future seemed more promising, however. The conclusion of the Revolution witnessed an effort to bring to fruition a legacy of Col. James Innes of New Hanover County, who by his will in 1760 had set aside money for a "Free school for the Benefite of the Youth of North Carolina." In 1783 the General Assembly chartered the Innes Academy, appointing trustees to utilize the bequest of Innes, accept donations on behalf of the school, obtain buildings, and hire teachers. However, five years later no action had been taken, and the legislature appointed additional trustees, giving them essentially the same charge. Also in 1788, Catherine Martin, who had recently immigrated from Germany, and the Reverend Mr. Stewart proposed opening schools in Wilmington. Martin, who had "a liberal Education in all kinds of needlework," directed her efforts toward young ladies. Later in the year the Reverend Stewart advertised his intention to offer Latin and Greek, English grammar, and "the principles of Religion, natural, and revealed," presumably to young men.[50]

Education more broadly encompassed newspapers, an indispensable means of obtaining information. Only four news sheets appeared in North Carolina before the Revolution—two in New Bern and two in Wilmington. In 1764 Andrew Steuart, disappointed in his attempt to become the public printer of the province, located in Wilmington and launched *The North-Carolina Gazette and Weekly Post Boy*. At Steuart's death, occasioned by drowning while swimming in the Cape Fear River, Adam Boyd, a clergyman of Pennsylvania birth and "a gentleman of fine literary and classical attainments," purchased Steuart's press. Boyd commenced *The Cape-Fear Mercury*, which he published from 1769 until he enlisted in the First North Carolina Battalion in 1776. In addition to the Wilmington region, the paper circulated as far as Anson, Mecklenburg, Rowan, Surry, and Guilford counties.[51]

Although newspapers increased in number after the Revolution, Wilmington belatedly acquired a news sheet. In March 1788, one Bowen and Caleb D. Howard established *The Wilmington Centinel, and General Advertiser*. Because the newspaper business offered at best a minimal income, economic success for printers rested upon a combination of activities that included job printing, book selling, bookbinding, and retailing products. Bowen and Howard sold writing paper, wrapping paper, pasteboard for bonnets, sealing wax, ink powder and stands, and books, including *The Chorister's Companion* and *The American Singing-Book*. Such activity failed to satisfy Bowen. After a traveling exhibition of waxworks appeared in Wilmington, he purchased some of the figures and inaugurated his own tour. The *Wilmington Centinel* ceased operation in March 1789, when Howard went to Fayetteville, entering into a partnership with John Silbey to publish the *Fayetteville Gazette*.[52]

The lack of an adequate postal system hampered newspaper publishers and the general public alike in their efforts to communicate with the world beyond Wilmington. Carolinians generally relied upon friends, expresses (private carriers), and packet boats in the coastal trade to transport letters and papers. Briefly, in 1739, a mail route was arranged to connect Virginia and South Carolina by way of the North Carolina coastal region, but only in 1770 was a permanent postal service realized. The route traversed the King's Highway, from Virginia through Edenton, Bath, New Bern, Wilmington, and Brunswick Town to South Carolina. The system was unreliable, and British postal inspector Hugh Finlay spent three months in North Carolina in 1774 trying to correct the inadequacies of the service. At the time, he arranged for a post between Wilmington and Cross Creek (present Fayetteville), the first east-west route in the province.[53]

Soon after declaring independence, the Continental Congress reestablished an American post along the same coastal route. Postal inspector Ebenezer Hazard visited Wilmington in 1777 to reinstate service. However, given the uncertain state of the postal system, William Hooper in 1779 sent a letter to Edenton by a friend and left "its further progress ... to the chapter of accidents." In 1783 a Mr. Brison, who represented the national government, moved to place the route on a firm footing as he traveled through Wilmington to Savannah, Georgia. Nonetheless, in 1788 a number of men in Wilmington and Fayetteville undertook privately to subsidize a post between the two towns, and by early 1789 a weekly round trip mail route materialized. The mail served not only private interests but local newspaper publishers who depended upon the receipt of papers throughout the state and nation for their news. The *Wilmington Centinel* in 1788 rescheduled its publication for Thursdays "in order to give our readers the latest intelligence we may receive by the post, who arrives on Wednesdays."[54]

Recreation, convivial association, religion, and education served to divert attention from a constant preoccupation with health. The southern coastal region was notoriously unhealthy, in large part because low, swampy regions contributed to malaria, or the ague, and fever. Malaria, however, was more a debilitating disease than a killer. It weakened the system, reducing resistance to other diseases that in turn caused death. By enervating its victims, malaria adversely affected the quantity and quality of labor. By hastening death from other diseases, malaria affected social and familial relationships. The resulting premature deaths, orphans, and high rates of remarriage spawned a society of open and mixed households. Moreover, the prospect of short lives may have produced a tendency toward a freer, more unrestrained life-style, especially among males. When possible, the wealthy went to the seacoast or sounds, or, in the instances of Cornelius Harnett and the John Burgwin family, traveled to Rhode Island to escape the "summer heats."[55]

Devastating, too, were epidemics, particularly those of smallpox and yellow fever, to which port towns were peculiarly susceptible due to their exposure to the outside world. Legislation in 1751 instituted quarantine regulations to protect the port of Wilmington and the colony from sickness abroad. According to that law, the commander of Fort Johnston would question captains of incoming ships to determine if contagions were on board. If so, or if the commander were not satisfied after his inquiry, he could prevent the vessel from proceeding until he notified the commissioners of pilotage for the Cape Fear River and they had given instructions for quarantining the ship. Despite precautions, periodic reports of epidemic sickness, including smallpox, emanated from Wilmington and New Hanover County.[56]

The afflicted could utilize the expertise of physicians, whose training varied immensely. Throughout the colonies the ratio of doctors to population approximated 1 to 600, and in urban areas (for example, New York in 1750) the ratio dropped to 1 to 350. At least twenty-four doctors practiced in Wilmington before 1778, which in any given year probably would have provided the town with a better ratio than the New York figure. Among the Wilmington practitioners were Armand John DeRosset, Sr., and Moses John DeRosset, father and son. Rebecca Green linked three physicians: she was the daughter of Dr. Samuel Green; she first married Dr. John Mortimer; and, after his death, she then married Dr. James Geekie. After the war, Archibald Maclaine counted himself fortunate that a Dr. Claypoole, who had studied under the eminent Dr. Benjamin Rush of Philadelphia, moved to Wilmington, for by medicines and a "rich and generous regimen" that consisted of vegetables and "animal food," the physician relieved Maclaine of a troublesome internal "disorder." Of course, the choice of physicians was critical. Maclaine reported a few months later that William Hill, Brunswick merchant and revolutionary, had died "of obstinate quackery."[57]

Those unwilling or unable to use the professional services of a physician relied upon their own knowledge of medicine, supplemented perhaps by such popular manuals as *Every Man His Own Doctor; or, the Poor Planter's Physician*, first published in 1734 in Virginia and reprinted two years later by Benjamin Franklin in Philadelphia. In that guide the author provided remedies for ailments that included ague, consumption, gout, sore throat, and yaws. His prescriptions consisted mostly of local "medicines," such as bear oil, deer dung, garlic, honey, mint, mustard, and sage. Andrew Steuart, publisher of the *North Carolina Gazette* in Wilmington, printed and sold in 1765 John Westley's *Primitive Physick, or an Easy and Natural Method of Curing Most Diseases*. Physicians and lay people alike who preferred more prosaic, European remedies could call at M. R. Wilkins's store on the corner of Front and Market streets, where he offered a variety of medicines, including tarter emetic, laudanum, opium, tincture bark, calomel, and paregoric, among many others—as well as tooth powder and brushes, and, perhaps best of all, "A Chest of Excellent Hyson Tea."[58]

Life was tenuous and the efficacy of medical attention problematic, but Wilmingtonians in 1789 enjoyed amenities unavailable to many North Carolinians. Wealth that accrued to the merchants and planters in the area translated into fine homes and lavish life-styles. As North Carolina's principal port, Wilmington represented a "window" to the world. While the state, to a great extent, remained rural, provincial, poor, and ignorant, achieving an undesirable reputation for its torpidity and cultural barrenness, Wilmington was a vibrant, thriving, cosmopolitan town. Through their continual contacts with the Atlantic coast, the West Indies, and Great Britain, Wilmingtonians remained abreast of the latest modes of dress, styles of furniture, and political occurrences. Located on the principal highway through the state, and along the south Atlantic coast, Wilmington beckoned to touring companies and traveling artists. And a constant influx of immigrants—merchants, professionals, artisans, and sailors—some transient and some permanent, augmented white and black residents to create a wonderfully diverse, dynamic population.

3
A Developing Economy

The evolution of Wilmington as a municipality depended greatly upon its status as a port, and more especially upon its ability to serve the economic needs of southeastern North Carolina. Although Wilmington was small, as were most southern colonial towns except for Charleston, South Carolina, function rather than size explained its importance as an urban community. Whether in Wilmington or in Charleston, the processes of exchange, collection, storage, and distribution of commodities signified a center of economic activity. Like Charleston, Wilmington linked an extensive interior region to a national and international economy.[1]

Wilmington, together with such other North Carolina port towns as Edenton and New Bern, and secondarily Bath, Beaufort, and Brunswick Town, represented the apex of North Carolina's urban chain. Smaller towns or villages to the interior—Cross Creek (Fayetteville), Tarboro, Halifax, Hillsborough, Salisbury, Charlotte, Salem, and many others—served as conduits of trade to the coast, although admittedly in many cases such commerce was directed through Virginia and South Carolina as much as to eastern North Carolina. Of course, these towns, even the largest—Wilmington, New Bern, and Edenton—remained small in size and population, principally because they all were little more than transshipment points (in addition to serving as centers of government) whose urban configuration would not necessarily have reflected their volume of commerce.[2]

As a transshipment point, Wilmington was admirably situated, occupying a position at the confluence of the two branches of the Cape Fear River, the only river in the state that empties directly into the Atlantic Ocean. Of its dual provenance, the most important is the Northwest branch, or simply the Cape Fear River, which begins at the confluence of the Deep and Haw rivers in present Chatham County and travels southeast about 150 miles to join the Northeast branch of the Cape Fear. The Northeast branch originates in present Wayne County and meanders some 100 miles to its junction with the Northwest branch. At that point the river flows as a single stream to the ocean about thirty miles distant. The two branches of the Cape Fear River drain over a quarter of North Carolina's present one hundred counties.[3]

Guarding the entrance of the Cape Fear River are sandbars called Frying Pan Shoals, which stretch off the cape for some eighteen miles. While ingress from the east is restricted to several sloughs of a maximum depth of five feet through Frying Pan Shoals, large vessels might approach from the south and west. Crossing the bar, as the entrance is termed, is dangerous, particularly in the face of shifting and shoaling sands that leave the depth of the water uncertain. A second entrance to the Cape Fear River appeared in 1761 when a storm opened New Inlet across the peninsula, almost ten miles above the point of the cape.[4] Although New Inlet could accommodate light-draft vessels, larger craft necessarily continued to cross the main bar. However, the opening of New Inlet caused increased shoaling downstream at the bar, a process that eventually threatened ocean-going commerce involving deep-draft vessels on the Cape Fear River.

As Wilmington emerged as one of North Carolina's principal towns and ports during the next fifty years, it overshadowed its early rival, Brunswick Town. By 1762, the latter paled in comparison to Wilmington in the estimation of one visitor. Another in 1775 saw in Brunswick Town a small village that was "very poor—a few scattered houses on the edge of the woods, without street or regularity." Saving Brunswick Town from virtual extinction was the "Flats," a sandbar in the Cape Fear River at the mouth of Town Creek, about equidistant between Brunswick Town and Wilmington. Larger ships calling at the river had to lighten their load at Brunswick Town before ascending the Cape Fear to Wilmington, and conversely, take on a full cargo at Brunswick Town. That, in turn, required the presence of British customs officials in Brunswick Town to enter and clear vessels.[5]

Before the Revolution, Brunswick Town and Wilmington constituted the principal ports of the Cape Fear region, or the customs district known as Port Brunswick. Almost a half century after its first permanent settlement in America, and coinciding with the settlement of North Carolina, the English government instituted a concerted policy to regulate the commerce of its burgeoning empire. That effort, beginning in the Cromwellian era but pursued more vigorously upon the restoration of the Stuarts in 1660, was embodied in a series of parliamentary statutes called Navigation Acts. Dominated by mercantilist conceptions that particularly emphasized the importance of trade for a national prosperity and military superiority, the English sought by the legislation to direct colonial commerce so that it might best serve and sustain the empire, especially the mother country.[6]

In order to effect the desired policy, the navigation legislation created customs districts with designated ports of entry in the various North American colonies whereby shipping might be properly regulated. During the first fifty years of the colony's existence, when settlement was confined principally to the Albemarle region, two customs districts sufficed for North Carolina. Port Currituck included the area of Currituck Sound, while Port Roanoke, with Edenton as its port of entry, encompassed the Albemarle Sound. As the colony expanded southward, ports Bath, Beaufort, and Brunswick were established to accommodate the growing provincial trade.

As early as March 1731, probably originating with the appointment and arrival of George Burrington, North Carolina's first royal governor, Port Brunswick became the official port of entry for the Cape Fear. The district encompassed the watershed of the Cape Fear River—in effect, the southeastern region of North Carolina—and included the ports of Brunswick Town and Wilmington. Shipping through Port Brunswick steadily increased during the four decades before the Revolution. Forty-two vessels left the river in 1734. By 1754 as many as a hundred ships annually entered Port Brunswick, according to Governor Arthur Dobbs, who once saw sixteen craft on the river at one time.[7] During the decade preceding the Revolution, Port Brunswick's import and export trade in terms of tonnage easily exceeded that of any other North Carolina port district, and constituted about 40 percent of the colony's total commerce.

Much of the trade of Port Brunswick moved through Wilmington, but all entrances and clearances were recorded with the customs officials seated in Brunswick Town. Historian Lawrence Lee attempted to calculate the approximate trade of Wilmington and Brunswick by assuming that vessels of less than one hundred tons proceeded to Wilmington, while others used the facilities at Brunswick Town. Lee believed that during the year, from April 5, 1767, to April 5, 1768, almost three times as many vessels cleared Wilmington as did Brunswick Town. But the total tonnage of the Wilmington vessels was less because the Wilmington trade was aimed at colonial coastal ports and the West Indies, whereas 87 percent of the vessels leaving Brunswick Town went to Great Britain.[8]

For three decades after the establishment of Port Brunswick, the trade of the district was confined primarily to the North American coast and the West Indies. From the northern colonies came manufactures, mainly cloth, utensils, tools, gigs, sulkies, and considerable amounts of foodstuffs, among which rum, molasses, sugar, and salt were the most prominent. The islands also sent rum, molasses, brown sugar, and salt to the province. In addition, smaller quantities of fruit, coffee, ginger, and mahogany, as well as a few slaves, cleared the West Indies for North Carolina. One hundred and twenty-five bondsmen entered Port Brunswick during the year ending April 24, 1775. Moderate amounts of manufactured goods—iron utensils, earthen wares, and linens, among others—also came from the West Indies, though undoubtedly most originated in England.[9]

Overseas commerce involving Port Brunswick increased gradually. According to Governor Dobbs in 1763, one-third of the English goods consumed in North Carolina came directly from the mother country. Because Brunswick Town was the premier deepwater port in the colony, most of the English trade centered in the Cape Fear. During the five-year period ending January 5, 1773, 139 of 215, or 65 percent, of the ships that entered the province from England went to Port Brunswick. Of the remaining, 49 went to Port Roanoke, 22 to Port Beaufort, and 5 to Port Bath; none went to Port Currituck. From England and Scotland came mostly manufactured goods, particularly cloth. Wearing apparel, shoes, and hardware were also prominent imports.[10]

It is well to remember, however, that much of the tonnage entering North Carolina toward the approach of the Revolution, perhaps one-fourth, came in ballast. For the year ending April 24, 1775, 2,588 of 8,386 tons, or 31 percent, of the tonnage entering Port Brunswick arrived in that fashion. And that figure understates the total, for many ships undoubtedly brought less than a full cargo to port. Because the northern colonies generated a greater demand for British goods than the southern colonies, British vessels might come to North Carolina by way of northern ports, at least partly in ballast, to seek a homeward-bound cargo.[11]

By the outbreak of the Revolution, Port Brunswick's export trade in terms of tonnage also surpassed that of the other customs districts in North Carolina. Moreover, due to its deep harbor and the nature of its surrounding economy, Port Brunswick's trade was increasingly directed toward transatlantic commerce. By 1768, when one-third of North Carolina's exports in terms of tonnage was destined for the British Isles, 60 percent of Port Brunswick's outward-bound trade moved in that direction. More than one-fourth of its shipping headed for the West Indies. One-tenth cleared for the mainland North American colonies. Only an occasional vessel was bound for southern Europe or Africa.[12]

Export tonnage from Port Brunswick, while exceeding that of other North Carolina ports, fell far short of the tonnage leaving Charleston,

South Carolina, and the larger northern mercantile centers. In fact, however, Charleston and Virginia ports probably shipped much of North Carolina's produce. According to one estimate, the value of North Carolina exports in 1770 leaving through the province's own ports was £100,000; another £75,000 was carried overland to Virginia for export; an additional £20,000 left via Charleston; and perhaps £5,000 more went to Pennsylvania and other northern colonies. Thus North Carolina ports handled about half of the colony's external trade. In similar fashion, perhaps 50 percent of the province's imports passed through its ports, a fourth came by land from South Carolina, and the remainder was brought from Virginia and more northerly colonies.[13]

Exports from Port Brunswick were diverse, but centered upon naval stores and wood products. Among the eastern seaboard colonies, North Carolina was England's largest supplier of naval stores on the eve of the Revolution, and enjoyed the parliamentary bounty designed to encourage the exportation of such goods. In 1768 one North Carolinian lamented the colony's reliance upon naval stores while planters in South Carolina reached a "pitch of opulence" with their rice, indigo, and hemp, commodities that North Carolina was equally capable of producing. However, the extensive pine forests and North Carolina's comparatively small slave population rendered reliance upon naval stores more feasible.[14]

Naval stores, variously defined but basically consisting of tar, pitch, rosin, and turpentine, derived from the longleaf pine. Crude or common turpentine was the resin collected from boxed, living trees. When crude turpentine was distilled, it produced spirits, oil of turpentine, and a residue called rosin. Burning pine wood in kilns produced tar. Boiling tar in open pits or in iron cauldrons yielded pitch, thicker than tar but whose consistency depended upon the length of the boiling process. Three barrels of tar produced two barrels of pitch. The seemingly endless tract of longleaf pines along the coast, and superb water transportation, made the pine derivatives a mainstay of the economy.[15]

Naval stores quickly became a major component of North Carolina exports. They went primarily to England. In 1772 only one-tenth of those products were shipped elsewhere, mostly to New York and Philadelphia, from whence they were probably transshipped to the mother country. England relied heavily upon the American provinces, importing only 11,403 barrels of naval stores in 1772 from other sources, mainly Russia and Sweden. Since North Carolina was the principal source of English naval stores, and the Lower Cape Fear annually supplied half those products, southeastern North Carolina, Wilmington, and Port Brunswick occupied a unique and valuable position within the British Empire.[16]

North Carolina also produced a variety of wood products, including sawn lumber (boards, plank, scantling), shingles, staves, heading, hoops, hogsheads, posts, oars, masts, spars, yards, and even house frames. Most important were boards, shingles, and staves. Most of the boards, plank, and scantling were pine and were cut in the colony's numerous sawmills, which produced two and a half to three million board feet annually. Cypress shingles and oak staves were laboriously cut by hand. Through Port Brunswick went approximately 70 to 75 percent of the province's exported sawn lumber, 25 percent of its shingles, and 10 percent of its staves. More then 90 percent of the exported wood products went to the West Indies.[17]

In addition to naval stores and wood products, a number of less significant exports found their way through Port Brunswick. Some provisions were sent to the West Indies. However, most foodstuffs were retained in the province to feed the local populace. Another exportable crop of increasing importance at the end of the colonial era was tobacco. As its growth shifted from the Albemarle region to the south and southwest to become the chief crop of the "middle parts" of North Carolina, some found its way down the Cape Fear River through Port Brunswick. George Washington, on his southern tour in 1791, reported that 6,000 hogsheads annually were exported from Fayetteville, presumably via Port Brunswick.[18]

Though far less significant than in South Carolina and Georgia, the cultivation of rice and indigo provided additional agricultural exports for North Carolina. About 1730, a traveler observed rice swamps along the Northeast Cape Fear. During the 1740s planters began to experiment with indigo, though only a few planters ever produced enough to make the effort worth their while. In the province the production of rice and indigo was confined almost exclusively to the lower reaches of the Northeast and Northwest branches of the Cape Fear River below Wilmington. Thus over 95 percent of the rice and over 80 percent of the indigo exported from the colony cleared Port Brunswick.[19]

To bring their produce to market along the inland waterways, the colonials used a variety of craft. Merchant James Murray's advice to a friend in London in 1741, "If you intend to do any business here, a Cooper and a Craft that will carry about 100 barrels will be absolutely necessary," was apropos three decades later. Loyalist Maurice Nowland at Fayetteville counted among his lost property during the Revolution "1 boat for transporting products to Wilmington." Canoes (varying in size, with some propelled by sail as well as oar) and perriaugers (larger than canoes, capable of carrying eighty to a hundred barrels of tar, and sometimes taken on

3—*A Developing Economy*   57

coasting voyages) were popular. Yawls, small sloops, and bayboats also sailed the rivers and streams. For commercial purposes, however, the flatboat and raft were most important.[20]

Turpentine and rosin were transported on flatboats that might carry fifty to a hundred casks, or on rafts bearing several hundred barrels. The rafts consisted of a framework of large timbers divided by crossbeams. Small saplings subdivided the sections into spaces about the length of a rosin barrel. The barrels were secured to the saplings by means of pliable hickory withes. On top of the barrels were boards covered with dirt or clay, which formed a deck on which raftsmen lived and cooked while floating downstream to market.[21]

The flatboats and rafts depended upon the current for motive power. Heavy oars, or poles, twenty to thirty feet long and mounted on two-foot fulcrums at either end of the craft, were used to steer the boat. Floating with the current meant slow travel. Between tides the raftsmen had to lay to, "having no power to move but by the force of the stream." The trip from Hallsville, ninety-two miles from Wilmington along the Northeast Cape Fear, required a week for a flatboat and perhaps ten days for a raft. Yet to one observer it was the best mode of transport, and had been "adopted by all the people up the country."[22]

At Wilmington the cargoes were delivered to commission houses in return for goods and credit. Rafts were dismantled and their timbers sold "for a trifle." Flatboats were usually loaded and then taken upriver against the current by means of poles worked from both sides of the boats as well as from the ends. A swift current might occasion warping the craft by fastening ropes to trees on the banks. In any case the work was extremely difficult, sometimes impossible when the water level was low. At that point wagons might be dispatched to haul the cargo overland. Upstream travel might take two to three times as long as that going in the opposite direction.

The rivermen or watermen who took the rafts and flatboats up and down the rivers were held in low esteem. One observer referred to them as "the poorest set of people" whom he saw in the province. He felt that they generally were "drunkards, and can be of little use in any other way; yet these get half-a-crown a day, and 3 gallons of rum per week." Many of the watermen were slaves who were familiar with every twist and turn of the rivers and creeks. In his will of 1768 Wilmington merchant John DeBois directed his executors to purchase four slaves to work his boats. Some fifty years later, bondsman Harvey Jarman was hired from his master for $300 per year and the usual allowance of food and clothing to work on the Northeast Cape Fear.[23]

Diversity also characterized the craft engaged in the Cape Fear import-export ocean trade. During the year ending July 3, 1775, 112 vessels entered Port Brunswick. They included brigs, sloops, schooners, ships, and snows. Outnumbering all types, and constituting 37 percent of the vessels calling at the port, were the brigs equipped with two masts (a fore mast with square sails and a main mast partly square and partly fore-and-aft rigged). Most of the brigs were small; two thirds were less than 100 tons. The remainder ranged upward in size to the 200-ton *Kernington*, sailing from Hull, England. Also appearing regularly at the port were sloops and schooners, which numbered 27 and 20 respectively during the year under consideration. The sloop was single-masted, fore-and-aft-rigged; the schooner, two-masted with main and fore sails suspended by gaffs. In the Cape Fear trade they ranged from 10 to 60 tons and were manned by crews numbering from two to six.[24]

The largest vessels calling at Port Brunswick were the ships and snows. The ships, three-masted and square-rigged, accounted for one-sixth of the craft entering the port. They averaged 130 tons and included the largest merchant vessel to visit Port Brunswick on the eve of the Revolution, the 230-ton *Hector*, owned by Brunswick Town merchant John Quince. Making infrequent appearances at the port were the snows, carrying two masts resembling the fore and main masts of the ships, and just behind the main mast a third mast bearing a trysail. During the year preceding the Revolution, only three snows called at Port Brunswick. They ranged from 65 to 120 tons and carried from six to ten crew members.[25]

Among other attempts to protect and improve the commerce of the Lower Cape Fear (and that of North Carolina generally) were the establishment of an inspection system to ensure the quality of North Carolina exports, the promotion of a more balanced economy, and the creation of towns to serve as centers of trade. The General Assembly resorted to an inspection system, begun in the proprietary era and expanded and improved in late years, to relieve North Carolina of the reputation of producing and exporting inferior products. Legislation fixed inspection sites in every county. Among the numerous items specified for inclusion under the inspection law were naval stores, staves, shingles, lumber, deer skins, rice, indigo, and pork—all potential exports whose improved quality would certainly have benefited the Cape Fear region, a prime producer of those commodities.[26]

Dependent upon pine derivatives, the economy of the Lower Cape Fear fluctuated with the price of naval stores in Great Britain. From producers to merchants and governor, residents of the province complained incessantly about the small returns from naval stores, as well as the high cost of imported goods. In part, the difficulties stemmed from the British navigation legislation which restricted colonial trade to channels most profitable to the mother country and the empire as a whole. On the other hand, the colonials also bore some of the blame. Carolinians were notoriously careless in their preparation of naval stores; and, in fact, colonial products rarely approached the quality of Scandinavian and Russian naval stores purchased by England (at exorbitant prices). In their objection in 1770 to Carolina pitch and tar, English importers recommended a proper observance of the strictures of the parliamentary bounty act and the local inspection system as the means to improve Carolina exports.[27]

Governors Johnston, Dobbs, and Tryon encouraged North Carolinians, especially those in the Cape Fear region, to expand their economic base by considering the cultivation of silk, flax, indigo, and hemp. To further the concept of diversification, the provincial legislature offered bounties on the production of hemp, flax, potash, and pearl ash. Cotton was early grown in the Lower Cape Fear. Some was exported, but most was used locally. According to one observer, "under proper management" cotton "would be an article of great consequence." Still, on the eve of the Revolution, Carolinians depended primarily upon naval stores, timber products, livestock, and food for commercial export.[28]

A major deterrent to Wilmington's growth as a port was the inability of the Lower Cape Fear to attract the backcountry trade. North Carolina's frontier commerce gravitated to Petersburg, Virginia; Charleston, South Carolina; and, to a small extent, northward as far as Pennsylvania. The pattern of backcountry migration was an influential factor in channeling the area's trade, as was North Carolina's geography, which made travel connections with neighboring colonies easier than with the east coast. Aggressive marketing, particularly by prominent Charleston merchant Henry Laurens, captured much of the backcountry trade, for the Charlestonians offered higher prices and better credit facilities.[29]

Potentially the most important of the frontier settlers were the Moravians, or the Brethren of the *Unitas Fratrum*, who began to migrate from Pennsylvania to North Carolina in 1753. They purchased and settled a tract of land called Wachovia near present-day Winston-Salem. Needing an outlet for the produce of their "Oeconomie," or communal economic system, the Moravians considered Wilmington. The opportunity came at a critical juncture for the port. Had the Brethren been persuaded to open a channel of commerce with the Lower Cape Fear, others in the west may well have followed. Moreover, the timing was significant, coming as it did when lines of trade and communication were in their formative stages. However, most of the backcountry business was siphoned off to adjoining colonies, inhibiting the development not only of Wilmington and the Lower Cape Fear but also of the entire province. The adverse patterns of trade continued to retard North Carolina's economic development long after the Revolution.[30]

Also detracting from Wilmington's trade were the poor roads in the eastern part in of the province, which were generally inferior to those in the west. The road from Wilmington to South Carolina was described as "nothing but a sandy bank" in 1734; forty years later it was termed "the most tedious and disagreeable of any on the Continent." Particularly difficult was the causeway that traversed Eagles Island opposite Wilmington. North of the town the Duplin Road was admirable for a brief distance, then deteriorated into swampy morasses. The highway along the coast to Snead's Ferry and New Bern was sandy, barren, and gloomy. Affording access to roads across the numerous watercourses in the region were bridges and ferries. Bridges, often in a state of disrepair, sometimes impeded traffic. So did ferries over the Cape Fear at Wilmington and over the Northeast Cape Fear at present Castle Hayne, at least until a drawbridge was erected about 1767 at the latter site.[31]

In order to lure backcountry trade to the east coast, the General Assembly made several efforts to extend roads from the western settlements to the Cape Fear during the decade prior to the Revolution. The prospects of the Moravian trade, following the appeals of Governor William Tryon and the opening of the Moravian town of Salem, prompted the General Assembly in 1768 to authorize a public road from the "Frontiers of the Province through the counties of Mecklenburg, Rowan, Anson, and Bladen, to Wilmington and Brunswick." Upon the failure of the road to materialize, the legislature in 1771 passed a similar statute which was designed for "the Advancement of Trade and Commerce." Additional legislation envisioned a road from the Dan River to Campbellton on the Cape Fear River to draw traffic from Guilford and Chatham counties. And a third road was authorized to connect Charlotte, a recently chartered town in Mecklenburg County, to Elizabethtown in Bladen County.[32]

Towns had long been envisioned as stimulants to trade, though urbanization materialized slowly. In the southeast, in addition to Brunswick Town and Wilmington, New Exeter, located on the Northeast Cape Fear some twenty-five miles above Wilmington, was incorporated in 1754 at the urging of inhabitants of New Hanover, Onslow, and Duplin counties who wanted to encourage trade along that section of the river. South Washington (now Watha), located on the same river a few miles above New Exeter, soon appeared. And in 1773 Elizabethtown in Bladen County, acclaimed "a healthy, pleasant Situation, well watered and com-

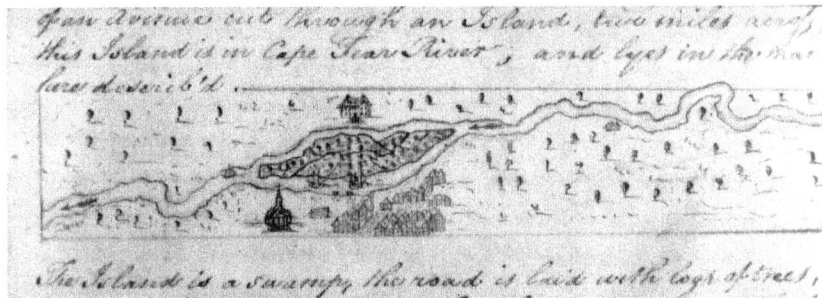

Top: Map by British postal inspector Hugh Finlay, 1774, showing the causeway leading through Eagles Island in the Cape Fear River opposite Wilmington, perhaps the worst stretch of road in early North Carolina. Courtesy of the North Carolina Office of Archives and History, Raleigh.

Bottom: The ferry that transported people and vehicles back and forth from Eagles Island to Wilmington, a slow, often unreliable, but necessary conveyance over waters too wide to ford or bridge. Drawing courtesy of the New Hanover County Public Library, Wilmington.

modious for Commerce," was incorporated after many years of informal existence. It provided a river landing on the Northwest Cape Fear between Wilmington and Campbellton.[33]

The most important urban nexus between the Lower Cape Fear and the backcountry was Cross Creek in Cumberland County. Cross Creek, a village located near the Northwest Cape Fear, had arisen in the 1750s, and was the southeastern terminus of a road authorized in 1755 to connect Orange Court House (subsequently Hillsborough) with the river. In 1762 the General Assembly incorporated Campbellton, located about a mile east of Cross Creek at the junction of that creek and the Northwest Cape Fear. That town was designed to divert North Carolina's backcountry trade from South Carolina and Virginia to the east coast, primarily to Brunswick Town and Wilmington.[34]

Campbellton and Cross Creek served Wilmington admirably as transshipment points from the interior. Roads from the backcountry converged on Cross Creek; produce came from as far as Salem, Hillsborough, Salisbury, and Charlotte. According to one doubtlessly exaggerated report, forty to fifty large wagons a day could be seen in Cross Creek, bringing beef, pork, flour, corn, hides, butter, tallow, and other goods. As a result, Wilmington merchants established stores or kept agents in Cross Creek to purchase the produce and send it by raft down the Cape Fear River. The two settlements were merged in 1778 as Campbellton, and, in 1783, named Fayetteville in honor of the Marquis de LaFayette. The Cumberland town soon became one of the largest urban communities in North Carolina and a commercial competitor of Wilmington before the Civil War.[35]

Like many of the Atlantic coastal towns, Wilmington was laid out in grid form and contained two major streets. One extended along the river's edge—Front Street (later, Water Street was cut between the river and Front Street). The other was perpendicular to the waterfront through the middle of town—Market Street. The first accommodated fishing, warehousing, and manufacturing activities; the second provided sites for services, businesses, and institutional buildings. The intersection of the two near the water was the focal point of the town. Perched on the hills overlooking the river were homes of the wealthy, who chose locations with proper drainage, attractive views, and refreshing breezes. The less well-to-do lived in low-lying areas. Still, all classes lived in close proximity, and all might easily walk the few blocks comprising the town, producing a pedestrian environment and creating a sense of community among the town folk.[36]

Despite the ability to draw upon the trade of the Northwest and Northeast rivers, and the resulting increase in exports via Wilmington, the town remained relatively small, largely because Wilmington continued to serve as a transshipment point, funneling the natural resources of North Carolina into the Atlantic market. The size of a port town depended not only upon a favorable geographic location and a sufficient export trade, but also upon its ability to serve an entrepreneurial, decision-making function, which would feature specialist brokers, insurance underwriters, and a manufacturing population to process goods in transit. With that kind of entrepreneurial activity, the port could transcend the limits of its trade and take on a life of its own, as did Boston, New York, and Philadelphia.[37]

From the beginning, Wilmington's economy revolved principally about commerce. Merchants from Atlantic towns and the British Isles spearheaded the development of the town, accompanied by a variety of support craftsmen and service people. Among the early residents of Newton and Wilmington were shipwrights, millwrights, tailors, cordwainers, blockmakers, carpenters, barbers, hatters, and physicians. Later, some small manufacturing appeared in the form of a turpentine distillery, owned by Cornelius Harnett and William Wilkinson (and located between present Walnut and Red Cross streets), and a tannery on Second Street, owned by John Lyon. Peruke makers, coppersmiths, and saddlers added to the diversity of later businessmen. During the colonial era, business operations were small, and in Wilmington merchants dominated.[38]

A distinctive feature of colonial Wilmington was the concentration of Scottish and Scots-Irish merchants in the town. Those merchants not only conducted much of Wilmington's trade, but also contributed to the port's commercial success abroad. They brought European, particularly British, commercial contacts with them. The Scots also helped to extend Wilmington's influence into the hinterlands, and vigorously pursued the North Carolina backcountry trade.[39]

Notable among the later Scottish merchants was Robert Hogg, who moved from Scotland to Wilmington in the 1750s. He soon helped to establish the firm of Hogg and (Samuel) Campbell. James Hogg, Robert's brother, arrived in 1774 and briefly worked at branch stores in Cross Creek and Hillsborough, two of several businesses established by Hogg and Campbell beyond Wilmington. At its dissolution in 1778, the partnership of Hogg and Campbell claimed assets amounting to £18,330 sterling. In the main, members of the mercantile community, including the Scots, appeared to be local operators, largely independent of Charleston and the overseas influences that controlled the northern counties of North Carolina and tidewater Virginia.[40]

Temporarily disrupting the lifeline of trade on which Wilmington depended was the American Revolution. The war for independence originated in the form of urban, often mercantile, protests against restrictive British commercial measures, in conjunction with denunciations of perceived British transgressions of American civil liberties. Wilmington and the Lower Cape Fear assumed a leading role in the revolutionary struggle in North Carolina from the Stamp Act crisis to the departure of the British occupation troops in 1781. At the outset, merchants, sailors, and others directly or indirectly dependent upon trade resented discriminatory and coercive parliamentary legislation that threatened to injure the local economy so thoroughly absorbed in commerce. For those individuals, political independence meant economic freedom.

Although the Revolution sprang from diverse sources, the colonial desire to pursue economic goals reasonably unfettered by the mother country cannot be overlooked. The Navigation Acts probably imposed an insignificant burden on the colonies, though the southern provinces suffered most from the mercantile restrictions. More important, the British effort after 1760 to enforce more stringently the commercial legislation, even to the point of simply inconveniencing shipping, was abrasive. And, of course, the invidious effort of the British to tax by means of navigation laws was anathema to many colonials. In fact, the Revenue Act of 1764 not only sought to tax Americans but favored British West Indian trade at the expense of that of the mainland colonies.[41]

Parliament in 1764 exacerbated a long-standing Carolina grievance by the passage of the Currency Act, which forbade the colonial issue of legal tender paper currency. North Carolina's rapidly expanding population, and an increasingly complex economy, necessitated an enlarged medium of exchange. Specie, or hard money, was too scarce, and commodity money, commodity notes, and simple credit were not always sufficient to bridge the gap. From the Cape Fear in 1775 Alexander Schaw declared that, "there is no specie in the province.... Nothing in the stile of a banker or money merchant was ever heard of." Governor Josiah Martin described the "majority from the southern region" of the province as a people "almost universally necessitous and in debt," a condition ascribed by many colonials to British restrictions on the emission of currency. While other issues ebbed and flowed, the Currency Act, with its attendant constitutional disputes, engendered continuing resentment in North Carolina.[42]

The Stamp Act of 1765 made taxation manifest, and heightened the cost and difficulty of entering and clearing shipping. In the face of colonial protests, the inability of the British to distribute stamps halted commerce on the Cape Fear River, because stamps had to be affixed to ships' papers in order to legitimate trade. A Cross Creek merchant complained that he could neither sell nor ship goods to Wilmington. Are we "Free Men of Slaves?" he asked. "Rouze" and "open your Port and Courts," he admonished Wilmingtonians. According to a report from Wilmington, "The trade of this river at present is entirely ruined!" The British had seized vessels for lack of stamped papers, and other ships were discouraged from putting into port. Those vessels could have carried off a vast quantity of tar and turpentine in Wilmington, "which, in a few weeks, will be running through our streets."[43]

Non-importation brought the repeal of the Stamp Act in 1766, but Parliamentary impositions and restraints were unrelenting in the ensuing years. The Townshend taxes of 1767 brought forth another, though less successful, effort to use non-importation to force Parliament to reconsider that legislation. The Tea Act of 1773 ignited an initial protest in Boston (and elsewhere along the coast later), to which the British responded with the Intolerable Acts in 1774. The colonials countered with the Continental Association, a non-importation, non-exportation, non-consumption agreement adopted by the first Continental Congress later in the year. Local committees of safety appeared to enforce the trade sanctions against Britain, which greatly diminished Wilmington's commerce.

Parliament reacted to the colonial challenge early in 1775 by passing the Restraining (or Fisheries) Acts, which severely curtailed provincial trade and fishing privileges. Exempted from the statutes were New York and North Carolina, presumably to avoid antagonizing the substantial numbers of loyalists within those provinces. The Wilmington–New Hanover Committee of Safety angrily denounced the exemption and retaliated by prohibiting all exports from Wilmington and New Hanover that might benefit the British army and navy in northern ports, Newfoundland, and elsewhere. In the Prohibitory Act, passed late in 1775, Parliament declared the colonies to be in a state of rebellion, outlawed all colonial shipping, and subjected provincial vessels to seizure by the British navy.[44]

At the onset of the war with England, privateering appealed to North Carolinians. As early as February 1776 a privateer was being fitted out in Wilmington, but merchants in New Bern and Edenton seemed to be more active in the spoliation of British shipping. Still, several prizes were brought to the Cape Fear, including in 1780 two armed brigs, one from St. Kitts, the other from Greenock, worth £10,800 sterling; and, in February 1783, a large Jamaican vessel loaded with rum and sugar.[45]

However, British naval vessels and privateers periodically brought commerce to a standstill in the Cape Fear. In May 1777, two British men-of-war crossed the bar to destroy a number of vessels at anchor in the river. British privateers also sailed the coast, practically stifling trade during the summer of 1779. The interdiction of commerce led to skyrocketing prices in Wilmington, if goods could be had at all. North Carolina's defensive naval operations little deterred the enemy.[46]

Wilmington emerged from the Revolutionary War prepared to

resume its position as a port of commanding consequence for North Carolina, but Brunswick Town numbered among the casualties of the independence movement. Deserted in 1776 after the British invaded the Lower Cape Fear, Brunswick never recovered. North Carolina's fifth provincial congress in 1776 ordered the collector of Port Brunswick to keep his office in Wilmington, which became the unofficial port of entry for the shipping district. At the same time, Brunswick lost its legislative representative in the General Assembly. In 1779 the legislature moved the seat of Brunswick County from Brunswick Town to the relative safety of Lockwoods Folly. Four years later a visitor described Brunswick town as "completely ruined and demolished." Some pilots eventually made their homes there, for it was convenient to New Inlet. However, at the end of the War of 1812 there were only two or three buildings left. Subsequently, Brunswick Town faded into memory, leaving only a few ruins as a reminder of its more prosperous days.[47]

Wilmington, however, anticipated a quick resumption of trade with England, the West Indies, and the American mainland. In order to implement commercial legislation and promote the shipping industry, North Carolina retained essentially the same machinery that had been used in the colonial era. The provincial congress in December 1776 appointed "collectors," or naval officers, to enter and clear vessels at the ports of entry. Naval officers subsequently were named by joint ballot of the two houses of the state legislature and commissioned by the governor. Commissioners of navigation and pilotage for the various ports were appointed by law. The county courts continued to select inspectors of commodities. The General Assembly retained the five colonial ports of entry, though substituting Port Wilmington for Port Brunswick in 1789, and designating Wilmington as the seat of the port.[48]

The state also addressed the pilotage system that had been established in 1751 for the Cape Fear River in order to facilitate shipping. Legislation in that year appointed five prominent residents of the Lower Cape Fear to be self-perpetuating commissioners of pilotage. They would examine and license pilots (to a maximum of seven) and dismiss those deemed guilty of "misbehaviour" in office. The law also provided a table of fees for pilotage service based on the draft of the vessels being guided over the bar and along the river. In "thick weather," when captains of vessels fired guns to inform pilots of their arrival, the commander of Fort Johnston was empowered to return the signal, dispatch pilots, and collect fees from the ship captains for the expended powder.[49]

The pilotage legislation of 1751 also provided for quarantine regulations to protect the colony from sickness abroad. The commander of Fort

Johnston was required to question each ship captain to ascertain possible contagions on board. If the commander was not satisfied, the vessel could not proceed farther until the commissioners of pilotage had been notified and had given directions for quarantining the vessel. Such precautions may have reduced the incidence of imported disease, but it failed to protect Wilmington altogether, for periodical reports of epidemic sickness, including smallpox, emanated from the town and New Hanover County.[50]

During the ensuing decade, the "great Increase of the Trade of [the] Cape Fear River" moved the legislature to reconsider the pilotage system. In 1764 it defined more carefully the responsibilities of the pilots, raised their number at the bar to twelve, admonished them strongly to obey the law, and reiterated the quarantine procedure. The statute increased the number of pilots serving the river from the bar to Brunswick from seven to eight, and allowed the commissioners to appoint a maximum of four pilots on the river between Brunswick and Wilmington. Because many pilots failed to guide vessels along the river, fines were prescribed for their neglect of duty. Fees for pilotage were raised in 1764 and again in 1766.[51]

Pilotage for the Cape Fear River was briefly neglected upon the realization of independence, but in 1777 the General Assembly rectified that oversight by reestablishing a system similar to that of the colonial era. The legislation prescribed a schedule of pilotage fees, appointed six self-perpetuating commissioners of navigation and pilotage, and permitted the commissioners to license pilots. The pilots were bonded for proper performance. Ship captains were required to notify the commissioners of smallpox or other contagious diseases on their vessels in order that quarantine proceedings might be followed. The next year the legislature raised pilotage fees "to encourage such good men as are capable and willing to act as pilots," and to compensate those who risked such wartime dangers as capture by the enemy.[52]

Pilots assumed a military as well as commercial importance during times of war. When Spanish sloops appeared off the Cape Fear in 1748 during King George's War, pilots unwittingly went to their aid, only to be taken prisoner and forced to lead the enemy into the river. During the French and Indian War, Cape Fear pilots were more cautious, waiting for ships to cross the bar to ascertain their identity before committing themselves. When the British captured one of the Cape Fear pilots during the Revolution, the Wilmington–New Hanover Committee of Safety assumed control of the local pilots, determining who would serve and the location of their stations, and providing, when necessary, for the support of their families.[53]

At the end of the war, in 1783, the General Assembly again addressed the pilotage system, because the "imposition, extortion, insufficiency and negligence" of the pilots had "greatly injured" the state's commerce. More pointedly, the legislature considered pilotage and navigation of the Cape Fear River the next year because inadequate payment of pilots forced many to quit or move to other states for employment. In the latter statute the legislature limited the number of pilots to ten, five from the mouth of the river and New Inlet to Brunswick, and five from Brunswick to Wilmington. Fees were elevated, bonds were required for proper service, and fines were imposed on ship masters and pilots who failed to comply with the law. In addition, pilots were allowed to build houses on the public grounds surrounding former Fort Johnston (in current Southport), so that they could be conveniently near the mouth of the river.[54]

As indispensable as they were, pilots aroused ambivalent feelings among the populace. The men often neglected to respond to ships seeking to cross the bar at the Cape Fear, failed to take vessels up and down the Cape Fear River, and sought to reduce competition with their fellows by pooling their efforts. That collaboration proved "to be extremely injurious to commerce," and the legislature banned partnership arrangements in 1771. However, the admonition had little effect, for by the mid–1780s it was "customary with the pilots of the Cape Fear to be equally concerned in the pilotage of vessels" coming to the river. Again the legislature prohibited partnerships, an injunction slightly relaxed in 1787 to permit no more than two of the Cape Fear bar pilots to work together.[55]

The General Assembly variously attempted to improve the navigation of the Cape Fear River and to protect the river channel. In 1784 the lawmakers proposed to build a lighthouse on Bald Head Island to assist mariners in navigating Frying Pan Shoals and entering the river. But not until 1789 did the legislature authorize construction of the lighthouse on land donated by Benjamin Smith of Brunswick County. The General Assembly in 1790 transferred the land to the federal government, which assumed responsibility for the construction and completed the Bald Head Lighthouse in 1795. In 1764, and again in 1784, the North Carolina legislature made provisions for erecting beacons and buoys at the mouth of the Cape Fear, and for marking the river channel. The lawmakers responded to the malicious removal or destruction of the markers by making such actions subject to stiff fines. And by statute, ship captains were forbidden to dump ballast from their vessels into the water along the river.[56]

Although the General Assembly in 1784 deemed a harbor master essential for the supervision of the shipping at Wilmington, it made the commissioners of navigation and pilotage responsible for the duties of that official until money could be raised to hire a harbor master. Five years later the legislature appointed Robert Scott to the position. The commissioners of navigation defined his duties and determined his fees. Legislation in 1802 made the commissioners thereafter responsible for appointing a harbor master for Wilmington.[57]

The efforts by the state to stimulate shipping contributed to a rapid revival of commerce. In the late 1780s North Carolina's volume of shipping surpassed that of the late colonial period. Trade was sluggish in 1783, but in the following summer alone, some 64 vessels, mostly British, were seen on the Cape Fear River. During 1788–89 more vessels than ever before reached the Cape Fear, and the trade of the entire state had never been greater. The British still played a significant role in the Cape Fear commerce. Of the 218 vessels that cleared Port Brunswick in 1788, 60, or 28 percent, were British. Two Swedish and one Danish craft rounded out the foreign-owned ships.[58]

In terms of the tonnage of shipping, the state's exports in 1788 had doubled that of 1769. Wilmington led all ports, clearing 38 percent of the state's export tonnage. Destinations, however, changed. Half the tonnage was bound for the West Indies, two-fifths for other American states, and little more than a tenth left for Great Britain. Though more important after the war, the West Indian trade was conducted on a different basis. Since the British closed their ports to American exports, North Carolinians traded with the French, Dutch, and Danish islands. Still, British vessels carried North Carolina goods to the West Indies.[59]

Following the Revolution, the flow of exports from Port Wilmington, as it became known in 1789 when it was officially changed from Port Brunswick, found Wilmington specializing in naval stores, wood products, provisions, and tobacco. The loss of the British bounty on naval stores depressed that industry. Exports of tar, turpentine, and pitch declined in comparison with pre–Revolutionary totals; the exportation of lumber and provisions surpassed prewar levels. North Carolina flour and rice were almost exclusively products of the Wilmington shipping district. The port also accounted for more than half of North Carolina's board and scantling exports. The West Indies remained the principal market for lumber products and provisions, though an increasing proportion of those goods went to the northern states.[60]

The most striking change in the export trade in North Carolina and the Lower Cape Fear was the increase in tobacco shipments. That commerce rose from 360,000 pounds in 1768 to 6,000,000 pounds in 1790. Before the Revolution, tobacco was exported principally from Port Roanoke. After the war, three-fifths of the state's tobacco that was shipped via water passed through Port (Brunswick) Wilmington, a reflection of the spread of the cultivation of tobacco into the central and southern regions of North

Carolina. Fayetteville proved to be a major transshipment point from the interior of the state to the coast.[61]

The origin of imported goods also changed after the Revolution. The importance of Great Britain declined; that of the West Indies rose significantly. Although the percentage of total import tonnage arriving from the American states remained about the same as before the war, New England's prominence declined, whereas trade with New York, Philadelphia, Baltimore, and Charleston expanded. The nature and variety of imports, however, changed little from the colonial era.[62]

Wilmington's mercantile community, mirroring the populace of the town itself, was in a constant state of flux, a condition exacerbated by the Revolution. New faces constantly appeared in the town as old ones departed. Merchant John Burgwin returned after the war following a judicious, self-imposed exile. Among the recent arrivals in mercantile circles were Philip Spaulding and Henry Dayton, who operated stores on Market Street. Apparently, the most active of the immediate postwar merchants was Amaziah Jocelyn. In addition to running a wholesale, retail, and commission store at a site near the public market, Jocelyn also established an "Intelligence-Office," a forerunner of the chamber of commerce, where he hoped to advertise real estate, ships for charter, and employment opportunities, and at the same time to provide information to the public concerning current prices for goods in the Wilmington market, exchange rates, and customs duties in the port. In addition, Jocelyn offered to lead an effort to deepen the channel of the Cape Fear River at the Flats. He sought private subscriptions for the project while promising to investigate machines used in the northern states to clear river channels.[63]

Although the economic changes of the Revolution seemed relatively minor compared to independence and the formation of republican governments in the United States, the economic consequences of dependence bordered on the disastrous. Per capita gross national product declined significantly, perhaps not reaching prewar levels until the 1790s or early 1800s. For North Carolina, the wartime economic dislocations were reflected in severe inflation, the loss of the British West Indies export market (at least directly and legally), and recession years during the mid–1780s. Exports declined along with per capita income. However, Frederick William Marshall overstated the case when he wrote, "The land itself, the people of property, commerce, public and private credit, the currency in circulation, all were laid waste and ruined." Actually, economic recovery in the state, particularly in the commercial sector, was fairly rapid, and the 1780s should not be described as "critical," at least for North Carolina.[64]

4

Colonial Politics

Wilmington's economic importance quickly translated into political prominence. After its incorporation by the General Assembly, the town eclipsed its rival, Brunswick Town, and became one of the most populous urban areas in the colony at the time of the Revolution. Men of wealth and eminence, as well as those aspiring to the same, moved to the town and the Lower Cape Fear. Among them were royal governors Gabriel Johnston, Arthur Dobbs, and William Tryon, whose presence in the region led to the focus of provincial government on the town.

More immediately, however, at the town's inception in 1739–1740, North Carolina and the British colonies along the Atlantic coast were embroiled in the War of Jenkins' Ear with Spain, which in 1744 expanded to become part of King George's War, a global conflict that pitted England against France and Spain in the Atlantic world. In 1741 the English planned an attack on Cartagena, a Spanish fortress in Colombia, and sought colonial aid. The colonies responded with thirty-six companies of one hundred men each. North Carolina contributed four companies, including one under the command of Colonel James Innes from the Lower Cape Fear. The English siege of Cartagena was a fiasco, undermined by poor leadership, disease, and a formidable fortification. Only twenty-five survivors from the Cape Fear company, including Innes, returned.[1]

All the while, Spanish vessels menaced commercial shipping at the mouth of the Cape Fear River, seizing several ships as they entered or cleared the river. As the war escalated in 1744, the North Carolina legislature ordered the construction of several coastal forts to protect against enemy incursions. Among them was Fort Johnston, meant to guard Brunswick Town and the Cape Fear. Work on the fort had barely begun when the Spanish in September 1748 sailed up the river and occupied Brunswick Town for three days. Local men in the area, including sailors and slaves, regrouped and counterattacked, driving the Spanish from the town to the safety of their boats on the river. Eventually the enemy left, but only after their principal ship, the *Fortuna*, sank following a violent explosion that destroyed the vessel, with a loss of ninety lives and considerable property. The retaliatory action by the Brunswick men not only saved their town but also thwarted any intention by the Spanish to sail farther upriver to threaten Wilmington.[2]

Although King George's War ended in 1748, its conclusion proved only a respite in the contention among the European powers. Beginning in 1754, the English and French colonials to the north inaugurated the French and Indian War, which merged two years later into the European conflict known as the Seven Years' War. At the outset of the war, Colonel Innes and North Carolina troops were sent to Virginia but saw no action. Innes continued to Maryland, where he built Fort Cumberland on the Potomac. Fortunately, the foreign threat to the Lower Cape Fear was negligible, for Fort Johnston was not completed until 1764, a year after the termination of the war, and British naval protection was virtually nonexistent. Still, as a precaution, residents of the area outfitted two privateers for their protection. The late Spanish entry into the war in 1762 caused concern for shipping interests, but the war concluded in 1763 without any material damage to the Lower Cape Fear.[3]

While engaged in the wars with Spain and France, North Carolina also exhibited severe internal tensions that left the colony in a state of civil conflict in the late 1740s and early 1750s. Permanent settlement and organized government in North Carolina originated in the Albemarle area, spread to the Pamlico by the end of the seventeenth century, and then to the Neuse region in the early eighteenth century. After the Tuscarora War, 1711–1714, the southern part of the province was opened to development. However, the older counties in the Albemarle retained a disproportionate number of representatives in the lower house of the General Assembly. Because there was no permanent seat of government, the governor, his council, and the legislature customarily met in private residences, and then in the towns of Edenton and Bath. Following the recovery of New Bern at the end of the Tuscarora War, and the settlement of the Lower Cape Fear in the mid–1720s, southerners keenly felt the discrimination in legislative apportionment and the difficulty of attending legislative sessions in the north, which required traversing a hostile terrain, traveling abominable roads, and crossing wide rivers.

Governor Gabriel Johnston, who needed to break the northern stranglehold on the assembly in order to secure payment of his salary and the passage of a new quitrent law, sought southern aid. In 1741 he called for a session of the legislature to meet in Wilmington, hoping that the difficulties of travel would dissuade the northerners from attending. Although the ploy did not work at that time, Johnston persevered. With the aid of Wilmingtonian William Faris, a prominent legislator whom Johnston had rewarded with a vice-admiralty judgeship, the governor again called a legislative session for Wilmington in November 1746. When the Albemarle delegates boycotted the meeting, the southern-controlled General Assembly passed legislation that equalized representation among the counties and established the permanent capital of the province in New Bern. Northerners protested, refused to abide by statutes enacted by the General Assembly, and instituted a civil protest that bordered on anarchy. Resolution of the conflict occurred only after the death of Johnston and the appointment of a new governor, Arthur Dobbs, who arrived in the colony in 1754 with the news that the crown had disallowed the legislation pertaining to representation and the location of the capital. The colony returned to the status quo.[4]

William Faris, who assisted Johnston, served as Wilmington's first legislative representative in the General Assembly of the colony. Using the example of England, where boroughs were allowed representation in Parliament, the North Carolina General Assembly permitted nine towns before the Revolution, including Wilmington, to send delegates to the lower house of the legislature. The number was reduced to six during the Revolution, and raised to seven with the addition of Fayetteville in 1789. Rationalizing borough representation was the need to recognize the interests of urban communities whose peculiar concerns might be overlooked in a predominantly agrarian society.[5]

From its incorporation, Wilmington enjoyed the right of legislative representation. Qualifications for delegates included residence in the town at least three months prior to election, and ownership of a house in Wilmington with one or more brick chimneys. Qualifications for voters also included residence in the town for at least three months, and occupancy, not necessarily ownership, of a house at least sixteen by twenty feet in dimensions. Faris, formerly a merchant of London, operated a store on Market Street for the firm of Faris & Lindsay, and owned a tar house and wharf on Princess Street. Following Faris, Lewis Henry DeRosset, merchant and planter, served Wilmington in the lower house from 1746–47 to 1752. Like Faris, DeRosset evidenced a sense of civic responsibility, serving as county sheriff and justice of the peace, and as a member of the governor's council from 1752 to 1775.[6]

As distinguished as were Faris and DeRosset, however, Cornelius Harnett, Wilmington's last representative before the Revolution was the most renown of the town's colonial legislators. Harnett, who served from

1753 through the last session of the colonial General Assembly in June 1775, sat on various committees, the number of which increased with the years of his service. He was a fixture on the committee to settle public accounts, which he often chaired. Other prestigious committee assignments included those on propositions and grievances, privileges and elections, and public claims. Statutes for the inspection of commodities, the regulation of the fees of the public officers of the colony, and the establishment of a town at Cross Creek reflected his efforts. In 1764 the Lower House placed Harnett on a committee to meet with the governor's council, or Upper House of the legislature, "to settle the Decorum" between the two houses, which often were at loggerheads, and on a committee to provide a liaison between the Lower House and the province's colonial agent in London. According to historian Jack P. Greene, Harnett was unquestionably one of the most important leaders in the North Carolina Lower House in the prerevolutionary years, sharing a position of preeminence only with John Harvey of Perquimans County.[7]

Harnett's service coincided with the glorious British victory in the French and Indian War, which left England in control of the northern and eastern portions of North America, but presaged the dissolution of the British empire. Imbued with a newfound sense of wealth and power, England attempted to strengthen its control over the American colonies along the Atlantic coast by enforcing more rigorously laws governing trade, by restricting westward colonial migration, and by imposing taxes on the provincials to ease the financial burden of imperial administration in the colonies. After enjoying a century and a half of lax oversight by British colonial authorities, the Americans rejected the new policies, leading to confrontation and ultimately to revolution in little more than a decade following the Treaty of Paris in 1763.

Wilmington became a focal point of the opposition to the British in North Carolina, in part due to its commercial orientation, which would suffer from revised British trade policy, and in part due to animated political leaders who spearheaded the resistance movement in North Carolina. Cornelius Harnett, in the General Assembly, led the opposition to the Sugar Act in 1764, which imposed taxes in the form of tariffs on certain colonial imports. The legislature recognized those tariffs as an invidious means of "taxation without representation." Also in 1764, Carolinians objected to the Currency Act, which denied the colony the right to emit paper money and called for the sinking of outstanding currency. Since specie, or hard money, was extremely scarce, and too little paper was available, the Parliamentary law threatened to stifle trade.[8]

Worse was the hated Stamp Act in 1765, which blatantly imposed a variety of taxes on the colonials. Subject to taxation were ships' papers, legal documents, playing cards, dice, newspapers, and college diplomas, among many other items. The law required payments of taxes in specie, and the trial of violations in vice-admiralty courts where the accused were denied the benefit of trial by jury. Opposition appeared in the form of the Stamp Act Congress in New York to protest the law and to institute a non-importation agreement or embargo of British imports as a means of forcing the British to repeal the statute. Organizations called Sons of Liberty sprang up in the seaport towns to thwart the implementation of the Stamp law.

The brunt of the resistance to the Stamp Act in North Carolina centered on Wilmington and Lower Cape Fear. On October 19, 1765, coinciding with the issuance of the "Declaration of Rights and Grievances" by the Stamp Act Congress, several hundred people gathered in Wilmington to protest the law, hang in effigy an inhabitant of the town who favored the act, and burn a large bonfire. The group brought men from their homes to the fire, where they were required to drink a toast to "Liberty, Property, and No Stamp Duty." All retired about midnight. On October 31, the eve of the effective date of the Stamp Act, another crowd gathered in Wilmington to bury symbolically an effigy of "Liberty." Just before the interment, the group discovered that Liberty possessed a pulse, placed the effigy in an armchair before a bonfire, and ended the evening with a general celebration.[9]

Although the Stamp Act became effective on November 1, stamps did not arrive until November 28. Meanwhile, Dr. William Houston, a resident of Duplin County who had been appointed without his knowledge as Stamp Receiver for the Cape Fear, traveled to Wilmington on private business. According to Houston, "The Inhabitants immediately assembled about me & demanded a Categorical Answer whether I intended to put the Act relating [to] the Stamps in force. The Town Bell was rung[,] Drums [were] beating, Colours [were] flying and [a] great concourse of People [were] gathered together." Houston was taken to the courthouse, where he tendered his resignation as Stamp Receiver "to quiet the Minds of the inraged and furious Mobb...," as well as to save himself. The usual celebration followed.[10]

Governor William Tryon next tried to placate the opposition in the Lower Cape Fear. On November 18, 1765, he invited prominent merchants and other gentlemen from the region to meet at his house, Bellfont (formerly Russellborough), just north of Brunswick Town. There he urged acceptance of the Stamp Act, but his guests replied that the law abridged their rights as British subjects and refused to submit. When the stamps

(November 20.)   T H E   (Numb. 58.)

NORTH-CAROLINA GAZETTE.

WILMINGTON, November 20.

ON Saturday the 19th of laſt Month, about Seven of the Clock in the Evening, near Five Hundred People aſſembled together in this Town, and exhibited the Effigy of a certain HONOURABLE GENTLEMAN; and after letting it hang by the Neck for ſome Time, near the Court-Houſe, they made a large Bonfire with a Number of Tar-Barrels, &c. and committed it to the Flames.——The Reaſon aſſigned for the People's Diſlike to that Gentleman, was, from being informed of his having ſeveral Times expreſſed himſelf much in Favour of the STAMP-DUTY.——After the Effigy was conſumed, they went to every Houſe in Town, and bro't all the Gentlemen to the Bonfire, and inſiſted upon their drinking, LIBERTY, PROPERTY, AND NO STAMP-DUTY, and Confuſion to Lord B-TE and all his Adherents, giving three Huzzas at the Concluſion of each Toaſt.——They continued together until 12 of the Clock, and then diſperſed, without doing any Miſchief.   And,

On Thurſday, 31ſt of the ſame Month, in the Evening, a great Number of People again aſſembled, and produced an Effigy of LIBERTY, which they put into a Coffin, and marched in ſolemn Proceſſion with it to the Church-Yard; a Drum in Mourning beating before them, and the Town Bell, muffled, ringing a doleful Knell at the ſame Time;——But before they committed the Body to the Ground, they thought it adviſeable to feel its Pulſe; and when finding ſome Remains of Life, they returned back to a Bonfire ready prepared, placed the Effigy before it in a large Two-arm'd Chair, and concluded the Evening with great Rejoicings, on finding that LIBERTY had ſtill an Exiſtence in the COLONIES,——Not the leaſt Injury was offered to any Perſon.

On Saturday the 16th of this Inſt. WILLIAM HOUSTON, Eſq; Diſtributor of STAMPS for this Province, came to this Town, upon which three or four Hundred People immediately gathered together, with Drums beating and Colours flying, and repaired to the Houſe the ſaid STAMP-OFFICER put up at, and inſiſted upon knowing, " Whether he intended to execute his ſaid Office, or not?" He told them, " He ſhould be very ſorry to execute any Office diſagreeable to the People of the Province." But they, not content with ſuch a Declaration, carried him into the Court-Houſe, where he ſigned a Reſignation ſatisfactory to the Whole.

As ſoon as the STAMP-OFFICER had comply'd with their Deſire, they placed him in an Arm-Chair, carried him firſt round the Court-Houſe, giving three Huzzas at every Corner, and then proceeded with him round one of the Squares of the Town, and ſat him down at the Door of his Lodgings, formed themſelves in a large Circle round him, and gave him three Cheers: They then eſcorted him into the Houſe; where was prepared the beſt Liquors to be had, and treated him very genteely. In the Evening a large Bonfire was made, and no Perſon appeared in the Streets without having LIBERTY, in large Capital Letters, in his Hat.—— They had a large Table near the Bonfire, well furniſh'd with ſeveral Sorts of Liquors, where they drank in great Form, all the favourite AMERICAN Toaſts, giving three Cheers at the Concluſion of each. The whole was conducted with great Decorum, and not the leaſt Inſult offered to any Perſon.

B   ¶ Immediately

*—— Its Brow's the Title Page,
That ſpeaks the Nature of a TRAGIC Volume!*
    Shakeſ.

This is the Place to affix the STAMP.

NORTH CAROLINA GAZETTE, 1765

Excerpt from the *North-Carolina Gazette* (Wilmington), November 20, 1765, recounting the opposition in Wilmington to the Stamp Act. Courtesy of the New Hanover County Public Library, Wilmington.

4—Colonial Politics 77

arrived on board H. M. Sloop *Diligence* on November 28, Tryon ordered Captain Constantine Phipps to keep them on the ship for the present, and that is where they remained for the duration of the crisis. Meanwhile, the lack of stamps stalled shipping on the Cape Fear River, as it did the operation of the courts. Mercantile affairs came to a standstill.[11]

Tryon's next opportunity to seek public support for the Stamp Act occurred in Wilmington on December 20, upon the ceremonial publication of his commission as governor of the province. Tryon had arrived in North Carolina in 1764 as Lieutenant Governor, and had assumed the governorship in 1765 upon the death of Arthur Dobbs. However, his gubernatorial commission arrived later in the year. Captain Phipps brought Tryon from Brunswick Town in his barge or dinghy "with all the parade peculiar to that kind of Gentry...." The mayor, aldermen, and "other Gentlemen" of Wilmington greeted Tryon at the Market Street wharf, and the New Hanover County regiment of militia lined the streets leading from the dock to the house in which Tryon stayed. A discharge of seventeen pieces of artillery saluted the governor, and captains of ships in the harbor unfurled their colors. However, the pomp and pageantry quickly dissipated when Tryon, in his address, stressed "the Necessity of America's helping her Mother" and asked the people to "receive the Stamps."[12]

The crowd responded with a "general Hiss," which changed to a cheer when the captain of a merchant vessel raised the Irish national flag, apparently a tribute to the deceased governor Dobbs, a native of Ireland. Phipps moved to take the flag, which so infuriated the townspeople and militia that they threatened to burn the captain's small boat, probably the vessel used to bring Tryon to Wilmington, unless the colors were surrendered. After Phipps complied with their demand, the mob placed the flag in the boat, dragged it around town, and finally launched it. Following a harangue by an exasperated Tryon, the mob gathered around several barrels of punch and an ox that had been provided by the governor for refreshments. They broke open the barrels and let the punch flow through the streets, put the head of the ox in a gallows, and gave the body to the slaves. But even the "Negroes disdained to taste the Bait of Slavery which was [la]id for their Masters...." Phipps threatened to go to Brunswick Town and bring up the *Diligence* "in order to blow the Town to pieces."[13]

Wilmingtonians and those of the Lower Cape Fear thus successfully defied the governor, in part because the British lacked a satisfactory peacekeeping agency and were unable to restrain the crowd. Sheriffs, constables, and municipal leaders all joined the protesters, rendering the governor's position untenable, short of full-scale violence. Phipps never effected his threat to destroy Wilmington. And on behalf of Wilmington, mayor Moses John DeRosset attempted in part to exonerate the townspeople by asking Governor Tryon not to "lay the whole Blame of every Transaction relative to the Opposition made to the Stamp-Act on this Borough when it is so well known that the whole country has been equally concerned in it." The governor accepted the apology, declaring that he was "willing to forget every Impropriety of Conduct" that the mayor, aldermen, and town of Wilmington "have shown personally towards me in the late Commotions." Nevertheless, Tryon retaliated for the embarrassment by moving the seat of government to New Bern. When he arrived in North Carolina, Tryon apparently intended to make Wilmington the capital of the colony, and purchased Bellfont with that idea in mind. After the Wilmington debacle, the governor persuaded the legislature in 1766 to denominate New Bern the permanent capital and to build a magnificent statehouse and governor's residence in that town—Tryon Palace.[14]

Wilmingtonians were also in the vanguard of a final demonstration of armed resistance in February 1766 that resulted in the opening of the ports of the Cape Fear to commerce. On February 18, after Captain Jacob Lobb of H. M. Sloop *Diligence* seized two merchants ships for failure to carry stamped papers and the colony's attorney general ruled that the ships should be sent to the vice-admiralty court in Halifax, Nova Scotia, for final disposition, numerous residents of the southern counties gathered in Wilmington, where they organized as the Sons of Liberty and pledged to prevent "entirely the operation of the Stamp Act." The following day, as many as a thousand men, including Cornelius Harnett, the mayor and aldermen of Wilmington, and other inhabitants of the town, converged on Brunswick Town to confront Tryon. Although the governor refused to be cowed, the mob eventually retrieved the two captured ships and forced royal customs officers and all other public officials in the region to swear that they would never issue stamped paper. At that point the river was open to commerce. Tryon contemplated asking the home government for troops to quell the disorders, but that action became unnecessary when Parliament repealed the Stamp Act in March 1766.[15]

The Stamp Act was dead, but the British quickly imposed additional taxes on the colonies in the form of tariffs in 1767. The Townshend Act placed duties on the importation of lead, glass, paint, paper, and tea. Again the colonials instituted non-importation to attempt to coerce the British into rescinding the taxes, though the effort lacked the efficacy of that in 1765–1766 to oppose the Stamp Act. The counties of the Lower Cape Fear endorsed trade restrictions in September 1769, even before the General Assembly took similar action in November of that year. In response to a

4—Colonial Politics 79

call for cooperation from South Carolina, a general meeting of the Sons of Liberty from New Hanover, Brunswick, Onslow, Bladen, Cumberland, and Duplin counties convened in Wilmington in June 1770, at which time the representatives reaffirmed non-importation, appointed local committees in Wilmington and the counties to enforce the agreement, and called for a meeting in Wilmington in July "to consult upon such measures, as may appear most eligible, for evincing their patriotism and Loyalty in the present critical Situation of affairs." At the July gathering, Harnett, chairman of the Sons of Liberty in the area, wrote the Sons of Liberty in South Carolina:

> We beg leave to assure you, that the inhabitants ... are convinced of the necessity of adhering strictly to their former resolutions, and you may depend, they are as tenacious of their just rights as any of their brethren on the continent, and firmly resolved to stand or fall with them in support of the common cause of American liberty.

Regardless of their intentions, however, shipping remained uninhibited, and Governor Tryon contended that non-importation was a failure. Parliament, in a conciliatory gesture in 1770, repealed the Townshend tariffs, except for the levy on tea, and for two years relations between the mother country and colonies improved.[16]

Diverting attention from the imperial scene at the juncture was the internal crisis in North Carolina known as the Regulator Movement. Inhabitants of the western counties, or backcountry, who felt burdened by inequitable representation in the General Assembly, unjust and onerous taxes, and corrupt local officials, began to seek redress for their grievances in the mid–1760s. Obtaining little satisfaction from the provincial government and Governor Tryon, the Regulators prepared to go to the Superior Court meeting at Hillsborough to air their demands. Tryon, with eastern militia, marched to the Orange County capital, met the Regulators, and managed to defuse a dangerous situation without bloodshed. However, it proved to be a temporary truce, for two years later the Regulators returned to Hillsborough, terrorized the town, and disrupted the court. Rumors circulated that the Regulators next intended to descend upon New Bern, the capital, where they threatened to "lay the Town in Ashes...."[17]

Once more Governor Tryon organized eastern militia for a foray into the backcountry to confront the Regulators. On a visit to Wilmington he found the people in the Cape Fear region "unanimous and spirited in this Cause, and the Officers successful in recruiting." Tryon and his force confronted and routed the Regulators at the Battle of Alamance in May 1771.

Participating in the battle were a militia company from New Hanover County and an artillery company of sailors from Wilmington, the latter commanded by Robert Schaw, Wilmington merchant and town commissioner. Dr. Thomas Cobham of Wilmington was one of the physicians attending the governor's troops. Upon hearing of the engagement at Alamance, though unaware of the decisiveness of the victory over the Regulators, Archibald Maclaine, William Hooper, and Robert Hogg, a committee representing citizens of Wilmington, informed Tryon that they were collecting money to raise a body of men to reinforce the governor if necessary. Tryon thanked the committee but assured them that his army was "fully sufficient to restore peace to the country, without putting the public or individuals to any additional expence by raising new forces."[18]

Imperial difficulties began anew in June 1772 when Rhode Islanders destroyed the *Gaspee*, a British revenue cutter, and the colonies in 1773 began to form committees of correspondence to speed communication and propaganda among them, including news about the *Gaspee* and the Tea Act of 1773. Patterned after Massachusetts town committees, the committees of correspondence represented the onset of colonial extralegal organizations that eventually replaced the British governmental apparatus. Josiah Quincy, Jr. of Boston traveled the east coast trying to raise support for the committees of correspondence. He arrived in Wilmington in late March 1773. On the second day in town he dined with William Hooper and about twenty other men, and spent the evening and night with Cornelius Harnett, "the Samuel Adams of North Carolina except in point of fortune," according to Quincy. At that time Quincy found a ready rapport with Harnett and Robert Howe, a prominent planter who owned Kendall Plantation on the Cape Fear River below Wilmington. According to Quincy, "The plan of Continental correspondence [was] highly relished, much wished for[,] and resolved upon, as proper to be pursued." The General Assembly in December 1773, no doubt at the urging of Harnett, created a committee of correspondence that included Harnett and Hooper.[19]

In addition to Harnett, William Hooper emerged as a leading opponent of British policies in Wilmington by 1773. Born in Boston, educated at Harvard, and having studied law under James Otis, Hooper had moved to Wilmington in 1764. Despite delicate health, Hooper necessarily traveled throughout the province in all seasons and weather on legal business. At Hillsborough in 1770 he had been dragged through the streets by the Regulators. In addition to his house on Second Street between Market and Princess, he owned several stores in Wilmington and a summer residence, Finian, on Masonboro Sound. In 1766 he was elected recorder of

William Hooper (1742–1790), lawyer of Wilmington, early advocate of resistance to England, and one of North Carolina's signers of the Declaration of Independence, 1776. Courtesy of the New Hanover County Public Library, Wilmington.

the borough of Wilmington. In 1773 Hooper apparently made a conscious effort to engage in provincial politics, for as Quincy noted, he was a "Whig" or radical, who was "caressed" by that group, and who sought election under their influence. And Hooper was successful, representing New Hanover County in the General Assembly from 1773 through its last session under royal government in 1775.[20]

Wilmingtonians moved into the forefront of the Revolutionary movement in North Carolina following the passage of the Tea Act by Parliament in 1773, which precipitated a series of "tea parties," beginning with the one in Boston in December of that year. Parliament retaliated with legislation known as the Intolerable or Coercive Acts, designed to punish the colonials. After Massachusetts issued a formal invitation to the colonies to hold a intercolonial congress to meet in Philadelphia in 1774 to consider a response to the Intolerable Acts, Wilmingtonians, led by Hooper, met on July 21 to call for a North Carolina provincial congress to select delegates to the continental congress. Hooper served as one of North Carolina's representatives to the first Continental Congress, and was reelected to the second Continental Congress which met in 1775. A year later, with Joseph Hewes and William Penn, he signed the Declaration of Independence on behalf of North Carolina.[21]

North Carolina held five provincial congresses from August 1774 to October-November 1776. The second congress ratified the proceedings of the first Continental Congress, the third and fourth congresses established provisional governments for the colony of North Carolina, and the fifth congress drafted a constitution for the independent state of North Carolina. Unrepresented in the first congress, the town of Wilmington sent Harnett to the succeeding three, and Hooper to the fifth. Serving with Harnett in the third congress was Archibald Maclaine, Wilmington attorney

Monument erected at the intersection of Market and Fourth streets in Wilmington by the North Carolina Society of the Carolina Dames of America to recognize the "Colonial Heroes of the Lower Cape Fear." Courtesy of the New Hanover Public Library, Wilmington.

and town commissioner, who came to the colony from Scotland by way of Ireland and owned considerable property in town, including a residence on Second Street south of Dock. Hooper represented New Hanover as a county delegate in the first four congresses, and Wilmington in the fifth.[22]

Doubtlessly Wilmington's most active patriot was Cornelius Harnett, the "Samuel Adams of North Carolina." In August 1775 the third provincial congress created the Provincial Council as a provisional government for the colony after royal governor Josiah Martin had fled New Bern, the capital, and had taken refuge on board the warship *Cruizer* in the Cape Fear River. Harnett became the president of the Council. When the fourth provincial congress replaced the Provincial Council with the Council of Safety, Harnett again was chosen president. According to historian R. D. W. Connor, "Harnett thus became the first chief executive of North Carolina independent of the Crown. Governor in all but name, he exercised greater authority than the people have since conferred upon their chief executive...." And following the establishment of an independent state government in 1776, Harnett was elected to the Council of State, an advisory body to the governor. It was a short-lived tenure, however, because early in 1777 the legislature elected Harnett to replace Hooper in the Continental Congress.[23]

In the meantime, Harnett also chaired the Wilmington–New Hanover Committee of Safety, one of many local associations designed to enforce the dictates of the Continental Congresses and ultimately to engineer the Revolutionary movement. The first Continental Congress adopted the Continental Association, a series of resolutions embodying non-importation, non-exportation, and nonconsumption agreements that meant to bring economic pressure to bear on the British. The congress also declared that the colonials should adopt life-styles of industry, frugality, and morality that befitted a people contending for their liberty and republican government. To that end the congress urged the creation of local committees of safety to enforce its mandates and, in the process, reveal "foes to the rights of British-Americans" who would be ostracized by friends of "American Liberty." The committees of safety proved indispensable in effecting the Revolution.[24]

Although some committees appeared in the wake of North Carolina's first Provincial Congress, most arose in response to the directive of the Continental Congress. In Wilmington on November 23, 1774, one of the first committees of safety in North Carolina was organized "to carry more effectively into Execution the resolves of the late congress held in Philadelphia." On January 1, 1775, New Hanover County formed a committee that merged with that of Wilmington, though they later drifted apart. The Wilmington–New Hanover committee tried to coordinate the patriot effort to oppose the British, to reinforce the revolutionary spirit among other committees, and to render assistance against British military threats as the occasion warranted. It reminded the Brunswick County committee that a ship, recently arrived from Glasgow and anchored in the lower reaches of the Cape Fear River, violated the non-importation agreement. A letter to the Bladen committee thanked that group for apprehending two men suspected of spying for the British. And the Wilmington–New Hanover committee congratulated its Cumberland counterpart "on the favourable disposition of their Committee & County to support the Common cause of America."[25]

Enforcement of non-importation and non-exportation fell principally to the committees in the port towns. Cargoes that arrived after the non-importation deadline of December 1, 1774, were auctioned, and the proceeds were earmarked for the aid of Boston, whose port had been closed by the British after the tea incident. Wilmington merchants dutifully reported the arrival of cargoes. Several violations of the shipping directive involved slaves, at which point the committee, with two exceptions (one for Cornelius Harnett), ordered the bondsmen reshipped and demanded proof from the importers that reshipment had occurred. Nonexportation became effective on September 10, 1775. As a result, the Wilmington committee forbade the loading of vessels after that date "on pain of [incurring] the displeasure of the public." When informed that several ships already loaded and cleared to leave before September 10 had been delayed, the committee, following congressional instructions, allowed them to depart. It also authorized a Captain Magill of the sloop *Ranger* to clear for New York with a cargo of deerskins. Otherwise, no other vessels left Wilmington without the committee's permission.[26]

Ultimately, the safety committees pressed the decision for independence upon the populace. By use of intimidation and public ridicule, they silenced the loyalists and swelled the ranks of the revolutionaries. Perhaps the most effective weapon wielded by the Whigs was the association or "test," a written statement of principle that proclaimed American rights and denounced British tyranny. More specifically, the association rejected British taxation and pledged to follow the dictates of the Continental Congress and North Carolina provincial congresses. People were forced to declare their sentiments and publicly sign the association. Wilmington used the resolutions of the Continental Congress of 1774 as its first test; other committees soon followed. Subsequently, the various committees formulated their own associations, usually an elaboration of the Continental Association proposed by the Continental Congress. Often the associations served as models for other committees: Cumberland used that of Wilmington.[27]

After Lexington and Concord in April 1775, the declarations within the associations became more strident, contending that the Americans were justified in exercising force to resist force, and calling for the patriots to pledge to sacrifice their lives and fortunes to secure freedom and safety. Wilmington drafted two additional associations in March and June 1775. The latter referred to "a Wicked and despotic" British government that, by its actions, offered sufficient justification "to drive an Oppress'd people to the Use of Arms." Therefore, the committee declared that it was "the Duty of Good Citizens" to resist "force by Force..." and stated that the people were "Ready to sacrifice [their] Lives and fortunes to secure ... [the] freedom and Safety [of their country]." Associations adopted by the Pitt and Tryon committees echoed those sentiments.[28]

The committees pushed the collection of signatures ruthlessly. Not only did the members of the committees sign the associations themselves, but they also presented the documents to the people, sometimes at large or by way of the militias. Janet Schaw, a Scotswoman visiting the Lower

Cape Fear in 1775, graphically described the pressure exerted on recalcitrants. A committeeman or militia officer went to a plantation where the owner was invited to sign the association or suffer the consequences—destruction of crops, livestock, and home; seizure of slaves; and perhaps bodily harm. According to Schaw, "Not to chuse the first requires more courage than they are possessed of, and I believe this method has seldom failed with the lower sort [of people]." In Wilmington the militia intimidated those who refused to sign. On one occasion Schaw found several loyalists surrounded by local soldiers. When an officer was asked by what authority he required approval of the association, he pointed to his soldiers and said, "there is my Authority, dispute it if you can." The loyalists stood their ground until two o'clock the following morning, when they were released. The standoff was ineffective; on another visit to Wilmington a few days later, Schaw found it "intirely deserted by the Tories, some of whom are out of the country, and others gone out of the way...."[29]

Mandatory militia service was another important means used by the committees to secure support for the Revolution. When called to the musters, men had to declare their loyalty; many may have served reluctantly but remained in service for fear of retribution from their fellow citizens. In July 1775 the Wilmington safety committee demanded that every white man capable of bearing arms enroll in one of the two local militia companies, and that anyone who had not signed the association must do so immediately. The committee considered failure to participate "as a Declaration of Intention inimicable to the Common cause of America." Governor Martin confirmed the success of this tactic when he reported that "Scotch Merchants at Wilmington who so long maintained their loyalty have lately been compelled ostensibly to join in sedition by appearing under Arms at the Musters appointed by the Committees...."[30]

Among those suspected of disloyalty to the American cause was Dr. James Fallon, a Wilmington physician. When the Wilmington committee discovered that Dr. Fallon was the author of a two-page tract critical of the American cause, it ordered his arrest. Little time passed before Col. James Moore, a militia officer, warned the committee that Dr. Fallon was a "dangerous Person among the Soldiers," and that he could not keep the physician in the guardhouse any longer for fear of "injuring the common cause and running the risk of the public safety." Despite strict orders to the contrary, Dr. Fallon apparently was able to leave the guardhouse freely, entertain visitors, and conduct a regular correspondence. The committee then put Dr. Fallon in the public jail, with orders to the sheriff and jailer directing that the physician receive no visitors and that his correspondence be censored by the committee. Such determination had the desired effect: two weeks later the doctor indicated a willingness to submit to the committee and offer security for his proper deportment.[31]

In addition to dealing with dissidents, the committees began to assume a defensive military posture by amassing gunpowder, lead, flints, and weapons whenever possible. In January 1775, following a royal proclamation banning the exportation of gunpowder from England to the colonies, the Wilmington committee ascertained the amount of powder in the town and began collecting money with which to purchase all that was available. The committee justified its action as being necessary for "the worst Contingency." The collection of military stores began in earnest in the summer of 1775, following the outbreak of fighting in Massachusetts, and continued into 1776. The Wilmington committee confiscated small cannons and handguns from the populace, purchased lead, and engaged men to make musket balls, cartridges, and gunpowder.[32]

The military preparations proved prescient, particularly for the Lower Cape Fear region, which more than any other area of North Carolina, assumed a critical importance in the Revolution. The strategic value of the area inhered in three interrelated factors: the Cape Fear River offered large, oceangoing vessels, including British warships easy access inland from the sea; large numbers of loyalists, particularly Highland Scots, inhabited the Upper Cape Fear valley; and royal governor Josiah Martin, after his ejection from the capital in New Bern in late May 1775, sought refuge first at Fort Johnston and then on board the *Cruizer*, a British vessel stationed in the river below Wilmington.[33]

Ensconced on the *Cruizer*, Governor Martin wasted little time trying to regain control of the colony. The governor's first priority was to strengthen Fort Johnston, a bastion that had been constructed during the French and Indian War to guard the Cape Fear River. Concerned that the fort might become a center for British military operations and a haven for runaway slaves who might be enticed to the British side by promises of freedom, the Wilmington safety committee proposed to destroy Fort Johnston. On July 19, 1775, Col. Robert Howe led some five hundred men, mainly from the militias of Brunswick and New Hanover Counties, on an assault that quickly overwhelmed the lightly manned fort and burned the structure. The Wilmington safety committee tendered its thanks to the participants in the expedition and celebrated its first victory over the British.[34]

Although Fort Johnston had been demolished, the British threat was hardly diminished. By proclamations and personal correspondence, Governor Martin denounced the revolutionaries and tried to rally those who remained loyal to the king. Among the Highland Scots of the Upper Cape

Fear valley he had allies; and the Wilmington committee noted with alarm in late July 1775 that the governor intended to visit the backcountry, where, it was asserted, he intended to collect men and kindle the flames of a civil war. In November the Brunswick safety committee ominously announced that another warship, accompanied by troop transports, had arrived on the river.[35]

In response, the Wilmington committee heightened its defensive preparations. Upon the request of the Brunswick committee, it sent carriage guns to defend Brunswick Town from possible attack. To protect Wilmington, the committee empowered three of its members to sink boats in the river channel to block the British access to the town by water. The committee also undertook the construction of breastworks below Wilmington to guard the town's land exposure. Finally, the committee sought gunpowder from the New Bern committee, and troops from the western counties. As 1775 closed, the people of Wilmington were prepared for the worst.[36]

Their apprehensions were well founded. Governor Martin asked his superiors in England for soldiers who would come to the Cape Fear region and join those who remained loyal to the Crown, particularly the Highland Scots in the Upper Cape Fear valley. Together the troops and loyalists would take the Lower Cape Fear and Wilmington, and gradually extend royal authority throughout the province. The home authorities agreed. Meanwhile, Wilmingtonians, alert to the plans of the governor, evacuated women and children, threw up breastworks throughout the town and along the river, and sought militia from surrounding counties for protection. Although the *Cruizer* appeared on two occasions, no harm was done and the crisis abated after the Scots were defeated at the Battle of Moores Creek Bridge on February 27, 1776.[37]

Martin's plan had gone awry when the Scots marched on Wilmington before the British troops arrived, leaving the Scots to face the overwhelming numbers of patriot militia in the area. At the end of March, the long awaited soldiers, under Sir Henry Clinton, appeared, but the first group was too small to constitute a major threat. However, in May some four to five thousand additional troops, under command of General Charles Cornwallis, arrived. To their dismay, no significant force of loyalists stood ready to assist them. Thus the British contented themselves with burning and pillaging the lower reaches of the Cape Fear, never directly threatening Wilmington. They departed late in May for Charleston, leaving behind several men-of-war to blockade the river.[38]

The transition to independence led to the denouement of the committees of safety, particularly following the April 1776 meeting of the

Fourth Provincial Congress, which created the Council of Safety to serve as a de facto government for North Carolina until the end of the year, when a constitution established a formal government for the new state. Although the committees of safety faded, yielding to a more powerful central authority that guided political and military affairs in North Carolina, the town and county organizations had served an indispensable function in effecting the revolution. Initially the committees were the extralegal means of protest by which the Continental and provincial congresses attempted to intimidate the British and impose their will upon the people. Subsequently the town and county safety committees became, in effect, counter-governments that gradually discredited legitimate authority, assumed the functions of duly constituted local governments, and provided an opportunity for the transfer of individual loyalty to the Revolutionary cause. Governor Josiah Martin expressed well the impact of the safety committees when he lamented, "usurping some new authority every day, executive, judicial or legislative, as the case might be, their powers soon became practically unlimited.[39]

Knowing from previous wars that the unguarded coast invited enemy attacks, and realizing that little assistance could be expected from the Continental authorities, the Provincial Congress in 1775 created a navy to protect the sounds and the Cape Fear River. The force consisted of three armed brigs and two row galleys. The three sailing vessels were two-masted brigs, commissioned the *King Tammany*, the *Pennsylvania Farmer*, and the *General Washington*, the last destined for the Cape Fear. The 120-ton *Pennsylvania Farmer* carried sixteen guns and 110 officers and men. The *King Tammany* was smaller, mounted with only twelve guns. The records reveal neither the size, armament, nor complement of the *General Washington*.[40]

None of the ships served to deter the British threats. The state occasionally used the *Pennsylvania Farmer* and the *King Tammany* for commercial voyages to the West Indies and for privateering. The *General Washington* proved useless. John Forster, one of the commissioners in charge of fitting out the vessel, reported in 1777 that he was unable to man the *General Washington* because the seamen of the area had gone to other ports or had enlisted in the Continental Army. But even if sailors had been available, Forster had no money to pay them or to purchase supplies for the ship. Although consideration was given to sending the *General Washington* on a privateering mission, which might lure sailors and underwrite expenses, the notion was dismissed by those who wanted the vessel to remain and protect the commerce of the region.[41]

The failure of the brigs to defend the coast as originally planned led to the decision to sell the *General Washington*. The sale was scheduled for

Wilmington in February 1778, at which time "guns, stores, tackle, apparel and furniture" would be auctioned. Apparently the transaction never occurred, for in April several British prisoners were imprisoned on the *General Washington*, and the governor of the state was notified that they were willing to serve on the ship. The final demise of the *General Washington* is unknown, though one historian has conjectured that it might have been the armed brig destroyed by a British raiding party along the Cape Fear River in February 1781.[42]

Despite the failure at Moores Creek Bridge and the departure of the troops from the Lower Cape Fear in the spring of 1776, there remained in Wilmington and North Carolina numerous British sympathizers, loyalists or tories, who opposed the revolutionary movement and hoped for a reconciliation between the colonies and their mother country. While the decision to remain loyal or to rebel was a very personal one, loyalists often had been born abroad and had immigrated to America after 1763; examples included the Highland Scots, who arrived in large numbers in North Carolina as late at 1775. Other distinguishing characteristics of loyalists included support for the Church of England, pursuit of the mercantile trade, and occupation of a government office. In short, a close attachment to the mother country through religion, commerce, and politics tended to orient men toward England. In the North Carolina Confiscation Act of 1779, for instance, merchants constituted 45 of the 68 men whose property was slated for sequestration.[43]

Wilmington proved a hotbed of loyalism, due particularly to the influence of the mercantile trade in the port. According to a visitor in 1775, all the merchants were British or Scotch-Irish, who "disapproved of the present proceedings. Many of them intend quitting the country as fast as their affairs will permit them...." Among those merchants was Robert Hogg, a native of Scotland and a town commissioner, who first cooperated with the local safety committee but left the colony in 1775 when more extreme measures were advocated. To avoid the confiscation of his property, he returned to Wilmington in 1778 to request citizenship and the restoration of his assets, and died in 1780. At least forty-four merchants lived in the town and its environs on the eve of the Revolution, including Hogg. More than half were unsympathetic, if not openly hostile, to the rebel cause. Ten appeared before the Loyalist Claims Commission, twelve fled to England, and two died in battle fighting the Americans.[44]

From the outset, revolutionaries proved unable to crush the loyalist opposition. Pro-British activities often escaped the notice of the safety committee, and surely the Scots at Moores Creek, though defeated, had been equipped and financed by merchants at Cross Creek and Wilmington. Even after the departure of many loyalists early in the war, brigadier general of the militia John Ashe wrote Governor Richard Caswell in 1777 that so many residents of Wilmington were "disaffected," he had ordered as many of the county militia as he thought reliable to watch the town. The following year William Hooper claimed that the loyalists in Wilmington were making "observations ... painful to men who love our cause." And despite the best efforts of the safety committee and militia, as late as 1780 some twenty men in Wilmington still had not taken the oath of allegiance to the state. The loyalists remained true to their principles and only awaited the chance to demonstrate their allegiance to the Crown. The British occupation of Wilmington in 1781 offered them that opportunity.[45]

After Cornwallis failed to take Charleston in 1776, the British turned their attention entirely to the northern and mid–Atlantic states. Finding little success after several years, they refocused on the southern states. The British captured Savannah, Georgia, late in 1778, re-royalized Georgia, and proceeded into South Carolina. Charleston fell in 1780, and many of its residents, including some of the "first Families," moved to Wilmington before seeking safer haven. At the same time, "universal alarm and anxiety" filled Wilmingtonians as they rightly anticipated an enemy movement to the north. The British marched through South Carolina, winning significant victories over the Continentals but never pacifying the state. Leaving South Carolina behind, Cornwallis, who had been given command of the southern forces, and Governor Martin moved to extend British control into North Carolina, feeling that state was the key to retaining British gains in Georgia and South Carolina. To support his offensive against General Nathanael Greene, commander of the Continental troops, Cornwallis planned to establish a post in Wilmington. Not only could the port supply his army but it could serve as an escape route to the sea, should that option become necessary. In addition, troops in Wilmington might serve as a source of protection for loyalists, and inspire them to action, for the British intended to rely upon adherents of the Crown in order to pacify fully the state.[46]

Cornwallis ordered Lieutenant Colonel Nisbet Balfour, commander at Charleston, to send an expedition to the Cape Fear, where Cornwallis thought it would be "of the utmost consequence for our own Security & for the effect it will have on the minds of the People in N. Carolina." Balfour named Major James Henry Craig to head the expedition, which consisted of a naval complement of three warships and support vessels, plus 300 troops. When the force reached the Lower Cape Fear in late January 1781, Wilmingtonians were alarmed. Those who did not flee surrendered. North Carolina Governor Abner Nash correctly expressed the state's reaction when he wrote that the occupation of Wilmington "will distress us very much, as we are unprepared to receive them." The British presence in Wilmington altered the course of the war in southeastern North Carolina. It hindered the recruitment of Continental troops in the area, and, more importantly, it intensified loyalist activity, which in turn made rebel control of the countryside tenuous at best, particularly after Craig purposely sent out raiding and foraging parties to wreak havoc upon the patriots.[47]

Craig, meanwhile, generally met a ready welcome in Wilmington, where the loyalists were "pretty numerous and influential." When Craig circulated a petition requiring inhabitants "to be admitted to a dependence upon Great Britain," only two men, Thomas Maclaine and John Huske, refused to sign. The major proceeded to name Samuel Campbell, merchant and former town commissioner, commander of the Loyal Militia. Campbell later went to Charleston, where he was colonel commandant of the militia for the Southern District. Ultimately his property in North Carolina was seized, and Campbell went to Nova Scotia. Dr. Thomas Cobham also aided the British. Upon the occupation, he joined the British forces and was appointed surgeon to the naval hospital in Charleston. He remained with the hospital after the war, when it was moved to New Providence in the Bahamas. Upon his discharge in 1786, Cobham relocated to England. His property likewise was seized and sold by the state of North Carolina.[48]

Craig achieved a reputation for dealing harshly with the local people. How one fared in Wilmington depended upon one's loyalty to the Crown. The pro–British, like Campbell and Cobham, seemed to prosper, while Elizabeth Parker, a resident of Wilmington for seventeen years, ran a successful boardinghouse with the "assistance of some neighboring Loyalists." Mary Boyd, wife of patriot Adam Boyd, who had published the *Cape-Fear Mercury* and enlisted in the army, found herself "in a constant state of alarm" and had to depend upon her slaves for support. Although several men fled Wilmington, among them William Hooper, their wives remained at the mercy of Craig. According to Hooper, his wife and other ladies were expelled from town and "suffered to carry with them nothing but their wearing apparel...." Craig refused the women carriages but offered a boat. He then forbade the boat to proceed, causing the women to return to shore and stand in the sun "for several hours" before changing his mind again and dispatching the vessel. However, as Mrs. Hooper made her way to Hillsborough, she "greatly profited by her Journey in point of health. The back country and exercise ... repaired her shattered constitution, and the fatigue of a few months is amply compensated by

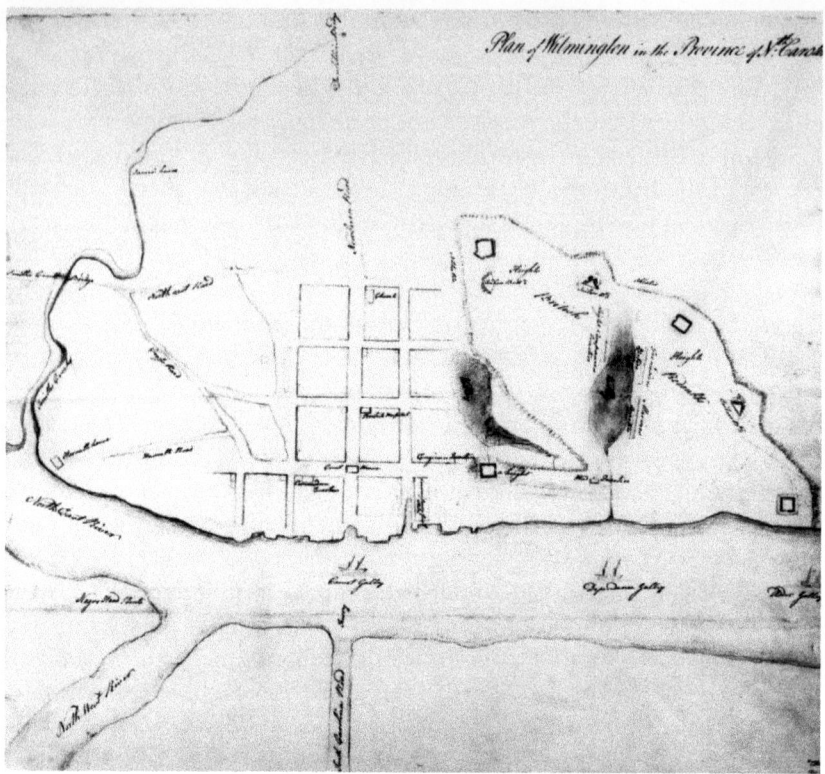

Map of Wilmington during the British occupation, 1781, showing British quarters, fortifications, and warships stationed in the Cape Fear River. Courtesy of the North Carolina Office of Archives and History, Raleigh.

the accidental consequences of it," according to her husband. Less fortunate was Cornelius Harnett, who had fled to Onslow County but was captured by the British and brought back to Wilmington, where he suffered under his confinement and later died from the rigors of his imprisonment.[49]

Joining Craig in Wilmington was Cornwallis, who spent two and a half weeks in the town in April 1781. The general and his army had entered North Carolina in the vicinity of Charlotte, and ultimately defeated Greene and his troops in the Battle of Guilford Court House in March. It was a pyrrhic victory for Cornwallis, who lost one-fourth of his men and found himself without supplies. Thus, he marched to Wilmington, which he reached on April 9; there he remained at least part of the time in the Burgwin-Wright House on the corner of Market and Third streets. When Cornwallis departed on April 25, he left his sick and wounded. Craig was under orders to leave Wilmington when Cornwallis reached Virginia, but the major decided to remain because the British presence would assure the loyalists of a base of support. As Craig pointed out, the principal loyalist grievance throughout the war was that the British military would arrive in an area, call upon the king's friends to announce themselves, and then desert them, leaving them to the mercy of the rebels. Wrote Craig, "I am pretty confident even with what force I have I could encourage & support them so as to become Masters of the Country & disarm the rebels...."[50]

Although the loyalists did not become "Masters of the Country," they and the British military vied on even terms with the rebels for several months for control of the Lower Cape Fear. Craig also ventured on successful raids as far as Duplin County, where he defeated his opposition in the Battle of Rockfish Creek, and to New Bern, where he remained for two days. When the patriots finally massed militia under command of General Griffith Rutherford north of Wilmington, and news arrived of Cornwallis' surrender at Yorktown in October, Craig prudently decided to evacuate Wilmington, taking his regulars and loyalists. It was a hurried departure. Loyalist Rigdon Brice "lost most of his Baggage & Effects." John Mackay left "Goods & Effects of considerable value ... on the wharfs, & what he put on board the Transports was Plundered & destroyed by the Soldiers, Sailors, or Negroes, on the passage." Arthur Benning, his wife, and children left "without anything but their Wearing Apparel." As Craig and the British set sail for Charleston on November 14, Rutherford and his troops entered the town, able to see the sails of the departing vessels as they moved down the river.[51]

Although the Revolution forced the departure of many loyalists, the movement for independence divided the patriots. The debate over the state constitution of 1776 revealed the dichotomy of views, perhaps best described as "conservative" and "radical." Conservatives favored a powerful executive, protection for property, an independent judiciary, and restricted suffrage—an elitist conception of government. Radicals envisioned a more democratic polity, including a powerful legislature, a weak executive, diminished property requirements for voting and holding office, and a bill of rights. In drafting a state constitution, the fifth provincial congress compromised but produced an essentially democratic frame of government that recognized the principle of popular sovereignty in a constitution that was accompanied by a bill of rights.[52]

Meanwhile, in 1776–1777 the Continental Congress in Philadelphia undertook the task of drafting a constitution to bind the thirteen states in a formal national union. Harnett, elected to the congress in 1777, like North Carolina's other delegates, showed extreme concern over the need to protect the rights of the states and the individuals within them. Nonetheless, Harnett approved the Articles of Confederation that emerged from Congress in late 1777. Realistically, he viewed the Articles as providing "the best Confederacy that could be formed, especially when we consider the Number of States, their different Interests, Customs, etc." The state legislature at first refused to ratify the Articles of Confederation, fearing national encroachment upon states rights, but under the constant prodding from Harnett reversed its decision and approved the constitution in April 1778. When the last of the states ratified the Articles of Confederation in 1781, a national government organized to replace the Continental Congress.[53]

In North Carolina and Wilmington the Articles proved a source of contention between the radicals and conservatives. The former appreciated the democratic aspects of the government, and more particularly, the safeguards provided for state autonomy and individual rights. Conservatives deplored the evident ineptitude of the national government, the embarrassments suffered in foreign affairs, and the failure to protect property rights and guard against such popular excesses as Shays' Rebellion in Massachusetts. While the radicals, led by Timothy Bloodworth, dominated New Hanover County, the conservatives, led by Archibald Maclaine, controlled Wilmington, though not without opposition.[54]

Reflecting the temper of Wilmington's politics during and after the Revolution were the elections for borough representatives to the General Assembly. Conservatives William Hooper (1777–1779, 1780–1782), Archibald Maclaine (1783–1787), and Edward Jones (1788–1792) proved victorious. Hooper enjoyed the confidence of the town after he returned from his stint as a North Carolina delegate to the Continental Congress. When Hooper moved to Hillsborough, Maclaine proved unbeatable, though he faced opposition from radical John Walker. The election in 1782 found twenty-four votes evenly divided between Maclaine and Walker. The sheriff cast the deciding ballot in favor of the former. The small number of votes probably reflected wartime conditions, for eighty-three votes had been counted in 1780. Citing the press of professional and personal obligations, Maclaine declined reelection in 1787, favoring Joshua Potts or, failing Potts, Edward Jones. Potts won by a single vote, but his election was disallowed, and Jones succeeded him.[55]

The municipal elections were often tempestous affairs. Wrote Maclaine in 1783, "The violence, the chicane, and the brutality of Walker (Maclaine's opponent), Tom Bloodworth and their commissaries, were excessive; & had not my friends as well as myself attended very close, many of those who voted would have been frightened away." Several times between 1780 and 1790 the General Assembly heard complaints about irregularities in the Wilmington town elections. Although the House of Commons denied challenges in 1780, 1784, and 1788, it vacated Hooper's seat in 1782 and invalidated the election of Potts in 1787. Walker claimed that Potts was not a freeholder, owning in 1786 no property "more than one Poll and a pair of Cheer Wheels." The House seemed to dismiss that claim when it upheld the eligibility of Potts, but it declared the election illegal because a number of non-taxpayers had voted while suffrage had been denied to bona fide citizens who had paid their taxes. Wilmington's electorate was clearly divided between the radicals and conservatives, and Walker was a tenacious opponent, though he failed to secure election.[56]

From the inception of the Confederation government in 1781, efforts had been made to strengthen the national authority. That movement culminated in 1787, when a convention representative of twelve states met in Philadelphia to draft the federal Constitution to replace the Articles of Confederation. As radicals dominated North Carolina, the state greeted the new constitution cautiously. North Carolina was the seventh state to call for a ratifying convention, and the twelfth to meet in convention. The elections in August 1787 for the state legislature portended trouble for a stronger national government. Maclaine evaluated the results from the conservative perspective: "We have a set of fools and knaves in every part of the State, who seem to act as by concert; and are uniformly against any man of abilities and virtue." From Maclaine's perspective, men of "abilities and virtue," including himself, supported the new constitution.[57]

Although the elections produced an apparent radical majority in the General Assembly, the legislature called for a state convention to meet in Hillsborough in July 1788 to consider the ratification of the Federal Constitution. Elections for convention representatives were held in March. The proponents of the Constitution, called Federalists, waged a vigorous campaign before the March elections to ensure a victory over the opponents of ratification, who were styled Antifederalists. Maclaine had "little or no doubt [of the approval by] our State ... the people, if left to themselves, are in favor of a change."[58]

Neither side, however, was willing to allow the people to make the decision unassisted. Leading the opposition in Wilmington were John Huske and a Col. Read, who "joined all the low scoundrels in the country, and by every underhand means, are prejudicing the common people against the new constitution," according to Maclaine. For their part, Maclaine and the Federalists in Wilmington subsidized the establishment of a newspaper in Wilmington, the *Wilmington Centinel*, to propagate their views. For a while, the editors of the newspaper, Bowen and Howard, duly trumpeted the Federalist cause, but subsequently Bowen left the partnership and Howard became "a rank anti-federalist."[59]

When the Hillsborough Convention met in July, the Antifederalists had an overwhelming majority. In the March elections, Wilmington chose Maclaine to represent the town, but the county delegation, which included John Huske, was unanimously Antifederalist. When the Hillsborough Convention met, the Antifederalists easily outnumbered the Federalists and sought to take a quick vote on ratification, claiming that the delegates were prepared for a decision and that delay would merely waste the public's money. The Federalists objected, hoping to gain support by postponing a ballot and using their superior oratorical skills. The Antis relented and agreed to consider the Constitution section by section. During the course of the week-long, relatively one-sided debate, Federalists, led by William R. Davie, James Iredell, Samuel Johnston, Archibald Maclaine, and Richard Dobbs Spaight, bore the burden of explaining and defending the Constitution.[60]

Maclaine addressed the convention more often than any delegate except Iredell, who represented Edenton. The Wilmingtonian answered Antifederalist objections to the phraseology of the preamble to the Constitution, to biennial elections for members of the lower house of Congress, to the right of the vice-president to cast a tie-breaking vote in the Senate, to the power of the president to appoint officers of the government when Congress was not in session, and to fears that the power of impeachment might extend to the states and that the jurisdiction of the federal judiciary might impair the sovereignty of the states. More broadly, he responded to the Antifederalist demand for a bill of rights to protect individual and states rights by claiming that, "the powers of congress are expressly defined; and the very definition of them is as valid and efficacious a check as a bill of rights could be, without the dangerous implication of a bill of rights." In the process he chastised the opposition for caviling at the finest government ever contemplated, and pointed out that, "it must be a matter of serious alarm to every reflecting mind, to be disunited from the other states."[61]

The Antifederalists paid no heed and, after the Federalists had exerted their best efforts, carried a resolution by a vote of 184 to 84 that neither ratified nor rejected the Constitution. Instead, they proposed to send to the national government a series of amendments designed to check federal power, protect states rights, and safeguard special interests of North Carolina, and a bill of rights to secure personal liberties. It was a bold move because eleven states had already ratified the Constitution, more than enough to ensure the inauguration of the new government without

North Carolina's presence. The Antifederalists were willing to remain outside the Union in order to pressure the government to accept their demand for amendments and a bill of rights.[62]

Upon the institution of the United States in April 1789, North Carolina became, in effect, a sovereign state. Meanwhile, a swift and striking change of opinion occurred in the state. The establishment of an orderly national government headed by the respected George Washington, and the promise of amendments to protect personal liberties and states rights, allayed the fears of some Antifederalists. For their part, the Federalists mounted an "educational" campaign that emphasized the prospect of discriminatory tariff duties against the state, the need for protection against the Indians in the West, and the embarrassment of North Carolina's alignment with Rhode Island, which had also rejected the Constitution. And, on the whole, the formation of the new Union left North Carolina no realistic alternative to joining the nation.[63]

The movement to reverse the action at Hillsborough began with the decision of the General Assembly in November 1788 to call for a second ratifying convention in Fayetteville. Already Wilmingtonians had held a public meeting on the matter in October. After Read and Huske exerted their best effort, they left the scene, and those who remained voted unanimously for a new convention. Elections in August produced an overwhelming Federalist majority. Again Wilmington elected a Federalist, William H. Hill, and New Hanover County sent a solidly Antifederalist delegation, including Huske. After three days of unrecorded debates, the Federalists in the Fayetteville Convention carried a motion to adopt the Constitution by a vote of 194 to 77.[64] What prompted some men to favor the Constitution and others to reject the document is intriguing. Neither wealth nor political experience greatly distinguished the Federalist from Antifederalist leadership. Fundamentally, Federalists and Antifederalists differed in their outlook on life. Federalists, representing the lawyer-merchant-planter elite, exhibited a commercial-urban orientation, as opposed to Antifederalists, who spoke for the mass of self-sufficient farmers in the state. While Federalists thought that the Constitution nicely blended authority with liberty, establishing the principle of popular sovereignty while checking popular excesses, Antifederalists saw an inordinate concentration of power in the new government. They particularly feared that undue consideration had been given to commerce, which small farmers, who represented the majority of the state's population, viewed as antithetic to liberty and the common good. Their precapitalistic mentality led them to distrust such "nonproductive" economic pursuits as commerce.[65]

Federalists in the eastern, mercantile communities of North Carolina, including Wilmington, rejoiced at the prospect of joining the Union under a government that could protect American interests abroad and property at home, promote a sound currency, and regulate trade throughout the country. In retrospect, the desire to protect individual and states rights, tempered by selfish state interests, shaped North Carolina's role in national politics during the Revolutionary era. Even the Conservatives or Federalists were aware of the need to shield the state from an overbearing national government, as well as against undue pressure from New England. Still, Federalists felt the need to replace the Articles of Confederation with a more powerful, active government which would serve to promote their conception of a "good" society, one controlled by an aristocracy and emphasizing commercial endeavors. But the ratification of the Constitution failed to crush the Radical or Antifederalist temperament in North Carolina. That element soon came to dominate politics in the state, though the Federalist spirit remained strong in Wilmington.

II.
The Maturing Years, 1789–1861

5
The Growth of a Town

Wilmington emerged from the Revolutionary era as one of the most populous towns in North Carolina, a state whose urban residents approximated only two percent of its total population throughout the antebellum era. From about a thousand inhabitants in 1790, Wilmington's population grew to 1,689 in 1800, a distant second to New Bern's 2,467. By 1820 the number of Wilmingtonians increased to 2,633. Yet the town had slipped to fourth in population, behind New Bern, Fayetteville, and Raleigh respectively. Nonetheless, the growth of Wilmington was impressive, especially given the decline in New Hanover County's population from 1810 to 1820. As a result, in 1820 Wilmingtonians constituted 24.2 percent of the residents of the county.[1]

After 1820 population growth in North Carolina slowed perceptibly, particularly during the decade of the 1830s. Hard times following the Panic of 1819 lingered for some two decades, reinforced by the Panic of 1837. Many Carolinians, seeking improved economic opportunities, moved to the Gulf Coast region. An Emigration Society organized in Wilmington in 1835 to secure information about Texas. Later in the year, the *People's Press* advertised the publication of *A Journal of a Tour in Texas; with Observations on the Laws, Government, State of Society, etc., etc.* At the same time, other North Carolinians sought to escape the baneful influence of slavery, principally to the free states of the Old Northwest Territory. The Nat Turner Insurrection and its severe repression caused several Wilmington families to move or to contemplate leaving the town. One, who considered emigrating to Ohio, wrote that he could not bear the thought of his children living in a slave state in the future. Despite the outmigration, Wilmington's population rose from 2,633 in 1820 to 5,335 in 1840, making it the most populous town in the state at the time. The town's residents made up 40.1 percent of the county's total in that year.[2]

While Wilmingtonians continued to grapple with the institution of slavery, the economic future of their town brightened considerably after 1840. Improvements in the navigability of the Cape Fear River and completion of the Wilmington and Weldon Railroad in 1840 led to boom times in the port. The *North State Whig* in Washington, North Carolina, editorized in 1850: "Look at Wilmington. But yesterday she was a dirty little village. To-day she stands a proud, enterprising city. What has made her what she is from what she so late was? Her internal improvements." As a result, the number of Wilmington residents rose to 9,552 in 1860, easily outstripping the urban populations of New Bern (5,432), Fayetteville (4,790), and Raleigh (4,780) on the eve of the Civil War. And at that time 44 percent of the inhabitants of New Hanover County lived in Wilmington.[3]

As North Carolina's principal port, Wilmington stood as a window to the world. In 1845 a Wilmington newspaper declared that the port city was "growing populous and mighty[,]" attracting "persons from the surrounding country, from distant States, and foreign shores, of every age, condition and employment." Actually, that observation applied to Wilmington from its inception; the rapidity of immigration only intensified in mid-nineteenth century. French, Portuguese, and Germans numbered among the western European immigrants who found their way to the port. Dominque Torrie, a Frenchman, arrived from Charleston in 1806 to open a print store. John M. Cazaux and his wife and son moved to Wilmington in 1836 from Brooklyn, New York, to start a bakery and grocery busi-

The port of Wilmington, circa 1860, showing in the foreground a pen in the river for containing timber floated down the river and beyond various types of craft in the Wilmington harbor, including sailing ships, steamboats, rafts, and rowboats. Engraving courtesy of the North Carolina Office of Archives and History, Raleigh.

ness. Cazaux subsequently employed a fellow countryman as a clerk. Antone Morris, a native of Portugal, operated a bar and oyster salon, but soon went out of business because his customers refused to honor their charge accounts. John (no surname), another native of Portugal, was less fortunate. He was killed in 1839 by Lucy Ann Sutton, apparently as the result of a domestic dispute.[4]

Germans constituted a distinctive element of the Wilmington populace in the two decades prior to the Civil War. Although North Carolina early contained significant numbers of Germans, apparently Jacob Wessel from Charleston was the first of that nationality to reside permanently in Wilmington. His arrival in 1840 was followed by the A. E. Mindel family and one Ehrhardt from New York in 1841. Other Germans from Charleston and Philadelphia appeared in Wilmington during the next few years. By 1852, Germans were sufficiently numerous to organize the German Volunteers, a militia company consisting of 57 officers and men. Six years later an estimated 400 to 500 Germans lived in Wilmington. Among them were enough Lutherans to form St. Paul's Evangelical Lutheran Church in 1858. In addition to the militia company and church, Germans established a "Mozart Verein," or Mozart Club, in 1860.[5]

Evidencing the Scotch, Welsh, and Irish segments of the population were the celebrations of St. Andrew's, St. David's, and St. Patrick's Day. In November 1800, "NATIVE and SONS OF NATIVE NORTH BRITONERS" of Wilmington observed St. Andrew's Day by inviting all the "fashionable company" within twenty miles of the town to a ball and supper at which some two hundred ladies and gentlemen were entertained "to their most perfect satisfaction, not a single cloud hovering near the sun of Festivity." Six years later the Wilmington St. Andrew's Society gathered at Dick's Hotel in November for a sumptuous repast. The following March a number of Wilmingtonians and men from the surrounding area similarly enjoyed a fine meal at Dick's Hotel as they celebrated St. David's Day. Later that month, "a few Sons and Descendants of St. Patrick" dined at Mrs. Dorsey's Tavern in honor of the day, drinking seventeen formal, and numerous volunteer, toasts, interspersed with appropriate songs. While remembrance of St. Andrew's and St. David's Day seemed to fade over the years, observance of St. Patrick's Day assumed an increasing importance.[6]

Wilmington also contained a small but growing Jewish community. At least as early as 1800, and perhaps during the colonial era, Jews appeared in the port. The earliest were Sephardic Jews, of whom Aaron Lazarus was the most outstanding. Arriving from Charleston, South Carolina, at the turn of the nineteenth century, Lazarus became a prominent and prosperous businessman. He owned a store and several warehouses, and co-owned Wilmington's first steam planing mill and the town's largest mercantile firm before mid-century. The early Shephardic Jews gradually disappeared, their numbers diminished by death, migration, and conversion to Christianity. Other than Lazarus, the most prominent Jewish citizen early in the nineteenth century was Jacob Levy, "the prince of auctioneers," who reportedly had a wonderful sense of humor. Remembered one non–Jew, Levy "was to be sure a Jew, but had nothing of their reputed faults; for he was all liberality, and generosity; a warm heart and benevolent soul...."[7]

An Ashkenazic Jewish community replaced the Sephardic Jews after mid-century. Immigrating mainly after 1848 from Germanic areas of Europe, principally Bavaria, but also from Hanover and Westphalia, the Ashkenazic Jews, like their predecessors, embraced white Southern culture, becoming slaveowners and eventually supporting the Confederacy. Virtually no evidence of anti–Semitism can be found in antebellum Wilmington, as Jews were readily accepted in town affairs. Although their numbers were small, approximately 74 in 1860, Jews exercised considerable influence in Wilmington's business community, owning 11 of 18 clothing firms and 6 of 19 dry goods companies in town.[8]

The obvious attraction of Wilmington and the resulting cosmopolitanism of the town is revealed both in life and death. Of 68 white craftsmen in the building trades in 1850, five came from Europe, 20 from other states, and 38 from North Carolina. Ten years later, of a total of 120, the figures were 10, 22, and 88, respectively. Mortality statistics offer further evidence of the diversity of the town's population. Of 33 (of a total of 36) white adult Wilmington Catholics buried in the Wilmington parish from 1845 to 1860, 25 were natives of Ireland, while seven came from England, Scotland, Germany, Nova Scotia, and Santo Domingo. One had been born in Wilmington. In 1860, 11, or 7.7 percent of those who died in Wilmington, had been born beyond North Carolina—three in Ireland, three in Massachusetts, two in Virginia, two in South Carolina, and one in Maryland.[9]

In fact, numerous antebellum residents of Wilmington had relocated from other states of the Union or from other areas of North Carolina. Representative of the many immigrants was James Cassidey, native of Salisbury, Massachusetts, who became one of Wilmington's principal shipbuilders. From Glastonbury, Connecticut, came Zebulon Latimer, who prospered in the dry goods business. James F. Post, born in New Jersey, moved to Wilmington in 1849, where he became the "premier mid to late–19th century builder architect" of the town, responsible in part for

Town Hall/Thalian Hall and the Bellamy Mansion, according to one architectural historian.[10] Yet, "Among the many great men who have adorned the life of our community, and contributed to the prosperity of this section of the State, no man has surpassed in usefulness Edward B. Dudley," wrote local historian James Sprunt. Born in Onslow County in 1789, Dudley moved to Wilmington in 1815, immediately represented the town in the General Assembly, later served in Congress and, in 1836, became the first popularly elected governor of North Carolina. More than any other, Dudley was the progenitor of the Wilmington and Weldon Railroad. No wonder that Wilmingtonians accorded him several public dinners and mourned his passing in 1855 by suspending business in town on the afternoon of his funeral, lowering flags on ships and public buildings to half-mast, and participating in a lengthy funeral cortege to Oakdale Cemetery, where Dudley was interred.[11]

Whatever the origin, Wilmington's population fluctuated greatly during the course of the year. The port bore the reputation of an unhealthy place, which Presbyterian minister Artemus Boies in 1819 deemed the principal drawback to the town. Merchants from the north who had settled in Wilmington customarily returned to their native lands in May, reappearing in October. By late June the rest of Wilmington's population was thinning as "families [were] going to the Sound, Smithville, and many to the springs in this state," according to one Wilmington woman. Smithville, "perched upon a bluff and embosomed among the umbrageous oak, many grass lawns, and shady walks," appealed to many. Others sought the healing properties of mineral waters or springs, which simultaneously offered an escape from the oppressive heat of the town and the opportunity to meet and mingle with people of like social class. Wilmingtonians frequented Shocco Springs in Warren County, arguably North Carolina's most popular resort east of the mountains, as well as Rockingham Mineral Springs, Hickory Spring, and Jones White Sulphur and Chalybeate Springs. The more adventurous left the state to take advantage of various Virginia springs, Nahant (Massachusetts), Niagara, and Saratoga. Wilmington merchant Platt K. Dickinson and his wife spent many a summer in Saratoga, and in 1859 they intended to "stay some time, as we require the water...."[12]

Residents of Wilmington, while sometimes critical of their surroundings, seemed to appreciate their town, but the port engendered a mixed reaction among strangers. After a sojourn in Rhode Island following her husband's death, Phila Cohen Lazarus Calder wrote, "My return to Wilmington is indeed a subject of congratulation. No words can convey the comfort and relief I feel in being once more 'at home.' The North accorded me none of the advantages which were so alluring in prospective." Among those who visited Wilmington, Mrs. Anne Royal called it "The garden spot of North Carolina." After many caustically critical observations about the rest of the state, Mrs. Royal found that Wilmington had "grown up in the cultivation of every virtue, and every accomplishment." (After having traveled throughout most of the United States, Mrs. Royal deemed only Camden, South Carolina, comparable to Wilmington.)[13]

Mrs. Royal, however, proved exceptional in her laudatory observations about Wilmington, for most visitors found the town highly dissatisfying. Susan D. Nye in 1815 concluded that Wilmington was "a dreary place. The buildings are bad and apparently going to decay." Mortimer DeMott in 1837 found the town well laid out, but the streets had been "built up without taste or consulting even convenience." Wilmingtonians lacked "energy & enterprise and as to public spirit it is practically a scoff...." He found "nothing here but Southern pride, and Northern hounds for plunder...." Jaundiced perhaps by a difficult trip from Virginia along the Wilmington and Weldon stage and railroad line in 1838, Fanny Kemble described Wilmington as "a place I could sooner die than live in—ruinous, yet not old,—poor, dirty, and mean, and unvenerable in its poverty and decay."[14]

A lack of adequate public accommodations served to estrange many visitors to Wilmington. Hotels were few, sometimes nonexistent, and strangers perforced relied upon boardinghouses in their absence. Susan Nye found her lodgings excellent, but her landladies were "gay to a fault," perhaps because they were widows and childless. Mortimer DeMott criticized the decrepit furnishings, unappetizing meals, and "miserable" attendance at his boardinghouse. After paying "the landlady $16 for incomoding me [for] as many days," DeMott left Wilmington "with as much pleasure as I ever went thence."[15] English actress Frances Anne (Fanny) Kemble, her two children, a nurse, and another woman found a hotel when they reached Wilmington, but the manager told them that they would have to share a single room with two beds. Thought Kemble:

> This unheard-of proposition, and the man's cool impudence in making it, so astonished me that I could hardly speak. At last, however, I found words to inform him that none of our party were in the habit of sleeping with each other, and that the arrangement was such as we were not all inclined to submit to. The gentleman, apparently very much surprised at our singular habits, said, "Oh! he didn't know that the ladies were not acquainted" (as if, forsooth, one went to bed with all one's acquaintances!) "but that he had but one room in the ladies' part of the house." To our common dormitory we therefore repaired, as it was impossible that we could any of us go any longer without rest.[16]

5—The Growth of a Town

Wilmingtonians recognized the lack of adequate facilities for the traveling public, particularly for such a large and growing town after 1840. Frederick Law Olmsted, when arriving in Wilmington from Fayetteville in the early 1850s, found two public houses at the time, but they were "so crowded with guests, and excessive business duties so prevented the clerks from being tolerably civil…" that he immediately booked passage on a steamboat for Charleston, South Carolina. At about that time a movement was under way to erect a hotel, either by private subscription or by a corporate undertaking. However, the proposal for a hotel had to compete with the need for a town hall, a public cemetery, and a theater. Eventually, after the realization of the other desiderata, the Wilmington Hotel Company was incorporated in 1859. But construction had not begun late that year when delegates and visitors to the meeting of the state Presbyterian Synod in Wilmington overwhelmed the town. The City Hotel, the lone establishment of its kind, could accommodate only a fraction of the influx. The others fended for themselves. And the erection of the new hotel remained problematic.[17]

Although Wilmington never obtained adequate hotel facilities before the Civil War, the town enjoyed an economic resurgence and construction boom during the late antebellum era, fueled by the completion of the Wilmington and Weldon Railroad, the deepening of the Cape Fear River channel below Wilmington to admit larger ships, and the increasing steamboat traffic on the river between Wilmington and Fayetteville. Editorialized the *Chronicle* in 1845, "We are determined not only to give you a good lead, sister cities of North Carolina, and this is not said in a spirit of boasting, but intend maintaining our undisputed supremacy." Among the amenities of which Wilmington could boast by the end of the antebellum era were gas lights, which began to replace candles and camphor oil lamps in the homes and street lamps filled with whale oil that served "to do little more than make the darkness visible." Legislation in 1851 incorporated the Wilmington Gas Light Company, which was so successful that it declared a dividend in 1857. Before the Civil War, Wilmington, Raleigh, New Bern, and Charlotte among North Carolina towns offered gas illumination.[18]

Wilmingtonians crowded into lodgings, large and small, as the population of the town rose over the years. Some of the dwellings reached impressive size. P. W. Fanning in 1847 advertised two homes in the northern section of Wilmington that apparently had been built on speculation. Both contained two stories with two additional attic rooms, and front and rear piazzas, and one boasted "all necessary closets and conveniences about the house…." An array of outbuildings, gardens, and walls often accompanied the individual houses. Representative was "Myrover House" on Orange and Front Streets, which belonged to William Mitchell. It had a kitchen, stable, carriage house, and corn crib. In advertising the sale of his house and lot in 1835, David Treadwell noted that the property contained a well with "most excellent water" and a garden with a variety of fruit trees. Years later, one Wilmingtonian recalled that "many a town lot was really a half-acre farm." Of course, at either end of the housing spectrum were the single rooms, kitchens, and tenements of the poor, and the magnificent town houses (such as the Zebulon Latimer House and the Bellamy Mansion) occupied by the wealthier elements of Wilmington.[19]

Within and beyond those homes Wilmingtonians played out their lives. Children were reared, though not always to the satisfaction of their parents. Lydia Hall severely chastised William, her son, who wanted to leave his apprenticeship as a clerk, writing that she feared that he would "never attain wisdom enough to discern your own ignorance, ... and your case is a very pitiful one indeed [for] no person as ignorant as you are can expect wages equal with those who have diligently strove to learn all that was necessary in that line [of work]." Happier occasions, however, found Kate (Catherine Douglass DeRosset), daughter of Dr. Armand J. DeRosset, Jr., marrying Gaston Meares in 1850. Those who responded to the six to seven hundred invitations created a "dense squeeze," even in the spacious DeRosset house, and bountiful tables filled with delicious edibles rendered one attendee "apprehensive of becoming both a jelly and jam before I got home." And from those marriages families were begun anew.[20]

Family life found women at a distinct disadvantage. Husbands often left home for extended periods on business, prompting Mrs. Armand J. DeRosset, Jr. to write plaintively to her spouse about how much she missed him and how difficult it was for her to care for their young children. Of course, a lady of Mrs. DeRosset's social standing had the benefit of help around the house, and could console herself with numerous friends and shopping. Her household may even have taken advantage of washing machines and sewing machines (including the Singer brand) that were advertised in the newspapers. The latter, however, failed to impress Wilmingtonians, or at least the men, one of whom wrote:

> The very best sewing machine that a man can have is a wife. It is one that required but a kind word to set it into motion, rarely gets out of repair, makes but little noise, [and] will go for hours without ... the smallest personal supervision being necessary.... In fact, you may leave the house for days, and it will go on working just the same. In short, no gentleman's establishment is complete without one of these sewing machines in the house.[21]

5—The Growth of a Town

Many wives rejected such backhanded compliments, however, and some found the rigors of married life too difficult to endure. Husbands inserted notices in the newspapers periodically to announce that wives had left "bed and board," though in the case of Hannah Ritter, her husband, Moses, announced that if she returned, he would "support her as usual, or procure a good house for her reception." Although William McMaster in 1805 claimed that his wife had departed without provocation, he had previously squandered the fortune in land and slaves that she had brought to the marriage and was currently paying one Neil Beard, Sr. $75 annually to board his wife and their two children.[22]

More serious than eloping wives was the crime that bedeviled Wilmington. Mail theft, forged checks, counterfeit bank notes, and numerous robberies, including that in 1835 of two hound dogs belonging to Archibald McRae, alarmed residents. A dispute at the theater one Saturday night in 1844 between Thomas Holden and A. L. D. Johnson prompted the latter to visit Holden's house the next morning, at which time Johnson shot Holden in the legs with a round of small shot, which was very painful, though not fatal. The following year Lucinda Burnett killed Serena Trade with a pair of tongs. Two men in 1859, Williams and Kiple, were convicted on five separate counts of theft, which included purloining a knife, bullet mold, gold locket, jewelry, and brace and bit, for which they received 39 lashes and six months imprisonment. In the same month, one Samuel Simmons was hanged for premeditated murder before a large crowd. As the *Journal* noted, "There is ... a strange fascination that draws men and women, too, to the contemplation of such affairs."[23]

Wilmingtonians also contended with the baneful effects of fire and disease. Too often interrupting the bustle along the waterfront or leisurely household activity were the ringing of the town's alarm bell and the shout of "Fire." Small fires occurred with startling regularity; major conflagrations in 1798, 1806, 1819, 1840, 1843, and 1845 burned large portions of Wilmington. The flames in 1798, which started in a house on the corner of Front and Dock Streets, consumed most of the buildings from the south side of Market to Dock Street, and from the river to Third Street, sparing only a few houses on the hills beyond Third. Eight years later fire devastated "a great part of the town," prompting the General Assembly to exempt from taxes in 1806 the property of those who had sustained losses. Following the onset of the panic of 1819, and a yellow fever epidemic in the summer, a huge fire in November 1819 devastated Wilmington. It destroyed the four blocks bounded by Water, Princess, Second, and Dock Streets, consuming an estimated 300 structures, including the recently built Presbyterian church, at an estimated loss of $600,000 or more. One of those blocks burned again in 1828, with damages estimated at over $100,000.[24]

Although small blazes took their toll in the 1830s, three fires inflicted considerable damage in the early 1840s. That in 1840 swept over the two blocks bounded by Market, Princess, Second, and Water Streets, excepting the Cape Fear Bank but burning the courthouse. A huge blaze in 1843, aided by a southerly gale of a wind, swept the northern part of town beyond Princess Street between the river and Second to the Wilmington and Weldon Railroad depot buildings. It spared only a dozen buildings while destroying some of the most elegant homes in the town, large quantities of county produce on the river wharves, and all the railroad buildings, five locomotives, and several train cars. The fire in 1845 left the block bounded by Market, Front, Dock, and Water "a mass of smoking ruins," with the exception of two buildings. The loss of some 40 to 45 structures, plus merchandise, was estimated at $100,000.[25]

The fires originated variously, some accidentally, and some, perhaps, were set intentionally. A candle left in the pantry of Mrs. Smith's boardinghouse in 1830 apparently was responsible for a small blaze. A pitch pot on a flatboat started a fire at a wharf in 1834. A month later, lightning struck the house of Mrs. Cowan, creating a small fire. Turpentine distilleries, two of which were burned in 1846, were particularly susceptible to destruction. Also vulnerable were steam sawmills. The Cape Fear Steam Saw Mill and Samuel Beery and Sons' steam sawmill, both located on Eagles Island, went up in flames in 1829 and 1849, respectively. And the increasing number of steamboats on the Cape Fear River constituted a hazard: sparks from the *Sun* started three, perhaps four, fires in one day in 1860; cinders from the *Kate McLaurin* set fire to cotton on the wharf of the Cape Fear Ocean Steamship Navigation Company in 1861.[26]

Beyond the accidental incidents, townspeople thought that many of the fires resulted from arson. After an attempt to fire the town in 1807, the commissioners offered a $500 reward for information leading to the apprehension of the guilty party. And convinced that the devastating fire of 1819 was the work of an incendiary, the commissioners offered $1,000 for information about the perpetrator. In 1825 a black man was incarcerated on suspicion of arson, but usually the supposed arsonists went undetected. And that only heightened suspicions. Incendiaries were blamed for three blazes in 1845, and the local newspaper noted that several unsuccessful attempts had been made to set fires. In 1857, in the most destructive blaze in the decade before the war, the *Herald* claimed that there was no doubt that the fire had been set, and hoped for the detection of the "villain or villains who have thus applied the midnight torch."[27]

5—The Growth of a Town

In moments of distress, Wilmingtonians looked to charity, both external and at home. After the disastrous fire in 1798, the *North Carolina Journal* of Halifax opined that while many families would find refuge in the country, others would need aid from the "opulent cities" of the nation. Following the fire in 1819, the *Raleigh Register* observed that, as Wilmington had helped others in time of need, surely aid would be forthcoming for the North Carolina port. However, after the fire in 1843, a committee appointed at a Wilmington town meeting to collect money for the sufferers locally obtained $750 in a week, including $100 from the Odd Fellows, which money was to be distributed by the town commissioners.[28]

Fortunately, many Wilmingtonians protected their property with insurance. Reports of the fires in three decades before the Civil War indicated that fire insurance covered from one-fourth to one-half of the losses. The principal underwriters were the North Carolina Mutual Insurance Company, the Hartford Fire Insurance Company of Connecticut, and the Phoenix Insurance Company of London. Other carriers patronized by Wilmington were located in Providence, Rhode Island, New York, Philadelphia, and Baltimore. The 1840 blaze found insurance compensating for at least $130,000 of the $300,000 in damage, though unfortunately for Dr. Louis J. Poisson, his policy had expired the day before the incident, and he had neglected to extend his coverage.[29]

For their part, the commissioners encouraged or even mandated the erection of fireproof buildings after blazes to prevent mishaps in the future. They only permitted the construction of fireproof structures in the block destroyed in November 1845, under penalty of $1,000, and seven years later prohibited any wooden buildings in the burned district of February 1852. Not all citizens welcomed the change, for brick added greatly to the expense of construction. After the fire in 1843, some contracted for brick buildings, while others opted for wood. And, in fact, brick did not always withstand the flames. The fire in November 1845 destroyed more than thirty such structures.[30]

Health in antebellum America, as in the colonial era, was always problematical, and Wilmington's geographic location rendered the town even more susceptible to contagions. Dr. John Hill aptly encapsulated the port's situation:

> The general aspect of the country, throughout the lower part of our state, is low, flat, and barren; and the margins of our rivers consist of swamps, subject to inundation from every tide.... On the opposite bank of the river is an island containing many thousands of acres of ... swamp.... The parts of the town adjacent to the river are but a few feet elevated above its surface. The wharves are ... badly constructed, and are always

> overflowed by storms and frequently by high tides. In the vicinity of the square…, there one of these wharves in an unfinished state, partly filling up with decaying vegetable matter, which, enclosed within logs and successively acted upon by the tides, exhibits a most loathsome and putrefaction source of disease. Our docks are notoriously filthy, and our cellars are so low and damp, as in wet season to require daily bailing.

Dr. Hill neglected to mention the several small streams "with swampy margins" that ran through the sand hills on which Wilmington was situated, contributing to low-lying areas and standing water. He also failed to note that Wilmington's status as a port doubly jeopardized the health of the town. From abroad, such contagious diseases as yellow fever and smallpox entered by shipping from Atlantic and Gulf states and the world at large.[31]

Despite precautions, the commissioners of navigation and pilotage for the Cape Fear River admitted that vigilant action could not protect altogether the citizenry in the course of trade with other ports. In fact, yellow fever visited Wilmington in 1796, 1819, and 1824. When smallpox threatened in 1802 and 1816, the Commissioners of Navigation and Pilotage advised residents to undergo kine-pox inoculation, the recent discovery of Edward Jenner. In the mid-thirties a mild epidemic of smallpox occurred. The infected were moved to the recently opened hospital at Mt. Tirza below town. A few cases of smallpox were reported in 1846, 1849, 1851, and 1854. In 1851 the town commissioners of Wilmington arranged with local physicians to provide free vaccinations, paid for by the town, for all who were unprotected.[32]

Although yellow fever and smallpox seldom visited Wilmington, the town bore a reputation as a sickly locale. However, in the estimation of Wilmington physicians and longstanding residents of the town, health improved over the antebellum years, mainly due to the elimination of streams, lagoons, and standing water, and to the enhancement of the riverfront along Water Street. Such efforts particularly helped to combat bilious fever, a principal affliction during the early years of the nineteenth century. According to the *Herald*, bilious fever "generally made short work of a stranger, sending him to the graveyard in about a week." Locals feared the fever as well. But by the late 1850s, many northern merchants in Wilmington who customarily left town in May and returned in late October to escape the sickly season, as well as many native Wilmingtonians who also sought safe haven elsewhere, felt comfortable in staying home during the summer and fall months.[33]

Nonetheless, contagions remained, and in his address to the North Carolina Medical Society in 1852, Dr. James H. Dickson catalogued the illnesses with which Wilmingtonians had to cope. Principal among them were bilious fever, typhoid fever, pleurisy and pneumonia, dysentery, cholera infantum (colitis, the great scourge of children), scarlet fever, measles, and whooping cough. Less threatening were "eruptive fever," jaundice, and paronychia, an epidemic of which occurred in 1851. Respiratory diseases more often attacked blacks because they were more exposed to the elements. Scarlet fever, once rare, appeared in epidemic proportions in 1846, 1848, and 1852. Wilmingtonians also had endured two or three epidemics of measles within the past decade. And Dr. Dickson overlooked influenza, an epidemic of which had struck Wilmington in the summer of 1843.[34]

In any year, Wilmingtonians were subject to a number of illnesses and other threats to their well-being. During the calendar year ending June 30, 1860, 143 Wilmingtonians died, including 22 from consumption, 14 from pneumonia, and two from pleurisy. Another 22 succumbed to bowel-related ailments. Whooping cough, typhoid fever, measles, and scarlet fever claimed five, four, four, and one, respectively. Otherwise, dropsy or anasarca (nine), inflammation of the brain (seven), and heart disease (five) proved most lethal. Those figures encompassed the white and black population of Wilmington, but burial records from Oakdale Cemetery from 1858, 1859, and 1860, which included interments only of whites, reflect similar results. Consumption was the leading cause of death (26 of 226 total deaths in the three years), followed by bowel-related disorders (21), scarlet fever (12), pneumonia (11), whooping cough (seven) and typhoid fever (five). Bilious fever indeed had abated, taking only four lives over the three years.[35]

Children suffered the most grievously, as any mother would attest. After trying for a week and a half to correspond with her daughter, Mrs. Armand J. DeRosset, Jr., finally wrote that the "whole time has been taken up with nursing children a little sick ever since I came home...." The preceding week her baby had suffered chills and fever every day.[36] The table at the top of page 114, including the 141 deaths in the calendar year ending June 30, 1860, for which ages were given, shows the risk to children.

Statistics from Oakdale Cemetery from 1858 through 1860 tend to reinforce these figures, showing that 43 percent of the interments were those of children under five years of age. As a rule, in North Carolina from the colonial era to the Civil War, if one could only survive infancy and early childhood, a relatively long life might ensue.

The summer and early autumn months bore the reputation as the most sickly time of the year. Deaths that occurred during the calendar year

Table 1
Deaths by Ages

Age	Number	Percentage
0–4	69	.49
5–9	9	.06
10–19	9	.06
20–29	15	.11
30–39	7	.05
40–49	7	.05
50–59	15	.11
60–69	5	.04
70 and over	5	.04

Source: Eighth Census, 1860, Mortality Schedule–3, North Carolina, New Hanover County, microfilm, State Archives, Raleigh, N.C.

ending June 30, 1860 (for whom 142 were dated by month), as well as those interments at Oakdale from 1858 through 1860, hardly reinforce that observation, however, as shown by the table below. The trend may have been toward a healthier summer and fall season, as many Wilmingtonians believed.

Table 2
Deaths by Months

	Wilmington for the Year ending June 30, 1860		Oakdale Cemetery for 1858, 1859, and 1860	
Month	Number	Percentage	Number	Percentage
January	10	.07	22	.10
February	9	.06	14	.06
March	5	.04	20	.09
April	4	.10	19	.08
May	26	.18	18	.08
June	18	.13	21	.09
July	11	.08	25	.11
August	9	.06	21	.09
September	11	.08	26	.12
October	13	.09	21	.09
November	6	.04	11	.05
December	10	.07	8	.04

Sources: See Table 1; *Journal* (Wilmington), January 21, 1859, January 2, 1860, January 16, 1861.

Wilmington benefited from the presence of numerous and skillful physicians in the antebellum era to combat imported contagions and indigenous diseases. A Dr. Cohen from Germany in 1805 stood ready to treat rheumatic pains, venereal diseases, fits of various kinds, cancers, dropsy, and all kinds of sores. Like most physicians, he treated the poor gratis. The number of physicians increased with the rising population of the town. The 1820 census listed seven physicians in New Hanover County, though not all were necessarily residents of Wilmington. By 1834, five practicing physicians lived in the town—Armand John DeRosset, Sr., Armand J. DeRosset, Jr., William P. Hort, John W. Watters, and Louis J. Poisson. Joining them soon was Dr. James H. Dickson, who in 1835 performed a subcutaneous Archilles tenotomy on his younger brother, and has been credited with introducing that surgical procedure in the United States. Other notable physicians who arrived in Wilmington in the 1830s and 1840s included Drs. John D. Bellamy, William J. Harris, James F. McRee, and John L. Meares. Rarely did physicians specialize, though in moving to Wilmington in 1851, Dr. William S. Langdon specifically advertised the practice of obstetrics among the branches of medicine that he pursued.[37]

The medical profession in North Carolina comprised not only medical school graduates but also preceptorial trainees without the M.D. degree, apothecaries (who prescribed medicines usually sold in their shops), and simply impostors. Concerned about the integrity of their profession, medical doctors in 1849 reorganized the North Carolina Medical Society, no doubt strongly influenced by the formation of the American Medical Association in 1847. (A North Carolina Medical Society had briefly appeared between 1799 and 1804.) Preceding the state organization were eleven county medical societies, one of the first of which appeared in New Hanover.[38]

Although Wilmington doctors did not help to inaugurate the North Carolina Medical Society, they quickly became active in the organization. Eight were listed as permanent members in 1852. In 1860, 10 of 233 permanent members and 5 of 18 honorary members of the society lived in Wilmington. Of the 10 Wilmington physicians, 5 had been born in the town, another in New Hanover County, 2 elsewhere in North Carolina, 1 in Georgia, and 1 (A. Medway) in Hungary. Five obtained their medical degrees from the University of New York, 2 from the University of Pennsylvania, 2 from Charleston Medical College, and 1 from Yale.[39]

Among Wilmington's honorary members were two of the most respected members of the profession in North Carolina. Armand John DeRosset, Sr., who died in 1859 at age 91, began practice in Wilmington about 1790, had been commissioned a surgeon in the Third Regiment of the North Carolina Militia in the War of 1812, and continued to see patients until a year before his death. Like most physicians, he was an active member of society and the business community, serving as a director for the Bank of Cape Fear and investing in the Wilmington and Weldon Railroad. Dr. James F. McRee, who died in 1869 at age 75, not only was "an accomplished chemist, [but] a bold, daring, and skilful surgeon, unrivalled in his diagnosis and prognosis," according to his obituary. He was also a classical scholar who read Latin and French as easily as he did English. Moreover, his knowledge of botany was unrivalled in the Lower Cape Fear, where he served as the authority on matters relating to that biological science.[40]

Supplementing the resident doctors were occasional itinerant physicians who visited Wilmington to promote a product or practice. Dr. C. P. Crane arrived in 1854, demonstrating his treatment of pulmonary diseases by the "inhalation of Medical Vapors" into the lungs. When Dr. Robert Hunter of New York appeared in Wilmington in 1860 to treat throat and lung diseases, particularly consumption, he encountered some opposition from local medical professionals. They apparently objected not only to his credentials but to his advertising his treatment through the newspaper rather than through medical journals.[41]

Visiting physicians and some early resident doctors also sold medicines, along with druggists and retail merchants. In addition to the usual assortment of medicines, Dr. Andrew Scott in 1806 offered kine-pox vaccine for inoculation against smallpox. Dr. Laroque & Son in 1816 advertised not only their professional services but also "fresh" medicines. In starting his practice in 1838, Dr. Robert F. Purnell opened a wholesale as well as retail drugstore, offering to sell medicines to other physicians and country merchants. Most of those physicians also provided chests of medicine for ships and plantation owners.[42]

Medical therapy changed slowly over the first half of the nineteenth century, and most physicians favored the usual emetic and purgative, along with bloodletting and blistering. Tarter emetic (tartrate of antimony and potash) was prescribed for fevers; the emetic ipecacuanha or ipecac, for eruptive diseases such as measles. Calomel, castor oil, and epsom salts headed the list of purgatives. If the patient did not respond to emetics and purgatives, physicians might draw blood, either by lancet or by leeches. Localized pains, such as in pleurisy and pneumonia, might entail the use of blister plasters. However, during the influenza epidemic in Wilmington in 1843, a local newspaper advised against extreme measures such as bloodletting, and counseled instead that the afflicted draw deep breaths from a vial of spirits of hartshorn or ammonia to clear the lungs. Wilmington physicians never embraced homeopathy, though an article in the

Daily Herald in 1860 noted its growing number of adherents in the nation.[43]

Those unwilling or unable to secure the services of a physician could avail themselves of a host of medicines or remedies at various retail outlets, including bookstores. Thomas Loring in 1818 was the Wilmington outlet for Lee's Original Family Medicines, which included Elixir (for respiratory ailments and "approaching consumptions"), Antibilious Pills, Grand Restorative, Nervious Cordia (for nervous disorders and much more), Worm Destroying Lozenges, Infallible Ague and Fever Drops, Restorative Tooth Powder, Genuine Eye Water, Anodyne Elixir (for headaches), and Indian Vegetable Specific (for venereal complaints). Over the years, Wilmingtonians might also purchase West India Head-Ache Drops, Dr. Relfe's Asthmatic Pills, Beckwith's Anti-Dyspeptic Pills, Sanford's Liver Invigorator, and Cherokee Remedy, the last an unfailing cure for gonorrhea and all diseases of the urinary organs. And Mexican Mustang Liniment for sprains, burns, and "Pains in any part of the body an external application can reach," worked as well for humans as it did for horses.[44]

Although the general practitioner advised patients about dental care and pulled teeth, dentistry as a specialized branch of medicine reached North Carolina at the beginning of the nineteenth century in the form of the itinerant. The early dentists took rooms at local boardinghouses or hotels and advertised a "short stay," a "very limited stay," or a sojourn of a "few days." Z. Florance from Charleston appeared in 1803, offering his liquid and dentrifice for preserving the teeth and gums. Two years later John Le Tellier removed teeth using "BRUFF'S Patent Perpendicular Extracting Instruments." W. R. Scott in 1833 inserted one or a whole set of artificial teeth; Dr. Pleasants in 1837 brought a "BEAUTIFUL COLLECTION OF TEETH" from France for that purpose. If the teeth could be saved, R. D. Addington plugged them with gold or silver. He also restored diseased gums, aligned teeth, and removed tarter and stains.[45]

Although itinerants continued to visit to the 1850s, Dr. William Ware in 1833 established a permanent practice in Wilmington which he pursued for almost two decades. Ware, a member of the American Society of Dental Surgeons, fabricated false teeth. At mid-century, Dr. B. A. Kennedy, graduate of the Baltimore College of Dental Surgeons, opened an office in Wilmington. During the late 1850s several professionals made the port a permanent residence, including Thomas B. Carr, M.D. and D.D.S., who extracted teeth for $.50 to $1.00, provided an entire set of false teeth on a fine gold plate for $150, and kept the best dentrifices and toothbrushes available. In 1860, resident dentists Drs. B. F. Arrington, A. J. Shriver, and John H. Freeman, all of whom advertised surgical (operative) and mechanical (false teeth) services, offered Wilmingtonians of means an opportunity to cope with their dental difficulties.[46]

Crime, fire, and disease often rendered life all too brief. Samuel Jocelyn wrote a heartrending letter to his daughter Betsy to tell her that her younger sister Clara had died suddenly. A chill, thought not to be serious at the time, was followed by a high fever, convulsions, and death within twelve hours. Jocelyn did not know how to offer Betsy consolation, "for alas we want it more than you. [T]o lose such a charming little innocent in so sudden[,] unexpected manner is beyond our fortit[ude] to support. Every moment she rises to the mind." Others succumbed to accidents. Lighting in 1839 killed Elizabeth Hamilton at the house in Wilmington in which she was staying. At least eight of the 143 deaths in Wilmington in 1860 were attributed to accidents, including one who was poisoned, one who was kicked by a mule, one who died in a boiler explosion, and three who drowned. In fact, the Cape Fear River claimed many lives over the years, as attested by the coroners' inquests. Often the victims were sailors, like the three young men from Virginia, Rhode Island, and New York, aged 26, 21, and 21 respectively, who perished in 1859, along with a 17-year-old Wilmington boy, when a small vessel in which they were sailing overturned in the river. But landlubbers were not immune. One N. Dry drowned while bathing in the Cape Fear.[47]

One of the most unfortunate deaths in antebellum Wilmington resulted from a duel in 1856 fought between Dr. William C. Wilkins and Joseph H. Flanner. At a political rally, Wilkins, a Democrat, contended that the merchants of the American Party would sacrifice the public interest for the sake of profit. Flanner, an American, quickly responded in language that infuriated Wilkins, who challenged Flanner. The two met near Fair Bluff, South Carolina (as duelling was illegal in North Carolina), where they fought with pistols at ten paces. On the third exchange, Flanner killed Wilkins, cutting short the promising career of a thirty-year-old physician. As one Wilmington woman observed, "I had hoped that the age of duelling was over with and that it was no longer considered cowardly to refuse a chal[l]enge. [F]or my part I should think it required much more moral courage to refuse than to accept one; but our young Americans think differently."[48]

For diversion from melancholy events, Wilmingtonians turned to games of chance. Declaring that billiards and backgammon were played "to an excess" in Wilmington in 1792, the state legislature required that the New Hanover County court license all establishments that offered billiards and backgammon "for pay." Some three decades later the county sheriff seized the billiard table of Dominique Cazaux for nonpayment of taxes. In the mid–1830s a group of Wilmingtonians strongly protested the appearance of a gambling hall where roulette and faro were standard fare. At that time, more than a hundred citizens affixed their names to a pledge not to frequent gambling establishments in Wilmington, and "as far as practicable [to] discountenance any person who is in the habit of doing so."[49]

Still, most Wilmingtonians probably embraced "gambling" in the form of lotteries, a popular form of raising money for various causes from the Revolution to about 1840. State-authorized lotteries in North Carolina especially benefited educational institutions and internal improvements. They also aided the Masonic Order and church construction in Wilmington. In addition, the Wilmington town commissioners on their own initiative in 1800 undertook a lottery to raise money to build a market and clean the dock in Dock Street. Duncan Livingston resorted to a raffle, or private lottery, in 1799 to dispose of several personal items; a merchant in 1836 used a raffle to sell 25 sets of gold earrings and matching brooches and other jewelry. Even after the legislature banned lotteries, North Carolina newspapers carried advertisements of lotteries throughout the United States, as well as the Royal Havana Lottery.[50]

Wilmingtonians also took advantage of a variety of public entertainments to mitigate the demands and disappointments of life. Just before the turn of the nineteenth century, a lecturer who also played the guitar appeared in the port town. A waxwork exhibition, a Mr. Rannie (who was a ventriloquist, magician, and tumbler), and Mr. Carter (a magician) followed. During the late 1830s, Il Diavolo Antonio offered an "exhibition" at the courthouse. He was followed the next year by Mr. Love, polyphonist. "General" Tom Thumb appeared in 1845 and 1851. The 1850s also offered Prof. Wye, billed as the world's youngest magician, ventriloquist Signor Biltz and his "Learned Canary Birds," and Sig. Donnetti and Col. Wood's troupe of "Educated Dogs, Monkies and Goats."[51]

The circus became a prominent feature of public life by the 1830s, though traveling exhibits of wild animals had been common since the turn of the century. Frost and Co., equestrians, raised the ire of their landlady in 1837 when the troupe left town without paying for their lodgings. The next year a circus and menagerie, featuring an elephant, lions, tigers, leopards, camels, hyenas, condors, and ostriches, promised a performance in which nothing would "offend the ear of the most fastidious," and all would be conducted "with the utmost order and decorum." Admission of ladies required the accompaniment of a gentleman. The famed Robinson and Eldred Circus toured in the 1840s and 1850s, and in 1860 two companies visited Wilmington—Robinson and Lakes Great Southern Menagerie and Circus, and Nixon's Royal Circus (mainly equestrians) from London. The performers, animals, riding exhibitions, clowns, music, and often paintings that comprised the circuses appealed to all, young and old.[52]

Wilmingtonians especially enjoyed dancing. Although some harbored reservations about the waltz and cotillion (in which dancers switched partners indiscriminately), and the Baptist Church in 1829 "disapproved [of] members attending theaters and balls," most remained undeterred, attending soirees offered by dancing masters in town, military balls, and dances that honored guests of the town or recognized a festive occasion. A dance in 1831 honoring the 1st Artillery, U.S., found the room "handsomely decorated with flags swords guns & bayonets all tastefully arranged a la militaire." Chalked figures marked the floor with the American eagle in the center. A chandelier was fashioned of various sized hoops in which bayonets were fixed, the sockets of which served as candlesticks, and bayonets as reflectors. Evergreens interspersed the whole. At the other end of the social spectrum, sailors appreciated a good jig as well. One Captain Braddock, at his own expense in 1799, provided a dance for his crew.[53]

Other forms of entertainment proved equally delightful. On a cold, sleeting day in December, Ada Amelia Costin took tea with one of her friends. In more favorable climes, young people enjoyed parties at the Sound, traveling from Wilmington in wagons. The newly married Kate DeRosset Meares and her husband accepted an invitation to a "married folks' party." And for the well-to-do, like Kate Meares, shopping was always a pleasure. More adventurous Wilmingtonians took railroad excursions, sometimes to Lake Waccamaw for a picnic, and steamboat excursions along the Cape Fear River to Smithville, Fort Caswell, and the ocean. Popular, too, were moonlight river trips featuring food, drink, and lively music, two of which were held within a week in June 1858. Other outdoor activities included fox hunting, for the woods around Wilmington abounded in that quarry, and yacht racing on the sounds, eventually including regattas organized by the Carolina Yacht Club.[54]

Horse racing continued to engage Wilmingtonians of means, as well as those who enjoyed the excitement and possessed small sums to wager. The Wilmington Jockey Club at the turn of the nineteenth century organized three-day races featuring one-, two-, and three-mile heats for purses of $600 or more. Participating horses were restricted to those who had "not been regularly trained and kept as ... race nagg[s] hitherto." The club maintained its racing schedule over the years. In 1833 William M.

West's filly Lady Sumner, sired by the famed Sir Archy, had no competition on the third day; she "galloped over the [three-mile] course and took the purse—$360." During the 1840s the club utilized the Clarendon Race Track, located about three miles east of town. At the end of the antebellum era, trotting matches took place at the Currie track, probably on the Currie farm about one mile east of Wilmington. A widely advertised trotting contest in 1860 featuring a Wilmington mare and Weldon mare failed to come off at the Currie track because the Wilmington horse had to be withdrawn due to rheumatism in her right hind leg. A substitute was quickly found, but the Weldon mare had no difficulty in defeating an opponent who was not "in what might be called exact trotting trim."[55]

Throughout the year Wilmingtonians enjoyed various informal and formal holiday observances. While many exchanged greetings of "Happy New Year" on January 1, that day was set aside for slave hire for the ensuing year, making it "unquestionably the least agreeable of all days of the year" (in the estimation of the *Daily Herald*), because townspeople and country folk clogged the streets as they made arrangements for labor.[56] A week later, however, on January 8, militia companies often paraded in the streets in recognition of the anniversary of the American victory over the British in the Battle of New Orleans during the War of 1812. January 8, 1829, held particular significance, for two months later President-elect Andrew Jackson, the Hero of the Battle of New Orleans, took office. The discharge of thirteen cannons inaugurated the day, followed by another (indicating the current number of states) at noon. A "large and respectable company" enjoyed a hearty meal with accompanying toasts at Mrs. Gregory's Hotel in the early afternoon. In the evening, transparencies drawn by a local artist depicting the Battle of New Orleans and Jackson attracted a number of spectators. A single discharge from a cannon at nine o'clock concluded the festivities of the day.[57]

During the antebellum era, Wilmingtonians recognized Valentine's Day. Both sexes flooded the mails with notes of various shapes and sizes that displayed Cupids, hearts, and arrows, and contained suggestive verses, most of which were harmless, though some were coarse and vulgar. Although merchant S. W. Whitaker in 1854 advertised "a beautiful assortment of Valentines" for sale, the practice of sending Valentines seemed to decline after mid-century.[58] Still, the *Herald* in 1857 carried an open verse to "John" from "Mary Valentine":

TO JOHN
As one who watches by the open sea,
Straining her sight for some expected sail—

> Trusting each rolling billow wild and free,
> Will bring its form within her vision's pale—
> Until her aching orbs begin to fail,
> And waning twilight settles into dark—
> Still sits she there, unheeding of the gale—
> For one she loves is in the looked for bark—
> And hope within her breast give[s] place to rising fears,
> And eyes, long used to weep, are filled with scalding tears.[59]

Even prior to the death of George Washington, his birth date, February 22, occasioned patriotic remembrances. The day opened and closed with the firing of cannons. In the interim, the celebration usually entailed the mustering of the volunteer military companies, and often the militia, which spent the morning and early afternoon marching through the streets, executing maneuvers and, in the case of one "rifle company" in 1845, demonstrating the techniques of "bush fighting." At two or three in the afternoon the military companies would gather for a fine meal and merriment at Masonic Hall or the Carolina Hotel. By the end of the antebellum era, however, the spirit of the day had waned, giving poignance to the editorial of the *Journal* in 1855: "The time can hardly ever arrive when the birth-day of Washington can come or go unmarked or unnoticed. Such a thing would portend no good for the country."[60]

On February 27, 1857, Wilmingtonians celebrated the eighty-first anniversary of the Battle of Moores Creek Bridge. Occasioning that particular observance was the decision by residents of Wilmington, New Hanover, and surrounding counties to erect a monument on the battlefield to the Revolutionary patriots who defeated the Scots in 1776. Accordingly, the mayor of Wilmington ordered businesses to close. The Wilmington and Weldon Railroad, and two steamboats, the *Flora McDonald* and the *Spray*, prepared to transport dignitaries, military companies, the Howard Fire Company, and townspeople to the vicinity of the battlefield for the laying of the cornerstone of the monument, speeches, food, and festivity. All returned home about eight o'clock in the evening "Under the light of the twinkling stars, and the silvery beams of the crescent moon...."[61]

Although April Fool's day began to assume some significance toward the end of the antebellum era, elders failed to appreciate the antics of children.[62] All, however, enjoyed May 1, a day on which local bands offered music, and military companies paraded through the streets. Students at the Odd Fellows Academy marched in procession to the school, and after demonstrating their academic prowess, crowned a Queen of May according to "immemorial custom." Afterward, the "Instructress" at the academy served the queen and her subjects a "collation" at her house. In 1856 military companies from Fayetteville and Raleigh visited Wilmington, parading until late at night and leading one resident to exclaim, "Such commotion and excitement I never saw in our town." But all behaved remarkably well, for not one became intoxicated.[63]

No public occasion was more elaborately or festively observed than the Fourth of July. Early in the nineteenth century the celebration was a "political" occasion for which members of the Republican and Federalist Parties gathered separately to enjoy sumptuous repasts with appropriate toasts.[64] Later the community joined in nonpartisan celebrations, sometimes subsidized by appropriations from the town treasury. A committee made arrangements about a month in advance. The day customarily began with the ringing of bells, hoisting of flags, and discharging of cannon. At nine o'clock a procession formed on Front Street. In the following order— bands, military companies, clergy, Revolutionary War veterans, orator and reader, committee of arrangements, United States military officers, Freemasons, firemen, mechanics, engineers of the railroads, ship masters and sailors, "Strangers," New Hanover County sheriff and clerk of court, justices of the peace, Wilmington magistrate of police (mayor), town commissioners, town guards, teachers and students of academies, citizens— the procession marched to a selected church for an appropriate service, followed by a reading of the Declaration of Independence, an oration for the occasion, and a huge meal.[65]

The celebration of the Fourth assumed an increasingly gala atmosphere as the years passed. The magistrate of police (mayor) requested townspeople to suspend business in order that all could participate in the celebration. Steamboat excursions were undertaken, principally to Smithville, but also to Fort Caswell and Bald Head, and simply to cruise the river. Railroad excursions took Wilmingtonians to Lake Waccamaw. Others left town for the sound, where they watched regattas at Wrightsville, sponsored by the Carolina Yacht Club. The German Volunteers in 1859 enjoyed a picnic at Hilton. And the Thalian Association mounted productions in the evening, including a benefit in 1849 to raise money for the construction of the Washington Monument. Accidents occasionally marred the day. One man fell into the river in 1855 while watching the fireworks display and drowned. Two years later another died as the result of a premature explosion of a cannon.[66]

Toward the end of the year, Wilmingtonians took time from their labors to observe Thanksgiving. Though not a national holiday, the governor of the state customarily designated a day in late October or early

November for public thanksgiving, often corresponding to days set aside in other states for a similar observance. Businesses and schools closed. Some went riding in the country, some went hunting, and others visited friends and neighbors. Many "lounged about the streets, and held up the corners...." Churches were open to those who desired to recognize the day for its true meaning, a day that greatly resembled Sunday. The Grand Lodge of North Carolina, International Order of Odd Fellows, which met in Wilmington in November 1857, celebrated Thanksgiving by marching in procession with the Cape Fear Lodge to the Methodist Church on Front Street for an oration. The Odd Fellows ended the day with a supper and dance.[67]

Wilmingtonians concluded the year with a celebration of Christmas. Children arose on that wonderful day to inspect their stockings and they hoped to enjoy small change and presents from Santa Claus. Afterward, church services, turkey dinners, the exchange of gifts, and visitations marked the occasion. The explosion of squibs, torpedoes, rockets, and all kinds of fireworks added noise (and danger), not only to the day but to the week between Christmas and the new year. In 1854 the town commissioners invited members of the North Carolina legislature to pass the holidays in Wilmington. Many took advantage of Wilmington's hospitality, which included a steamboat excursion and a cotillion party at the Carolina Hotel. Performances by the local Thalians and MacKenzie's Vaudeville Troupe added to the festivities of the season. Those who overindulged in spirits "enjoyed the official hospitalities of the town as dispensed at the guard-house." But there was time to recover, for business slowed markedly until the beginning of the new year.[68]

6

The African American Experience

Often participating in seasonal festivities and ceremonial activities, as well as observing those peculiar to their own culture, were African Americans, both slave and free. North Carolina had early committed to the institution of slavery. By 1830, slaves in the state had increased to one-third of the total population. At mid-century, twenty-seven percent of white families owned slaves, though two-thirds possessed fewer than ten bondsmen. On the eve of the Civil War, North Carolina also contained more than thirty thousand free blacks, a number surpassed only by Virginia among the southern states. Although North Carolina was an overwhelmingly rural state, approximately ten percent of the free blacks resided in urban areas.

African Americans, slave and free, comprised a large segment of Wilmington's residents during the antebellum era, certainly well more than half the town's population at the beginning of the nineteenth century. Yet, as their absolute number rose throughout the years, blacks became less significant. They constituted 58.3 percent of the populace in 1820 and 1830, dropped to 50.7 percent in 1840 and 1850, and dipped to 45.5 percent in 1860. By comparison, in 1860 blacks made up 56.6, 43.6, and 41.4 percent of the populations of New Bern, Raleigh, and Fayetteville, respectively, at the end of the antebellum era.[1]

Among the African American population in North Carolina was a growing number of free blacks. From 5,041 in 1790, they reached 30,463 in 1860. Relatively few lived in towns, given the overwhelmingly rural character of North Carolina. In 1800 New Bern, Fayetteville, and Wilmington (the most populous urban areas in the state) claimed 144, 67, and

19 free blacks, respectively. By 1820 the number of free blacks in Wilmington had risen to 102, or 4 percent of the town's inhabitants, but still trailed the free black population of Fayetteville (277), New Bern (268), and Raleigh (177). In 1860 only New Bern, Wilmington, Raleigh, Fayetteville, and Elizabeth City contained more than two hundred free blacks. And Wilmington's free black population, after rising from 356 in 1840 to 652 in 1850, declined to 573 in 1860.[2]

Natural increase, some immigration (particularly from Virginia), miscegenation, and manumissions drove the number of free blacks upward in North Carolina. In Wilmington, Magdalin Mary Toomer liberated Tamar in 1803 for "faithful and meritorious services...." Later a Wilmington resident of considerable estate acknowledged his paternity of two slaves, freed them, and left them a legacy of $250. His executors, fearing questions about the legality of the emancipation, obtained legislative recognition in 1812 of the freedom of the slaves. In 1855 numerous petitions to the General Assembly sought the emancipation of James Hostler, who earlier had saved the life of Thomas Hall Yates, a white. While the two were working more than twenty feet above the ground on a construction project, Yates apparently suffered a seizure, and Hostler, at his own risk, moved to prevent Yates from falling. In addition to Yates' petition, another, signed by 39 Wilmingtonians, attested to the exemplary character of Hostler. The legislature acquiesced, enacting a statute that liberated Hostler.[3]

Slaves in Wilmington seemed to enjoy a degree of autonomy that bordered on license, if not liberty. A Rhode Island newspaper in 1846 offered an external perspective: "There is probably no place in the world where slaves are treated with more lenity and indulgence than in Wilmington." Bearing out that assessment were slaves in town who served as jail keepers and naval stores inspectors. Others, like Peter, piloted ships in the Wilmington harbor. Peter was allowed to work by himself and solicit jobs in exchange for part of his income. According to a former slave, black artisans in Wilmington "hired theyselves where they pleased. They colle'ted they pay, an' the onliest thing the owner took was enough to support they fam'lies." Working or not, slaves purloined goods from their masters, which they vended to merchants in town. With the proceeds, if they chose, the bondsmen had no difficulty procuring alcoholic drinks, given "the indiscriminate and unlimited granting of ... licenses" to retailers of such beverages by the town commissioners.[4]

The General Assembly, seconded by the Wilmington town commissioners, continued their earlier efforts through legislation and ordinances to control the slave populace in the port. Statutes required slaves who

> The Board then proceeded to pass the following resolutions
>
> Resolved that no pass or permit shall be sufficient to protect any slave After the hour of nine P.M. unless it be stated in such pass the place or places to which the said slave is allowed to go or the errand on which he is sent, And the time he is allowed to be out; And any slave or slaves found with passes other than those described above shall be dealt with as though they had no pass.
>
> Resolved That [if] any slave[36] found without a pass or an insufficient pass, shall state to the guard that he is sent to any place or upon any errand upon sudden emergency, as for a physician or otherwise, it shall be the duty of the guard to accompany ~~him~~ the slave to the place or person designated, And if the statement of the slave be found untrue he shall be punished not exceeding fifteen lashes
>
> Resolved That all slaves offering insolence to the town guard in the performance of their duty, whither they have a pass or not, shall be punished by the Police officer not exceeding fifteen lashes

Resolutions by Wilmington town commissioners, December 22, 1847, that exemplified the restrictions imposed upon slaves, though apparently bondsmen often found means to evade such limitations. Courtesy of Nancy Beeler and Rush Beeler, eds., *Wilmington Town Minutes, 1847-1855* (Wilmington, 1997), 15.

hired out their labor to have their owners' consent in writing, register with the town clerk, wear a badge supplied by the town, and limit each job to twenty-four hours duration. Slaves were restricted in their work to Wilmington or an area within a half-mile of the town, to vessels in the river, and to wharves opposite the town. Given the supposed baneful influence of the free blacks on slaves, the General Assembly tried to prohibit the interaction of the two groups, banning intermarriages of free blacks and slaves, forbidding free blacks to entertain slaves in their homes at night, and proscribing slave owners from allowing their bondsmen to meet free blacks "for the purpose of drinking and dancing…." Additional legislation sought to prevent whites and free blacks from engaging in games of chance and gambling with slaves. Town commissioners established a nine o'clock evening curfew for slaves and relied upon the watch or town guard and police officials to maintain order among bondsmen.[5]

Not only slaves but free blacks found themselves increasingly subjected to regulations circumscribing their activities, leading to what historian John Hope Franklin has termed a "Free Negro Code" in North Carolina. Legislation in 1785 required free blacks in Wilmington to register with and obtain from the town commissioners a cloth badge bearing the word "FREE," which was to be worn on the left shoulder. Ten years later the General Assembly directed county grand juries, including that of New Hanover, to present free blacks who might "become dangerous," and upon trial and a guilty verdict, compel those free blacks to give bond for proper behavior. Subsequently, the legislature forbade free blacks from immigrating into the state. Laws passed in the legislative session of 1826–1827 provided for apprenticing free black children and imposed stiff penalties for vagrancy, which might lead to hiring out free blacks for as many as three years.[6]

A more fervent reaction followed the publication of *Walker's Appeal in Four Articles* (1829), written by David Walker, who had been born in Wilmington or its vicinity to a slave father and a free mother. Walker eventually moved to Boston, where he issued an emotionally charged pamphlet in which he called upon slaves to throw off their chains and secure their freedom by whatever means might be necessary. In Wilmington a "well-disposed free person of Colour" gave a copy of *Walker's Appeal* to the magistrate of police. That official told Governor John Owen that an investigation revealed that several free blacks and slaves "have for the few months past frequently discussed the subject of a conspiracy to effect the emancipation of the slaves of this place."[7]

The growing militancy of the abolitionist movement, as evidenced by Walker's pamphlet, occasioned a renewed effort by the General Assembly in its 1830–1831 session to control the actions of free blacks. Legislation banned the circulation of seditious publications designed to incite insurrections or conspiracies among slaves or free blacks. The General Assembly also curbed the movement of free blacks, limiting their ability to peddle wares outside their home counties and forbidding free blacks who left the state from returning after more than a 90-day absence. Another statute subjected ships entering North Carolina ports with free blacks aboard to quarantine for 30 days and proscribed any interaction between free blacks on board and blacks on land. According to Franklin, by 1830–1831, the "Free Negro Code" in North Carolina was almost complete.[8]

During the ensuing three decades additional restrictive legislation constituted "afterthoughts" to the Free Negro Code, and the state Constitutional Convention in 1835 took the significant step of disfranchising free blacks in North Carolina. Enabled to vote by the state constitution of 1776, free blacks became sufficiently numerous by the 1830s (or were deemed sufficiently threatening) that whites feared they might influence the outcome of elections. Both Owen Holmes and Lewis H. Marsteller, Wilmingtonians who represented New Hanover County in the convention in 1835, opposed disfranchisement. Holmes noted that previous legislation had been designed to "vex and harass" free blacks, and contended that disfranchisement would relegate them to the status of slaves. Holmes argued for retaining the vote for propertied free blacks of "good standing," as opposed to those who were "vicious and disorderly," in part because it might encourage free blacks to warn whites of slave unrest. However, by the narrow margin of 66 to 61, the convention decided to abrogate the free black franchise.[9]

Attesting to the "freedom" enjoyed by slaves was the establishment of the search or patrol system, instituted in mid-eighteenth century to try to prevent the concealment of weapons, to thwart possible insurrections, and to keep "order and good decorum among the negroes at public places...." County courts in North Carolina annually divided their respective jurisdictions into districts and appointed searchers or patrollers to inspect slave habitations. Briefly, in 1824, the General Assembly shifted patrol duty in New Hanover to the militia companies, but reneged on that experiment in 1827. The New Hanover County court in June of 1831 tried to make the patrol system more effective, requiring a search of slave dwellings at least once every twenty days, requiring slaves to carry passes that specified the places to which they were permitted to go, banning night gatherings of blacks, and providing punishments for violations of the regulations. Patrollers in Wilmington numbered from 10 to 14, and included such luminaries as Dr. A. J. DeRosset, Jr., Owen Fennell, and Thomas Cowan. By 1861, as Wilmington had expanded and grown more populous, the New Hanover County court divided the town into two districts, each patrolled by only three men.[10]

The slave patrol also attempted to maintain order among free blacks. When a free black in town was found using "impertinent, if not seditious language," the patrol "chastised him, jailed him, and when let out, chastised him again." A slave administered the flogging in both cases, and according to a local paper, "witnesses assert[ed] that it was never better done." The editor continued:

> This may be Judge Lynch's Law, but we think it a very good one. Nor has the patrol stopped here. They have extended their services into the tribe of free Negroes who have swarmed here from other sections and squatted in the perlieus [sic] of the city, and already have and now are in the act of abating much of that nuisance. The thanks of the public are due to them.[11]

Partial autonomy and family ties may well have encouraged slaves to seek permanent freedom—in effect, joining the ranks of free blacks. John Burgwin advertised in 1797 for two runaways—Frank (recently whipped and wearing a leg iron) and Ned. The former worked on Burgwin's wharf in Wilmington; the latter had just finished a term with Harris and Springs, Wilmington blacksmiths. Peggy, who ran away from Jonathan Stanly in

August 14   tf

TEN DOLLARS REWARD.

RAN AWAY from the subscribers about the first of March last, a negro named

GLASGOW,

better known by the name of Glasgow O'Neill. He is so well known in Wilmington, and the immediate neighborhood, where it is expected he is lurking; that a description of his person is unnecessary.— We will give the above reward of Ten Dollars, for his delivery to us at the works near the Big Island, or to the Jailor in Wilmington.

                          TAYLOR & WILLIAMS.

July 24   tf

Ten Dollars Reward.

RAN AWAY from the subscriber, on the 10th instant, a negro woman named LUCY, aged about 30 years, very black, and walks lame in consequence of having been frost bitten — She formerly belonged to Jonathan Avery, and is well known in Wilmington and its vicinity. All persons are forewarned from harboring or carrying her away, as the law will be rigidly enforced——The above reward will be paid on her delivery to me, or the Jailor in Wilmington.

                        JOHN M. VAN CLEEF.

August 14   tf

Advertisement for the apprehension of slave runaways in the *Cape Fear Recorder*, October 16, 1824. So "well known" was Glasgow that he needed no physical description, but Lucy was identified by her owner, as were many runaways, in order to facilitate their capture. Courtesy of the New Hanover County Public Library, Wilmington.

1819, was "well known about Wilmington, and on the sound...." The owner of Sarah in 1819 felt that she would find safety in Wilmington, Greenfields (to the south of town), or Joseph Eagles' plantation, "at each of which place[s] she [had] relatives." Two years later James Usher concluded an advertisement for two men by stating, "further description is needless, as they are well known in this place and on the sound." Kitty, who left the service of Jesse Bowden in 1851, had a husband in Brunswick County, where Bowden thought she might be found, if she were not in Wilmington or its "suberbs."[12]

Slaves who avoided their captors and posed a threat to public safety risked outlawry, meaning that they could be "kill[ed] and destroy[ed] without accusation or impeachment of any crime...." Mathews, member of an outlawed group in 1797, was so severely wounded in his capture that the *Wilmington Chronicle* feared that he "would have eluded the vengeance of the law; it is now, however, conjectured that he will live long enough to make a public exit." Another in Mathews' band was captured, given a trial, and hanged at Gallows Hill. Three years later the New Hanover County court outlawed six men and a woman, who were "lurking in the swamps, woods, and other obscure places causing injuries to the inhabitants of the state." And slave owners were not always anxious to retrieve obstreperous runaways. Robert Brown in 1821 offered a reward for the apprehension of Cupid or "for his HEAD."[13]

As a thriving port, Wilmington offered a means of permanent escape for slaves who sought their freedom by obtaining passage to the North and beyond. And advertisements for runaway slaves in the Wilmington area reflected that apprehension on the part of slave owners. David Greer in 1803 assumed that Frank would attempt to board a ship to make his escape. Four years later, in advertising for Moses, John Barclay pointedly forbade all "masters of vessels [from] carrying him off, as the law will be rigidly enforced against them." Samuel Noble in 1809 warned ship captains against taking runaways Jack and Peter or allowing their crews to conceal the slaves. Such fears were well based, for Wilmington became a vital part of the Underground Railroad in North Carolina during the antebellum era, providing a sea route by which slaves might gain their liberty.[14]

Blacks engaged in maritime activities, free and slave, represented the key link in the flight to freedom. From the colonial era, African Americans figured prominently in fishing and boating along North Carolina's numerous waterways, as well as in Atlantic shipping. Blacks worked as draymen in towns, stevedores on the docks, pilots along the rivers, and cooks, stewards, and sailors on ships. Sometimes directly, but often through intermediaries such as rivermen and those who worked in town, runaway slaves in Wilmington and in the country found sympathy. Among those who aided runaways was Peter, a slave of a Wilmington merchant, and two Quakers, Fuller and Elliot. Peter piloted oyster sloops belonging to the Quakers, which gave the trio "an opportunity to lay and devise plans for getting many [slaves] into Canada...." Runaways contacted

Fuller and Elliot through Peter, who might have been approached by other watermen or by various blacks in Wilmington's wharf district.[15]

Although the extent and success of the operations of Peter, the Quakers, and others to funnel slaves through the port to freedom can never be truly known, whites became alarmed, particularly after abolitionist agitation in the North heightened in the 1830s. Authorities in Wilmington in 1833 apprehended Edward, a black steward on the brig *Fisher*, for concealing a slave girl with the intent to take her beyond the state. Two years later the captain, mate, and two sailors of the schooner *Butler*, bound for Fall River, Massachusetts, were arrested when a runaway slave boy was found on board their vessel. And on the eve of the Civil War, four black sailors were jailed for attempting to aid John, a slave, in making his escape to New York on board the schooner *George Harris*. From New York the sailors planned to take John to Boston, the port from which they had shipped.[16]

Successes, most of which went undocumented, doubtlessly outnumbered failures. Arriving in Boston about 1850 was a vessel from Wilmington aboard which a female slave belonging to George W. Davis of Wilmington had been hidden by the first mate without the knowledge of the captain. Although the authorities in Wilmington strongly suspected that the slave was aboard, intensive searches failed to reveal her hiding place. Even though the slave was detected in Boston, the first mate managed to take her ashore to safety. Still, leaving Wilmington did not guarantee freedom. While sailing to New York from Wilmington in 1850, the captain of the schooner *Minerva Wright* discovered two slaves hidden on board. He left the men in Norfolk, Virginia, from which the local sheriff returned them to North Carolina. In 1853 and 1854, local officials in Boston captured fugitive slaves from Wilmington on board the brigantine *Florence* and the schooner *Sally Ann* respectively.[17]

Whites, of course, recognized their vulnerability. According to the Wilmington *Aurora*, black sailors were, "all of them, from the very nature of their position, abolitionists, and have the best opportunity to inculcate the slaves with their notions." Given the opportunities available to stevedores to hide runaways, a correspondent to the *Journal* argued that, "we must have *white* men in the place of *negroes* engaged in that business." Wilmington authorities prohibited slaves from piloting or stevedoring on ships belonging to free blacks, but the need for black labor doomed any effort to replace African American stevedores with whites. Still, the commissioners of navigation and pilotage for the Cape Fear River regularly ordered the fumigation of ships leaving Wilmington, and eventually contracted with private agents to board, search, and smoke or fumigate vessels in order to locate stowaways.[18]

While runaways constituted the loss of valuable property, and outlying slaves, individually or in groups, represented an annoyance or occasional threat to the public safety, insurrections evoked terror among whites. Gabriel Prosser's plot in Richmond in 1800, a potential uprising in northeastern North Carolina in 1802, and Denmark Vesey's conspiracy in Charleston in 1822 rested uneasily on the minds of white Wilmingtonians. Still, the Nat Turner insurrection in Southampton County, Virginia, took North Carolina and Wilmington by surprise. Turner, a self-ordained preacher and slave, began a campaign of bloodshed on August 21, 1831, that quickly spread panic through the northeastern counties of North Carolina. A week later a degree of calm had descended upon those counties, but rumors of slave plots spread to western and southeastern parts of the state. Duplin and Sampson Counties were caught up in the hysteria by early September, when rumors of a slave conspiracy led to the incarceration, trial (often extralegal), and occasional execution of bondsmen.[19]

Wilmington reacted calmly at first to the news of the Virginia insurrection, but evidence gathered at the trials of slaves in Duplin and Sampson Counties increasingly seemed to implicate bondsmen in the port. Then Isaac Scott, a free black, told Wilmington authorities of a suspected plot which involved a number of African Americans in Wilmington, including Dan, also a free black, who was accused of showing a keg of powder to the conspirators. Several slaves were subsequently arrested. After a large number of whites volunteered to protect the town, Wilmington's town commissioners appealed to Governor Montfort Stokes for aid. Stokes permitted the officials to use arms from the state arsenal to protect the town and county.[20]

Subsequently, hysteria overtook Wilmington on September 12 when an explosion was heard in the distance and a rumor spread that two hundred slaves had gathered within twenty miles of the town. Streets filled with women and children carrying mattresses and prized personal possessions as they made their way to the safety of a militia post. Moses Ashley Curtis, an Episcopal minister, found more than a hundred people crowded in one of the buildings, all "half dead from fear." Many had fainted, and one "was jabbering nonsense in a fit of derangement." Wilmington men patrolled the streets that night, but Curtis was unmoved. He went home and, to calm his wife, slept with a loaded musket. However, he recorded in his diary, "What contemptible fuss for nothing at all except a want of reason and judgment." The following morning a company of militia returned from the supposed encampment of the armed slaves and reported that the noise the previous evening had been caused by some "revelers" who had discharged a piece of field artillery.[21]

When their fears abated somewhat, Wilmingtonians, like whites in other areas, began to seek out black "conspirators." Following numerous arrests and forced confessions, slaves revealed to Dr. James F. McRee, a local magistrate, that blacks in Duplin, New Hanover, and other counties, numbering perhaps 4,000, planned an assault on Wilmington on October 4. They intended to set fire to the Methodist and Baptist churches, located at opposite ends of the town. While the men worked to extinguish the blazes, the slaves were going to kill as many women and children as possible, after which they intended to engage the militia. If the insurrectionaries could not hold the town, they planned to rob the banks and board ships for Santo Domingo. The episode had a profound impact on Wilmington. After earlier rejecting a move to the free states, one resident wrote, "now there is no sacrifice, no exertion, which we would not make to effect such a removal, for this place will never be better."[22]

In addition to those who felt the need to leave the South, others supported the American Colonization Society. Organized in 1817 to raise funds to transport free blacks and liberated slaves to Africa, the society obtained donations in Wilmington and occasionally used the port as a base from which to ship blacks to Africa. The society in 1825 received $10 from the Presbyterian church and $80 from other donors. During the ensuing three and one-half decades, the Presbyterian, Baptist, and Methodist churches, the Reverend Adam Empie of the Episcopal church, the "Colored People of Wilmington," and Dr. James Dickson contributed to the organization. Two general collections in the 1850s produced $99.50 and $30 respectively for the Society. Thomas Buchanan, agent for the society, went to Wilmington in 1838 to fit out an expedition for Liberia. Fourteen years later the secretary of the society announced that the organization intended to send a ship from Wilmington to Liberia, for which almost a hundred applications for passage had already been received. Despite the apparent sympathy shown for the society, on the eve of the Civil War one Wilmington newspaper criticized the organization as wasteful in its expenditure of money and ineffective in realizing its goals.[23]

Although some were willing to attack the problem of slavery by deportation, there was little objection to the institution of bondage itself. And as abolitionism took a more militant turn in the North, Wilmingtonians responded in kind. At the prompting of the Intendant of Charleston, South Carolina, residents of Wilmington in 1835 held a town meeting which approved of resolutions condemning "reckless fanatics, enrolled as *Anti-Slavery Societies*." Promising to protect "inviolable and CHARTERED RIGHTS," it created a committee of vigilance, composed of 24 of the town's leading citizens, to "guard with vigilance all the channels of communication with the non-slaveholding States," and to examine all suspicious persons and papers. Within a week the committee was called to inspect several boxes of books received by the Methodist Church to determine if the volumes contained incendiary, abolitionist literature. In ensuing years Wilmingtonians held town meetings to denounce the liberation of a slave in Boston while in the company of his master and efforts by Bostonians to thwart the implementation of the Fugitive Slave Act. According to the *Wilmington Advertiser*, "Any indifference manifested by us on such [occasions] is suicidal, and gives the strongest ground for apprehending the dissolution of this Union."[24]

Not only were Wilmingtonians concerned about abolitionist efforts to flout the law and liberate slaves; they also remained sensitive to the possibility of slave uprisings, particularly in the tense atmosphere following John Brown's raid in 1859 and the election of Abraham Lincoln in 1860. Late in 1860 Solon Larkins, a teenager, was arrested and charged with treason for writing to an abolitionist society in New York and asking for $200 to support a planned insurrection on December 22 by 100 slaves, 40 free blacks, and 40 whites. Revelation of the letter caused "great excitement in Town and the surrounding Country," but an extensive investigation revealed the plot to be a fabrication. The young man just wanted to extort money from the abolitionist society. While one Wilmington newspaper referred to the matter as a "boyish freak," another deemed it a serious matter whose author "ought to be made to feel the consequences of his conduct." However, a Wilmingtonian observed that Larkins's "Family connections in this Place which is very numerous & influential will screan him" from punishment.[25]

Regardless of their fears, white Wilmingtonians remained greatly dependent upon slaves and free blacks, who provided a critical mass of labor for the town and port. Traditionally, January 1 of each year constituted the day for conducting the sale and hire of slaves for the coming twelve months for both Wilmington and New Hanover County. During the year the settlement of estates and the press of business occasioned additional transactions. Moreover, professionals who trafficked in slaves, buying and selling blacks, periodically appeared in Wilmington. Ansley Davis, from Petersburg, Virginia, advised the public in 1847 that he intended to remain in town for an extended period, during which he wanted to buy a "large number of slaves of both sexes," aged 14 to 30, for whom he would pay the "highest cash market price." Later that year James T. Morris advertised as a broker for the sale of slaves, claiming that, "there shall be no pains spared ... to make the above property bring its value, either in this or another market." M. Cronly, prominent broker and auctioneer of slaves in the 1850s, used the old county jail on the corner of Second and Princess Streets to confine bondsmen entrusted to him.[26]

African Americans were particularly prominent in Wilmington's maritime industry, where they served as boatmen, pilots, seamen, stewards, and cooks. They evidenced their indispensability, at least in the case of free blacks, when the General Assembly in 1830 compelled ships employing free blacks to ride quarantine in an effort to prevent runaway slaves from finding passage on those vessels. In the resulting opposition to the law, a correspondent to the *Cape Fear Recorder* declared:

> In nine cases out of ten, no white sailor can be employed as cook or steward; and in such a case, a captain would either have to go without either of these necessary adjuncts or sail to some other state. If [Wilmington-owned ships] carry a free coloured man out in that capacity they cannot bring him back, and but few will engage on these terms.[27]

As a result, the legislature soon repealed the statute.

African Americans, slave and free, worked in myriad other occupations, serving as barbers, blacksmiths, butchers, coopers, distillers, hostlers, iron moulders, millers, saddlers, seamstresses, shoemakers, tailors, tanners, wagoners, weavers, and wheelwrights. Along the waterfront, stevedores loaded and unloaded ships; women peddled fish and oysters, sold meals to sailors, and offered to wash clothes; and draymen waited for a call to transport goods back and forth to the docks. Blacks were especially important in the furniture and building trades, working as cabinetmakers, carpenters, joiners, masons, and plasterers. Remembered a former slave, "We had a lot of them artisans 'mongst our folks." According to the census of 1850, 34 of the 97 free residents of Wilmington listed in the building trades were free blacks. In the estimation of architectural historian Catherine W. Bishir, "Blacks were important to the building industry in every eastern North Carolina town, but probably nowhere did they enjoy such success ... as in Wilmington."[28]

Representative of the craftsmanship of African Americans in Wilmington were the impressive Town Hall/Thalian Hall and Bellamy Mansion, both finished just before the outbreak of the Civil War. One slave recalled that "mos' all the fine work 'round Wilmin'ton was done by slaves. They called 'em artisans. None of 'em could read, but give 'em any plan an' they could foller it to the las' line." And the son of the first owner of the Bellamy Mansion wrote that all the carpentry work on the building "was performed by negroes, chiefly free negroes. The masonry and plaster work, the cornices and other ornamental work on the walls was also done by negroes." Actually some whites did work in the building trades, and occasionally with African Americans. When scaffolding collapsed at a building in 1846, three whites, two slaves, and a free black carpenter fell. Solomon Nash, the free black, was deemed by the white community a "respectable man of his class, ... [who] carried on a large business on his own account."[29]

In addition to Nash, other prominent free black builders in Wilmington included James Sampson, James Boon, and members of the Artis and Howe families. Sampson, reportedly the son of a wealthy Sampson County planter, had been taken to Wilmington in 1819 at the age of eighteen, where his father liberated him and established him in the carpentry business. Sampson subsequently trained many young blacks, free and slave, and was one of a few builders in North Carolina, white or black, who amassed property worth $20,000. James Boon began his career as an apprentice to a Franklin County carpenter. He worked for planters in Franklin and Halifax counties, and then joined his brother in Wilmington in 1848. Before he traveled to Wilmington, however, Boon obtained an endorsement from William Jeffreys, a prominent white, that served as a recommendation for work and "a pass during all lawful hours" while the carpenter lived in Wilmington.[30]

African Americans also fashioned some of the furniture that graced public and private buildings in Wilmington. White cabinetmaker John Nutt in 1798 advertised the sale of a slave who had been bound to him to learn "the business of cabinet work, and Windsor chair making." Later that year Nutt warned the public against the clandestine use of his "negro apprentices to repair riding Chairs or other work, which tends to my injury particularly as the materials to complete such jobbs must be purloined from me by [the] apprentices." When John, who may have been an apprentice of Nutt, was advertised for sale in 1801, he was described as a chair and cabinetmaker "who is so well known in Wilmington ... that a description of his qualities is unnecessary."[31]

The extensive black presence in the Wilmington work force engendered competition with whites and consequent criticism, if not violence. After 1831, whites complained, and correctly, that legislation in that year which forbade slaves "to go at large" as free men, make contracts, and keep houses independently went unenforced in Wilmington. More specifically, white draymen pointed out that while the town required them to pay an annual $10 fee to conduct their businesses, slaves paid nothing, leaving the whites at a competitive disadvantage. Eventually the town commissioners equalized the fee and imposed annual charges on other slaves, including hucksters, male and female laborers, and washwomen.[32]

Most alarming was an incident that occurred one night in July 1857 when several whites demolished the framework of a house under construction by black artisans, leaving a placard stating that "a similar course would be pursued, in all cases against all buildings to be erected by negro contractors or carpenters...." While the actual demolition had been undertaken by a few men, some believed that they were part of an "organized association" of 250 or more. White artisans denied any conspiracy but objected to competition by slaves (not free blacks), because slaves received basic care from their masters and therefore were able to underbid whites for work. Moreover, whites alleged that slaves illegally engaged in contractual work.[33]

A town meeting quickly followed the incident. A number of "gentleman" in "strong terms" deplored the destruction of the building, and castigated white contractors, mechanics, and laboring men as "abolitionists," "dead rabbits," and "plug uglies." The participants in the meeting adopted resolutions requesting the mayor to offer a reward for the conviction of the perpetrators. They also tendered their services to the mayor in the future to prevent a recurrence of "a similar outrage, ... even at the hazard of our lives." White artisans held their own meetings, returning the epithets "to the authors and vendors for their own digestion," and disavowing any attempt to create trouble. The artisans also observed that in the past several instances of the illegal destruction of private property (blowing up log cabins and mausoleums, and destroying stills and residences) had gone unnoticed. But in the future the artisans promised to seek redress of their grievances through legal channels.[34]

The incident, whose circumstances were doubtlessly influenced by the high cost of living in Wilmington and the adverse impact of the recessions of 1854 and 1857, revealed the tensions in town between the "gentlemen" and the working class, between capital and labor, between slave owners and non–slave owners. Concerned about the possible divisiveness engendered by slavery, the *Journal* reminded the artisans that all lived in a slaveholding state and community, and that they must "regard this matter as southern citizens of a southern State." At such a critical time in the late 1850s, the paper went on, the artisans ought not to engage in behavior that undermined the institution of slavery. Those who had immigrated to Wilmington must have understood its environment. If a choice had to be made between slavery and those who opposed the institution, the *Journal* editorialized, "we would retain out institutions and our property."[35]

Although the *Journal* appropriately established the parameters of the argument, the newspaper begged the question of equity. As the artisans rightly contended, they found no protection from the laws by which slaves contracted and hired their services because evasions of those statutes were "so accessible to Negroes and their Masters and PROTECTORS, that they are valueless and ineffectual...." Indeed, legislation governing all activities of slaves—maintaining quarters apart from their masters, interaction with free blacks, economic controls—largely went unenforced. A statute in 1835 requiring the town commissioners to appoint an agent to supervise slave contracts was not implemented until twenty years later. Slave owners, whether through indifference or economic necessity, refused to cooperate in the enforcement of regulatory laws and ordinances.[36] When white artisans protested the use of slave labor in the building trades in 1857, they, in effect, attacked the system, evoking a vitriolic response from the "gentlemen" of Wilmington.

While slaves contributed immeasurably to the economy of Wilmington, their lives were not totally consumed by work. In the yards and streets, children gathered for ball and other games. However, some families observed a measure of segregation, for one slave recalled, "we chil'en was told to play in our own yard and not have nothin' to do with the free issue chil'en or the common chil'en 'cross the street, white or colored, because they was'nt fitten to 'sociate with us. You see our owners was rich folks." Boys pitched pennies, played marbles, rolled hoops, played ball, raced, and flew kites. Men—slaves and free blacks—played games of cards, dice, and ninepins, at which they often bet small amounts of money.[37]

Slaves and free blacks also enjoyed music, even to the extent of becoming professional musicians and organizing bands. Throughout the antebellum era most of the musicians hired for entertainment were African Americans. Many slaves achieved a reputation for proficiency on the fiddle. In the census of 1850, two free blacks listed their occupation as fiddler; in 1860, three. Philip Bazadier (a slave or free black) was one of perhaps only two trumpeters in Wilmington before mid-century. Blacks also organized bands, including Allen's Rosebud Brass Band, formed in the mid–1850s and headed by Allen Evans, a slave or former slave who owned Allen's Barber Shop. Frank Johnson's Band, though led by a white, included blacks.[38]

The musicians and bands provided music for the community on diverse occasions. Dances commanded the services of fiddlers. Bands played airs on Washington's Birthday, May Day, and July 4, as well as at militia gatherings. As troops prepared to embark for service in the Mexican War in the 1840s, "very early in the morning, ... old Philip Bassadier, ... sounded his horn at the corners of the streets. Then the Negro drummers beat the reveille in front of the courthouse...." The fifer and drummers were directed to march down the line, and volunteers were ordered to fall in behind them. Blacks often accompanied whites on steamboat excursions to provide music for the revelers and in 1855 may even have taken a boat of their own in conjunction with two steamers transporting white Wilmingtonians.[40]

During the Christmas season, slaves not only provided music but also celebrated a unique entertainment known as John Kuner (John Kooner, Jonkonnu, John Canoe). Derived from a festival of West African origin, John Kuner emerged in the islands of the West Indies, particularly Jamaica, from which it gravitated to the American mainland (though in the case of North Carolina, the custom may have been brought directly to the colony from the Guinea slaving coast). Around Christmastime, numbers of men arrayed themselves in outlandish clothes, donned horrific looking masks, and danced through the streets, stopping at houses or before interested onlookers to sing and afterwards seek pennies or small gifts for their performances. While the John Kuners delighted adults and children, the curmudgeonly editor of the *Daily Journal* remarked in 1851, "Christmas is Coming, in fact it is almost come, and were it not for the ... noise and confusion and the 'Kooners,' or however otherwise the confounded word is spelled, and the firecrackers, and all the other unnamed abominations, we should be much inclined to rejoice thereat."[41]

The John Kuner tradition seemed to wax and wane in Wilmington. In 1854 the "kooners" paled in comparison to those "of olden times, nothing like the 'Kooners' that used to be about some years ago," editorialized the *Journal*. Three years later "the colored population was in high feather, and John Kuner appeared in all his pristine splendor." Yet the following year, and in 1860, "John Kuner [was] fading out," "feeble," "getting ridiculous," and "nowhere now," according to the newspapers. Nevertheless, blacks continued the tradition beyond the Civil War, perhaps to the 1880s. Eventually, young white boys appropriated the custom, which they pursued with relish into the twentieth century.[42]

While the holiday season offered relaxation and merriment to Wilmington blacks, religion played a fundamental role in the lives of African Americans throughout the year. Laboring under bonded servitude, and unable to express themselves fully, slaves used religion as an outlet for the release of emotions and frustrations. They retained elements of their African heritage, religious and otherwise, but the prohibition of the slave trade in 1808 meant that they came under ever greater pressure to adapt, at least with modifications, to the cultural constructs of whites.

In turn, slave owners and churches in Wilmington made an effort to Christianize slaves, or to expose them to religious services. Blacks often attended the church of their master's choice. Their names were listed in the marriage and death records of St. James Episcopal Church. Episcopalians eventually erected St. Paul's Church on the corner of Fourth and Orange Streets to offer free seating to blacks and the opportunity for interracial worship. Numerous slaves also attended First Baptist Church. By 1845 the Baptists contemplated the establishment of a separate "African congregation." Subsequently, blacks gradually assumed a semi-independent role in the church and organized their own worship service. Their membership in 1863 comprised 165, as opposed to 225 whites in the Baptist church. And St. Paul's Evangelical Lutheran Church, under construction in 1859, contained room specifically for 50 African American worshipers.[43]

The Methodists, however, led by Bishop Francis Asbury in the course of his famous circuit-riding ministry, spearheaded the effort in Wilmington to bring Christianity to blacks. And the Methodists were successful, though they endured persecution for their efforts, including assaults and arrests. The first Methodist church in Wilmington, founded just before the turn of the nineteenth century, embraced both blacks and whites, but the former were numerically superior. In 1803, Asbury declared that membership consisted of 878 "Africans, and a few whites." Over the years, African Americans continued to constitute the bulk of the membership of the Methodist church. Possibly in the 1830s, dissident blacks in the Front Street Methodist Church formed their own congregation, and by 1855 black Methodists in Wilmington outnumbered whites, 1,268 to 497.[44]

In their religious worship, and in their daily lives, blacks, bonded and free, managed a surprising degree of autonomy. Harsh, restrictive legislation was often evaded, due in part to the recalcitrance of the African Americans, and in part to the unwillingness of whites to enforce their own town ordinances and legislative statutes. There were limits. In the course of training black youths in the building trades, James Sampson opened a school for the instruction of free blacks and, occasionally, slaves. When discovered, the school was closed, and Sampson barely escaped a public whipping.[45] Indeed, slaves seemed to have enjoyed more indulgence than free blacks, as indicated by the incident in 1857 when slave owners reacted angrily to whites who tore down a building under construction by slaves. The story of blacks in antebellum Wilmington was one of many themes: lives of bondage or semi-bondage; lives that were inseparable from those of whites with whom they necessarily lived in close proximity; and yet lives characterized by an incessant and often successful desire to gain some measure of freedom.

7

Fellowship, Fraternity, Association

While African Americans longed for release from their constraints, whether bondage for slaves or the restrictions imposed on free blacks, the white populace in Wilmington organized to enjoy a wide range of communal endeavors. Characteristic of Wilmingtonians in the antebellum era, and Americans in general, was a penchant for association. Whites in the port town sought one another's company for varying reasons, ranging from social camaraderie to military protection to charitable endeavor. As a result, a number of voluntary associations arose, including social clubs, fraternal orders, benevolent societies, mechanics' groups, militia companies, and churches.

Representative of the social gatherings were the Ninepenny Whist Club and the Wilmington Whistling Society. Thirteen Wilmington men organized the Ninepenny Whist Club in 1801 for the purposes of eating, drinking, and playing cards. Most of the men shared an interest in commercial affairs and evidenced a Federalist bias in their politics, but the purpose of the club was merriment. The group disbanded about 1807 because "the meetings became too hilarious to suit the taste (or conscience?) of the more moderate members...."[1] At approximately the same time, the port also hosted the Wilmington Whistling Society, composed, among others, of auctioneer Jacob Levy, shipwright James Telfair, lawyer Edward Jones, and Scottish gentleman Andrew Cutlar, who met in Dorsey's Tavern. At each meeting individual members whistled previously agreed upon tunes. The best performer, as adjudged by a committee, treated the company with wine that evening. Like the Ninepenny Whist Club, good humor and hilarity were the order of the day.[2]

The decade before the Civil War found Wilmington hosting a number of quizzical organizations that presumably consisted of whites, though some may have borne a relationship to the African American John Kuner tradition. The Don Quixote Invincibles and the Great Moguls usually appeared during the Christmas season, presenting a "grotesque, ridiculous, unique, fanciful" public display in the streets that resembled the John Kuners in their outlandish costumes and music. The Moguls also paraded in the summer, unofficially as part of the July 4 festivities. An unnamed group, "Clampsus Vitus," posted a notice of a meeting in 1856 for the initiation of new members and business of "special importance," at which the "R. G. Musician[s], will be in attendance with their instruments in bright condition." The "Red Men," or "Waccamaw Tribe," an "association dressed up in Indian costume, or what is supposed to be such," appeared in public in 1858. And on Christmas eve in 1860 the "Wild Goose Club" met at "Rendez-Vous No. 1." Members, or "Wild Geese," were ordered to be "punctual and come prepared as we shall take a high flight tonight. By order of the Gander. Quank! Quank!"[3]

Masonry thrived in Wilmington after the Revolution. The North Carolina Grand Lodge in 1791 recognized Wilmington's St. John's Lodge as the oldest in the state. Five years later the state legislature incorporated it as St. John's Lodge No. 1. In the same year, St. Tammany's Lodge, No. 30, appeared in Wilmington when several members of St. John's No. 1 petitioned to withdraw and form a new lodge. According to legend, the petitioners objected to the overindulgence in alcoholic beverages by members of St. John's, but no evidence exists to justify such speculation. St. Tammany's entertained North Carolina Grand Master William R. Davie and Grand Senior Warden John Louis Taylor in May 1796, and on December 27 joined St. John's to celebrate the feast of the anniversary of St. John the Evangelist. The General Assembly incorporated St. Tammany's No. 30 in 1805.[4]

Throughout the antebellum era the Masons in Wilmington and visiting members of the order gathered every December 27 to observe "St. John's Day." Often preceded by a band (the German Brass Band in 1854), they marched through the streets in their aprons and regalia to their destination, usually the Presbyterian, Methodist, or Episcopal church, where a suitable sermon was given by the resident minister. In the early nineteenth century, the Concord Chapter, No. 6 (changed from No. 1), of Free Masons apparently replaced St. Tammany's Lodge. Members of St. John's Lodge, with visiting Masons, in a solemn ceremony in 1804 laid the cornerstone of Free Masons Hall on Orange Street, which served St. John's Lodge and later the Concord Chapter until 1841–1842, when it was superseded by a new Masonic Hall on Front between Walnut and Red Cross Streets. In 1852 local Masons entertained the Grand Royal Arch Chapter of North Carolina, after which the members of the Grand Chapter enjoyed an excursion on the steamboat *Calhoun* to Smithville.[5]

A popular fraternal, benevolent society that arose to accompany the Masons was the International Order of Odd Fellows, whose first lodge appeared in North Carolina in 1841. The following year the Cape Fear Lodge, No. 2, organized in Wilmington and was incorporated by the General Assembly in 1843. Clarendon Lodge, No. 45, an offshoot of Cape Fear Lodge, No. 2, formed in 1852. On May 13, or thereabouts, the Odd Fellows, accompanied by one or another of the many bands in town, paraded through the streets to celebrate their anniversary in "a spirited manner." Their "glittering decorations ... dazzled the eye" as they made their way from Odd Fellows Hall on Princess, between Third and Fourth Streets, to a church to hear an oration. Subsequently, they often arranged for a steamboat excursion down the river in which there was music, dancing, "crowds of pretty girls," and "plenty of good eating." During the 1850s, aided by an ever expanding railroad system, the Grand Encampment of Odd Fellows in North Carolina several times gathered in Wilmington for its annual meeting.[6]

Beyond the Masonic and Odd Fellows orders, the militia and volunteer military companies, which supplemented the militia, offered camaraderie as well as satisfying a necessary public service. In addition to musters, the Wilmington troops joined other companies of the New Hanover County regiment in periodic reviews called by the brigadier general of the North Carolina Militia. At those times, officers were expected to "feel a proper degree of responsibility for the appearance and discipline of their respective regiments, armed and accoutered agreeably to law." By the 1830s the population of New Hanover County was sufficient to justify a division of its militia into the Upper and Lower Battalions, the latter embracing Wilmington companies.[7]

However, during the antebellum era the militia system fell into some disrepute. Largely responsible, according to Robert Rankin, judge advocate for the New Hanover Regiment, was the inability of militia officers to obtain copies of the militia laws of the state, none of which had ever been furnished to the officers. Consequently, they were "uncertain how to proceed on the most important matters of a Military Nature, producing the most fatal lethargic tendency...." Moreover, Rankin contended that "the long list of exemptions [from military service] including the most respectable of the community that ought to stand in the Militia ranks is the mark of contempt and degradation" to the militia. Matters had not improved on the eve of the Civil War, when the "worn-out militia system" had "fallen under very general ridicule," according to the Wilmington *Journal*. Militia service was unpopular and officers unqualified. Still, as the Wilmington *Herald* pointed out, the "bum-a-litia," as the little boys called them, served well in the war with Mexico and still commanded respect.[8]

Cushioning the decline of the general militia was the appearance of volunteer companies, which generated a greater sense of pride, discipline, and camaraderie than the ordinary militia. Early in the nineteenth century the town boasted three volunteer military companies—the New Hanover Troop of Light Horse, the Artillery Company, and the Wilmington Volunteer Corps of Light Infantry. The 1830s found the New Hanover Horse Guards, the Independent Artillery Company, and the Wilmington Volunteers supplementing the militia. The Clarendon Horse Guards, a cavalry company, organized in 1844, the same year that the Volunteers disbanded. As one older historian wrote, the volunteer companies came and went, but the militia "rolled on forever."[9]

The decade before the Civil War witnessed the appearance of new volunteer companies and an increased interest in military service, particularly as the dissolution of the Union loomed. Although the Clarendon Guards apparently had ceased to exist by 1853, the appearance of the German Volunteers and the Wilmington Light Infantry Company in that year gave Wilmington "two handsome and efficient volunteer companies." Flags were presented to the companies at the time of their organization, accompanied by appropriate addresses by the donors and recipients, including a thanks to the "fair givers" of the standards. Soon joining the German Volunteers and the Wilmington Light Infantry were the Rifle Cadets. The election of 1860 and increasing sectional tension produced additional companies, including the Cape Fear Riflemen, composed of mechanics and working men in the town, and the Horse Artillery.[10]

Bedecked in resplendent outfits, the volunteers made an imposing appearance. Privates of the Wilmington Light Infantry sported a full dress cap with white plume, gilt eagle, and the letters "W.L.I." on the front; dress coat of blue black trimmed with buff; epaulettes of buff fringe; and pants two shades lighter than the coat, with buff stripes down the outer seam of both legs. The officers' uniforms differed in having a red and white plume, sash and sword, and ornaments on the collars of the coats. And the dashing presence elicited gushing approval. Editorialized the *Wilmington Advertiser*, "What exercise is more manly than the drill? What constitutes the quietude and security of our firesides, but the frequent display of the ability, and readiness to *preserve* it?"[11]

The Wilmington Light Infantry maintained a high profile in the community, both militarily and socially. The company staged a target shooting contest in 1855 on the anniversary of the signing of the Mecklenburg Declaration of Independence (May 20, 1775), and in 1857 took the steamer *Flora McDonald* to Fayetteville, where it joined the Oak City Guards from Raleigh, the Fayetteville Independent Company, the Lafayette Light Infantry, and the Fayetteville Cadets from the host town for shooting contests, lavish meals, and speeches. That same year the Wilmington Light Infantry gave a military ball at Mozart Hall, which was described as "the event of the season." In May 1860 the Wilmington Light Infantry celebrated its seventh anniversary by embarking on a picnic to Belvidere plantation about two miles across the river from town. Less than two weeks later the Light Infantry undertook a moonlight excursion by steamboat up the Cape Fear River, accompanied by a brass band and a string band, which provided music for dancing.[12]

Public service from a different perspective emanated from Wilmington women who participated in the nationwide movement to raise money to purchase Mount Vernon, home of George Washington. Ann Pamela Cunningham organized a national fund-raising effort in 1853 to buy the mansion and surrounding area for preservation. Three years later the Virginia legislature chartered the Mount Vernon Ladies' Association of the Union, which led the organization of local chapters through the nation. The Wilmington chapter organized by 1857, at which time it raised awareness of its project by sponsoring a series of lectures featuring such local luminaries as lawyer George W. Davis, author Griffith John McRee, and Methodist minister Dr. C. F. Deems, as well as nationally known politician and orator Edward Everett. It addition to raising money by memberships, which cost a dollar, the Wilmington women put a box in the post office in which the public could place donations to the Mount Vernon Fund. Wilmingtonians contributed significantly to the successful effort to save Mount Vernon.[13]

Self-improvement prompted some Wilmingtonians to respond to the call of temperance, adopting either an attitude of moderation in the use of alcohol or total abstinence. Temperance societies appeared in North Carolina about 1822, an expression of the general reform movement that swept the nation at the time. The Wilmington Temperance Society organized at least by early 1833. It was spearheaded by Protestant ministers and met in the Baptist, Methodist, and Presbyterian churches of the town. According to Presbyterian minister Thomas P. Hunt, a number (varying from 38 to "nearly" 50) of habitual drunkards formed their own "Temperance Society" in 1833 in satirical opposition, holding meetings on Sunday in which they ridiculed religion and denounced temperance. A sharp debate ensued over the details of the Rev. Hunt's report. And as the matter gained national notoriety, many regretted the adverse publicity accorded Wilmington in the incident.[14]

By the mid–1840s, Wilmington exhibited three temperance organizations—the Washington Temperance Society, the Auxiliary Washington Society, and the Wilmington Total Abstinence Society. As a boy attending Laura Rankin's school at that time, Nicholas W. Schenck recalled that the Washington Temperance Society was "in full blast those days."[15] Joining the early temperance societies was Rock Spring Tent, No. 180, International Order of Rechabites (of Wilmington), which organized in 1845, enrolled 120 members the following year, and obtained incorporation by the legislature in 1849. The Rechabites mixed pleasure with business in their annual meetings, taking a cruise in 1848 down the Cape Fear River on the steamboat *Wilmington*, "accompanied by a large concourse of ladies...." In 1851 Rock Spring Tent No. 180 celebrated its anniversary in conjunction with the Topsail Tent and the Hanover Sons of Temperance, marching from their headquarters to Mozart Hall to receive the Sons, and then to the Baptist church on Front Street to hear a sermon. A year later an imposing procession of temperance groups "wound through the principal streets" of Wilmington, making "a very handsome appearance, to which the adornments of the costumes of the Rechabites greatly contributed."[16]

Interest in temperance seemed to wane by the mid–1850s. The Washington Temperance Society reorganized twice, once in 1848 in time to hold a celebration at Christmas at the Methodist and Baptist churches and again in 1851, before finally succumbing. Publishers tendered prospectuses in 1846 for two temperance newspapers in Wilmington, the *Philanthropist* and the *Temperance Sentinel*, and in 1852 for the *Standard of Temperance*, also slated for Wilmington, but apparently none received sufficient encouragement to inaugurate a paper. Although references to temperance organizations abated after 1853, advocates of temperance held a meeting in Wilmington in March of 1854, preparatory to a Temperance Convention in the town, for the purpose of nominating candidates to the General Assembly to represent the cause of temperance. And the following year a temperance lecturer from Ohio spoke to crowded assemblages on two nights.[17]

Various organizations attested to Wilmingtonians' enjoyment of music. The Harmonic Society, formed before 1809, provided musical concerts and music for community events. A glee club, probably organized for political purposes during the presidential campaign of 1848, held forth at least until 1857. And in 1860 a Mozart Club offered vocal music to the town. During the twenty years prior to the Civil War, several bands appeared—the Wilmington Band, Frank Johnson's Band, the Amateur Brass Band (which became the Wilmington Cornet Band), and Allen's Rosebud Brass Band. Blacks comprised many of the bands, which played airs for holiday festivities, for militia, political, Masonic, and temperance parades, for dances, and for steamboat excursions.[18]

Businessmen, mechanics, and planters sought to protect and promote their respective interests through associative endeavors. Late in the antebellum period, Wilmington merchants organized a chamber of commerce for the purposes of promoting trade, arbitrating disputes, establishing uniform commercial regulations, and representing the sentiment of the town if necessary to state legislators. Although contemplated (as a board of trade) at least as early as 1839, a chamber of commerce emerged only in 1853. Quickly the mercantile houses that composed the chamber, at least forty-two in number, moved to establish shipping rates for river traffic from Fayetteville to Wilmington, to permit the purchase and sale of spirits of turpentine without an additional charge for the barrel, and to order the purchase of turpentine and tar directly from producers rather than from the inspectors of those products. Members of the chamber also agreed in 1855 that they would henceforth dine at 4:30 in the afternoon instead of 1:00 P.M., as had long been "the custom of an afternoon" in Wilmington, in order to avoid an interruption in business hours and to enjoy a more leisurely meal later.[19]

Artisans or mechanics in Wilmington faced continual competition from skilled slaves (and free blacks) who might be hired out by their masters or who might be allowed to hire their own labor. The mechanics frequently complained to the legislature, and organized as the Incorporated Master Mechanics in 1808 to protect their interests. The General Assembly responded with legislation from the 1780s throughout the antebellum era that attempted to regulate free black and slave labor, but to little avail, for the statutes were loosely enforced at best. In 1857 the frustration of whites erupted when, during the night of July 27, white mechanics partially destroyed a house under construction by black workers and left a note that the same fate would befall other buildings erected by black laborers. Recriminations followed. A gathering of mechanics in turn disavowed the violence but asked for proper enforcement of existing laws regulating the contract and hire of blacks.[20]

Adding to the diversity of organizational efforts in Wilmington were agricultural societies, which, of course, included county residents but received their principal impetus from Wilmingtonians. Although always

7—Fellowship, Fraternity, Association   149

one of the largest urban areas in North Carolina, Wilmington, like all towns, was removed only by a few blocks in any direction from the countryside. Moreover, many wealthy inhabitants of Wilmington owned plantations. Among them was Dr. John Bellamy and Griffith J. McRee. The Cape Fear Agricultural Society, organized about 1810 and incorporated in 1813, constituted one of the first county agricultural organizations to appear in North Carolina. It met in Wilmington and certainly included Wilmingtonians. However, the society, like so many others that formed in the first quarter of the nineteenth century, folded within a few years.[21]

Planters and farmers of New Hanover reorganized in 1854–1855 in the wake of a revived effort in North Carolina to launch county societies and, in 1852, a state agricultural society. At the outset, men of agriculture from New Hanover and Brunswick cooperated in the formation of the New Hanover and Brunswick Agricultural Society, but subsequently New Hanover established an independent society. In 1860 the New Hanover Agricultural Society decided to purchase thirty acres of land east of current Greenfield Lake to serve as a fairground. Still, the tardy formation of the New Hanover society, the belated establishment of a fair when other county societies (including those of Duplin and Onslow) had long held such educational gatherings, and a paucity of attendance at meetings betokened a lack of interest among New Hanover farmers in agricultural improvements or, at least, organization.[22]

Relieving the stress of business and toil in everyday life was organized religion. Interest proved sporadic. Early in the nineteenth century a visitor from New England, accustomed to attending church, wrote deprecatingly of finding not more than a hundred worshipers on the Sabbath in Wilmington. In the 1820s a Wilmingtonian observed, "The churches of the town [only the Episcopal and Methodist were open at that time] were attended but little." And complaints appeared in the newspapers about those who kept businesses open on Sunday, and noisy children in the streets whose play disturbed worshiping congregations.[23]

However, the Great Revival at the turn of the nineteenth century, ministerial visitations (particularly those of Methodist Francis Asbury), camp meetings, and a revival in the late 1850s maintained or rekindled interest in religion over the years. Camp meetings, often associated with the Methodists, were usually held at Town Creek or the site of old Brunswick Town in Brunswick County. For a week-long camp meeting in May 1836, the steamboat *Clarendon* was chartered to take persons to Town Creek, leaving each morning at seven o'clock and returning each evening.[24]

The Revival of 1858 in Wilmington, reflecting a Northern urban phenomenon engendered by the Panic of 1857 and the growing political crisis, stimulated interest in religion. It emphasized interdenominational unity and avoidance of controversial issues. Meetings were held in the various churches of the town, morning, noon, and night, attracting whites and blacks. The Front Street Baptist Church held interdenominational sunrise prayer services. The revival fostered the Wilmington chapter of the YMCA, increased church membership, and eventuated in the construction of several churches. By 1860, fourteen churches had been erected or were under construction in the town, including the Seamen's Bethel, where religious services were provided for the mariners in port.[25]

The Episcopalians, successors to the Anglican (who had erected St. James Church on Market Street prior to the Revolution) represented the oldest element of organized religion in Wilmington. However, the church reportedly was desecrated by British soldiers during the war, and services were discontinued from the beginning of the conflict to 1795. At that time St. James revived, aided by legislation in 1796 that authorized members of the church to elect wardens, and by legislation in 1812 that permitted members of the church to raise $3,000 by lottery for repairs to their building. In 1819 Wilmington hosted the state convention of the Episcopal Church. Twenty years later, in 1839, St. James demolished its meetinghouse and began construction of a new church at the same location, much to the dismay of "P Q," a correspondent to the *Wilmington Advertiser*, who preferred the simplicity of the old building and expressed regret that worshipers needed "the effect of architectural elegance to inspire devotion." The new edifice was impressive. Representing a stylish Gothic Revival design by Thomas U. Walter, it set a new architectural standard for Wilmington's future churches.[26]

During the 1850s the Episcopalians constructed two additional churches in Wilmington. The vestry of St. James in 1852 resolved to form another parish and erect St. John's Episcopal Church on the northeast corner of Red Cross and Third streets. The cornerstone was laid late the following year, but the church apparently was not finished until 1860. Meanwhile, Episcopalians undertook the construction of St. Paul's in 1858, sighted initially at Fourth and Orange streets and built under the auspices of Bishop Thomas Atkinson. It offered free seating to a racially mixed congregation. After the Civil War, St. Paul's served as a mission to blacks, many of whom eventually left in 1869 to form their own congregation. St. Paul's then moved in 1914 to its present location on Market and Sixteenth Streets.[27]

Through the numerous Scots and Scotch-Irish in Wilmington, the Presbyterian Church had long exerted an influence upon the local populace. A congregation formally organized in 1817, and two years later erected

7—Fellowship, Fraternity, Association

St. James Church on Market Street. Representing a Gothic Revival design, it established a new architectural standard for future Wilmington churches. Drawing courtesy of the New Hanover County Public Library, Wilmington.

First Presbyterian Church on Front Street. Forty-seven pews were sold for $10,250; another nineteen were reserved for visitors and the poor. Although the church almost immediately burned, it was rebuilt in 1821 at the same location, aided perhaps by a $6,000 lottery authorized by the state legislature. In 1858 fourteen members of the First Presbyterian congregation bought a lot on Chestnut Street and proceeded to erect St. Andrew's Presbyterian (or Second Presbyterian) Church. The following year a Presbyterian synod convened in Wilmington, bringing numerous strangers to town, according to an Episcopalian who remarked that, "All the Churches have been thrown open to them except ours and the R[oman] C[atholic], ... and Predestination ... [was] preached thoroughly." On the eve of the war in April 1861, a third Presbyterian Church, located on the corner of Third and Orange Streets, was dedicated.[28]

An influx of German immigrants into Wilmington in the two decades preceding the Civil War resulted in the organization of a Lutheran congregation in the town in 1858, the only evidence of Lutheranism in the state outside the lower piedmont region. The following year the congregation laid the cornerstone of St. Paul's Evangelical Lutheran Church, located at the corner of Market and Sixth Streets. The walls and most of the brickwork of the proposed Gothic Revival structure, which contained room for as many as fifty blacks along with the white congregation, had been finished by 1860. However, the Civil War and its aftermath prevented the completion of St. Paul's until 1869.[29]

The Baptists and Methodists, which became the leading denominations in North Carolina, early appeared in Wilmington. First Baptist Church organized in 1808 with twenty members, who met in a frame building on the corner of Front and Ann Streets. The church had ceased to function by 1813. In 1833 the Baptists reorganized, and worshiped in a church on Front Street that was dedicated in 1838, and at which the North Carolina Baptist State Conference convened in 1851. Toward the end of the antebellum era the Baptists purchased a lot on the corner of Market and Fifth Streets on which they proposed to build an early English Gothic structure. Slow funding and the war delayed completion of First Baptist Church until 1870.[30]

Methodism made its principal appeal to the poorer element of society and, in the eastern region of North Carolina, particularly in the towns of Wilmington and Fayetteville, to blacks. Circuit rider Bishop Francis Asbury struggled mightily to bring Methodism to North Carolina, in the process making several visits to Wilmington. A church reportedly was formed in the port in 1797 under the leadership of William Meredith. According to minister William Capers in 1813, "Negroes ... almost exclusively composed the congregation.... The whites were very poor or barely able to support themselves with decency." The racially mixed composition of the church membership brought derision, and sometimes violence, upon the Methodists. Reportedly, Methodist meetinghouses were burned in Wilmington.[31]

Eventually the Methodists occupied a large wooden building on the corner of Front and Walnut Streets called the Methodist Meetinghouse. After succumbing to fire in 1843, Front Street Methodist Church, a "commodious place of worship," was rebuilt of brick and dedicated in 1845.

First Baptist Church on Market Street, a Gothic Revival structure whose completion was delayed by the onset of the Civil War. Drawing courtesy of the New Hanover County Public Library, Wilmington.

During the rebuilding of Front Street Church, a need was felt for a place of Methodist worship south of Market Street. Services were conducted in a building near the intersection of Second and Castle, which became a mission of the Front Street Church. Eventually a Methodist church was constructed on Fifth Street on land (in the woods at the time) donated by Miles Costin between Church and Castle Streets.[32]

In the early nineteenth century Roman Catholics in North Carolina were few in number and confined mainly to towns in eastern North Carolina, particularly New Bern and Washington. Prospects for Catholics brightened when John England in 1820 became the bishop of Charleston. Touring North Carolina in 1821, Bishop England found twenty-two Catholics in Wilmington, who worshiped with Protestants—Methodists, Episcopalians, and Presbyterians—in town. In the wake of the appearance of Bishop England, St. Thomas Parish was erected in Wilmington, and Catholics began to gather as a group. Until 1847 they used the Presbyterian church, courthouse, theater, and Masonic Hall for worship. Under a missionary, the Very Reverend Thomas Murphy, who was stationed in Wilmington in 1846, St. Thomas Catholic Church was erected and dedicated in 1847. Located on Dock between Second and Third Streets, it borrowed from the Gothic design of St. James.[33]

Beyond the Protestants and Catholics, Wilmington's Jews added to the religious diversity of the port. The early Sephardic Jews were too few in number to form a minyan. Many, including Aaron Lazarus and Jacob Levy, chose to worship at St. James Episcopal Church. An increased Jewish presence, spurred by an Ashkenazic immigration, resulted in the formation in 1852 of Chevra Kadisha to gather funds for a burial ground. Attesting to the success of the organization was the dedication in 1855 of the Hebrew Cemetery within the newly opened Oakdale Cemetery. After the Civil War an Orthodox Jewish congregation formed in Wilmington, opening a synagogue briefly in 1867. Five years later a Reform congregation organized, which built and dedicated the Temple of Israel in 1876.[34]

Churches, among other organizations, played a role in assisting the less fortunate in Wilmington who depended upon the beneficence of the public. Poor relief, which had been primarily a function of the Anglican parishes before the Revolution, became a more secular matter after the war. Legislation called for the election of wardens of the poor in the counties and provided for the imposition of county taxes for the maintenance of the poor. By law, the poor were deemed the unpropertied, those incapable of earning a living by reason of physical or mental incapacity to labor. Included in that group principally were the mentally handicapped, invalids, cripples, and aged. In general, the care of the poor by the wardens consisted of a combination of granting allowances to individual paupers, boarding paupers with private families, and placing paupers in the poorhouse. In 1860 the counties of North Carolina spent $83,486 for the support of 1,922 paupers, 33 of whom (30 Americans, 3 foreigners) were in Wilmington.[35]

The General Assembly in 1785 authorized the erection of poorhouses in selected counties in the state, and in 1793 empowered the wardens of the poor in any county to build a facility for paupers. After the wardens of the poor of New Hanover in 1797 approved the construction of a poorhouse to be located in Wilmington, the county treasurer advertised for bids for erecting the proposed 50-by-16-foot structure, which would be divided into four rooms and be accompanied by two brick chimneys. Over the years the wardens of the poor hired superintendents for the poorhouse and provided them with lodging. The New Hanover County poorhouse, once hailed as one of the best in the state, had fallen into "a miserable dilapidated condition," according to reformer Dorothea Dix, who visited North Carolina in the late 1840s. A grand jury in 1851 agreed. Although the exterior was sound, the wards exhibited a "miserably filthy ... condition," indicating "the most culpable disregard of health[,] cleanliness, or comfort" of the tenants.[36]

In addition to the legal poor, there were many others in Wilmington who depended upon private philanthropy—poor children, women (often widows), mechanics, and sailors. Playing a prominent role in offering charity for children and females were well-to-do women in Wilmington. The General Assembly in 1817 incorporated the Female Benevolent Society, the third in the state (following similar organizations in New Bern, 1812, and Fayetteville, 1813), which aimed to assist orphans and children of the poor, particularly to provide them with "a moral and religious as well as a common education."[37]

While the work of the Female Benevolent Society in its early years remains moot, the Ladies Working Society of St. James Episcopal Church in Wilmington, incorporated in 1833 by the General Assembly, assumed the responsibility of providing a free school for the poor. In conjunction with a Juvenile Female Working Society, the women held fairs to raise money, which was used for charity and for repairing the church. Women of the Presbyterian Church also held fund-raising festivals at which they sold edibles and potables for the benefit of civic and church affairs.[38]

In the mid to late 1840s a "Ladies Benevolent Society" had succeeded the Female Benevolent Society. Directress Catherine G. Kennedy headed the society, which was incorporated in 1852 for the purpose of alleviating the suffering of the poor and sick.[39] The group divided the town into districts, to which members were assigned to investigate "meritorious claimants upon their bounty." In addition to seeking donations of money and material goods, including wood during the winter, members of the society offered sewing instruction to poor women and girls to provide them with a skill and source of income. The society obtained the use of the basement of the Seamen's Home on Front Street, which it called a

"Depository," at which the girls could offer their needlework for sale and where residents were encouraged to take their clothes for alterations. In 1860 the ladies made plans to establish a home for indigent widows (which materialized in 1879 as a residence for the elderly and remained open until 2000).[40]

Relieving the suffering of the poor was an arduous task for the Ladies Benevolent Society, made more difficult by a lack of support. Although single women in Wilmington increasingly sought alms, having been forced out of work by automation (according to the chief directress), there were only seventy-three members (six of whom were men) in the society in 1859. Since annual dues were a dollar, the society depended greatly upon donations. Altogether, it had $293 available in 1859, of which it spent $238. Undermining perhaps the effectiveness of the society but reinforcing its goals were additional ongoing charitable efforts in Wilmington. In 1855 wood was donated anonymously to "the suffering poor" of the town. And a newspaper notice in 1857 informed readers that they could leave donations for the relief of the poor at the store of Brown and Anderson. At that point some $350 had been distributed to furnish fuel, clothing, and food to the needy.[41]

On occasion, artisans or mechanics organized for mutual support and sustenance. Legislation in 1795 offered the opportunity for indigent and aged mechanics in Wilmington to establish a charitable relief fund. The General Assembly virtually reenacted the statute in 1815, after which a Mechanical Society was established, but the organization must have been short-lived. However, in 1824, after an association had been formed to raise money for "unfortunate, afflicted and disabled" mechanics and their families, "to whom chance or misfortune may render assistance necessary," the legislature incorporated the Mechanics' Benevolent Society of Wilmington to effect those charitable intentions.[42]

Mariners likewise required support. Landlubbers seemed to look upon the seafarers as simple-minded men, almost childlike in their behavior, who needed protection for their own preservation. Such safeguards were all the more necessary because sailors were strangers in their ports of call, without family and friends, and at the mercy of unscrupulous characters. Of course, the public concern for sailors was not altogether altruistic, for Wilmingtonians admitted that they were "well aware of the importance of Seamen...." They provided the labor for the lifeblood of the town—shipping—and their misfortunes would "greatly injure the trade of this port, and lessen the Commercial importance of the State."[43]

Taverns and sailor boardinghouses posed particular threats to the welfare of sailors, and, by extension, the commonweal of Wilmington.

7—Fellowship, Fraternity, Association 157

The boardinghouses beckoned to the seafaring sojourners, but too often only to fleece the unwary. Wilmington merchants and townspeople in 1817 complained to the General Assembly about the establishments which frequently were scenes of boisterous behavior and immorality that "shock[ed] the delicacy of the community." Moreover, the proprietors "too frequently" took advantage of the "unsuspecting and confiding nature" of the sailors so that "it is a truth amounting almost to a proverb that few Sailors leave the port with a cent in their pockets." As a result, the legislature permitted the Wilmington town commissioners to license the sailor boardinghouses, require bonds for proper behavior from their owners, and, in effect, limit the number of such businesses in the town.[44]

Another alarming problem for seamen, and one which also impinged directly upon the port community and its commerce, was the health of mariners. Often sailors arrived in Wilmington suffering from various maladies. According to a critic, in less serious cases the collector of the port attempted to provide for the ill, packing the sailor "off to some sailor tavern, where his sick ear is regaled with the midnight reveling of his unsick companions, or mayhap he is more fortunate and finds an asylum in the hut of some negro woman, where at least, his fevered brain will not be racked with the clanking of gill measures and beer pots." When the deadly contagions of yellow fever and smallpox threatened, mariners were quarantined on board their ships, enduring the most inhumane conditions until all were well or had died. Without a hospital, not only did the sailors endure privation but the entire port suffered from the injunction of shipping.[45]

For its part, Congress quickly recognized the need to provide medical care for American merchant and naval seamen. In 1798 Congress enacted legislation for the "Relief of Sick and Disabled Seamen," in effect, establishing the Marine Hospital Service (forerunner of the United States Public Health Service). The statute required the deduction of 20 cents per month from seamen's wages—"hospital money"—with which to establish a Hospital Fund to provide care for sailors in hospitals or other institutions in American seaports, or, by authorization of the President of the United States, to construct hospitals for seamen. Dissatisfaction with the legislation of 1798, and the perceived special needs of the United States Navy, led Congress in 1811 to pass a law to establish navy hospitals, financed in part by $50,000 taken from the Hospital Fund. North Carolina failed to benefit from any of the federal legislation until the construction of the Marine Hospital at Portsmouth in 1846.[46]

Meanwhile, the North Carolina General Assembly early addressed the need to care for ailing seamen. Recognizing the insufficiency of funds raised by parish taxes and the wardens of the poor in counties like New Hanover, in which there were ports (Wilmington), the legislature in 1789 imposed a levy on captains and crews of vessels entering North Carolina (though later exempting masters and sailors who were residents of the state) to help sailors who "frequently suffer[ed] from the want of proper means in sickness...." Finding the Collector or Naval Officer at the port of Wilmington reluctant to part with the money thus obtained for ill sailors, the legislature in 1794 authorized the wardens of the poor in New Hanover County to sue for any funds that they thought might be available.[47]

However, when North Carolina joined the Union late in 1789, its commerce became subject to the jurisdiction of the United States. State legislation was superseded by the federal statute in 1798. Finding that the hospital money raised by the federal government proved inadequate for the care of unwell sailors, the state in 1804 and 1817 moved to supplement federal moneys with its own impositions, subject to ratification of Congress. The national legislature approved the state levy of 1817, but only for five years.[48]

While marine hospitals appeared throughout the United States, North Carolina and its chief port were overlooked. A correspondent to the *People's Press* in Wilmington in 1833 urged townspeople to act, observing that, "Justice advances an unanswerable claim; interest presents a powerful motive, and humanity pleads in the strongest terms." Sailors paid their hospital dues and deserved a return on their money. Wilmington's prosperity depended upon its commerce, and commerce in turn depended upon the facilities and advantages that the port could offer. Captains and crews, if they had a choice, would be reluctant to frequent a port which lacked the means to care for ill sailors. And the correspondent alluded to the practice of quarantining sick men on their own ships, where they lacked medical assistance, and to captains who left sick hands along the river as they departed the port, dooming the men to an almost certain death.

When North Carolina congressmen in 1834 and 1835 failed to obtain funding for the construction of a hospital in the vicinity of Wilmington, Wilmingtonians took the initiative. At meetings held in April and May, 1835, Edward B. Dudley, prominent Whig politician and future governor of North Carolina, among others, spearheaded an effort to organize a society to collect funds to underwrite a hospital for seamen in the Wilmington area. When the group asked the secretary of the treasury of the United States if the federal hospital money that had been collected at the port could be used for the Wilmington hospital, the secretary refused. Nonetheless, the Wilmingtonians persevered, opening a hospital by October 1835 at Mt. Tirza(h), on a 150-acre plot of land belonging to Dudley, located about three miles south of the town along the Cape Fear River.

The General Assembly, in its legislative session of November-December 1835, evidenced its support by incorporating the Wilmington Marine Hospital Association to provide "for the relief of sick and disabled American seamen," noting that the Wilmingtonians had "already purchased land and prepared suitable houses for that purpose...." By resolution, the legislature appropriated the money collected by the state under the auspices of the statute of 1817, $1,752.40. Also in 1835, the General Assembly enacted legislation that imposed levies on all seamen entering the port of Wilmington (except those serving on coasting vessels within the state), the proceeds of which would be given to the Wilmington Marine Hospital Association. However, the law, made subject to the approval of Congress, was never ratified by the national legislature and hence was not implemented.

The hospital remained open for several years, as the Wilmington Marine Hospital Association struggled to continue its operation. Dudley formally sold the Mt. Tirza land to the association in 1836 for $1,000. At that time the association implored the federal government either to take control of the hospital, appropriate $8,000 to $10,000 for the maintenance of the institution, and allocate the hospital money collected at the port to the association, or ratify the North Carolina legislation of 1835 to provide supplementary funding, but the national authorities were unmoved. Still, the hospital continued to function at least through September 1838, by which time it had become "tenantless." Memorials by the Wilmington Marine Hospital Association to the secretary of the treasury in 1844–1845 indicated that the hospital had been "abandoned for years for want of means to sustain it...."[49]

Although the hospital had closed and the Wilmington Marine Hospital Association apparently ceased active operations by 1849, Wilmingtonians continued to demand a marine hospital for their port. Two petitions on the subject were sent in 1846 from Wilmington to Washington; the state legislature unanimously adopted a resolution in 1852 instructing North Carolina's congressmen to seek the establishment of a marine hospital along the Cape Fear River; and the commissioners of navigation and pilotage for the Cape Fear River in 1854 memorialized the secretary of the treasury for action.

The national government finally yielded to the entreaties of the Wilmingtonians. In 1855 Congress authorized an appropriation of $40,000 to purchase land and erect a marine hospital and accompanying "pest house" for sailors with contagious diseases. The collector of customs at the port immediately advertised for suitable property, but Wilmingtonians differed over an appropriate site. Some wanted both hospital and pest house built at Mt. Tirza; others desired the construction of the hospital in town, leaving the pest house at Mt. Tirza. Eventually the federal government bought the Mt. Tirza site for $5,000, and the North Carolina General Assembly confirmed the purchase of the property at Mt. Tirza for the hospital and pest house in 1857 and 1859 respectively. But the whole matter led an exasperated secretary of the treasury to avow, "Never was [I] so bedeviled in the whole course of my life. I've got a good mind to put them both on Bald Head." The contract for the hospital was let by June 1857, and by early 1860 the hospital had been built but, lamented the *Daily Herald*, had not opened. And apparently the pest house was never erected.[50]

Strongly advocating the erection of the marine hospital, and more generally promising assistance to sailors in port, was the Seamen's Friend Society, which may have organized briefly as early as 1835 but which was incorporated by General Assembly statute in 1852 and organized the following year. In attempting to elevate "the social, moral and religious condition and character" of sailors, the society intended to establish a sailors' boardinghouse (to replace the iniquitous public institutions) and a mariner's church or Seamen's Bethel. Within a year the society had purchased the Commercial Hotel on the southwest corner of Front and Dock Streets for the Seamen's Home, though the $7,500 price, plus an additional $800 for repairs, left the society greatly in debt. Until the opening of the home, G. W. Williams kept a few sailors who sought a temperance environment in his home. The Seamen's Friend Society sponsored the Cape Fear Marine Total Abstinence Society, which met weekly at the Seamen's Bethel.[51]

The Seamen's Friend Society sought to erect a church in conjunction with the Seamen's Home. Captain Gilbert Potter, a charter member of the society, at his own expense built the Seamen's Bethel, which he donated to the society. The Bethel, which adjoined the Seamen's Home, was dedicated in November 1859. Ministers from the various churches in Wilmington preached periodically at the Bethel, and the society sought to raise money to secure a chaplain for the church. In 1860 the women of the Cherry Street Mariners' Church in New York, who had learned of the Wilmington church's need for a banner to mark the location of the Bethel, sent a "Bethel Flag" to Wilmington.[52]

Meanwhile, the Seamen's Friend Society, despite a somewhat precarious financial existence, assisted numerous resident and transient sailors. In the year ending June 1, 1860, it housed 1,118 men in the Seamen's Home, including 165 who needed medical relief. Although 147 of

7—Fellowship, Fraternity, Association   161

Headquarters of the Seamen's Friend Society or the Seamen's Home, where local and transient sailors received material, medical, and spiritual assistance. Drawing courtesy of the New Hanover County Public Library, Wilmington.

the latter qualified for money from the federal Hospital Fund, 18 sick and disabled were maintained solely by the society. (The government excluded from its assistance foreign seamen on foreign vessels, and foreign seamen who had not served at least three years on American ships; as well as American seamen who lacked a "protection" or certificate of eligibility for assistance, who were afflicted with incurable diseases, or who were not paupers.) According to its president in 1860, Captain Charles D. Ellis, the society had collected $20,184.63 since its inception and had expended $20,166.15, leaving a balance of $18.48. But it had outstanding debts amounting to $1,590.66. Moreover, the Rev. William J. Langdon, the society's indefatigable traveling agent, had died in 1859. Nonetheless, after the interruption caused by the Civil War, the Seamen's Friend Society revived and continued its mission to serve sailors in the port.[53]

8

Education, Enlightenment, and Culture

Beyond it myriad organizations, Wilmington enjoyed a reputation as a center of culture in North Carolina. That distinction rested in part on the wealth of the residents, in part on favorable transportation facilities (including the principal highway leading through eastern North Carolina and the Wilmington and Weldon Railroad), and in part on the port status of the town that opened Wilmington to the rest of the world. While North Carolina labored under the appellation of the "Rip Van Winkle" state, Wilmington exhibited bountiful opportunities for the young to pursue an education, a newspaper press second to none in the state, and a longstanding tradition of fostering the arts, particularly the theater.

Opportunities for children to secure an education in Wilmington increased dramatically during the nineteenth century. In the early years schools opened and disappeared with regularity as itinerant educators tested the market and women—married, widowed, and single—sought a source of income. Thomas D. Hamilton in 1796 offered courses in "useful literature," as well as Latin; Robert Tate in 1800 offered instruction in English grammar, reading, writing, Oriental languages, and the sciences. A Mrs. Kenon in 1807 established an "English school," in which she taught reading, writing, arithmetic, geography, and more. During the 1830s at least five women advertised formal courses of instruction in Wilmington, including Miss Jessie B. Sampson's school for young ladies (in which the schoolmistress provided instruction in English, French, music, drawing, painting, "Fancy work," and waxwork).[1]

The most popular school for boys in the 1830s was that taught by Jesse Mulock, who offered courses in elementary and higher education. His pupils might be exposed to orthography, reading, writing, grammar, geography, arithmetic, history, philosophy, chemistry, rhetoric, composition, algebra, and geometry, as well as mensuration, surveying, and astronomy. Remembered one student, "Mr. Mulock's principle was thoroughness.... There could be no dodging nor evasion. The chinquapin was always ready for use and was in frequent demand." Perfection required students to stay after dark, so the boys brought candles, along with books, to school. Mulock even held classes on Saturday for "map-inspection, or a lecture on astronomy—a sort of dessert to the intellectual feasts of the other five days." Nonetheless, he was patient, helpful, and much admired.[2]

The decade prior to the Civil War found Wilmington practically teeming with schools. Miss Magee taught young ladies English, French, music, and painting; L. Holmes offered a classical school for boys in which he taught algebra, geometry, Latin, and Greek; Miss Harriet Moore kept a school for girls and small boys; Verina S. Moore provided a boarding and day school for young ladies. A young ladies' seminary in 1860, taught by Mrs. Mary E. Russell and Miss Clarinda L. Hall, provided students with instruction in English, modern languages, Latin, piano, singing, pencil drawing, and oil and pastel painting. In addition to the seminary, in 1860 at least twelve other private schools offered classes in Wilmington, including two academies.[3]

The academy movement that swept across North Carolina in the aftermath of the American Revolution bypassed Wilmington until the early nineteenth century. After the Innes Academy failed to materialize in the 1780s, the state legislature in 1803 appointed new trustees for the institution and authorized them to sell the property bequeathed by Innes for the school in order to purchase a more suitable site. Another two years elapsed, however, before a meeting of the trustees took place. According to historians of education and theater in Wilmington, the Innes trustees obtained property on North Princess between Third and Fourth streets and, in conjunction with the local Thalian Association, constructed a building that housed a theater on the first floor and an academy on the second, a structure thereafter referred to generally as the Innes Academy. However, it appears that a separate institution, the Wilmington Academy (as opposed to the Innes Academy), was responsible for constructing and opening an academy/theater complex.[4]

As the General Assembly attempted to reorganize Innes Academy in 1803, the legislators also incorporated Wilmington Academy, possibly the successor of an institution called the New-Hanover School, chartered in 1800. Monetary subscriptions had already been collected to finance the school. The legislature permitted the trustees to hold a lottery to raise an additional $3,000. The General Assembly later allowed those who offered financial support for the institution to elect a board of self-perpetuating trustees to manage the academy. The trustees in 1803 contracted for the construction of a large brick structure, seventy by forty feet, which would house both an academy and a theater. Meanwhile, the trustees opened a grammar school in May of that year under the direction of the Rev. Andrew Caldwell at a schoolhouse in Toomer's Alley. The proposed academy building remained unfinished in 1810, when the trustees asked all those who had agreed to underwrite the cost to pay their subscriptions. By 1812 the Wilmington Academy prepared to receive scholars.[5]

During the ensuing twenty years the Wilmington Academy apparently operated on an intermittent basis. It combined elementary training with advanced study, and by 1816, if not earlier, admitted boys and girls, at least for preliminary work. During the hot and sickly months of the summer and fall, the academy moved its instructional services to Smithville, "a healthy and pleasant situation." In 1833 the academy planned to reopen after an unknown period of closure, promising that no teacher would be permitted to "inculcate on the minds of the students *sectarian principles*," an indication perhaps of the reason for the earlier closure. As was customary in the schools, at the end of the academic session, students underwent an examination open to the general public.[6]

Unable to maintain the school, the trustees of the Wilmington Academy in 1843 leased the eastern end of their property to the local chapter of the International Order of Odd Fellows for the establishment of a new school.[7] Opening in October 1843, the Odd Fellows School contained male and female departments whose scholastic year consisted of two sessions of twenty-two weeks each. A classical department was added in 1846, at which time a student enrollment of approximately ninety boys and seventy girls evidenced the popularity of the school. According to the secretary of the Grand Lodge of North Caroline, I.O.O.F., the "full tide of [the] successful experiment" in Wilmington rested upon the adoption of the "Normal System of Education," which currently was popular in Prussia, and about which he wanted to learn more from the noted American educator Horace Mann.[8]

The instructors of the Odd Fellows School impressed students and the public alike. Robert McLauchlin of Baltimore was the first principal. His wife supervised the female department. At McLauchlin's death in 1845, his students "mourned him, because we loved him. He was strict and maybe severe, but never unjust...." Levin Meginney succeeded McLauchlin; a Miss Richardson took charge of the female department. Young girls wrote appreciatively about their studies under Richardson. The trustees

8—Education, Enlightenment, and Culture

The Wilmington Academy (from a plat of Wilmington by J. J. Belanger, 1810), a long-standing educational institution whose first floor served as a theater and second floor as a school. Drawing courtesy of the New Hanover County Public Library, Wilmington.

hired Robert Lindsay, a graduate of St. Andrew's University in Scotland, to head the classical department. Although a fine scholar, he ultimately found his calling in politics, later becoming the governor of Alabama. Both boys and girls practiced long hours for their public examinations at the end of the academic sessions, and impressed visitors with their singing, recitations, declamations, and blackboard work. Despite its popularity, the Odd Fellows School closed in 1849, for the local lodge believed that "the population and growing importance of our town requires the establishment of an Academy, founded on a more extended and permanent basis" than the current school.[9]

Two new academies soon appeared in Wilmington. Levin Meginney, former principal of the Odd Fellows School, opened the Wilmington Institute in 1850, a classical institution that contained male and female departments and enrolled young children as well. In 1853 George W. Jewett began the Wilmington Male and Female Seminary. Offering an English and classical education "usually taught in the Academies and High Schools of New England," from whence he came, Jewett promised that students would be "thoroughly fitted for College." Both schools ended their terms with highly popular "exhibitions" featuring declamations and vocal and instrumental music. They remained open until the beginning of the Civil War.[10]

Supplementing private instruction were free or charity schools and the public schools of the state of North Carolina. Before the advent of public schools in North Carolina, the Ladies Working Society of St. James Episcopal Church in Wilmington offered a free school for the benefit of the poor. Eliza Lord was the president of the institution. The society held a fair in 1833, a "novelty" at that time, to raise money for the school. By the end of the year the charity school, which was "untrammeled by sectarian regulations," opened. Supported by donations and funds raised by additional fairs, the school operated at least through 1839. The Presbyterians in Wilmington likewise maintained a free school, probably Hunt's or Hart's Free School, from the mid–1830s to the early 1840s.[11]

The Union Free School represented another, but short-lived, effort to provide education for those who needed assistance (and did not want to attend public schools). In 1857 three Wilmington men underwrote the school, which was located in a building on south Sixth Street between Nun and Church. Students assembled each morning on the second floor in the auditorium for a reading of the Scriptures, prayer, and announcements. The Union Free School was popular, enrolling an average of 134 scholars per month, almost evenly divided between males and females. Dramatic appeals for financial assistance, "A hundred outstretched arms, and scores of ... starving intelects [sic] imploringly supplicate that sustenance at our hands ... without which they surely die — or live but to become abhorrent skeletons of neglected, depraved humanity," were unavailing. The school operated at least through February 1860, when a lack of funds apparently forced its closing.[12]

After many years of debate and delay the North Carolina General Assembly in 1839 passed legislation to establish a public school system. An essay in the *People's Press* in 1833 contended that the "means of education ought, of right, to be placed within the reach of every American citizen," for public schools were "as essential as public prisons, and were more of the former instituted, there would be less occasion for the latter." The legislature offered each county the opportunity to participate in the school program. Upon a favorable vote (469 to 39) in New Hanover in August 1839 to establish schools, the county court in September divided the county into school districts and named ten men to be a board of school superintendents. Subsequently the court imposed the necessary taxes to supplement annual state appropriations that were distributed according to the "federal" population of each county. As the sixth most populous county (behind Wake, Guilford, Chatham, Randolph, and Orange) in the 1850s, New Hanover received $3,416 from the state in 1859.[13]

Nevertheless, the public school system grew slowly, and the success of common schools before the war was questionable. In 1843 only 16 of the 35 districts in New Hanover County contained schoolhouses and enrolled students. Wilmington encompassed two of the inactive districts. Although commissioners had been appointed to find schoolhouses and hire teachers, they had taken no action. By 1847 at least, the Wilmington schools were open when Walter A. Merrill in the Second School District taught reading, writing, arithmetic, and geography in a three-month term that ended on July 9. Sixty-three boys and 42 girls attended, one for as few as five days and another for as many as 67 days, but averaging 36 and 37 days of instruction, respectively. Nevertheless, in the 1850s, S. D. Wallace, chairman of the board of superintendents, claimed that the common schools were "not patronized except by those who have not the means to send to other schools & hence the numbers that attend are limited & their character not very flattering." The deficiencies of the public schools in Wilmington may have explained the popularity of the Union Free School in the town.[14]

Beyond formal academic training, wealthier Wilmingtonians benefited from schools specializing in music, singing, and dance. Most of the instructors were transients, working a few months or a few years in Wilmington before seeking employment elsewhere. And only in the two decades before the Civil War did the opportunities to gain an acquaintance with the fine arts measurably heighten. Alexander C. Miller in 1804 offered training in music and painting; Miss Beze in 1809, instruction in music, French, drawing, and needlework. John Marek in 1833 advertised instruction in vocal music, religious and non-religious, and instrumental music, as well as lessons for violin, guitar, piano, violoncello, French horn, flute, and clarinet. At a public concert designed to display his talents, Marek received plaudits from the local newspaper publisher.[15]

Music instruction was rare until the 1840s, however, when numerous men and women offered their services to the public. Among them was Mrs. Sarah Ann Cooke, organist at St. James Church, who taught from 1841 to 1846. Before coming to Wilmington she had received a "thorough musical education" in England and had had twelve years' experience in the United States. She offered lessons on pianoforte and organ, and in singing. In 1855 John H. Whitney of Boston, a Mrs. Cushing, a Miss Dailey, and a Mrs. Whitaker competed for students seeking lessons on the piano. In 1860 Maurice Bode taught piano, organ, thoroughbass, and singing; a Miss Medway, pianoforte, thoroughbass, and singing.[16]

Singing schools were exceedingly popular, particularly among young people, toward the end of the antebellum era. Again, most singing masters were itinerants who stayed several weeks to train students for a final concert. Mr. D. Kemmerer, who taught juvenile singing schools in 1855 and 1856, needed sixteen lessons before he was ready to present his students in highly successful concerts. As many as one hundred students enrolled under his direction. A Mr. Sheetz advertised his school in 1858 at the Front Street Methodist Church. The following year a Mr. Griswold instructed gentlemen in "solo and concerted Singing, embracing English, Irish, and Scotch ballads, Quartetts, Trios, [and] Duets..." in which he featured "The Proper method of bringing out the voice, its management [and] general style of singing...." Griswold also offered ladies and gentlemen a course of twelve lessons at their private residences.[17]

At least as appealing to Wilmingtonians as music and singing was dancing. Teachers of dance appeared early in the town, at least from 1797, when Richard Coleman announced his evening school from candlelight to nine o'clock. In addition to offering the then-current and newest dances—cotillions, waltzes, country dances, fandangos, polkas, redowas, and Spanish dances—teachers emphasized the ancillary benefits of their classes, which included proper deportment, manners, and grace. Most instructors were male, but Madam Blake in 1852 taught ladies and gentlemen (separately), as well as "misses and masters."[18]

Two of the most popular instructors in the late antebellum era were J. Word and J. L. Frensley. The former taught classes at Mozart Hall, though he also offered lessons at private residences if classes of eight could be obtained. In 1851 Word returned from the northern states with a variety of "new and fashionable Dances," which included "the beautiful Gortilza, introduced this season for the first time." J. L. Frensley taught between 1854 and 1858. Reflecting his success was the large number of pupils who attended his school. At the end of each term a soiree was held at which students demonstrated their prowess to parents and friends. Initially, the soirees were held at Mozart Hall; the last, in 1858, took place in the new town theater.[19]

Several teachers offered instruction in modern languages in addition to the schools and academies in town. Many were Frenchmen, including a Mr. De Chanla in 1809, who had spent seven years at the University of Paris and advertised classes in French and Latin. Another was a young French gentleman who in 1838 offered his services on "liberal" terms because he wanted to become proficient in the English language. Although not a native of France, J. T. Norcem in 1852 claimed that he would show testimonials of his ability to teach the French language as "thoroughly as any Parisian." Beyond the French language, I. A. Printens in 1833 taught Spanish, and William Henry Bauer in 1855 taught French, Spanish, Italian, and German.[20]

Wilmingtonians also enjoyed tutelage in more specialized subjects. Papen Labazdier and Carter Jones instructed gentlemen in the art of using the small sword and broadsword respectively. Jones also opened a "Military School" in 1836 in which he taught infantry and light infantry tactics. A Mr. Tousley and William M. Pelot provided instruction in bookkeeping. Tousley also taught penmanship; a Mr. Chapman, "common writing" and stenography. A mother and daughter, immigrants from France, and more recently from New York after finding the weather in the north too cold, sought to sustain themselves by teaching embroidery, music, painting, and French.[21]

Playing an indispensable role in enlightening the populace was the newspaper. The history of the newspaper press in Wilmington fairly reflected that of the industry in North Carolina during the antebellum era. News sheets appeared and disappeared with startling regularity as a lack of public support or the failure of subscribers to honor their commitments doomed most enterprises. Newspapers usually attached themselves to one or another political party for support; in turn parties needed organs of propaganda, particularly during the hard fought campaigns between Democrats and Whigs in the era of the second party system. And not until that time, in the 1840s, when coincidentally Wilmington became the most populous town in North Carolina, did the port achieve a permanent press. A growing population and expanding economy subsequently supported two dailies, two weeklies, and a tri-weekly newspaper simultaneously, which distinguished Wilmington as a leader in the newspaper coverage in the state.

After the demise of the *Wilmington Centinel, and General Advertiser* in 1789, Wilmington apparently lacked a newspaper until 1795, when James Carey established the *Wilmington Chronicle; and North Carolina Weekly Advertiser*. John Bellew succeeded Carey, but Allmand Hall purchased the printing office of Bellew in 1796 and the following year issued *Hall's Wilmington Gazette*, whose title changed to the *Wilmington Gazette* in 1799. The *Wilmington Gazette* faced competition for an unknown period of time from the *Cape Fear Herald*, which began publication in 1802, and from the *True Republican*, for which there are surviving issues from its origin in 1809 through November of that year. Although Hall sold the *Wilmington Gazette* to William S. Hasell in 1808, the paper continued under that title at least until 1816, when it was advertised for sale.[22]

As the *Wilmington Gazette* closed its operations, Thomas Loring inaugurated a long career in newspaper publishing in Wilmington when he started the *Cape Fear Recorder* in May 1816. Before the *Recorder* ceased operation in 1832, at least three other papers, including the *Wilmington Herald*, a Universalist paper (discontinued in 1827), the *Liberalist*, and the *Wilmington Reporter* (published at least from 1827 to 1829) appeared. H. S. Ellenwood in late 1832 began the *Wilmington Advertiser, and Merchants' and Farmers' Gazette*. Loring reemerged in the newspaper business in January 1833 when in partnership with P. W. Fanning he started the *People's Press*. Upon the quick retirement of Fanning, in May 1833, Loring took sole possession of the paper and merged it with the *Wilmington Advertiser* to form the *People's Press and Wilmington Advertiser*. Finding subscriptions declining, Loring closed the paper in 1836, only to open another immediately under the title *Wilmington Advertiser*, which he sold five months later to Frederick C. Hill. After five years Hill advertised the sale of the *Wilmington Advertiser*, the last extant issue of which appeared in May 1841.[23]

After a long and fitful start, newspapers finally achieved a permanence in Wilmington during the two decades prior to the Civil War. Wilmington businessman Asa A. Brown started the *Wilmington Weekly Chronicle* in 1839. He sold the paper in 1851 to Talcott Burr, Jr., who renamed it the *Wilmington Herald*, publication of which was interrupted by the Civil War but resumed in its aftermath. Sometime in the early 1840s a paper titled the *Messenger* appeared to accompany the *Chronicle*. It was sold in 1844 to David Fulton and Alfred J. Price, who founded the *Wilmington Journal*, which continued publication through the Civil War. The *Journal* on September 8, 1851 undertook the publication of the first daily newspaper in North Carolina, the *Daily Journal*. The *Herald* followed with a daily in 1854.[24]

Two additional newspapers supplemented the *Herald* and the *Journal* in the 1850s. Thomas Loring returned to Wilmington from a stint of newspaper publishing in Raleigh to found the *Commercial* in 1846, which was both a weekly and a tri-weekly publication, apparently the first tri-weekly in North Carolina. Loring continued the paper at least until 1857. Henry I. Toole, a native of Edgecombe County, undertook the publication of the *Aurora* in 1849, which ceased upon his death in 1850. Together with the *Journal* and the *Chronicle*, the *Commercial* and the *Aurora* provided Wilmington with four papers at midcentury out of a total of forty-five papers published in the state. Wilmington's dailies in 1860, the *Journal* and the *Herald*, represented two of only eight daily newspapers published in North Carolina on the eve of the Civil War.[25]

Newspaper publishers depended greatly upon politics to generate interest in and support for their sheets. The advent of the party system in the United States in the 1790s—Federalists and Jeffersonian Republicans—and the second party system in the 1830s—Democrats and Whigs—practically required organs of propaganda to disseminate the views of the respective parties. Annual elections for state legislators through 1835, biennial thereafter, elections for United States representatives and senators, and quadrennial elections for president of the United States, not to mention contests for local and county offices, generated an ongoing interest in politics. Because the parties were fairly evenly matched in Wilmington and in North Carolina, particularly between the Democrats and Whigs before the Civil War, every vote was consequential. Newspapers assumed an enormously influential role in politics but in turn depended upon patronage from members of the parties for their existence.

From the outset Wilmington publishers were embroiled in politics. Allmand Hall at first tried to steer a neutral course, but when Samuel A. Clark became a half-owner in the paper in 1804, Hall and Clark announced that the paper "will henceforth be continued on the pure principles of REPUBLICANISM." When the *Wilmington Gazette* passed to William S. Hasell in 1808, it must have fallen into Federalist hands, for the next year the *True Republican* was started expressly as a vehicle for the Jeffersonian Party in Wilmington.[26]

The political controversies of the 1830s again produced advocatory news sheets. H.S. Ellenwood's *Wilmington Advertiser* reflected incipient Whig views, while Loring of the *People's Press* proved a trimmer. The latter had opposed Jackson and the Democrats but subsequently embraced the party. Upon the merger of the *Press* and the *Advertiser* in May 1833, Loring claimed that the "supineness of professed impartiality becomes tiresome and disgusting" and openly displayed his attachment for the Democrats. Three years later, however, after the Whig *Fayetteville Observer* struck the *People's Press and Wilmington Advertiser* from its exchange list, advertisers melted away, and subscribers dwindled, Loring closed the paper and started the *Wilmington Advertiser* which he claimed would be completely impartial in political matters. According to Loring at that time, an editor ought not have to express gratuitously "a violence that he does not approve, and cultivate prejudices and animosities, at variance with his principles and repugnant to his feelings," when his compensation was "nothing but ill will." Then, suddenly, Loring sold his newspaper.[27]

The following decades found editors more committed than Loring to a political role. Asa A. Brown in his prospectus for the *Wilmington Weekly Chronicle* in 1838 announced that his "political principles coincide with those entertained generally by the Whig party," including support for internal improvements and public education in North Carolina. When the *Chronicle* was sold in 1851 and changed to the *Herald*, its new owner continued its advocacy of Whig principles. Contrarily, the *Messenger* in the 1840s was a Democratic sheet, and the owners of the *Wilmington Journal* expected subscribers of the former to continue their support for the *Journal*, which claimed to uphold "the Constitution as it was left us by our fathers; [and] ... a strict construction of that Constitution, thereby ensuring the rights of the several States which compose the Confederacy" and to oppose uncompromisingly Whig measures—a United States bank, a protective tariff, a bankruptcy act, and internal improvements by the national government. In 1860, Wilmington's press nicely reflected the divided political populace of the town.[28]

Publishing a newspaper was an onerous experience and often a thankless task. Beyond the sheer physical exertion of setting type and operating presses, editors and publishers faced shortages of paper, problems of delivery, and difficulties of obtaining news. Allmand Hall in 1804 apologized for issuing the *Wilmington Gazette* on paper of "inferior size," noting that his seasonal stock of paper had not arrived in timely fashion. Three years later Hall complained of the exorbitant charges of the Fayetteville mail carrier who took the *Wilmington Gazette* to the upper Cape Fear region. Thomas Loring in 1835 regretted that the *People's Press and Wilmington Advertiser* had been "irregularly received" at several places in Duplin County and had not arrived at all at Rockfish. Delays in the delivery of the mail also deprived editors of the receipt of newspapers from other parts of the state and nation on which they depended principally for their information. Even after the arrival of the telegraph by 1851, the cost of the service was almost prohibitive, and the *Journal* and the *Herald* in 1860 agreed that they could use it only sparingly.[29]

Editors on occasion engaged their counterparts in heated controversies engendered by political differences and regional rivalries, including that between Wilmington and Fayetteville. Abusive language and sometimes physical violence ensued. Although relations among the Wilmington editors seemed reasonably cordial, that was not necessarily true beyond the port. Thomas Loring of the *Commercial* took offense at remarks by Edward J. Hale, editor of the *Fayetteville Observer*, and retaliated with articles that were "understood to impeach the legitimacy" of Hale. Later Loring, "having had time for cool reflection," issued a retraction in which he disclaimed "any wish injuriously to affect the reputation" of Hale and admitted that "no just ground exist[ed] for any such imputation...."[30]

The constant bane of newspaper publishers was the delinquent subscriber. Late in 1798, Allmand Hall asked subscribers who had started

8—Education, Enlightenment, and Culture

subscriptions in January 1797 to settle their accounts. Thomas Loring became so exasperated in 1834 that he published the names of several delinquents, one of whom owed for eighty issues. And failure to pay accounts resulted in the reduction of the size of papers or the closing of operations. Owners of the *Journal* in 1851 reminded readers that "Newspaper publishers are no doubt patriots—*we* are, but we are forced to confess that with all our patriotism we cannot afford to carry on business simply for the public good." At long last the *Journal* adopted "The Cash System" (requiring that subscriptions be paid in advance), as had many northern and some North Carolina papers. Subscription accounts were too small to dun when newspaper collection agents charged twenty percent for a collection fee and were unable to find many delinquents.[31]

Yet the *Journal* and its rival the *Herald* persevered and apparently prospered. The papers constantly upgraded their operations. The *Herald* enlarged its paper in 1854. Both the *Journal* and the *Herald* bought steam-operated presses as hand presses gave way to steam after midcentury. In the late 1850s the *Journal* moved into a two-story, fireproof brick building with basement and attic on Princess Street. That the owners of the *Journal* could afford such a fine structure "out of the profits of a printing office, so rarely occurs, especially in North Carolina, that we look upon it almost as one of the wonders of the nineteenth century," recorded the envious editor of the *Herald*. The printing establishment was located on the second floor, where there was a private office for the editor, a business office, and a compositor's room, the last 39 feet long and 36.5 feet wide, with an 11-foot ceiling and 13 windows that offered "a flood of light" and a refreshingly cool atmosphere in which to work in the warmer months of the year. In 1860, the *Daily* and *Weekly Journal* counted 600 and 1,700 subscribers, respectively; the *Daily* and *Weekly Herald*, 450 and 800, respectively.[32]

Newspaper publishers continued to depend greatly upon the postal service for the receipt of news sheets from other sections of the state and nation as well as for the delivery of their own papers. However, poor roads, inclement weather, and robberies often impeded the effective function of the postal system. A paucity of post offices and inefficient postmasters also rendered service problematic. The deficiencies of the mail system irked the publishers, who complained throughout the antebellum era about the post. Representative was the *Wilmington Advertiser* in 1838, which editorialized, "We are daily suffering from the Mail *derangement* in this section of the country." At the time of the Civil War many North Carolinians still used private carriers to convey mail.[33]

Wilmington struggled with the rest of the state to secure an adequate post. In 1800, sixty-eight post offices served North Carolina's sixty-one counties. At that time Wilmington enjoyed weekly mail service from New Bern and Fayetteville. The advent of railroads, particularly the Wilmington and Raleigh (Weldon), greatly speeded the arrival of news from the north, in addition to enhancing the dependability of the service. The Wilmington and Weldon Railroad in 1838 obtained a contract from the federal government to carry mail from Petersburg, Virginia, to Charleston, South Carolina, part of the coastal route from Washington, D.C. to New Orleans. It was a coup for Wilmington, because Raleigh had hoped that the Raleigh and Gaston Railroad might be selected to transport the mail through the state capital. And it was a victory secured by persistent lobbying led by Wilmington merchant Aaron Lazarus, who represented Wilmington's case to the postmaster general in Washington, D.C.[34]

Briefly, in the mid-1840s, the postmaster general threatened to revoke the Wilmington and Weldon's mail contract due to the unreliability of the steamers that ran between Wilmington and Charleston. A town meeting in Wilmington sought reconsideration, claiming that the steamers were fit for service and that the route was the most inexpensive available. The federal government relented. In addition to the northern and southern mails brought by railroad and its steamers, local service encompassed Smithville, Taylor's Bridge, Harrells, Onslow Court House (Jacksonville), and Fayetteville (served by two routes—one by Clinton and Warsaw and one by Elizabethtown). The construction of the Wilmington and Manchester Railroad, completed in 1854, offered mail service to points along that line, including Whiteville.[35]

By the late 1850s the "Great Northern and Southern Mail" from New York through Wilmington and Charleston to Florida and New Orleans again came under attack. Wilmingtonians held a town meeting at which the mayor was authorized to beseech the postmaster general to retain the coastal mail route. Certainly, Wilmington merited adequate postal service. In 1860 the net proceeds of the post office in the port not only were three times greater than those for Raleigh, the next most remunerative town in North Carolina, but equaled the combined revenues of Raleigh, Fayetteville, New Bern, and Chapel Hill. Nonetheless, mail "irregularities" continued, leading to the absence of timely news and the cancellation of newspaper subscriptions, and Wilmingtonians and their newspaper publishers could take comfort only in the fact that the difficulties were nationwide.[36]

Toward the end of the antebellum era newspapers began to depend for their news on the telegraph. The North Carolina legislature in 1847 recognized the incorporation of the Washington and New Orleans Magnetic Telegraph Company, organized by Samuel F. B. Morse and associates, which would run a line through the state. The next year an agent of the company visited Wilmington to arrange for a line from the port to Weldon. Not until May 1851, however, was a connection to Wilmington completed. Still, the cost of the new means of communication at the outset was daunting. The *Commercial* tried to provide the news without the use of the telegraph, for the publisher did not suppose that readers "desire we should be [put] to an extra expense merely to insert the word 'Telegraph' without necessity." As late as 1860, the *Journal* and the *Herald* complained of the monopoly charges of the telegraph company, regretted that no preference was given to the press, and perforce used the telegraph sparingly.[37]

In addition to news sheets, newspaper publishers provided the forerunners of libraries in form of reading rooms, the earliest of which may have been started by William S. Hasell of the *Wilmington Gazette* in 1808. The Raleigh *Star* wrote enviously in 1813, "There are reading rooms in Newbern, Wilmington, & Fayetteville, and they are the fashionable resort of all respectable people of those places." Thomas Loring opened a reading room, available day and night, immediately after starting the *People's Press* in 1833. By the end of the year he offered twenty newspapers from various North Carolina towns as well as news sheets from fourteen other states, two territories (Florida and Arkansas), and the District of Columbia, and more were shortly added. Reading rooms remained popular in ensuing years. A year after inaugurating the *Journal*, publisher David Fulton offered a reading room and exchange for the benefit of businessmen. Observed Fulton, there were no venues in which gentlemen could meet in the evening "unless the bar rooms may be considered in this light."[38]

Beyond the reading rooms, Wilmingtonians began to consider the benefits of "public" libraries. The exchange of books was primarily a private matter, as individuals loaned volumes to family, friends, and acquaintances, though, of course, books were mislaid in the process. Archibald MacRae felt moved in 1833 to ask those in the community to examine their collections and to return any books bearing his "*cognomen.*" At that time, however, William C. Jackson operated a "Circulating Library" in Wilmington, loaning books at 6¼ cents per week. A little more than a decade later "The Young Men's Lyceum and Mercantile Library Association" was organized, a forerunner of the Wilmington Library Association.[39]

Wilmingtonians moved belatedly to establish a library. The General Assembly had incorporated thirty-two library societies or companies in North Carolina between 1794 and 1848, at which time the legislature passed a general incorporation act for literary institutions and benevolent societies. A meeting in April 1855 led to the permanent organization of the Wilmington Library Association in June, at which time Dr. James H. Dickson was elected president. By the end of the year the association had opened its library and reading room in the rear of a building on Water Street. Pleas for books of every kind found a ready response, including sixty volumes donated by Thomas Loring. The assistance of women was sought, for husbands, sons, and brothers could meet at the library and "improve their minds, save their constitutions and purses, yea, even their characters, instead of hastening at the first cessation from business at night to the billiard saloons or a dozen other amusements infinitely worse for health and happiness."[40]

The Library Association languished for several years for want of adequate space but reorganized in October 1859, again under the presidency of Dr. Dickson. More ample quarters were available, because the town commissioners had offered two rooms in Town Hall/Thalian Hall for the use of the Library Association. And to generate interest, the association, sponsored a series of monthly public lectures offered by eminent residents and nonresidents. Dr. Dickson, who presented the first lecture, was followed by the Right Reverend Thomas Atkinson, George W. Davis, Griffith J. McRee, the Rev. J. S. Long, and the Rev. Calvin H. Wiley. The last, as state superintendent of public education, made such an eloquent plea for improving public schools in Wilmington that immediately after his address a committee was formed to consider and report on the subject. As for the library, it was opened to members from two to twelve in the morning and from six to ten in the evening.[41]

More generally Wilmingtonians also benefited from debating societies and lectures. Admittedly the debating society was short-lived, apparently confined to 1833, but public lectures became increasingly frequent in the late antebellum era. Among many who addressed the public were Mr. Estabrook and Dr. Barker, who lectured on phrenology in 1838 and 1859 respectively. Dr. Slater, in 1846, having spent two years in Mexico, described life in that country to Wilmington audiences. Mr. Spencer, in 1852, discussed ancient and modern magic. In the years that followed, the Rev. C. F. Deems spoke at the Front Street Methodist Church on the importance of merchants incorporating into their transactions the "rules of Christian ethics—to avoid the wild hunt after sudden wealth," and Dr. D. Brown Williams discoursed on "electro-psychology."[42] Interested and thoughtful Wilmingtonians clearly enjoyed ample opportunity to broaden their horizons.

Over the years increasing wealth and sophistication, predicated on

Wilmington's mercantile economy and openness to the world, produced a rich cultural tradition in the port town. Although many Wilmingtonians doubtlessly enjoyed fine literature, before the Civil War few engaged in its production. Johnson Jones Hooper, humorist, was born in Wilmington in 1815, and published his first story in the *Cape Fear Recorder* in 1830, a poem satirizing a British consul who fell into the harbor during the christening of a ship. But Hooper left the port soon thereafter, settling in Alabama, where he became nationally famous for his humorous tales, which included the adventures of Captain Simon Suggs, a dishonest gambler. Griffith J. McRee, who owned property in Wilmington and a plantation on the Northwest Cape Fear River, gained fame in 1857 for his two-volume edition of the *Life and Correspondence of James Iredell*. Although little recognized in North Carolina, McRee received attention beyond the state, including a praiseworthy missive from noted national historian George Bancroft. According to McRee's biographer, "In his skill and integrity as an editor of documents, McRee equaled or surpassed the standards of the time."[43]

During the antebellum era Wilmington homes reflected prevailing national and international architectural trends, though the surviving buildings stand as much as evidence of a serendipitous ability to avoid ravenous fires as representations of Wilmingtonians' architectural tastes. Representing the Federal style of architecture that spanned the late eighteenth and early nineteenth centuries are the Lazarus House (1819), built for wealthy merchant Aaron Lazarus, and the Cassidey House (1828), constructed for shipbuilder James Cassidey, which was later transformed into a stuccoed Italianate villa. The Cassidey House bears the impress of New England craftsmen, many of whom immigrated to Wilmington before the Civil War as the services of skilled workers were sought by Wilmingtonians.[44]

From 1820 to 1860 the Greek Revival, Gothic Revival, and Italianate architectural styles successively altered the Wilmington urban landscape. Representing Greek Revival is the DeRosset House (1841), commissioned by Dr. Armand J. DeRosset, Jr., physician and partner in a commission merchant house, which towers over the town at the corner of Second and Dock Streets. St. James Episcopal Church (1839) on Market Street introduced Gothic Revival to Wilmington, a style that seemed reserved almost exclusively for ecclesiastical structures, including the later St. Thomas Roman Catholic, First Presbyterian, First Baptist, and St. Paul's Evangelical Lutheran churches. Italianate, popular after midcentury, reached its zenith in Wilmington in the Zebulon Latimer House (1852) on Third Street, built for a prosperous dry goods merchant, and currently the headquarters of the Lower Cape Fear Historical Society.[45]

The Lazarus House, built circa 1816, on Mulberry (now Chestnut) Street. Built by businessman Aaron Lazarus, it is one of the few houses in Wilmington retaining original Federal/Adamesque stylistic elements despite extensive subsequent remodeling. Photograph courtesy of the New Hanover County Public Library, Wilmington.

Two of Wilmington's grandest buildings—Town Hall/Thalian Hall (1858) and the Bellamy Mansion (1859-1861)—appeared on the eve of the Civil War. New York architect and theater designer James M. Trimble provided the plans for Town Hall/Thalian Hall. James F. Post, a native of New Jersey who moved to Wilmington in 1849, was the supervising architect. Upon the completion of Thalian Hall, Post turned his attention to the Bellamy Mansion on Market Street, "a landmark of architectural classicism in the region, and ... the summit of self-expression for its owners, Dr. John Dillard Bellamy and his family," according to architectural historian Edward F. Turberg.[46]

When furnishing their homes, Wilmington residents, as their means permitted, kept abreast of the latest styles of furnishings, which in furniture meant Neoclassical from the late eighteenth through the middle third of the nineteenth century. Prominent among the early Wilmington artisans who fashioned such furniture was John Nutt, who moved from Charleston, South Carolina, and advertised as a cabinetmaker, chair maker, and riding-chair maker. Other Charleston cabinetmakers, including Henry Jocelin, took advantage of Wilmington around the turn of the nineteenth century. In 1806, Samuel Parmele, a New York cabinetmaker, opened a shop in Wilmington. Some of the men specialized in Windsor chairs, including Vosburgh & Childs from New York, who not only advertised in 1797 as Windsor chair makers, but also claimed to make elegant settees and to repair and paint old chairs.[47]

Unfortunately for local artisans, the Neoclassical style changed significantly the technology of furniture making, rendering such work better suited to the large shops of urban areas such as New York, Philadelphia, and Boston, which could engage in specialty work and carry a considerable inventory. Although Wilmington importers of furniture between 1820 and 1840 overwhelmingly favored New York, during those two decades some 449 individual pieces, 8 boxes, 81 bundles, and 4 unspecified shipments of furniture also arrived from Philadelphia. And in 1839 Talcott Burr, Jr., advertised that he would sell at auction "an invoice of BOSTON FURNITURE," including washstands, a secretary, bureaus, tables, and a clock. Still, at least one Wilmington cabinetmaker, Benjamin Gillott (Gillett), spoke disparagingly in 1816 of some of the imported furniture, claiming that his furniture "cannot fail of being preferred to the trash that is shipped here to be sold at auction." Regardless of Gillott's aspersions, Wilmingtonians had the opportunity to obtain fine furniture, either from local craftsmen or from abroad.[48]

In addition to the finely crafted furniture of the region, other forms of the visual arts, from funerary sculpture to painting, betokened the cultural tastes of Wilmingtonians. According to historian John W. Myers, "the visual arts have been an essential and lively part of the cultural life of the Lower Cape Fear." Masons offered to carve gravestones, the preeminent sculptural form in the colonies before the Revolution, and an artistic medium that continued to be refined as exemplified by headstones and monuments in the graveyard of the St. James Church and more particularly in Oakdale Cemetery after it opened in 1855. Painters left their marks on coaches, signboards, and fire-buckets, and by the Revolution artists traveled the east coast of the colonies, painting portraits for a living.[49]

Art in various media made its impress on Wilmingtonians in the antebellum era. F. J. Jocelyn, the first recorded itinerant artist in Wilmington, advertised his services in 1798. Many followed over the years, including J. J. Belanger, who not only painted portraits but also decorations on the walls of St. John's Masonic Lodge on Orange Street. Traveling artists such as S. Hirsh in 1855 continued to visit Wilmington to the eve of the Civil War, but by that time several had settled permanently in the town and had opened studios, including a Mr. Massalong in 1851 and

W. G. Browne in 1858. However, by the 1840s, daguerreotypists began to compete with painters for the attention of the Wilmington public. Among others, one Harrison, reportedly the best daguerreotypist in the state, had by 1853 established in Wilmington a gallery in which "beauty, with its diversity of expression and features, glows forth from the plate, ... and fascinates the eye...."[50]

Wilmington also benefited from traveling, as well a magnificent permanent piece of artwork. Joel Tatum's "Resurrection" in three scenes with an accompanying lecture appeared at Mozart Hall in 1849. The following year Wilmingtonians had a chance to see Pomarede's "Panorama of the Mississippi River" and the "Funeral Procession in Charleston of John C. Calhoun." Later in the 1850s Rossiter's "Captive Israelites," "The Return of the Dove to the Ark," and "Miriam the Prophetess," and J. Insco Williams' Bible Panorama, containing more than fifty scenes from the Bible, exhibited in town. Remaining permanently in Wilmington was the canvas drop curtain for Thalian Hall, a landscape with figures depicting ancient Grecian scenes. A gift from several Wilmingtonians, it had been painted by William Russell Smith, who also painted scenery and drop curtains for several theaters, including the Philadelphia Academy of Music and Edwin Booth's theater in New York. According to Myers, the presentation not only represented "an infusion of current taste and fashion from the larger centers of culture to the north, but also a commitment to the cultural enrichment of Wilmington ... on the part of prominent citizens."[51]

From an early date Wilmingtonians evidenced "a decided taste for the drama," according to a local writer. To satisfy that desire for theatrical entertainment and perhaps to provide supplemental actors for visiting professional troupes, a Thalian Association organized in Wilmington, reportedly in 1788, perhaps earlier, the oldest of its kind in North Carolina. The group reorganized as many as three times before the Civil War, the last in 1847, after which it received a charter of incorporation from the state legislature in 1849. Over the years the Thalian Association provided needed diversion, sometimes "To relieve the dullness that hereabouts pervades," according to the *Daily Herald* in 1855. At the same time the Thalians had to surmount such difficulties as the lack of an adequate wardrobe, the want of decorum in the theater, and, the principal obstacle to the success of amateurs, "the great and very natural difficulty of making boys look like girls."[52]

While Wilmingtonians appreciated the efforts of the local Thalians, they eagerly awaited the appearance of touring theatrical groups. From the 1790s to the mid-nineteenth century, the Charleston Theater Company provided much of Wilmington's entertainment.[53] However, located on the principal highway along the coast and, after 1840, accessible by railroad, Wilmington attracted northern troupes as well. Mr. Cromwell and his company from New York offered a comedy in 1804. Several actors from New York, Philadelphia, Norfolk, and Portsmouth theaters stopped in Wilmington in 1840 for a performance.[54] The completion of Thalian Hall in 1858 provided Wilmington with a fine facility to attract talent, including Fleming's Company in 1860 and the Bailey Varieties in 1861. The latter group first performed under a large tent on Boundary (Fifth) Street but subsequently moved to Thalian Hall, where they had much more room, and offered "Our American Cousin" to an appreciative audience.[55]

The theater season usually encompassed the winter and spring months, concluding in May, when, according to the *Journal* in 1851, "It is getting too hot" for such activity. Performances opened with a dramatic piece—tragedy, comedy, romance—and often concluded with a farce, though on one occasion, in 1804, a pantomime. In the interim the companies offered singing and dancing, including a "Fancy Polka" by Miss Eveline in 1852. Mr. Edgar of the Charleston troupe in 1797 asked that requests for particular songs be submitted in the morning of his performance and that he would honor them "in rotation as far as the ability of the company can extend." According to Joseph Jefferson, nationally known actor who played in Wilmington, "It was customary in those days, particularly with provincial companies, to vary the dramatic fare so as to suit the different tastes of the public. Comedy and tragedy were therefore dished up, and many may say hashed up." Of the varied fare to which Wilmingtonians were exposed, Edward Bulwer-Lytton's *The Lady of Lyon* seems to have been the most popular production.[56]

Professional concerts, rare before 1830, became increasingly common prior to the Civil War, particularly as European performers traveled to the United States. Wilmington hosted as many as ten concerts annually in the 1850s. The always popular family groups included the Ophean Family (two brothers and two sisters) in 1845 from "New England's sunny hills," who reappeared often.[57] Also in demand were such groups as the Swiss Bell Ringers, who played first in 1845 and continued to return as late as 1855.[58] Representing the variety of entertainment in the 1840s were Eliza and Emma Kilmiste, aged 4 and 6, accompanied by Wattie Ferguson, the "celebrated Scotch Piper"; a Mr. Templeton, "celebrated European vocalist"; a Mr. Collins, an Irish comedian and vocalist; and the Danseuse Viennoise, 48 in number.[59] Jenny Lind, the "Swedish Nightingale," passed through Wilmington in 1850 on the way to a concert in Charleston, South Carolina. Her manager, P. T. Barnum, refused an impromptu engagement in Wilmington because there was not a theater of sufficient size to justify a performance.[60] Though disappointed in not hearing Jenny Lind, patrons of music in Wilmington in 1853 welcomed Norwegian violinist Ole Bull, regarded as the equal of Paganini. In 1857 Miss M. M. Gibbs, the "Jenny Lind of the South," regaled Wilmingtonians. And the next year Sigismund Thalbert, considered one of the greatest violinists of the period, performed in the port.[61]

Minstrel shows proved the most popular entertainment for the masses during the late antebellum years. In the 1840s troupes with a routine of song, dance, and dialogue began touring the country. Perhaps the first to reach Wilmington was J. Morris's Concert and Olio Company in 1842 from New York. Numerous groups followed over the next two decades, including the Ethiopian Serenaders, the Plantations Melodists, Julien's Minstrels and Burlesque Opera Troupe, Kunke's Nightingale Opera Troupe, the Pee Dee Ethiopian Opera Troupe, the New Orleans Opera Troupe, Geo. Christy's Minstrels with their "Mammoth Company," and Buckley's Minstrels. After attending a performance of Buckley's Minstrels in 1860, the editor of the *Herald* advised, "Let all who love fun and laughter, and especially good music, go to-night...." Duprez and Green's Minstrels arrived in town in early 1861, playing among other tunes "Dixie," which had become "the most popular air of the day." In the wake of the popularity of the minstrel shows, Wilmingtonians organized their own minstrel troupe, the "Sound Serenaders."[62]

The 1850s found opera troupes performing in Wilmington with some regularity. Madame Rosa DeVries (Prima Donna of the Italian Opera Company) entranced audiences in 1855. The completion of Thalian Hall seemed to attract additional companies. The Excelsior Opera Troupe played in 1859, followed in 1860 by the French Opera Comique. The latter proved disappointing because its orchestra failed to appear. Later in 1860 only part of the Cooper English Opera Troupe had arrived on opening night, and they were late but managed to placate an audience "whose patience was becoming somewhat attenuated." The remainder of the troupe eventually appeared. They not only honored their commitment to three full performances but also offered a "Grand Operatic Matinee" on Saturday afternoon for the benefit of the ladies of Wilmington.[63] As the *Daily Herald* proclaimed, "We are a music loving people, and can appreciate good playing and music."[64]

The local Thalians and traveling troupes utilized several buildings in Wilmington for theatrical and entertainment purposes. The "Old '76 Coffee House" (or Tavern), a large, two-story building, named for the year in which it was constructed and located on east Front Street between

8—Education, Enlightenment, and Culture

Town Hall/Thalian Hall (City Hall/Opera House), a public structure on the corner of Third and Princess streets that combined government functions with civic entertainment. Designed by New York architect John M. Trimble, the theater opened in 1858, the largest south of Richmond, Virginia. Drawing courtesy of the New Hanover County Public Library, Wilmington.

Orange and Ann, may have housed theatrical performances along with political rallies, the ball given in the honor of George Washington in 1791, and other social events. Henry Halsey's "New House" and "Williams' Long Room" may also have accommodated performances. Most popular in the early nineteenth century was the lower floor of the Wilmington Academy, variously known as the "Theatre," the "Wilmington Theatre," and the "Old Drury" after the London theater, which seated from three to four hundred people. Supplementing the academy in the 1840s and 1850s were Masonic Hall, 124 Market Street, a "Splendid Hall, 50 feet by 30 feet, with an orchestra or gallery off one side," and Mozart Hall, 20 South Front Street, remembered by one Wilmingtonian as "a little room dignified by the name of Mozart Hall." Just before the Civil War the Wilmington Light Infantry Armory offered an alternative site for exhibitions.[65]

At the end of the antebellum period Wilmington finally obtained a satisfactory theater and entertainment hall. The limitations of the Wilmington Academy and other sites became too obvious after the refusal of Jenny Lind to sing for want of a sufficiently large hall. Joseph Jefferson found the "dusty old rat-trap of a theater" in the academy so badly in need of repair that three days were required to prepare it for an opening performance. The Thalian Association and the town commissioners in 1855 undertook to construct an edifice that served both as a theater and as a municipal building—Town Hall/Thalian Hall, also called the "Opera House." After the demolition of the old theater, the president of St. John's Masonic Lodge, No. 1, laid the cornerstone for the new building in an elaborate ceremony on St. John's Day in December 1855. The new theater and town hall edifice was finished in 1858, measuring 110 by 60 feet, with a stage 42 by 57 feet and an auditorium 45 by 57 feet. Two tiers surrounded the floor seats. Gas lights supplied the illumination. The theater opened on October 12. G. F. Marchant's Company of Charleston served as the first resident stock company, inaugurating a theater (and town hall) that Wilmington had long needed.[66]

9

Urban Government

As the white and African American populations grew during the antebellum era, making Wilmington the most populous town in North Carolina in 1860, urban government became increasingly complex. Residents so filled the original platted area of the town that the General Assembly greatly enlarged its limits in 1849, subject to alterations in 1851. Following an imperfect survey of the new area, the town commissioners in 1855 hired an engineer to resurvey the town, including the streets of the old portion as well as the new. All that remained was for the commissioners to secure authority from the legislature in 1855 to open streets in the new sections of town, making allowance for any existing structures.[1]

The governance of Wilmington continued to rest in commissioners elected by those townspeople who qualified to vote for members of the lower house of the state legislature. Polls were open on election day from noon to sunset after 1795 and from ten o'clock in the morning to four o'clock in the afternoon after 1843. The number of commissioners remained at five from after the Revolution until 1843, when the General Assembly raised the number to seven. The 1843 statute also reduced to one year the term of office for commissioner, which had been increased to two years in 1801. The change engendered consternation in many Wilmingtonians, who, among other objections, criticized the frequency of elections by which "a partisan spirit is ever excited, social feuds are engendered, and the harmony of the community seriously if not lastingly disturbed." The General Assembly in 1794 directed the commissioners to choose one of their number as magistrate of police, the title of which in 1855 changed to mayor, much to the delight of the *Daily Herald*, which felt that magistrate of police was "an expressionless phrase, and did not convey the true meaning of the duties of chief municipal officer." Regardless of the terminology, the magistrate of police or mayor was the principal executive officer of the town.[2]

Although the legislature early empowered three or more commissioners to constitute a court for the purpose of enforcing town ordinances, for the more expedient settlement of controversies within Wilmington the General Assembly in 1818 authorized the New Hanover County court to select one of its members to be a special magistrate (or justice of the peace) for Wilmington. The law required the magistrate to live in the town and to keep an office open at least three days a week. With certain exceptions, his authority extended only to the town limits. The county court in 1819 chose Montesquieu W. Campbell to be the first special magistrate.[3]

The legislature in 1852 made the office of special magistrate elective for a biennial term beginning in 1853. Elections were well contested. In 1855 Thomas Loring (369 votes) defeated W. T. J. Vann (119) and Alexander Lamont (14) for the position. However, Loring was not a sitting justice of the peace at the time, so the election was invalidated and the county court assumed the power to choose the special magistrate—Vann. Yet it appeared that Vann was ineligible because he held an appointment under the Treasury Department of the United States as a weigher and gauger for the port of Wilmington. Occupying the office of special magistrate apparently would have violated the clause in the North Carolina state constitution that prohibited dual officeholding. Nonetheless, Vann assumed the position and was vindicated by winning the town election in 1857 as special magistrate.[4]

Beyond the commissioners, including the magistrate of police and the special magistrate, law enforcement devolved upon a police officer and constables. The commissioners created the position of police officer in 1847 at an annual salary of $500 to pen loose animals, kill dogs whose owners had not purchased badges for them, and generally to enforce the ordinances of the town. Both the police officers and constables originally obtained appointments from the town commissioners, but the constabulary eventually became elective. By the end of the antebellum era, Wilmington had been divided into upper and lower districts, each served by two constables. Candidates advertised in the newspapers, promising "the strict and punctual discharge of the duties of office" and soliciting the support of "friends and fellow-citizens." Those elections were likewise competitive. In 1861 John Utley (234) votes and L. M. Williams (225) won in the upper division; S. Petteway (148) placed third. Biddle (205) and Hawkins (162) carried the lower division; Sholar (75) ran third.[5]

A town watch represented an effort to guard against the frequent outbreak of fires, to compel slaves to observe a 9:00 P.M. curfew, and to keep order on Sundays. At the outset the commissioners hired watchmen, but insufficient funds and the ineffectiveness of the paid watch led "patriotic" citizens in 1806 to organize the "Wilmington Night Watch," which enrolled 120 white adult male volunteers in groups of four, each assuming guard duty one day a month. The experiment lasted two years, at which time the commissioners returned to the institution of a hired guard, which was retained until the Civil War, though its effectiveness remained questionable. The guard constituted such a major expense for the town that the General Assembly in 1792 and 1811 allowed the commissioners to impose special taxes to underwrite the cost. In 1854 the commissioners augmented the foot guard with a mounted guard of two horsemen to ride along the outlying areas of town north and south of Market Street.[6]

Town commissioners assumed responsibility for public buildings and structures, particularly the market house and dock. Serving the Wilmington judicial district and New Hanover County, the courthouse and jail fell to the jurisdiction of the New Hanover County court. Yet, the location of the buildings commended them to the attention of the commissioners, who in 1806 also attempted to raise money by a lottery to fireproof the courthouse. Regardless of the success of the lottery, the courthouse burned in 1840, and the county magistrates met in Society Hall, a building in the rear of St. James Church, until the county erected a new courthouse on Princess Street.[7]

If possible, the jail, accompanied by stocks, proved more troublesome than the courthouse, not only because it deteriorated so rapidly but also because of its location amid the homes and businesses of the town. After appointing commissioners in 1804 to determine whether to repair the old prison or build a new one, the General Assembly agreed to the latter, authorizing the county to impose a tax for construction. In 1836 the county justices let contracts for building another jail, 38 by 34 feet, three stories high, with walls ranging from two to three bricks thick, that was located on Third and Princess Streets. Less than two decades later, after finding the jail too small and insecure, the New Hanover County court contemplated another. At the time, some Wilmingtonians urged that the new prison be built beyond the town limits where it would not "inconvenience" the public, but the county justices decided to rebuild the jail in the vicinity of the courthouse. In 1853 the court ordered the immediate construction of the facility for no more than $20,000, selling the old jail and imposing taxes on county residents from 1853 to 1857 to pay for the structure.[8]

Closely resembling the courthouse in appearance, except that its first floor was open and paved, was the town market, pejoratively called the

"Mud Market," which stood at the intersection of Second and Market streets. A second market house occupied the intersection below the courthouse. Many vendors distanced themselves from the market, selling fish, beef, port, and other products at their shops, at stands, or from boats at the public dock. That in turn entailed a loss of time in shopping, as well as being "able to get only what the *negroes* have left, after picking out the best." Derided over the years and deemed "a disgrace to humanity," the Mud Market was finally replaced in 1847. Still, the new Market House was not always well utilized, for by 1860 butchers, among others, who formerly used the public area had opened shops throughout the town.[9]

Nevertheless, the town commissioners closely supervised market operations. They reserved stalls numbered one through four for sale of the vegetables, five through twenty-four for meat, and twenty-five through thirty for fish. Stalls were rented to the highest bidder. Among other regulations, the commissioners forbade butchers to bring entrails of animals to the market, prohibited smoking tobacco in the market, required the meat stalls to be "cleanly scoured," and demanded that servants of butchers be "cleanly dressed" at all times. The commissioners also prohibited carts, mules, horses, and oxen of those buying and selling in the market from remaining more than a half-hour in Market Street outside the market. The police officer of the town served as the clerk of the market, enforcing the regulations promulgated by the commissioners.[10]

The town commissioners also exercised control over the activities of vendors in and beyond the market to protect the health and welfare of the public. Empowered to make regulations for weighing and measuring articles, they annually appointed a standard keeper who maintained the weights and measures for the market. By law, commissioners assized bread and periodically visited bakers' shops to examine and weigh bread offered for sale to the public. However, as the *Wilmington Journal* noted in 1855, such regulations seemed at odds with the laws of trade. Why should restrictions be placed on the manufacturing skill of the baker but no one else? Whether turpentine, butter, or bread, the price should be determined by the market, "a matter for the buyer and seller." However, when several people became ill in 1860 after drinking milk brought by a vender to town, more extensive regulation of the market appeared necessary.[11]

Accompanying the market was the public dock at the foot of Market Street at which fruits, vegetables, and meats, including fish, were vended from small vessels or taken to the market house, and at which naval stores and other exportable products were brought for sale. The commissioners were responsible for the maintenance of the dock and empowered to determine the rules of wharfage. As in the colonial era, the commissioners frequently ordered the removal of lumber, logs, and other bulky articles and obstructions from the dock, but without noticeable success. Compounding the problems caused by encumbrances was the lack of space between the dock and the buildings on either side which made it difficult for drays and other vehicles to pass back and forth.[12]

Toward the end of the antebellum era the town commissioners undertook their most daunting project—the construction of Town Hall/Thalian Hall. Impetus derived from the need for a new theater, because the old one, located on the first floor of the Odd Fellows Academy since the beginning of the century, proved inadequate for a growing populace that supported a local Thalian Association, as well as many itinerant shows. In tortuous fashion the town acquired ownership of the land on the northeast corner of Third and Princess streets, leading one historian to avow that the history of the lots "is fraught with more unrecorded deeds, lost agreements and preliminary deals than possibly any other piece of property in North Carolina." The commissioners, as empowered by law, sold $20,000 worth of bonds to purchase the site for Town Hall/Thalian Hall. Upon acquiring legal title to the land in 1855, the commissioners let a contract for construction.[13]

Yet the joint effort on the part of the town and the Thalian Society to bring the Town Hall/Thalian Hall to completion seemed interminable. When the Thalians desired a larger theater than envisioned by the original plans, the town tried to buy out the association. As a result, the Thalians agreed to shoulder the cost of modifying the plans, and that in turn required finding a new contractor. The cornerstone was laid in December 1855, and by April 1858 the theater was sufficiently complete to permit an exhibition by Frensley's Dancing School. The theater formally opened on October 12, 1858, but finishing touches were not concluded until mid–1859, when all the scaffolding came down and Wilmingtonians witnessed a truly magnificent structure. The Thalians, who had arranged with the town to lease the theater, proved unable to comply with their contract, and in 1860 the Thalian Association surrendered the hall to the commissioners.[14]

As the Town Hall/Thalian Hall neared completion, the mounting friction between North and South, and, following the election in 1860, the heightened threat of war found the town commissioners confronting the need for an armory and a magazine. In the spring of 1861 a town and county committee jointly worked to find a site for an armory in Wilmington in which to store military supplies. At the same time, the General Assembly ordered the Wilmington commissioners to provide one or more magazines in which to store gunpowder that might be brought to the town.[15]

In addition to public buildings, the construction and maintenance of streets and sidewalks proved troublesome in a town built on sand and crisscrossed by springs and streams. Throughout the antebellum era the town commissioners tried to level the streets, but grading sometimes occasioned bitter opposition. After a lengthy lawsuit decided in favor of a plaintiff, the town was forced to erect retaining walls at public expense after grading. Perhaps for that reason, as late as 1860 the eastern terminus of Market Street was deemed dangerous to pedestrians and riders for lack of proper grading. Low-lying portions of the town were filled, including the area along the riverbank, which permitted the construction of Water Street between the river and Front Street. Purchasing ballast stone, the authorities began to pave Front and Market streets. Sidewalks along Front and Market relieved those on foot from competing with traffic in the streets. Gas streetlamps provided illumination along the major thoroughfares after the mid–1850s. And residents contributed to the beautification of the town by planting trees along the streets.[16]

Still, sandy streets and deteriorating sidewalks constantly confounded the commissioners. According to the *Wilmington Advertiser*, a walk from the river up the south side of Market Street to St. James Church would lead a person to "imagine himself up to the neck in John Bunyan's Slough of Despond." Even on a calm day, sand invaded the eyes, nostrils, and teeth of the unfortunate traveler. Sidewalks required continuous repair. Even when sidewalks were available, horses were hitched so close to them that those on foot were compelled to run the risk of being injured by the animals or to go around them into the streets where lay excrement. And not only animals but people were guilty of fouling the avenues. One household reportedly used the street as a receptacle for its "filth and offal," creating a "mud hole and manure hill in one of [the] principal thoroughfares" of the town. The magistrate of police usually bore the responsibility for contracting for clearing the streets and waste removal.[17]

Traffic on the thoroughfares added to the difficulties of opening and maintaining the streets. Early in the nineteenth century the commissioners ordered drivers of drays and carts to lead their horses, and imposed fines on those "galloping ... a Horse immoderately." They also prohibited the driving of horses through the streets, claiming that it was "productive of danger ... especially to children." After the construction of the Wilmington and Weldon Railroad Bridge over the Northeast Cape Fear River, the commissioners limited those riding horses or conducting vehicles across the structure to a pace no faster than a walk. Still, ordinances were ignored, as indicated by a complaint from the *Chronicle* in 1841: "Is there no law against trotting and galloping horses in carts and drays through the streets of Wilmington? If there be such a law, it is almost daily violated...."[18]

Contributing to the congestion in the streets were the many drays, carts, and wagons, regulation of which fell to the commissioners. Perhaps to reduce the number of draymen in town, the commissioners imposed an annual $10 tax on those engaged in the business, leading white draymen to protest vigorously that this was an unfair levy that placed them at a competitive disadvantage with slaves pursuing the same vocation. Despite the tax, the number of drays increased over the years, leading the commissioners in 1857 to prohibit the vehicles from standing for any length of time on Water Street, on Market Street between Water and Front, and in any of the alleys of the town.[19]

Beyond the traffic, a constant vexation in all North Carolina towns was the animal population, particularly dogs. In 1806 the town commissioners authorized the constable to kill hogs and goats running at large and to impound horses, releasing them to their owners upon the payment of a dollar. Perhaps finding that stricture unduly harsh, the legislature the next year allowed the commissioners to impose taxes on owners of free-ranging hogs, goats, and other animals. Later, the General Assembly approved a fine in the very substantial amount of $10 on owners of such animals. Still, over the years hogs continued to roam freely, as did cattle. The town's police officer in 1857 "committed" two cows to the "Pound," notifying their owners that the animals would be sold if not claimed and fees paid.[20]

Dogs, the number of which kept by whites and slaves had so "increased as to render them a nuisance" and greatly elevated the danger of rabies, according to the legislature in 1817, proved the worst menace. Eventually the commissioners required owners to obtain badges or licenses for dogs and to muzzle the animals. Moreover, the commissioners authorized the police officer of the town, as well as citizens generally, to kill unlicensed and unmuzzled dogs. That led in turn to the following "doggerel" that appeared in a local paper:

> The dogs had a meeting and made this resolve[.]
> That they all connection with man would dissolve,
> Since the passage of the muzzle law bears on its face
> The total destruction of their persecuted race.
> The meeting was large and quite literary,
> For all of their prerogatives appeared very chary[.]
> Present—Tray and Dash, who moved Carlo for President
> Seconded by Trip, a much esteemed resident.

> Towser was appointed Secretary of the meeting,
> Who though a stranger met with a very warm greeting.
> Resolutions they passed consoling the families
> Of the Brothers who perished, and those deprived of their liberties[.]
> They all appeared sad and strongly of one mind,
> That unless a repeal, they'd propagate no more of their kind,
> For to subject one of their offspring to such a disgrace,
> Would be cruel, and might be considered a waste
> Of valuable inhabitants on a community.
>
> The assembly passed off to the satisfaction of all,
> With a unanimous vote to await another call,
> In case the framers of this law did not repeal,
> And thereby our wounded honor to heal[.]
> Respectfully submitted by Secretary Towser,
> With promise that next meeting shall be a Rouser.[21]

Owners of dogs included slaves, who either belonged to white residents or came from the surrounding countryside. State law required slaves who sought to hire their time to produce in writing consent from their owners and to obtain a badge or license from the town commissioners. Although white laborers on occasion complained of the competition offered by slaves, the scarcity of the former virtually dictated the use of black workmen. And the General Assembly permitted the commissioners to force bondsmen to work, for the alternative was the resort to theft in order to obtain the money to pay their owners. Legislation in 1835 authorized the commissioners to appoint an official to superintend slaves by registering and hiring the bondsmen, receiving their wages, and paying their owners—in effect, systematizing the process. However, not until a "Strong memorial" was presented to the commissioners in 1854, urging them to implement the law, did they appoint Thomas F. Gause agent to oversee slave laborers.[22]

In addition to laborers, the commissioners tried to cope more generally with the slave presence in Wilmington. White residents claimed that slaves found easy access to establishments retailing alcoholic drinks and created disturbances in the streets at night and on Sundays. In response, the commissioners ordered the constables to jail all nonresident bondsmen without passes, releasing them only when claimed by their owners. A 9:00 P.M. curfew was imposed on Wilmington slaves, who might be apprehended and punished by the police officer after that time if they did not possess passes from their owners.[23]

Always troublesome were the ordinaries, dram shops, and bars where spirituous liquors were vended. At the beginning of the nineteenth century proprietors of those establishments by law were required to obtain a license from the town commissioners rather than the county court in order to conduct their businesses. Town and county retailers of spirituous liquors in New Hanover were also required to pay an annual $25 tax for "the Advancement of Temperance and good Order in Society." Liquor dealers strenuously opposed the imposition as "unjust and burdensome" because it was much higher than a similar tax in adjoining counties. Moreover, they pointed out that the onerous tax led to evasion and smuggling, which in turn diminished revenue for the government.[24]

Despite restrictions, the sale of intoxicating liquors flourished. A Wilmington town meeting in 1852, reflecting the impact of the temperance movement in the county and state, recommended to the General Assembly that the legislature strictly control or ban altogether the traffic. In a special session in 1855 the town commissioners finally took action. The commissioners limited the number of licenses to retailers of spirituous liquors in small measures to ten annually and required each to pay a $300 tax. Moreover, the commissioners refused to grant a license to anyone who kept his bar or store open at any time on Sundays.[25]

Throughout the antebellum era the commissioners grappled with two continual hazards to community life—fire and disease. The determination of fire regulations and fire-fighting policy continued to inhere in the commissioners, who attempted—with little success—to require householders to keep fire buckets and to sweep regularly their chimneys. Legislation in 1791 empowered the commissioners and members of the fire company to blow up or demolish any structure during a fire to prevent the spread of the blaze. Fifteen years later that duty devolved upon fire wardens after the General Assembly authorized the commissioners to divide the town into wards and appoint a warden for each area. However, after a fire in 1821, a local newspaper reprinted the statute of 1806 and the names of the current fire wardens, who "are to be obeyed accordingly," an indication that Wilmingtonians had grown rather lax in their respect for authority.[26]

Fire companies which cared for and operated the engines provided the principal protection against fire. The General Assembly in 1791 incorporated the Wilmington Fire-Company, and in 1820 authorized the town commissioners to form as many fire companies as needed, though their collective membership was limited to sixty men. The legislature exempted members of the fire companies from militia duty, and in Wilmington it was well known that many joined the companies "to get clear of mustering...." Confirming that observation was the resignation en masse of the firemen in town after legislation in 1843 required their militia service. That, unfortunately, left the town vulnerable during the great fire of November 1845.[27]

Regardless of the availability of fire companies, Wilmington's citizens offered their help when conflagrations threatened. During the fire of 1845 both blacks and whites, guided by the fire wardens, successfully operated the fire engines and wielded fire hooks. Additionally, those of both races usually worked assiduously to remove household belongings and business inventory from buildings before the spread of fires. After a blaze in 1829, Henry B. Howard publicly thanked his friends for their efforts in saving his property and extended his appreciation also "to the coloured people, for whose exertions, he owes them a grateful and lasting remembrance."[28]

Over the years the commissioners gradually effected a Fire Department for Wilmington. An "Extinguisher Engine" was early obtained. The acquisition of new or additional engines and, very importantly, hose was often prompted by fires, such as the one in 1852, which revealed the inadequacy of current equipment. In 1861 two fire companies served Wilmington—the longstanding Howard Fire Company, which was reincorporated in 1859, and the Hook and Ladder Company No. 1. At that time the Fire Department consisted of the chief engineer, his assistant, seven fire wardens, and captains of the two fire engine companies. The commissioners elected one of the fire wardens as chief warden and another as his assistant. From the remaining fire wardens, one was chosen to superintend the demolition of buildings during a fire, and another to be his assistant.[29]

Despite the various conflagrations, the fire-fighting apparatus occasionally served well. Never were the engines "more effectively used," wrote the *Cape Fear Recorder*, than when extinguishing a blaze in April 1821. The fire companies with their engines appeared promptly at the scene of a fire in 1834, and "citizens, generally, manifested their usual alacrity on such occasions." However, a lack of water frustrated the best of intentions. Fires too remote from the river virtually burned themselves out unless the many springs about town could be tapped. The occurrence of two fires on Fifth Street between Chestnut and Walnut in 1860 found the engines unable to access the river, leading to the observation that the town needed a fire well or reservoir.[30]

Disease, together with fire, represented a constant threat to the tranquillity of Wilmington. The town's port status and low-lying site made it all the more susceptible to illnesses. The General Assembly authorized the commissioners of navigation and pilotage for the Cape Fear River to appoint a health officer to establish regulations for vessels entering the port of Wilmington. The commissioners ignored the directive, making the pilots who brought ships over the bars at the Cape Fear River and New Inlet responsible for ascertaining illness on board vessels and reporting to the commissioners. During an imminent threat of smallpox in 1816, the commissioners reiterated their stricture to pilots. Legislation in 1828 reaffirmed the authority of the commissioners to make and enforce quarantine regulations, and two years later the commissioners of navigation and pilotage imposed a general quarantine on all ships arriving from the Mediterranean, Africa, West Indies, and points south of Wilmington. Subsequently, when yellow fever threatened southern towns in 1854 and 1855, the town commissioners prohibited persons from the "infected" areas from visiting Wilmington, though, interestingly, the ban did not apply to travelers "who shall pass in regular course through the town." Residents of Wilmington who returned to town were quarantined for fifteen days.[31]

Municipal authorities also strove to protect the health of the community, and with some success. Empowered by law, Wilmington town commissioners turned their efforts principally toward filling low-lying areas in town where stagnant water collected, clearing lots overgrown with vegetation, removing rotting trash and debris from the streets, forcing landowners to drain their property, and ordering the cleansing or filling of cellars in structures close to the river. The last proved a never-ending battle. In 1803 the cellars of a number of buildings under construction between Market and Princess streets contained "stagnated water and putrefied substances, which ... [had] become so extremely obnoxious as almost to impede the passage of persons in their vicinity." In addition to standing water, lots overgrown with weeds and filled with rubbish endangered the public health, leading to directives to clean up such properties. By the end of the antebellum era the commissioners decided to divide Wilmington into seven districts, over which each of the seven commissioners was given jurisdiction and made responsible for giving "such orders as may seem to them necessary for the health of the town."[32]

Concomitant to concerns about the public health and hygiene was the need to find additional burial space for the deceased in a town whose population quintupled from 1789 to 1860. St. James' Cemetery, an adjoining public cemetery for which the town was responsible, and other burial areas filled fast. Moreover, some townspeople may have taken umbrage at imposing tombs or mausoleums. In late September 1845, not long after dark, a large brick structure built by John A. Taylor in St. James' Cemetery as a repository for his family's remains was destroyed in a violent explosion that shook Wilmington. Reportedly, the tomb was viewed as a "nuisance." By the early 1850s there was general agreement that sites beyond the town were needed for the interment of the dead.[33]

A number of prominent citizens, led by Dr. Armand J. DeRosset, Jr., Platt K. Dickinson, Oscar G. Parsley, Henry Nutt, and James Cassidey, successfully obtained a charter of incorporation in 1852 from the General Assembly as the "Proprietors of the Wilmington Cemetery," or the Wilmington Cemetery Company. Capitalized at $25,000, the organizers were responsible for purchasing and preparing a suitable site for a cemetery. From the proceeds of the sale of lots and burial fees the company would establish a permanent fund whose moneys would be used for the maintenance of the cemetery. Once additional funds realized from fees and the sale of lots were sufficient to reimburse the company for purchasing the land and improving the grounds, the stockholders were to transfer their interest in the cemetery to the owners of the burial plots, who were entitled to a number of shares commensurate with their number of lots. The lot holders at that point became the stockholders in the corporation.[34]

The Wilmington Cemetery Company bought land about a mile beyond the city limits, and by February 1855 was prepared to sell lots in Oakdale Cemetery. Initially, lots were sold at a minimum of $50 each, but demand was so great that many lots were sold at a premium, and the company realized approximately $10,000. The first burial was that of the daughter of Dr. DeRosset, one of the "Proprietors" of the cemetery. By the end of the year the company notified the public that interments might be made only by a permit, the cost of which ranged from two to eight dollars, depending upon whether the deceased was a child or an adult and whether private or public lots were used. In the springtime the "City of the Dead" presented a charming appearance and proved a favorite spot for visitors. In 1860 the company improved the road leading from Wilmington to the cemetery and opened a new one for better access. Upon the opening of Oakdale, the Wilmington commissioners limited burials within the town limits and in 1861 forbade them altogether.[35]

Blacks in the eighteenth and early nineteenth centuries may well have been buried in a section of the old town cemetery beyond St. James' Cemetery. As in the case of whites, an increasing population demanded additional burial space. In the 1840s, as he prepared to move to Louisiana, William Campbell, a white, deeded property to the town with the stipulation that it be used "for the colored population" of Wilmington. The area, Campbell Square, was bounded by Campbell, Red Cross, North Fifth, and North Sixth streets and contained the Campbell Square Cemetery or "Negro Burying Ground." The cemetery opened as early as 1847. The fee for interment in 1853 was one dollar for an adult and fifty cents for a child. In 1860 the town commissioners purchased fifteen acres of land adjacent to Oakdale Cemetery for the interment of African Americans, which subsequently became known as Pine Forest Cemetery. However, tombstones in that cemetery dating from the 1840s and 1850s indicate an earlier usage of the property for burials.[36]

Of course, myriad other matters came to the attention of the Wilmington commissioners. The numerous springs about town raised the possibility of creating an underground water system which would culminate in a reservoir at the courthouse. Eventually the town opted for constructing cisterns of 400 to 500 barrel capacity at the corners of Mulberry and Fourth, Market and Seventh, Orange and Fourth, and Nun and Second; building a tank at Jacobs Spring near the jail; and sinking a well near the railroad between Third and Fourth streets.[37] The commissioners forbade merchants from opening their stores on Sunday, maintained a town clock (actually the clock on St. James Church) and town bell, and issued invitations to prominent politicians to visit the town, including, in 1854, the entire state legislature for the Christmas season.[38]

Taxes and fees underwrote the expenses of town government. By law the commissioners were allowed to impose property and poll taxes that were collected by the New Hanover County sheriff at the time he collected county and state levies. The sheriff annually received a list of Wilmington residents and their real estate from the town clerk, who in turn was furnished that information by denizens and property owners. The General Assembly empowered the town commissioners in 1859 to appoint a tax collector for the town. Supplementing property and poll taxes were levies imposed on the retailers of spirituous liquors; on owners of hotels, billiard tables, livery stables, restaurants, bowling saloons, sailors, taverns, wagons, drays, and carts; and on tradesmen, cooks on ships, hucksters, laboring men and women, slaves living in the country but working in town, and washwomen. Commissioners also taxed transient tradesmen who kept stores in Wilmington. Fines and fees from cases tried in the county and superior courts augmented municipal revenues.[39]

The town, however, constantly labored under its financial obligations, usually concluding each year in debt and sometimes failing to pay its employees in a timely fashion. Occasionally the commissioners borrowed money via short-term notes to cover deficits. Financial difficulties were occasioned in part by the inability of the town to realize fully tax collections. Sheriffs were unable to obtain moneys from the poverty-stricken or those who had left the town. Throughout the antebellum era many failed to list their taxes, probably depriving the town of a third of its revenue. Moreover, listed property was often undervalued, leading to additional losses of tax moneys. On occasion the town lost the opportunity to collect fees. In 1806 the General Assembly permitted the commissioners to impose a one percent fee on auctioneers' sales in Wilmington for the use of the town, but in 1818 the legislature appropriated the proceeds to pay the salaries of the judges of the state supreme court, which had been established in that year. Wilmingtonians appealed for the return of the auctioneers' moneys, claiming that "upon the prosperity of the seaport towns of our state, measurably depends the prosperity and welfare of its population...." And the town reminded the General Assembly of the debilitating effects of the panic (or depression) of 1819, which particularly affected urban areas, and the devastating impact of the fire in Wilmington in 1819. Eventually the legislature relented.[40]

Municipal responsibilities, and hence expenses, increased with the growth of Wilmington. Absorbing considerable moneys were the town watch (including an extra guard during the Christmas holidays), fire protection and fire fighting (repairing fire engines, ringing the bell for a fire, paying those firemen who were first to their engine), work on the streets (clearing, hauling ballast stones, grading), caring for town slave laborers (vaccinations for smallpox, purchase of shoes), and sundry other matters (maintaining the clock on St. James Church, expenditures for observing the funerals of prominent individuals, expenditures for celebrating the Fourth of July). In addition, the town commissioners, as empowered by law, purchased stock in the Wilmington and Manchester Railroad ($100,000) and the Wilmington, Charlotte and Rutherford Railroad ($200,000) and borrowed $20,000 for the erection of the Town Hall/Thalian Hall. At the time of the Civil War, caring for the largest town in North Carolina had become increasingly onerous, not only for the town commissioners but also for the citizenry, who shouldered the financial burden of paying for municipal expenses.[41]

10

An Expanding Economy

The tribulations of Wilmington's town commissioners, who struggled to provide municipal services and to underwrite various financial obligations, largely reflected the economic fortunes of the port. As North Carolina entered the United States in 1789, a scattered, rural populace beset by poor roads, shallow rivers, and the Outer Banks, which inhibited external commerce, left the state impoverished, isolated, or dependent for markets upon Virginia and South Carolina. Wilmington, though favorably located for trade on the Cape Fear River and constituting North Carolina's only deepwater port of consequence, could not escape the debilitating embrace of the rest of the state. It virtually stagnated until 1840, when improvements to the navigability of the Cape Fear River, the increasing importance of steam navigation, and the advent of the railroad transformed Wilmington into the state's largest town and a major Atlantic port by the time of the Civil War.

Of course, as a port of national, even international, consequence, Wilmington responded to events arising beyond the borders of North Carolina. During the Napoleonic Wars the Embargo of 1807 depressed shipping in the port, and Wilmingtonians happily noted the relaxation of that stricture two years later. The War of 1812, despite British patrols in the Atlantic, found Wilmington bustling with privateers, one of which, the *Lovely Lass*, was owned by local investors. The privateers brought 3, 5, and 15 vessels to port for condemnation in 1812, 1813, and 1814 respectively. The *Lovely Lass*, however, was captured in 1813 by a British vessel off Montego Point in the West Indies, and the captain and crew were imprisoned in Nassau.[1]

Wilmington and the nation enjoyed a brief period of prosperity following the end of the War of 1812, but the panics of 1819 and 1837 led to depressed conditions for more than two decades. The Reverend Thomas

Wright wrote from Wilmington in 1819, "These are dreadful times with us for money." A year later many of the leading mercantile houses in the port owed "more or as much as they can pay." The collector of customs for the port, reputedly in debt to the federal government for $100,000, had resigned his position and disappeared. The panic of 1837 forced Wilmington banks, like so many throughout the country, to suspend specie payments, which were not resumed until early 1841.[2]

The recessions of the mid-1850s also adversely affected Wilmington. Opined the *Daily Herald* in January 1855, "Mr. Hard Times is here yet, and every body has become acquainted with him." Later that year Thomas Smith & Co. closed its mill "In consequence of the scarcity of Money, and the delay of our customers to pay their accounts...." The number of suits for debt brought to the New Hanover County court jumped fourfold. Banks suspended specie payments, and, in 1857, according to one newspaper, "upward of sixty vessels [are] now lying in the port of Wilmington, owing to the difficulty of procuring Freight."[3]

The economic life of Wilmington, which revolved about shipping, in turn depended heavily upon commission merchants, or factors, who took country produce—naval stores, cotton, foodstuffs—in Wilmington on consignment and tried to find the best market for their disposal. In turn, they procured goods from abroad for their customers. Prominent among the early commission merchants was John F. Burgwin. Between December 23, 1815, and January 13, 1816, at least eight vessels owned by Burgwin or containing cargoes for Burgwin & Co. docked in Wilmington. Most factors maintained offices in New York or other northern ports. Joseph R. Blossom made cash advances on produce consigned to him for sale in Wilmington or for shipment to Benj. Blossom & Son in New York. In 1860 commission merchants lined Water and Front Streets, but their number lacked John Hathaway, who died in 1859 after more than forty years in business in Wilmington, during which he had been universally esteemed for his integrity. Stores had closed on the afternoon of Hathaway's funeral, and the commission merchants in the port attended the services "in a body" as a measure of respect.[4]

The steadily increasing population of Wilmington demanded an increasing number of support personnel to provide the necessary goods and services to sustain the shipping community. Dry-goods merchants went north during the summer and early fall months to order the latest fashions. The stock began to arrive in September, though, as Mrs. Armand J. DeRosset, an inveterate shopper, observed in the middle of September 1859, there were "but very few persons in town as yet to purchase." The *Journal* in 1855 commended the "taste and discrimination of the Dry

Goods men" in their "skillful selection" but noted that shopping, as a result, would soon be "rather expensive." It had also become more laborious for the ladies of Wilmington. Over the years losses from exposure and theft compelled retail merchants in 1838 collectively to discontinue the longstanding practice of sending goods to women in their homes for consideration in order to relieve them of the stress of shopping in the stores.[5]

Wilmington boasted a variety of other stores to satisfy the needs of its inhabitants. Chandlers, booksellers and bookbinders, tailors, hatters, hairdressers and barbers, tobacconists, bakers, blacksmiths, painters and daguerreotypists, confectioners, watchmakers, lawyers, and physicians offered their services. Proprietors of bathhouses tendered hot and cold showers or baths; owners of livery stables cared for horses. In addition to ice, Dominque Cazaux in 1825 sold ice cream, punch, and lemonade at his ice house. R. Robinson opened a bottling business in 1853 for mineral waters, ginger pop, and all kinds of beverages. S. M. West in 1860 advertised "a large sample stock of superfine Under Garments for Ladies and Gentlemen...."[6] In addition to the numerous saloons in town, the Rock Spring Restaurant in 1846 and the Wilmington Empire Restaurant in 1854 catered to local residents and travelers, serving meals "at short notice, at any hour."[7]

For a town that served not only as a center of commerce but also as a hub of river and rail traffic, Wilmington appeared hard pressed to provide adequate lodging facilities for its many visitors. Boardinghouses abounded. James Carr promised, "Every attention will be given, and the best provisions and choicest liquors provided." In advertising his Merchants' Coffee House, I. C. C. Gunn agreed to take boarders for the day, week, or quarter. David Thally endeavored to make travelers as "comfortable as if they were at home" and maintained a livery stable for their convenience. Still, itinerants often found Wilmington's boardinghouses less than satisfactory.[8]

Boardinghouses supplemented the town's hotels, which also seemed wanting, at least in quality if not in numbers. One of the earliest and certainly best known was Dick's Hotel, operated by William Dick, who had relocated from Fayetteville. Thereafter a succession of hotels served Wilmington, including the North Carolina Hotel, the Wilmington Hotel, and the Clarendon House in the 1820s. Two decades later, after the advent of the railroad, which brought more visitors to town, the Commercial Hotel, the Hanover Hotel, the Rock Spring Hotel, the Wilmington (formerly Planter's) Hotel, the LaFayette (Washington and LaFayette) Hotel, and the Carolina Hotel supplemented the longstanding Clarendon House.

Still, a hotel proprietorship was a risky business, and most establishments constantly underwent new ownership. The Carolina Hotel changed hands at least three times between 1845 and 1855.[9]

A number of Wilmingtonians in the early 1850s spearheaded a movement to erect a new hotel to supplement the existing establishments, because travelers complained about the lack of suitable accommodations, and steamboat captains reported that passengers slept on the boats when steamers arrived too late to make railroad connections. However, many in town felt that the current hotels and boardinghouses were sufficient. Public meetings to promote the construction of a new hotel met a lukewarm reception. Finally, in 1859, prominent businessmen, including John Dawson and Oscar G. Parsley, obtained a charter of incorporation from the General Assembly for the Wilmington Hotel Company. By May of that year the company had selected a site for the hotel. Yet the projected cost of the lot and proposed hotel was $60,000, and the company lacked adequate funds to undertake the project immediately. Thus, in 1860, Wilmingtonians perforce remained satisfied with their several boardinghouses and hotels, including the City Hotel, the Rock Spring Hotel, and the Washington House, as well as the Farmers' House, the Mechanics' Hotel, and the Pilot House.[10]

Women played a vital role in the economy, mostly as homemakers but also in a more public capacity. The poor resorted to domestic service, laundering, and sewing. Two women worked in O. G. Parsley's steam sawmill in 1850. Educated, single women and widows often sustained themselves by teaching, both in public and in private schools. Beyond the basic elements of education, they taught music, dancing, French, and such "female" subjects as sewing, crocheting, and embroidery. A Mrs. DeNeale in 1855 sold fruits, candies, preserves, and sweetmeats, an "assortment ... undoubtedly the largest, and best ever brought to this market." Women were also proprietors of several of Wilmington's boardinghouses. A Mrs. McDonald operated the Marine Hotel early in the nineteenth century; Mrs. Elfe opened a boarding establishment in 1837, in which she also intended to run a day school. Women operated at least three boardinghouses in town in 1860.[11]

Female entrepreneurs proved most prominent in the clothing businesses, principally millinery but also in dressmaking and mantua making. Most milliners maintained New York connections and usually went north to obtain the latest fashions of the season. Mrs. Fairchild in 1806 offered "an elegant Assortment of Fashionable Split Straw Bonnets, Feathers, Plumes, &c." In 1851 Mrs. Shaw, Mrs. V. R. Peirson, and Miss Sarah Jane Taggart vied for the attention of millinery shoppers.[12] Mrs. Shaw also com-

10—An Expanding Economy

A turpentine distillery, representative of one of the principal industries in antebellum Wilmington, though a dangerous workplace in that it was susceptible to devastating fires. Drawing courtesy of the New Hanover County Public Library, Wilmington.

bined dressmaking with millinery, in which business in 1847 she "received the French Fashions monthly...." Mrs. Wilkinson in 1845 engaged in millinery and mantua making. In 1860 Mrs. B. M. Mengart exhibited and sold "needle and fancy work" from Berlin.[13]

In an economy oriented toward shipping and services, manufacturing played a small role. Occasionally, some reflected upon the dependence of the South upon northern manufacturers and felt that abundant raw materials and cheap labor, including slave labor, in the area might be utilized for manufacturing. After all, editorialized the *People's Press*, "Hundreds of children are advantageously employed in the northern factories." After the completion of the Wilmington and Weldon Railroad, by which cotton could be brought from eastern North Carolina to the port, consideration was given to the construction of a cotton mill in Wilmington. Interested businessmen held a meeting in 1845 to discuss the possibility and to obtain information about the operation of factories in Fayetteville and northern towns. Enthusiasm quickly waned, however, and the textile industry in North Carolina remained confined to the Piedmont section of the state.[14]

Manufacturing in the vicinity of Wilmington centered on shipbuilding, turpentine distilling, and wood products. Given the location of Wilmington and the availability of timber, a number of ships were constructed in the port during the antebellum era. The shipyards of James Cassidey in town and Samuel Beery and Sons on Eagles Island produced many of the vessels. Most were schooners, though sloops, brigantines, and steamboats came off the ways as well. In addition to the oceangoing and river craft, the Beerys in 1852 built a pilot boat, the *John C. Calhoun*, for two pilots in Charleston, South Carolina. Jesse J. Cassidey, who was given his father's business upon the retirement of James Cassidey in 1855, finished two racing craft in 1859, destined to be "additions to the already large fleet owned by the Carolina Yacht Club."[15]

In addition to shipbuilding, Wilmington (or, at least, New Hanover County) in 1810 and 1820 contained turpentine distilleries, "spinning machines," looms, a candle-making establishment, bakeries, and saltworks, all deemed manufacturing operations by the federal censuses of those years. In 1827 Wilmington boasted three steam-powered sawmills and a steam-powered rice mill. By 1850, when "manufacturing" had become more strictly defined by the federal government, Wilmington contained 34 manufactories, including 14 turpentine distillers, 10 saw or planning mills, 2 rice mills, 2 shipbuilding companies (Cassidey and Beery), and 1 business each devoted to saddle and harness making, copper manufacture (stills and roofing), barrel making, tanning, fishing, and machinery. Clearly, the orientation of manufacturing in Wilmington favored naval stores and wood products, as those raw materials were processed for export.[16]

Aiding the export trade of Wilmington and North Carolina was the continuation of the inspection system that had been started in the colonial era. The state legislature authorized the New Hanover County court in 1807 to appoint inspectors in Wilmington for ton timber; in 1818 for staves and heading; and in 1821 for provisions, naval stores, and lumber, in effect encompassing the principal exports of the Wilmington market. Legislation later required inspectors for each of the sawmills (apparently the steam sawmills) in the vicinity of Wilmington and for the inspection of flour. Naval stores, however, proved Wilmington's most significant export. In 1852 the county court was allowed to appoint eight or more inspectors for naval stores, whereas all other coastal towns were limited to six. By 1860 twelve naval stores inspectors served the port of Wilmington.[17]

The General Assembly in 1855 made the town commissioners of Wilmington responsible for appointing two inspectors of flour, provisions, and forage. The commissioners proceeded to draft regulations for the inspection, requiring flour to be put "in good barrels made of well seasoned timber, with not less than ten hoops, say three on each head and two on each bilge, and contain 196 pounds, exclusive of the weight of the barrel, which is hereby fixed at 19 pounds...." Flour was rated as "middling," "cross," "fine," "superfine," or "family" or condemned as "short weight," "sour," or "musty." Similar strictures were issued for pork, beef, and hay. Rice and wheat also fell within the purview of the inspectors. Two years later the legislature required that all cotton sold in Wilmington be weighed by the inspectors of flour, provisions, and forage, but returned the power of appointing the inspectors to the county court. A third inspector was mandated by statute in 1861, an indication of the increased importance of the export of provisions.[18]

As a center of commerce in North Carolina, Wilmington particularly needed adequate banking facilities to underwrite and promote trade and shipping. Yet the state was among the last of the original thirteen to charter banks when the General Assembly in 1804 established the Bank of Cape Fear and the Bank of Newbern. Many in North Carolina—and throughout the nation—opposed banking institutions because they smacked of corporate privilege, benefiting the few at the expense of the many. Others viewed banks as speculative enterprises, which during good times or bad might fold, erasing the hard-earned assets of those who had depended upon the institutions. Opponents of banks and their paper notes, or "soft money," preferred to rely upon specie or "hard money" for economic exchange. As a result, in inaugurating the Bank of Cape Fear, the commissioners of the bank issued a lengthy explanation of the benefits of banking enterprises in hopes of encouraging those in the region to support the institution.[19]

North Carolina's initial foray into banking became enmeshed in politics. Federalists controlled the Bank of Cape Fear and the Bank of Newbern. Jeffersonian Republicans provided the impetus for a rival bank, the State Bank of North Carolina, incorporated in 1810 and headquartered in Raleigh, with branches in Wilmington, New Bern, and four other towns. The Jeffersonians hoped that the State Bank would drive the older banks out of business, but that strategy failed. The banks in Wilmington and New Bern obtained extensions of their charters that increased their capitalizations. Competition from the Second Bank of the United States and a depressed economy in the wake of the Panic of 1819 eventually forced an end to the first wave of banking in North Carolina. The Bank of Newbern and the State Bank closed in the early 1830s.[20]

Banking facilities, however, remained indispensable, and the General Assembly responded in its 1833–1834 session by incorporating the Bank of the State of North Carolina (which had a branch in Wilmington, among other towns), and by extending to 1855 the charter of the Bank of Cape Fear, capitalized at $800,000. In 1847 the legislature incorporated the Commercial Bank of Wilmington with a capitalization of $300,000 (later raised to $350,000), but in the mid–1850s Wilmingtonians felt that their growing population and thriving trade merited additional banking capital in the port. Thus the General Assembly in 1855 incorporated the Bank of Wilmington, capitalized at $800,000. The Bank of Wilmington organized later in the year, giving the port four commercial banks at the end of the antebellum era—a branch of the Bank of the State of North Carolina, the Bank of Cape Fear (whose charter was again extended in 1855), the Commercial Bank, and the Bank of Wilmington.[21]

Supplementing the four commercial banks was the Wilmington Savings Bank, chartered in 1855 and opening in May of that year. It was "especially created for the benefit of the masses" to offer a safe haven for the deposits of small savers, and through its loan policies to ensure "a more general diffusion of its funds among persons in moderate circumstances." Within six months 122 depositors had placed $6,908.82 in the Wilmington Savings Bank. The incorporating statute and amendments forbade the officers of the bank from receiving compensation, required that the bank's money be invested in the most conservative financial instruments, and prohibited the bank from issuing paper money. Stock shares cost $30, putting them within the reach of many citizens and thereby allowing the less affluent to become investors.[22]

Ultimately, of course, Wilmington's livelihood depended upon shipping. Despite the European wars of the 1790s and early 1800s, North Carolina commerce expanded. Registered tonnage in foreign trade increased 25 percent between 1790 and 1815. Since the state was not a major exporter, it was not greatly affected by the British and French commercial restrictions during the Napoleonic Wars. And the War of 1812 was a fillip for North Carolina, for foreign shipping apparently relied more heavily upon North Carolina ports due to the blockade of New England and New York ports during the conflict. In the process, Wilmington easily outdistanced its rivals in North Carolina. At the conclusion of the War of 1812 Wilmington accounted for virtually all of North Carolina's foreign trade and 80 percent of the value of the state's domestic exports by sea. New Bern, the next busiest port, shipped 6 percent of the state's domestic goods, followed in order of importance by Washington, Edenton, Camden, Plymouth, and Ocracoke.[23]

Despite some overland travel by road, and (after 1840) by railroad, the Cape Fear River and its tributaries provided Wilmington with the bulk of its exportable products. Below the town, small schooners, sloops, and a variety of other craft sustained river traffic. From the Northwest and Northeast Cape Fear rivers came rafts and flats with naval stores, timber, and other heavy items. Flats varied greatly in size. An advertiser in a Fayetteville newspaper sought four, two measuring 48 by 10 feet and two measuring 30 by six feet. Larger flats could carry from 300 to 500 barrels of turpentine. The *J. L. Cassidey*, from Lyon's Landing on the lower Black River, arrived in Wilmington in April 1851 with 326 barrels of rosin, 64 barrels of tar, and 64 barrels of turpentine. During the 1830s steamboats appeared regularly on the waters above Wilmington, particularly between the port and Fayetteville, and their numbers increased before the Civil War. However, all traffic, including steamboats, required adequate water, and low levels brought shipping to a halt on occasion.[24]

Water levels of the Cape Fear and its tributaries varied greatly. Reported the *Fayetteville Observer* in October 1845, the river "is at last in a navigable state.... It rose Saturday and Sunday upwards of 20 feet [due to a heavy rain]." Shippers along the river awaited the rising waters to float their produce downstream. Two months later the *Journal* noted that heavy rains had swelled the creeks and rivers, in consequence of which large quantities of timber and naval stores had come to Wilmington. The flow of trade slackened in the summer when the river was low, perhaps no more than eighteenth inches on the shoals.[25]

Consequently, the Wilmington commercial market opened in November, was "brisk" in December, and increased in volume in the first three months of the year. April witnessed a decline in business, a trend that became more pronounced in May. Local trade almost halted in June. The summer and fall months were "dull." During the slow seasons commission merchants exercised especial care. According to John F. Burgwin, merchants rarely dispatched vessels to Wilmington without notifying their correspondents in advance of the desired products. Four weeks' notice was deemed advisable in order to give the agent sufficient opportunity to obtain a cargo at a reasonable price and have it ready at the time of the arrival of the ship. Otherwise, "great detention and disappointment often happen...; as but seldom peculiar kinds of produce can be had on sudden notice."[26]

Over the antebellum years Wilmington's export trade varied little. Overseas commerce depended mainly upon the extractive forest industries of the region—naval stores and wood products. Tobacco exports declined significantly, but the prominence of cotton in the Wilmington market, particularly in the 1850s, more than made up for the deficiency of tobacco, and portended the importance of cotton for the Confederacy and Wilmington during the Civil War. Foodstuffs figured less prominently in Wilmington's trade on the eve of the war, except for rice and peanuts, exports of which increased during the 1850s. The produce of the Upper and Lower Cape Fear remained well suited to the West Indies. Lumber, flour, rice, shingles, staves, naval stores, and livestock left Wilmington, scattering "in as many directions as there are Islands." Imports of West

Indian sugar, rum, molasses, and coffee found a ready market in Wilmington.[27]

The coastal trade continued to form a crucial component of Wilmington's commerce. Most transactions involved New York and Philadelphia and, to a lesser extent, Boston, Baltimore, and Charleston. Packets connected Wilmington and New York as early as 1812. By 1833 packets also sailed between Wilmington and Philadelphia. In 1839 nine lines regularly linked Wilmington and the northern cities. Efforts to establish a packet to Baltimore failed in the 1840s but came to fruition in the following decade. Few European goods were brought directly to Wilmington. Rather, "custom" had introduced the practice of supplying the Lower Cape Fear with dry goods, hardware, iron, salt, crockery, and other items indirectly from the ports along the northern coast of the United States.[28]

Shipping activity in Wilmington increased steadily. On January 25, 1833, alone, a reported 70 vessels were in port. From 1838 through 1842, an annual average of 543 ships called at Wilmington. The number increased to over 700 by mid-century and reached 814 in the year ending May 6, 1854. Most were American-owned. For the year ending May 6, 1854, the number was 781 of 814; for the year ending May 1, 1858, 616 of 633. Non-American vessels were mostly British: 23 of 33 in 1854; 13 of 17 in 1858. Occasionally ships called from Belgium, Holland, France, Spain, Russia, Norway, Sweden, Germanic countries, Argentina, and Venezuela. Most ships were small. During the 1850s schooners comprised 75 percent of those reaching the port; brigs, 20 percent; barques, 5 percent. Galliots infrequently appeared. Although Wilmingtonians owned 27 percent of North Carolina's shipping tonnage, merchants continued to rely mainly upon outside shipping sources, finding it cheaper to hire vessels than to procure their own.[29]

Wilmington's commercial economy received a decided stimulus in the antebellum era from North Carolina's engagement in the "transportation revolution." Trying to counter the stigma of the "Rip Van Winkle State," and, more particularly, to combat a depressed economy (as well as competition from neighboring states), North Carolina joined the nationwide movement to advance transportation and communication. The transportation revolution embraced the improvement of roads, including turnpikes and plank roads, the utilization of canals, the enhancement of the navigability of rivers, and the application of steam power to travel on water (by steamboat and steamship) and on land (by railroad). Although advances in road construction and canalling little benefited Wilmington, improvements in the navigability of the Cape Fear River, together with the steam travel, transformed the port into North Carolina's largest town by the Civil War.

Overland transportation in post–Revolutionary North Carolina for the most part remained wretched. At the conclusion of the Revolution the General Assembly in 1784 virtually reinstituted the colonial approach to road construction and maintenance. County courts remained in charge, using overseers and road companies—in effect, commandeering the labor of those who lived adjacent to the highways. The system was inefficient, burdensome, and inequitable. In the estimation of one historian, the typical road force consisted of "ten or twelve men and an overseer, a little gray mule, a small plow, six dogs, three or four guns, and a few tools which often are not considered worth using at home." Such a gathering was hard on rabbits but little enhanced the roads. Thus Governor William A. Graham informed the state legislature in 1848, "our method of maintaining the public highways has made no advance beyond that existing in England, in the time of Phillip [sic] and Mary."[30]

Following the War of 1812, the General Assembly evidenced a more sustained interest in highway development, often supported by public funds. It directed the creation of roads, for which counties were responsible. It also chartered turnpike and plank road companies, trying to rely upon private entrepreneurial efforts to flesh out a system of highways in the state. Realizing the inadequacy of private capital, the legislature rendered assistance to such efforts in the form of grants of land, grants or loans of money, and the purchase of stock in companies. Occasionally the state funded roads solely at the expense of the public. But Wilmington and the coastal area of North Carolina little benefited from such largesse, as attention centered primarily on the Piedmont and Mountain regions, which were more sparsely settled, relatively poor, and marked by a more difficult topography. Still, as one observer aptly stated, all those roads, even the turnpikes, "were, at best, good dirt roads," and suffered in direct proportion to their traffic.[31]

Recognizing that deficiency, North Carolina enthusiastically embraced an alternative—plank roads—during the decade preceding the Civil War. Plank roads appeared in the state when the General Assembly responded to Governor Graham's criticism of the North Carolina highway system in the late 1840s by chartering the Fayetteville and Western Plank Road Company, the Wilmington and Masonboro Plank Road Company, and the Wilmington and Walker's Ferry Plank Road Company in 1849. Eventually the legislature authorized a total of 84 plank road companies, many of which converged on Fayetteville, which became the hub of the plank road movement in the state. The Fayetteville and Western was not only the first such road, but in the beginning it was a successful operation, which encouraged plank road construction elsewhere. Although the plank road movement proved a short-lived experiment, any success enjoyed by Fayetteville redounded to the benefit of Wilmington due to the trade nexus between the two river towns.[32]

Although Wilmington helped to initiate the plank road movement, the port did not realize the success of Fayetteville, in part because the Northwest and Northeast Cape Fear rivers served as admirable arteries of trade. The Wilmington and Masonboro and the Wilmington and Walker's Ferry companies apparently produced few results. More successful was the Wilmington and Top Sail Sound Plank Road Company, chartered in 1851 and organized in 1852. The twelve-mile road running east from Wilmington via Market Street through heavy sand toward the Onslow County line increased the flow of traffic from Onslow and the northern part of New Hanover County. The Wilmington town commissioners permitted the company to extend the plank road from the town limits through Market Street to Second Street after which the town assumed responsibility for maintenance. The company secured a charter in 1855 to extend the plank road to Sneads Ferry in Onslow, but no record exists of its construction.[33]

In addition to road construction and maintenance, bridging remained difficult, given the scattered population in the countryside surrounding Wilmington, numerous low-lying areas, and periodic floods that carried away existing structures. The lack of bridges, like poor roads, elevated the cost of transportation and sometimes prevented farmers from driving livestock to Wilmington for sale. To encourage the construction of an appropriate span over Smith's Creek, the General Assembly in 1808 invested John Blanks with a toll bridge at the site for fifty years to replace the previous structure. Hilton Bridge, the other major bridge in that vicinity, was rendered a "free bridge," open to all without charge, when Wilmington businessmen in the 1830s raised money through private subscription and a benefit performance by the Thalian Association to bridge the Northeast Cape Fear River. When replacing the bridge in the mid–1850s, the New Hanover County Court used public funds, aided by private subscriptions of $1,000, to continue the free bridge. Farther north, Heron's Bridge, or the "Big Bridge" as it was called, across the Northeast Cape Fear, was destroyed by the British during the Revolution but subsequently rebuilt. Of course, that bridge, like the others when non-operational, was replaced by a ferry. And travel west and south from Wilmington to Eagles Island and beyond always relied upon ferriage to cross the rivers, a slow, cumbersome, and expensive means of transportation.[34]

Canals also offered an opportunity to improve Wilmington's trade. North Carolina, in conjunction with Virginia, early experimented with the

Dismal Swamp Canal, which linked the Albemarle Sound with the Chesapeake Bay, but it was a qualified success. In the southeast the Cape Fear River attracted attention. Efforts first centered on Brunswick County, where the Smithville Canal Company, incorporated in 1805, intended to build a canal from Lockwoods Folly to the Elizabeth River, which emptied into the Cape Fear. That would have allowed Lockwoods Folly residents a safer passage to market in Wilmington, as opposed to exiting a narrow inlet to the Atlantic Ocean in order to reach the Cape Fear River. The effort was renewed in 1811 when the legislature permitted a company to raise $5,000 by lottery to build the canal. Four years later the Cape Fear Canal Company, authorized to charge tolls as means of recouping its expenditures, was permitted to cut a canal from Masonboro Sound to the Cape Fear River at the Haulover.[35] However, no substantive results derived from those efforts.

After the War of 1812, Archibald D. Murphey, the farsighted Orange County state legislator, proposed utilizing canals to help create an integrated internal improvements system in North Carolina that would divert trade from Virginia and South Carolina by concentrating traffic on North Carolina ports. In the southern region of the state Murphey suggested using canals to unite the Catawba, Yadkin-Pee Dee, Lumber, and Cape Fear Rivers, depending upon the last to provide an outlet for commerce. In 1816 the General Assembly incorporated the Lumber River Canal Company to construct canals to link the Cape Fear and Lumber rivers and the Lumber and Yadkin Rivers. In 1819, following a legislative attempt to revive the Lumber River Canal Company, stock subscriptions were sought in Wilmington, Fayetteville, Rockingham, Wadesboro, Allenton, and Rowan County, but without success.[36]

The failure to prosecute the early Yadkin, Lumber, and Cape Fear canal operations dampened enthusiasm for several years, but in 1845 the General Assembly sought again to establish a canal from the Cape Fear to the Lumber River, and in 1847 from the Cape Fear to the Yadkin River. The latter, involving the Yadkin and Cape Fear Canal Company, generated considerable interest, but cautious observers suggested surveying the route of the canal before inviting stock subscriptions to the company. To raise money for the survey, committees were organized in Moore, Montgomery, Randolph, Davidson, Rowan, Davie, Surry, Wilkes, and Stanly Counties, as well as in Fayetteville and Wilmington. However, the work never advanced beyond the proposal to survey the route, for it was undermined largely by the chartering of railroads by Virginia, South Carolina, and North Carolina that provided other avenues for the export of Yadkin Valley produce.[37]

Improving the navigability of the Cape Fear River to permit deeper draft vessels and steamer traffic added immeasurably to the economic potential of Wilmington. In 1792 the General Assembly chartered the Cape Fear Company to "render safe and easy" navigation of the Cape Fear from Fayetteville to the confluence of the Deep and Haw Rivers, a distance of some 98 miles. Legislation in 1796 superseded the previous statute by incorporating the Deep and Haw River Company to improve navigation from Averasboro in Harnett County above Fayetteville to the meeting of the Deep and Haw Rivers. Subsequently, the legislature in 1811 incorporated the Cape Fear Navigation Company to work on the Cape Fear from the mouth of Cross Creek at Fayetteville downriver to Wilmington. After the company had expended money from its stock subscriptions and a lottery authorized by the legislature, the courts of the counties along the river were instructed to appoint overseers and workers to remove obstructions from the river.[38]

Legislation in 1815 merged the Cape Fear Navigation Company with the Deep and Haw River Company, retaining the former's name. The resulting company received a state stock subscription of $15,000 and was authorized to work the entire length of the river, from its mouth to the Deep and Haw, and then as far as navigation was feasible. The Cape Fear Navigation Company opened its book for subscriptions in March 1816, purchased flats, equipment, and slaves, and commenced work in August, principally between Fayetteville and Wilmington. Improvements to the river by 1819 justified (in the estimation of the company) the imposition of tolls on vessels using the river, which in turn resulted in the payment of the company's first dividend.[39]

During the ensuing decade the Cape Fear Navigation Company concentrated its efforts on the river from Fayetteville to Wilmington, removing large numbers of logs, overhanging trees, and branches; sluicing; and building an occasional dam. In 1823 the General Assembly committed the state to subscribe to an additional $25,000 in stock—on two conditions. First, the company must yield its claim to the river below Wilmington, because the state wanted to undertake improvements in that area, believing that the cost involved was beyond the capability of the company. Second, the company would have to place its operations under the supervision of the Board of Internal Improvements and the state's civil engineer. The company quickly accepted the conditions of the state's proposed stock subscription. Almost immediately, however, opposition to the state's involvement in internal improvements threatened the subscription and forced the resignation of the civil engineer. That prompted the company to remind the legislature of the profitability of navigation improvements to stockholders, including the state, the utility of the operations for those using the river, and the necessity (as experience had shown) in North Carolina and around the nation for government support to ensure the success of internal improvements projects. Although the General Assembly persevered, a recession in the late 1820s prevented North Carolina from fulfilling its $25,000 commitment until 1833.[40]

The company appreciated the guidance offered by the state. Initially the president and directors had embarked upon a business that was "totally new—at all events, new to them—having no path marked out before them, they were under the necessity of exploring their way, guided only by the suggestions of their own minds...." The company proceeded to open the river from Fayetteville to Wilmington to regular steamboat traffic, in addition to rendering passage easier for the usual rafts and pole boats. The value of freight shipped on the river increased from an annual average of $26,410.81 between 1824 and 1828 to $28,613.97 between 1832 and 1836. Work went more slowly between Fayetteville and the junction of the Deep and Haw Rivers. At the end of the 1830s, the company contended that the river from Averasboro "afforded a tolerable navigation for such Batteaus [sic] as could pass the Canals and Locks at Buckhorn Falls to Fayetteville."[41]

The state continued to foster the economic development of the upper reaches of the Cape Fear River that in turn would have redounded to the benefit of Wilmington. Hoping to open access to the naval stores of the region, and particularly to the iron and coal deposits of Chatham County, the General Assembly in 1849 incorporated the Cape Fear and Deep River Navigation Company. In addition to charging tolls for remuneration, the company also received the privilege of operating boats on the river to transport passengers and freight. The state subsidized the venture. But from the outset, the company experienced difficulty in securing a competent contractor for the work. And despite an infusion of state money, the company seemed always in financial straits. Moreover, freshets posed a constant danger to any improvements.[42]

Despite repeated financial bailouts from the state in the 1850s, the Cape Fear and Deep River Navigation Company finally admitted defeat. It had collected only a minuscule amount of money from tolls in 1851–1852 on naval stores, wood products, corn, and nails. Some naval stores passed through its locks on the river in 1857. But shippers preferred to wait for high water to raft over the locks rather than to pay the tolls. The state purchased the company for $365,000 in 1859, changed its name to the Cape Fear and Deep River Navigation Works, and hired an engineer to finish the job. After additional state investment and considerable tribulation, the engineer in September 1860 claimed that the river was open to commerce. Yet a series of freshets in November severely damaged the operations. The legislature thereafter limited expenditures on the river and tried to sell the company. At the approach of the Civil War the governor suspended all work. The state failed to pursue river improvements after the war and found a purchaser for the works in 1873.[43]

The Cape Fear Navigation Company continued its efforts up to the Civil War, but the company commanded a far more limited scope of operations than that permitted by the original charter of incorporation. After abnegating the Cape Fear below Wilmington in 1823, the company in 1830 yielded its claims to the tributary streams above Wilmington and, in 1852, its claims to the Cape Fear above Fayetteville as a result of the formation of the Cape Fear and Deep River Navigation Company. Still, such divestitures left the Cape Fear company in control of the most profitable section of the river, that between Fayetteville and Wilmington. Criticism persisted, for one writer in 1845 asked why was navigation between the towns "more uncertain than it used to be! Where are the improvements and works of the 'Navigation Company!' What is that Company doing!" Annual reports of the company showed that it remained active removing logs, stumps, trees, and debris from the river channel each year. Freight subject to tolls in 1852, valued at $67,268.83, amounted to more than twice the value of freight in any year in the 1820s and 1830s. Steadily increasing traffic on the Cape Fear River in the 1840s and 1850s, particularly in the form of steamboats and their lighters, attested to the success of the Cape Fear Navigation Company.[44]

The state undertook the improvement of the channel and bar at the mouth of the Cape Fear River below Wilmington. The General Assembly initially underwrote the effort, which cost $39,730 between 1822 and 1829. The state engineer tried to enlarge the main channel of the river by closing minor channels and dredging shoals. Deeming the project too expensive, the General Assembly sought the support of the national government. Congress considered North Carolina's request favorably, appropriating $202,627 for river improvements from 1829 to 1839, to be undertaken by the U.S. Army Corps of Engineers. By the end of 1839, when federal funding ceased, the Corps had significantly deepened the river channel. As a result, Wilmington shipping noticeably increased.[45]

The Cape Fear below Wilmington again became the scene of federal activity in the 1850s, principally because the inability of larger ships to navigate the bar and river threatened the future of the port. Wilmingtonians spearheaded the effort, holding a meeting in 1852 to encourage the state's congressional delegation to support the effort. North Carolina's congressmen could only squeeze $20,000 from the national government in

1853, enough to permit the Corps of Engineers to begin preliminary work. To maintain enthusiasm for river improvements in Wilmington, a Committee of Thirteen was created in the port. In conjunction with local authorities, the committee invited A. D. Bache, superintendent of the United States Coast Survey, to Wilmington. At a public gathering in 1853 Bache pictured a dismal prospect for Wilmington shipping if improvements were not quickly forthcoming.[46]

The Bache-led meeting concluded with a resolution to collect $60,000 locally to supplement the $20,000 congressional appropriation. Within a month, subscriptions to raise the money had been pledged. The movement to seek additional funding received a stimulus from a river improvements convention in Wilmington in 1854. Numerous county gatherings from as far away as Guilford, Alamance, and Chatham and as near as Wayne, Bladen, Cumberland, and Sampson supported the effort and sent delegates to the Wilmington meeting. Governor David S. Reid chaired the convention, which memorialized North Carolina congressmen to continue to press for federal aid. Congress responded with an appropriation of $140,000 in 1854 to improve the entrance to the river by erecting jetties at Bald Head and by closing the beaches between Smith and Zeke Islands.[47]

Work on the project had commenced in 1853, based on the earlier appropriation of $20,000, and proceeded apace until 1857, when a three-day gale in September negated much of the jetty construction at New Inlet and, in fact, opened two new beaches south of the inlet. Government study commissions later in the year and in 1858 concluded that before the storm the works had been effective, that the jetties should be rebuilt, and that New Inlet should be closed in three years. Although work was not immediately resumed, the government gained valuable experience that guided its efforts after the Civil War in closing New Inlet.[48]

Congress funded other improvements to shipping along the Cape Fear River, including lighthouses and beacons. After the War of 1812 a beacon was erected at Federal Point to guard New Inlet. A lighthouse replaced the beacon in 1837. Congress appropriated $15,000 in 1816 to replace the lighthouse on Bald Head Island. The 109-foot structure was operational by 1817 or 1818 and remains the oldest standing lighthouse in North Carolina. Federal funding in 1848 provided for a series of markers and lights, from the main bar at the mouth of the Cape Fear River to Wilmington, to outline the river channel. The program included buoys, beacons, small lighthouses, and a lightship. All were in place in 1855, at which time the Cape Fear River and its channel were finally marked properly.[49]

Steam navigation greatly aided North Carolina's quest to improve its transportation network, and no section of the state benefited more than the Cape Fear region. The emergence of steam on North Carolina waters was an extension of the pioneering efforts of numerous American inventors and entrepreneurs of the late eighteenth and early nineteenth centuries. The first successful steamboat in the state was the *Norfolk*, owned by the Newbern Steam Boat Company, which arrived in New Bern in April 1818. The company hoped to use the *Norfolk* for passenger runs between New Bern and Elizabeth City, but the venture was abandoned in July 1818. During the ensuing four decades, however, steam vessels appeared throughout eastern North Carolina's sounds and rivers, but found their greatest success on the Cape Fear River.[50]

Coincident with the abortive efforts of the Newbern Steam Boat Company was the attempt of James Seawell and associates to institute steam navigation on the Cape Fear. The General Assembly in 1818 approved Seawell's petition for a seven-year monopoly on steam traffic between Fayetteville and Wilmington, provided that he maintain a steamboat on the river at all times and that he charge 10 percent less for freight than current rates. Seawell put two steamers on the river that year. The first was the *Henrietta*, built by Seawell in 1817–1818 on his plantation about three miles beyond Fayetteville and launched on April 30, 1818. The *Henrietta* made weekly runs between Wilmington and Fayetteville. The *Prometheus*, built in Swansboro by Otway Burns, famed privateer of the War of 1812, was towed to Wilmington, where it was outfitted with its engine and other equipment. Although the *Prometheus* provided transportation for President James Monroe when he visited Wilmington in 1819, the steamer soon disappeared, leaving the river to the *Henrietta*. Seawell and associates formalized their business arrangement by incorporating the Cape Fear Steam Boat Company in 1822. The company expanded its operations in 1823, adding the steamer *North Carolina* and three steamboat flats to the run of the *Henrietta*. By 1826, however, the Seawell monopoly on steamer traffic on the Cape Fear River had ended.[51]

When the Cape Fear River opened competitively after the expiration of Seawell's monopoly, aspiring entrepreneurs moved quickly to take advantage of the opportunity. The *Henrietta* remained on the river, apparently purchased by Doyle O'Hanlon of Wilmington and two Fayetteville businessmen, who in 1827 obtained a charter of incorporation from the General Assembly for the Henrietta Steam Boat Company. At the same time, the legislature chartered the Cotton Plant Steam Boat Company, composed of Wilmington and Fayetteville businessmen. The steamer *Cotton Plant*, built by Duncan Thompson, one of the incorporators, measured 108 by 16½ feet and was launched from Thompson's boatyard below Clarendon Bridge

The *Prometheus*, one of the first steamboats on the Cape Fear River, 1819. The vessel was built by Otway Burns in Swansboro, North Carolina, and towed to Wilmington, where it was outfitted with its engine. Drawing courtesy of the New Hanover County Public Library, Wilmington.

in Fayetteville in April 1826. The *Henrietta*, the *North Carolina*, and the *Cotton Plant* ran the river infrequently for the remainder of the decade.[52]

Additional steamers appeared on the Cape Fear in the 1830s. Joining the *Henrietta* and the *Cotton Plant* in 1831 was the *John Walker*, the first steamer built in Wilmington, which was used between Wilmington and Fayetteville until it succumbed to an explosion in 1836. As early as 1833 the *Clarendon* of the Clarendon Company entered the river trade but apparently was moved to the Savannah River in Georgia in 1838. The *Duncan McRae*, originally intended for service on the Pee Dee River in South Carolina, replaced the *John Walker* and may have been owned by Duncan McRae of Fayetteville, who in 1839 secured a charter for the Cape Fear and Western Steam Boat Company. And in 1836–1837, the steamer *Wilmington* of the New York Line, owned by one Captain Dougal of Wilmington, worked the river in conjunction with the sailing packets *Carolina* and *Caleb Nichols*. The packets undertook ocean transport between New York and Wilmington; the steamer *Wilmington* conveyed goods from Wilmington to Fayetteville.[53]

The following decades saw steamer traffic increase rapidly. The Henrietta company, after adding the *Fayetteville* in 1842 and the light-draft *Evergreen* in 1845, was reincorporated in 1847. The Cotton Plant company, of which O'Hanlon had become the proprietor, was sold in 1845 to a group of Fayetteville men, renamed the Merchants' Steam Boat Company, and incorporated in 1847 under that name. In addition to the steamer *Cotton Plant*, it owned the *William B. Meares*, launched in 1844 by O'Hanlon, and the *Rowan*, which appeared on the river in 1846. The Cape Fear Steam Boat Company, organized in 1848, put the *Gov. Graham* on the river in that year, received a charter of incorporation from the legislature in 1849, and was purchased by Dibble and Brother late in that year. During the 1850s the Cape Fear between Wilmington and Fayetteville fairly teemed with steamers. In 1851 eight worked the river, sometimes with timber rafts and as many as three lighters in tow. The *Fayetteville Observer* listed five major steamboat lines on the Cape Fear in 1854, at which time the number of steamers on the river had increased to 15. Although the number declined slightly in ensuing years, 13 steamers traveled back and forth between Wilmington and Fayetteville in 1857 and 1860 respectively.[54]

In the Wilmington harbor and downriver, steamers proved useful for salvaging and towing operations. In 1851 the steam tugboat *Fayetteville* went to the aid of the brig *Thetia* from England, which was lying off the main bar, "to lighter her up and bring her in." In 1857 the steamer *Henrietta* rescued the barque *J. W. Blodgett*, which ran ashore near New Inlet, and brought the vessel to Wilmington. A month later two steamers pulled the ship *John Ravel* off the bar of the Cape Fear River.[55] The most active of the steam tugs in the late 1850s was the *Mariner*, which may have belonged to the Wilmington Steam Tug Company, incorporated in 1855. When the *Col. John McRae* sprang a leak at Frying Pan Shoals after leaving Wilmington in November 1857, the *Mariner* brought the barque back to port for repairs. And in 1860 the *Mariner* salvaged goods from the wreck of the brig *Alexander Wise*.[56]

Steamer transport below Wilmington proved far less extensive than above the port. After its appearance in 1818, the *Prometheus* may have ventured to Smithville (present Southport) on occasion, and in 1832 one of the Cape Fear steamers may have been involved in carrying mail from Wilmington to Smithville. Later, if the *C. D. McNair* ran to Smithville in 1837 as proposed, it was a short-lived experiment. Perhaps precluding the need for such a connection were the steamships belonging to the Wilmington and Raleigh (Weldon) Railroad Company, which stopped at Smithville as they traveled to and from Charleston. The first sustained route between Wilmington and Smithville occurred when Wilmington merchant A. H. Van Bokkelin put the *Spray* on the run as early as 1853, advertising four trips weekly between the river towns, with stops at Orton. After the railroad steamships terminated their operations in 1854, Van Bokkelin obtained a charter of incorporation from the legislature for the Wilmington and Smithville Steamboat Company and continued the *Spray* on that route through October 1857.[57]

With the exception of canal traffic to Virginia, North Carolina rather tardily embraced interstate steam navigation. While steamships regularly plied the Atlantic waters soon after the end of the War of 1812, connecting northern and southern ports, including Baltimore, Norfolk, Charleston, and Savannah, ocean steamers only incidentally called on North Carolina. As early as 1821 and 1826, respectively, the *Commerce*, bound from Philadelphia to Georgetown, and the *Carolina*, Savannah to New York, put into the Cape Fear for wood. In the mid–1830s the *Virginia*, running between Norfolk and Charleston, visited Smithville, and the *Dolphin*, connecting the same ports, stopped at Smithville and then at Beaufort, passing through Core Sound and exiting by way of Ocracoke Inlet. At the end of the decade, steamers from Charleston occasionally called at Wilmington.[58] However, North Carolina's early oceangoing steam navigation centered almost entirely upon the steamship line of the Wilmington and Raleigh Railroad.

The General Assembly, in amending the charter of the Wilmington and Raleigh Railroad in 1835, permitted the company to operate steam ships in conjunction with the railroad. Although the railroad was not finished until 1840, the company moved quickly, putting two steamers on line in 1837 between Wilmington and Charleston. The *Boston* undertook a trial run in early May, but soon developed mechanical problems and resumed a regular schedule only in October. Joining the *Boston* two months later was the *North Carolina*, which impressed Wilmingtonians with its speed, for it was able to make a round trip to Charleston in 29½ hours, including a stopover in Charleston of 2½ hours. By providing a conveyance for passengers and freight to and from South Carolina, the company enhanced the potential use of the railroad. At the same time, the connection enabled the company to procure a mail contract from the United States government that provided needed revenue.[59]

Eventually the Wilmington and Raleigh put four steamers on line. The *Boston* proved unsatisfactory and was replaced by the *Gov. Dudley*, a 487-ton, New York–built craft that measured 175 feet on deck, 165 in the keel, and 24 feet in the beam. Rounding out the complement of four were the *C. Vanderbilt* and the *Wilmington*, which arrived in December 1838 and September 1839, respectively. Subsequently, the *Gladiator* replaced the

North Carolina, which sank after a collision with the *Gov. Dudley* in July 1840 about thirty miles northeast of Georgetown. The mail contract, which necessitated daily communication between Wilmington and Charleston after January 1, 1839, took its toll on the steamships. Although the company used four vessels, often only three were operational, while the fourth underwent repairs. The Wilmington and Raleigh discontinued the steamers in 1854 when the completion of the Wilmington and Manchester Railroad offered an uninterrupted rail connection through North and South Carolina to Charleston.[60]

Other than the railroad line, steamer connections between North Carolina and the Atlantic community continued to consist of sporadic contacts, principally with the Lower Cape Fear, which had always served Atlantic shipping as a port of refuge. Adverse weather forced the *Express*, Charleston to Philadelphia, to put in at Smithville in 1845. The *Jasper*, bound from Georgetown to Providence in 1854, stopped for water. By midcentury steamships irregularly came to Wilmington as merchants used them to supplement sailing craft. The *Propeller* of Baltimore brought goods to merchant George Harriss in 1851. Three years later the *Reliance* from Hartford, Connecticut, came to the wharf of William Neff and Son, and the *Calhoun* shipped merchandise to DeRosset and Brown. In 1854, at the retirement of the railroad steamers, Charlestonians attempted to revive a regular packet between their port and Wilmington, but subsequently only occasional steamers arrived from South Carolina, including the *Gen. Clinch* in 1857 and the *St. Mary's* in 1860. In the latter year the *Etiwan* from Georgetown also appeared in Wilmington; and the *Carolina* from Fernandina, Florida, periodically brought passengers and freight to the Cape Fear port.[61]

The establishment of interstate packets linking North Carolina to the Atlantic world began haltingly in Wilmington in the mid–1850s, and encompassed the Albemarle, Beaufort, and New Bern by the Civil War. In December 1854 Wilmingtonians greeted the *North Carolina*, a 700-ton steamship measuring 177 by 34 feet that intended to operate regularly between Philadelphia and Wilmington, but that trial proved disappointing. More successful was the establishment in June 1860 of a run by the *Parkersburg* between New York and Wilmington. Owned by the Cape Fear Ocean Steamship Navigation Company, which had been incorporated by the General Assembly in 1859, the *Parkersburg* made weekly round trips, requiring 65 hours each way, in which the steamship brought merchandise to Wilmington and returned with naval stores and a wide variety of other produce of the Lower Cape Fear. Competition for the Cape Fear Ocean Steamship Navigation Company appeared at the end of 1860 when the Wilmington and Weldon Railroad announced its intention to launch a line of "first class Steam Ships between Wilmington and New York, via Philadelphia."[62]

In addition to improvements to the navigability of the Cape Fear River and the advent of steam travel, the railroad contributed mightily to the economic growth and prosperity of Wilmington. The earliest successful railroads in North Carolina were Virginia lines connecting Petersburg and Portsmouth to the Roanoke River in the vicinity of Weldon. But in its 1831–1832 session the General Assembly chartered the Cape Fear and Yadkin Valley Railroad, designed to attract trade from the Yadkin Valley to Fayetteville and thence to Wilmington. Unfortunately, the proposed railroad exacerbated the rivalry between Fayetteville and Wilmington, because the former feared a loss of trade by a railroad to the New Hanover port. More than $100,000 in stock was subscribed in the Cape Fear region, about two-thirds of which was taken in Wilmington, but the total was far less than the $300,000 required by law to incorporate the company. Thus those who had collected the money notified subscribers in the spring of 1833 that they might obtain their funds due to the failure of incorporation.[63]

Hopes revived in Wilmington, however, when the General Assembly, in its legislative session of 1833–1834, chartered the Wilmington and Raleigh Railroad and empowered it to build a line from the port to the state capital. Inaction followed, and the company failed to organize; but in 1835 the legislature amended the charter, permitting the company to connect with the Virginia railroads in the vicinity of Weldon, allowing the road to operate steamships, and increasing its capitalization from $800,000 to $1,500,000 to accommodate the alterations. Wilmingtonians acted precipitately, subscribing to a quarter-million dollars of stock by the end of February 1836. Another $20,000 was subscribed by those living along the prospective route, which all agreed must be to Weldon rather than to Raleigh. The company started construction at both ends of the line, Weldon and Wilmington, connecting the track with stagecoaches. By May 1837 it had also purchased a steamboat, and others were in the offing. At that time the General Assembly agreed to purchase two-fifths of the stock in the company in four installments of 25 percent, each payable when corresponding private subscriptions had been paid. According to the president of the Wilmington and Raleigh, "The confidence imparted to the work by the action of the State, has had the most salutary influence; and individuals, no longer deterred by the apprehension of hazard, have been most free in manifesting that confidence, by large and liberal subscriptions."[64]

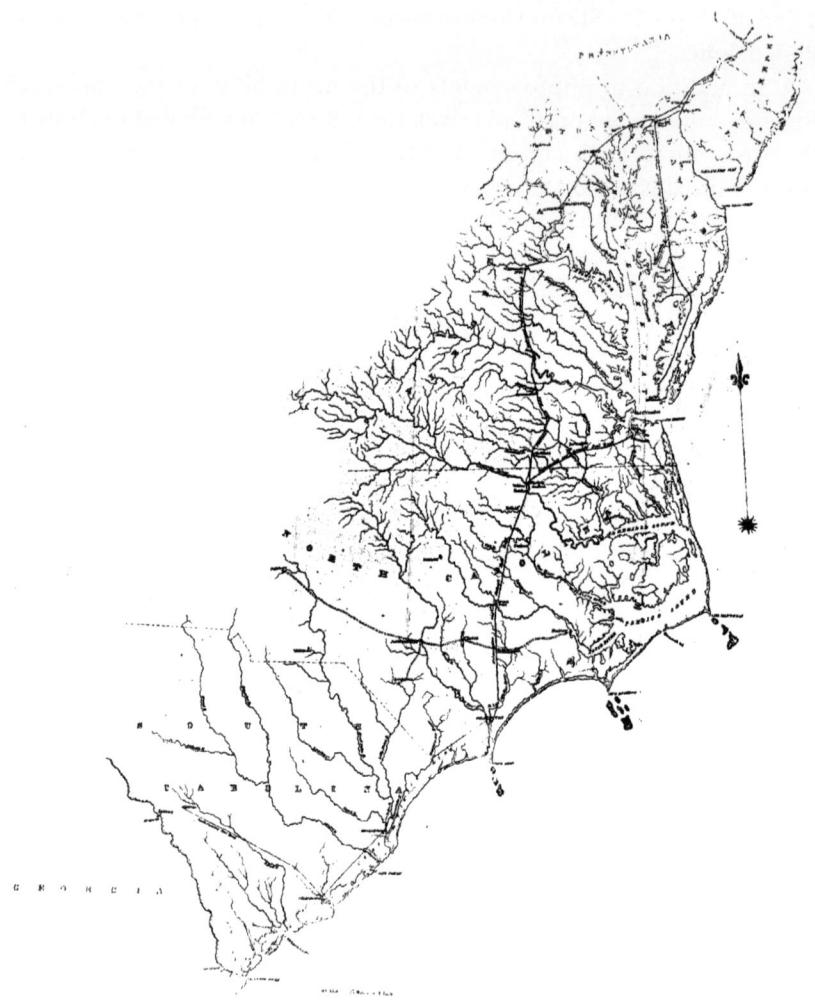

Map showing the route of the partially constructed Wilmington and Raleigh (Weldon) Railroad, 1838, whose completion in 1840 provided a connection by rail and water from northern states to Charleston, South Carolina. Courtesy of the North Carolina Office of Archives and History, Raleigh.

Meanwhile, the Wilmington and Raleigh began to lay track and tout the advantages of a route from Baltimore to Charleston, using trains, Chesapeake Bay steamers, Virginia railroads, and the Wilmington and Raleigh and its steamers to Charleston. English actress Frances Anne (Fanny) Kemble in 1838 passed through the state on the half-finished railroad from Weldon to Wilmington. Soon after twelve midnight, the train from Weldon stopped, and Kemble and her party were informed that they would have to take stage, "so in the dead middle of the night we crept out of the train, ... [and] walked a few yards ... [to] where three four-horses coaches stood waiting to receive us." The road traversed marshes "through which we splashed, with hardly any intermission, the whole night long." Below Waynesborough the next day the passengers were forced to alight to walk over the Neuse River bridge, which was deemed too rotten to support the coach and passengers together. About sunset Kemble reached the point where the tracks had been built from Wilmington. While waiting for the train, she was surrounded by "a troop of gazing boors.... A more forlorn, fierce, poor, and wild-looking set of people, short of absolute savages, I never saw." Kemble finally reached Wilmington at five o'clock the following morning.[65]

The last spike in the Wilmington and Raleigh was driven on March 7, 1840, completing a 161-mile railroad that reputedly was the longest in the world at that time. The cost of the road was determined to be $1,909,755.54, including the investment in four steamships that connected Wilmington and Charleston. The Wilmington and Raleigh immediately moved remunerative. From May 1 to November 1, 1840, receipts exceeded expenditures by $63,360.60, and net operating income continued to be positive throughout the decade. The railroad depended largely on passenger traffic and mail revenues at the outset, but freight transport increased during the ensuing decade. In 1855 the General Assembly changed its name to the Wilmington and Weldon Railroad to reflect the true geography of its line. Five years later the Wilmington and Weldon instituted a steamship line between Wilmington and New York in order to enhance its competitive position vis-à-vis Norfolk, Charleston, and Savannah, all of which had connections with northern ports.[66]

Wilmington's second railroad originated in the mid–1840s after the General Assembly chartered a rail line to connect the Raleigh and Gaston Railroad in North Carolina to South Carolina, which might ultimately provide a linkage to Charleston. Facing the possibility of an interior railroad from the North to Charleston, Wilmingtonians feared that their town might be bypassed and that the Wilmington and Weldon would be rendered a local railroad. Although the North Carolina-South Carolina road failed to materialize, Wilmingtonians explored the prospects of constructing a railroad from their port to the interior of South Carolina, at which a link might be found to Charleston. South Carolinians in Sumterville greeted enthusiastically a proposal to build a line from Wilmington to Fair Bluff (near the South Carolina line) to Sumterville, and then to Manchester on the Camden and Gadsden Railroad, which was then under contract. The General Assembly responded to that interest in 1847 by chartering the Wilmington and Manchester Railroad.[67]

The Wilmington and Manchester proved to be a project mainly of Wilmington and South Carolina residents. Those in Wilmington and its vicinity subscribed to some $200,000 worth of stock in the company. After considerable debate, Wilmingtonians sought and received from the General Assembly permission for the town commissioners to take an additional $100,000 worth of stock on behalf of the town. For its part, the legislature transferred one-third of the state's shares in the Wilmington and Weldon Railroad to the Wilmington and Manchester, allowing the sale of that stock to raise money for the Wilmington and Manchester. Work on the railroad commenced in 1849 in Brunswick County, west of the Brunswick River ferry, and concluded in 1854. At the outbreak of the Civil War the eastern terminus had been extended to Eagles Island in the Cape Fear River. The harbor steamer *George L. Champion* (until it burned in 1857) and *Clarendon* transported passengers and freight for both the Wilmington and Manchester and the Wilmington and Weldon Railroads among Wilmington, Eagles Island, and the west side of the river in Brunswick County.[68]

During the late 1850s the Wilmington and Manchester Railroad, faced a mixed future. The depressed economy, competition from newly opened railroads in neighboring states, and the reduction of steamship rates between South Carolina and Georgia and northern states cut into its business. However, a report for the fiscal year ending September 30, 1859, revealed a road that was paying dividends and reducing its bonded indebtedness. Receipts amounted to $427,000, of which 38 percent derived from freight transport, 11 percent from mail carriage, and most of the remainder from passenger traffic. Moreover, according to a correspondent to the *Daily Herald*, the construction of the railroad had contributed materially to the economy of Wilmington, and property values had been enhanced even more than originally predicted by its advocates. Of course, the times were "dull," but the railroads had materially softened their impact on Wilmington.[69]

As the Wilmington and Manchester neared completion, Wilmingtonians began to contemplate a road to tap the trade of western North Carolina counties whose commerce naturally gravitated to South Carolina. Charlotte proved agreeable. A convention in the Mecklenburg town in 1854 proposed a railroad from Wilmington to Charlotte; a subsequent meeting in Wilmington endorsed the idea. The General Assembly obliged in 1855 by incorporating the Wilmington and Charlotte Railroad to run from the vicinity of Wilmington through Lumberton, Rockingham,

Wadesboro, and Monroe to Charlotte. Later in the same session the lawmakers amended the statute to incorporate the Wilmington, Charlotte and Rutherford Railroad, raising the capitalization of the company from one to three million dollars, and permitting an extension of the line from Charlotte to Rutherfordton.[70]

The company organized in October 1855, but work progressed slowly, and only a portion of the railroad had been finished by the outbreak of the war. The state again offered financial assistance, providing a subsidy of $8,000 per mile. By a vote of 531 to 103, residents of Wilmington authorized the town commissioners to subscribe to $200,000 in company stock on behalf of the town. The first cargo of track for the railroad arrived in May 1859; the first locomotive appeared two months later. Still, only 24 miles of track had been laid from the eastern terminus by December 1859. In January 1861 the railroad extended to Moss Neck in Robeson County. Work from the western terminus was delayed, no doubt by fears in Rutherfordton that the railroad would hurt the community by taking away its wagon trade, a commerce deemed "necessary to sustain the prosperity of an inland town."[71]

The internal improvements movement and advances in transportation arguably benefited Wilmington more than any town in North Carolina, reinforcing its dominant position as the center of commerce in the state, as seen in Table 1.

TABLE 1
Tonnage Entering and Clearing North Carolina Ports
July 1, 1849–June 30, 1850

	Domestic		Foreign	
	Entrances	*Clearances*	*Entrances*	*Clearances*
Wilmington	11,555	19,718	9,115	11,380
New Bern	2,664	3,643		
Washington	2,118	1,372		
Edenton		131		
Camden	2,170	2,945		
Plymouth	1,205	2,175		113
Beaufort	473	755		

Source: *The New American State Papers*, 32:693–697.

Improvements to the navigability of the Cape Fear River from above Fayetteville to its mouth substantially enhanced the shipping potential of the port, more especially in conjunction with the advent of steam vessels. Railroads revolutionized land travel, and Wilmington, as the terminus of three lines, drew upon an even greater hinterland for trade. Compared to other south Atlantic ports, Wilmington held its own vis-à-vis Virginia but suffered in comparison with South Carolina and Georgia, as seen in Table 2.

Table 2
Tonnage Entered and Cleared at Major Atlantic Ports
July 1, 1849–June 30, 1850

| | *Domestic* | | *Foreign* | |
	Entrances	*Clearances*	*Entrances*	*Clearances*
Norfolk	6,415	18,283	7,866	8,482
Wilmington	11,555	19,718	9,115	11,380
Charleston	52,414	68,537	44,205	52,830
Savannah	11,883	21,039	45,134	51,524

Source: *The New American State Papers*, 17:664, 32:693–94, 697.

Nonetheless, Wilmington remained predominant in North Carolina, and during the Civil War revealed its indispensable value as a shipping entrepôt for the Confederate States of America.

11

Antebellum Politics

After North Carolina ratified the federal Constitution and joined the Union in 1789, the state politically embraced the new nation. The majority of the state legislature in 1790, the two United States senators, and four of five members of the House of Representatives had favored the Constitution. Significantly, the exception in the House was Timothy Bloodworth of New Hanover County, who represented the Cape Fear congressional district. Very quickly, however, North Carolinians began to revert to their staunch advocacy of states rights and suspicion of national authority.

That Antifederalist orientation became clearer in the early 1790s, a circumstance occasioned in large part by a division in the state—and nation—over the propriety of the financial program of Secretary of the Treasury Alexander Hamilton. Proponents of the Hamiltonian program, or Federalists, espoused a powerful, active national government that would foster commerce and industry, and protect property. Federalists also admired the orderly, hierarchical society of England, where civic virtue superseded individual self-interest and the people generally deferred to a wealthy, educated elite for governance. The opposition, styled Jeffersonian Republicans, Democratic Republicans, or just simply Republicans, represented the masses, admired French republicanism (though not its excesses), trusted more in the democratic political process, and viewed with suspicion national authority, preferring instead to rely upon state and local government.

As the Jeffersonian Republicans gradually took control of the state, the Federalists exhibited their greatest strength in three areas: the upper Cape Fear Valley, or the Fayetteville congressional district; the central coastal area around New Bern; and several borough towns, including Wilmington, that sent representatives to the General Assembly.[1] Still, Wilmingtonians early sympathized with the French during their war with

England in the 1790s. Despite President George Washington's Proclamation of Neutrality in 1793, Wilmington briefly served as a base for the French privateer *L'Aimee Marguerite*, which brought a prize to port late in the year. Upon the rumor that the privateer and its prize were to be seized, the pro–French Wilmingtonians rushed the vessels from port so hurriedly that the prize left one of its anchors. The next year the privateer was detained on the order of Washington, but residents of Wilmington and the county clearly supported the French cause.[2]

The undeclared war with France in 1798 and the refusal of the Republicans to support military preparedness led to a revival of the Federalist Party in North Carolina, though the Federalists still remained the minority party. Upon the political "revolution" brought by the elections of 1800, the Republicans took firm command of the national government. Their control over North Carolina was never again threatened, though the Federalists maintained a stronger political presence in North Carolina than in any other southern state.[3] Federalist opposition to the war with England in 1812 found sympathy in North Carolina, where many Republicans also objected to the conflict. Yet the successful conclusion of the War of 1812 greatly discredited the Federalists, who disbanded as a national organization after their loss in the presidential election of 1816.

Republicans and Federalists found support in Wilmington, though the latter controlled the town at the outset. Most, if not all, of Wilmington's borough delegates to the house of commons represented the Federalist Party. One of them was the very popular Joshua Grainger Wright, who served from 1792 to 1795 and from 1799 to 1808 and occupied the speakership of the house in 1807 and 1804.[4] Nonetheless, the Republicans formed a Republican Society of Wilmington to further their cause.[5] And newspapers emerged to support both parties. The *Wilmington Gazette*, Federalist to 1800, turned Republican from 1801 to 1808, then reverted to Federalism. During the Republican interlude, the *Cape Fear Herald* espoused the Federalist cause. And in 1809 the *True Republican* appeared as the propaganda organ of the Republican Party.

Although politics seriously divided Wilmingtonians throughout the antebellum years, most in the town united in welcoming prominent national visitors, among whom was George Washington, who appeared in April 1791 on his famous southern tour. The Wilmington troop of horse met the president about 12 miles from town; the "gentlemen" of Wilmington, about six miles from town. Upon reaching Wilmington, Washington received a triple salute, three rounds of fifteen shots each, from a battery of four cannons under the command of Captain John Huske. Washington then made his way to his lodging at Mrs. Ann Quince's house on Front Street "through an astonishing concourse [sic] of people of the town and country, whom, as well as the ladies that filled the windows and balconies of the houses, he saluted with his usual affability and condencension."[6]

Washington remained two days in Wilmington. During that time he dined with the leading citizens at a public dinner given in his honor. One evening he attended a ball at which there were illuminations, bonfires, and 62 ladies, according to his count. Indeed, the president appeared "equally surprised and delighted, at the very large and brilliant assembly of ladies, whom admiration and respect for him had collected together." Washington left Wilmington about six o'clock in the morning, taking a federal revenue barge across the Cape Fear River to the road to South Carolina. Gentlemen from the town attended the president, vessels in the Wilmington harbor displayed their national colors, and cannons roared, all accompanied by the "acclamations of the people, from the wharves and shipping."[7]

Political acrimony in Wilmington intensified in the early nineteenth century. While the Federalists were labeled "tories" and "aristocrats," Republicans were deemed "jacobins." The Fourth of July in 1802 found each party holding its own celebration of national independence (which actually occurred on Monday, the fifth, since the fourth was on Sunday). The Republicans listened to a reading of the Declaration of Independence, heard an address by party leader Timothy Bloodworth, and enjoyed a sumptuous meal at the courthouse, followed by numerous toasts. Federalists likewise enjoyed their own repast at "a table richly spread with the choicest viands" and concluded with appropriate toasts. No wonder that a toast by Thomas Cowan in 1809 upon the inauguration of President James Madison, "The Town of Wilmington—unanimity and friendship among its inhabitants," received approbation from many quarters.[8]

Continuing to divide Wilmingtonians—and Americans—was the conflict between England and France. The war of the 1790s between the two European powers concluded in 1800 but erupted once more in 1803 at the instigation of Napoleon Bonaparte. Again the Federalists evidenced sympathy for the British; the Republicans, for the French. Although both belligerents imperiled the maritime rights of the United States, the British with the larger navy proved the worse culprit, seizing American ships, setting up illegal blockades, impressing American sailors, and violating American territorial waters. Eventually Americans became convinced by the Battle of Tippecanoe in 1811 that the British were also arming the Indians on the Northwest frontier and encouraging them to beset settlers in the western territories.

Meanwhile, Americans were outraged in 1807 when the British man-of-war *Leopard* attacked the *Chesapeake*, an American naval frigate, killing several American sailors and impressing four others. At a town meeting in Wilmington in July 1807, Republicans and Federalists alike condemned the British action and passed resolutions to deny aid to British warships and to request the commissioners of navigation and pilotage to refuse pilotage service to British warships and privateers. The meeting appointed a committee to consider the defense of Wilmington in the event of a war with England. Expecting the worst, Wilmingtonians began collecting cannons, and with the assistance of a Philadelphia schooner conveyed the cannons to a site selected for a battery.[9]

The Jeffersonian-controlled Congress responded to the British attack of 1807 by imposing an embargo on all American shipping but the coastal trade. Although Wilmington Republicans earlier in the year had praised Jefferson and suggested that he run for a third term as president, the interdiction of trade was not altogether popular in the principal port of North Carolina. And not all abided by the embargo. The schooner *Hiram*, owned by Thomas Snead, left Wilmington reportedly bound for the West Indies with cargo of rice and flour. Snead disclaimed any knowledge of the voyage and any responsibility for the actions of the captain of the ship. After the furor against England had abated and Wilmingtonians realized the devastating impact of the embargo on shipping, most welcomed the abandonment of the embargo in 1809, even holding a public dinner "to celebrate the revival of COMMERCE."[10]

When neither verbal protests nor trade restrictions produced a satisfactory recognition of American rights, war ensued with the British. The War of 1812 found the United States woefully unprepared and North Carolina's long coastline an inviting target for the enemy (as had been the case during the wars of the eighteenth century). At the time of the *Chesapeake* crisis, federal gunboat Number 7, commanded by sailing master Thomas N. Gautier, protected Wilmington. Pleas from the citizenry secured the construction of three additional gunboats—numbers 166, 167, and 168, for the benefit of Wilmington. Moreover, at the onset of the war Wilmingtonians began constructing a fort on Clark's Island in the Cape Fear River below the town for protection. Fortunately, Wilmington's meager defenses were not tested.[11]

In the beginning of the war Wilmingtonians seemed to support the military effort of the United States. Yet, at a muster to seek volunteers or, if necessary, draftees to meet President James Madison's call for several thousand militia from North Carolina, no more than half the needed number of men appeared, and those were without order or discipline.

Wilmington merchants proved selfishly unpatriotic in taking advantage of military construction contracts to realize such great profits that they erected brick houses in town and drank the "best of wines." And during a crisis in 1813 one resident wrote that Wilmingtonians prepared "not to fight, but for flight, [for] safe creeks and swamps are diligently inquired after."[11]

Diverting attention from the local situation were occasional reports of a British presence along the coast. The British landing on Ocracoke in July 1813 produced general alarm. Mildly threatening in June 1814 were two British ships and a brig that stood off the main bar of the Cape Fear River for several days. Three pilots were captured but released. The following month the *Peacock* approached Federal Point but espied militia that had been mobilized and quickly departed. Not so fortunate were the sailors sent ashore south of Wilmington by the *Lacedemonian* to seek cattle. Leaving their barge laxly guarded, the entire British party was captured by local militia.[13]

Privateering was far more important than naval operations in the waters off North Carolina. It was also an immensely profitable undertaking. North Carolina ports outfitted four privateers; one each from Wilmington and Washington, and two from New Bern. Wilmington's *Lovely Lass* captured only one prize, a schooner carrying a cargo valued at $10,000. Subsequently the *Lovely Lass* was taken by the British vessel *Circe* of Montego Point in the West Indies in May 1813 after a nineteen-hour chase. Captain John Smith and his crew of sixteen were imprisoned at Nassau.[14] Wilmington, however, received numerous privateers and their prizes.[15]

After the War of 1812, which successfully confirmed the independence of the United States and brought suitable respect to the new nation, the Republicans dominated national politics. Tainted by its opposition to the war, the Federalist party disbanded as a national organization after losing the presidential election of 1816 to Republican James Monroe. Monroe, like Washington, undertook his own "Southern Tour," visiting Wilmington in 1819. The town, "in a good deal of agitation" over the visit, sent a company of cavalry to meet the presidential cortege in the vicinity of Scotts Hill and to escort the party into Wilmington about seven o'clock in the evening. Notwithstanding rainy weather, a number of townspeople gathered to greet the president, after which Monroe lodged with Thomas Cochran, who lived on Second Street between Chestnut and Mulberry. The following day Monroe visited the Wrightsville area and returned for a public dinner in the evening. At that time, appropriate addresses were exchanged between the magistrate of police and the president, followed by the usual toasts (including several drunk by the company after the president had retired). After remaining two nights in Wilmington, Monroe boarded the steamer *Prometheus* for Fort Johnston. He spent a night in Smithville, viewed the lower reaches of the Cape Fear River, and then sailed to Georgetown, South Carolina, to continue his tour.[16]

During the ensuing presidential election in 1820, Monroe successfully retained the office of president, for he had no opposition in a political atmosphere termed the "Era of Good Feelings." Only 103 New Hanover votes, most doubtlessly from Wilmington, were cast for Monroe in 1820 in his bid for reelection.[14] However, the election of 1824 shattered the Republican party, producing in its stead the Jacksonian Democrats and the National Republicans. The National Republicans in turn gave way to the Whig Party, formed by Henry Clay of Kentucky in 1833–1834 to wrest control of the national government from Jackson and the Democrats.[17]

The second party system featuring the Democrats and Whigs set the political stage for the ensuing two decades. In general, the Democrats claimed Jeffersonian Republican roots, espousing economy and limited government in both state and nation. At the national level the party opposed a high tariff, a United States bank, and the distribution of the sales of public lands, but favored the annexation of Texas and the Mexican War. Whigs advocated an active government, one that would promote education and internal improvements, particularly in North Carolina. Nationally, Whigs found themselves on the opposite side of the foregoing issues. Both parties organized statewide in North Carolina. The Democrats enjoyed their greatest strength in the eastern counties; the Whigs found support principally in the Albemarle region and the west. Socioeconomically, wealth characterized Whigs perhaps more than Democrats. At least that seemed true for Wilmington.[18]

During the quarter century before the Civil War the state was fairly evenly divided between the Democrats and Whigs. The latter won the presidential contests in the 1840s, dominated the governorship from 1836 through 1850, and usually controlled one or both houses of the state legislature to mid-century. But always the margins of victory were slim. After 1850, the Democrats gained ascendancy, winning presidential and gubernatorial elections, as well as control of the legislature. The disintegration of the national Whig Party after 1852 led to the formation in the mid–1850s of the American, or Know-Nothing Party, to which many former Whigs in North Carolina became attached. The Americans also made a pitch to Democrats, and a sufficient number of the latter joined the Know-Nothings that the party was rendered more than just Whiggery under another name. Although the Americans challenged the Democrats briefly in the mid–1850s, the xenophobia, anti–Catholicism, and secrecy of the Know-

Nothings undermined the organization. In North Carolina former Whigs attempted to revive their party with some success in the late 1850s, but their efforts foundered on the secession crisis and civil war.

While national and state politics underwent realignment during the early antebellum years, Wilmington was one of the seven borough towns that enjoyed legislative representation and continued to send a delegate to the North Carolina House of Commons until that privilege was revoked in 1835. Sixteen men occupied the Wilmington seat in the forty-six annual sessions of the legislature from 1789 through 1835. Averaging almost four terms, the Wilmington representatives provided the town with greater continuity in the legislature than did New Hanover County, whose senators and commoners averaged fewer terms. Joshua Grainger Wright (1792–1795, 1799–1808) proved the most popular Wilmington representative, followed by William W. Jones (1809–1815).[19]

Other than Wright and Jones, Joseph A. Hill represented Wilmington most often, serving in the legislative sessions of 1826–1828 and 1829–1831. Hill's election in 1826 evidenced the sometimes competitive nature of the local contests, for his opponents contended that his victory cost him and his friends $400 to $500. In 1831 Hill's opponents claimed that "the Mercantile and Mechanical interests of the place required a change," because Hill had favored agriculture over trade when they expected that the town's delegate would protect commerce. As a result, challenger Daniel Sherwood defeated Hill in the 1831 election by a vote of 111 to 109.[20]

Subsequent elections proved less exciting. After serving two years, Sherwood declined reelection, and Montesquieu W. Campbell, a past borough representative, offered for the office. His opponent was John D. Jones; Jones proved the easy winner, 141 to 27. In 1834 Sherwood again sought the borough seat, and was opposed by Edward B. Dudley, who had been Wilmington's representative in the General Assembly in 1816 and 1817. Dudley triumphed, 133 to 91, and defeated Sherwood in a rematch in 1835, 83 to 32. Serving in the 1834–1835 and 1835 sessions of the General Assembly, Dudley was the last borough representative from Wilmington.[21]

Wilmington and the other borough towns lost their representation when the Constitutional Convention of 1835 recommended the elimination of the borough franchise. Alterations in the state constitution had long been demanded, principally by westerners who felt that they were deprived of appropriate legislative representation in the General Assembly. In 1834, by a close vote in both houses of the legislature, the General Assembly decided to put the decision to hold a constitution convention before the people in a referendum. (Ironically, borough representatives provided the margin of victory in the house of commons.) In a strictly sectional vote in which the numerically populous western counties prevailed, the referendum was approved. A constitutional convention met in Raleigh in 1835.

Three men vied for the two seats accorded New Hanover County in the Constitutional Convention. (Boroughs were not granted delegates to the convention.) All the candidates were Wilmingtonians—Owen Holmes, Lewis H. Marsteller, and Joseph A. Hill. In the May 1835 election, Wilmington favored Holmes (120 votes) and Hill (119) over Marsteller (69); but countywide, Holmes and Marsteller were the winners. At the time, Holmes and Marsteller represented New Hanover County in the state senate and house of commons, respectively.[22]

Although legislative reapportionment was the principal concern of the convention in 1835, the delegates considered several other matters, including the propriety of borough representation in the legislature. Over the years many expressed doubts about the advantages of the privilege of borough representation, sentiments often shared by residents of the towns themselves. The eloquent William Gaston, resident of New Bern and representative of Craven County, defended special representation as needed to protect the commercial interests of towns in an overwhelmingly agricultural state, particularly in light of the existing town-county hostility that might preclude any consideration being given to urban concerns. Moreover, the General Assembly might be deprived of the often talented and able men elected to the legislature by the towns.[23]

The opposition, led in part by Owen Holmes, countered on all fronts. First, it stigmatized the existing system by equating the franchise of North Carolina towns to the "rotten boroughs" of England. Moreover, the slow development of urban centers in North Carolina seemed to negate the usefulness of any aid they had received in the past from the General Assembly. According to Holmes, "mere" merchants had never represented the town. And commercial matters, like those of agriculture, concerned the entire state, not just towns, and thus must be entrusted to the entire legislature. In a democratic polity the people must be trusted to recognize and support their most talented men, whether they lived in rural or urban areas. And the borough franchise was inequitable, giving a few voters in towns greater proportionate representation than those in the counties. [24]

An additional objection to borough representation centered on the "politics" or electioneering involved in the process. Holmes and others pointed out that corruption, "debauchery," and violence often accompanied town elections. According to Holmes, the evils of politicking were magnified in the commercial towns, for "Our population is of a more abandoned cast—we have more dependent and more pliable materials to work upon." He contended that sailors and other dependents went to their employers to determine how to cast ballots. "Nothing was more common, than, a day or two before the election, to house the voters as they housed their cattle."[25]

The disfranchisement of the towns was a foregone conclusion from the outset. Attempts to grant representation to Wilmington, New Bern, Edenton, and Fayetteville, and then just to Wilmington, New Bern, and Fayetteville, failed. The convention finally voted 78 to 50 to eliminate borough representation. Holmes and Marsteller joined the majority. According to the *People's Press and Wilmington Advertiser*, Holmes and Marsteller expressed the sentiment of the great majority of their constituents in New Hanover County, though probably not the majority of the residents of Wilmington. Still, the editor felt resigned to the loss, and opined, "If this measure shall produce a more complete unity of feeling between the citizens of town and country, the event will more than compensate for the loss of our representative."[26]

Following the Constitutional Convention of 1835, Democrats and Whigs prepared for the political contests of 1836. Because they were a new party, the Whigs failed to nominate a candidate for the presidency in 1836, leading to an easy victory for Martin Van Buren, who represented the Democrats. But the campaign of 1840, in which Whig William Henry Harrison contested the reelection bid of Van Buren, was a hard-fought battle. The Whigs seemed determined to wrest the presidency from the Democrats. Wilmington Whigs fashioned a full-rigged model ship, christened the *Constitution*, and took it to Raleigh, where it was presented to the county that showed the greatest increase in Whig voting in the presidential election over the recent gubernatorial election. In Wilmington, ladies of the Whig persuasion presented the party members with a flag or banner "as an emblem of their zeal." Whigs also constructed a log cabin, emblematic of Harrison's birthplace, on the north side of Market Street between Front and Second, where many rallies were held and much hard cider was drunk. Shortly before the election an explosion damaged the log cabin. Despite a $400 reward, the culprit was never apprehended. Nevertheless, the Whigs carried Wilmington in 1840 for Harrison by a vote of 277 to 265.[27]

The Democrats in Wilmington regrouped, however, and never lost another presidential election before the Civil War. As seen in Table 1, with the exception of 1852, the elections were well contested, but only in Wilmington. New Hanover County was staunchly Democratic. Wilmington Whigs provided between 77 and 94 percent of the total Whig vote in the county in the presidential elections. Still, every vote counted in the national contests because North Carolina was so evenly divided. For that reason political leaders of both parties worked for a full turnout on election day. And the outcome had an immediate impact on the state, and particularly on Wilmington, for the party that controlled the presidency controlled patronage. For example, in 1853, after Democrat Franklin Pierce assumed the presidency, two permanent inspectors—the weigher and gauger—three temporary inspectors, and the hospital physician for the port of Wilmington, all representing the previous Whig administration, lost their positions to Democrats.[28]

Nonetheless, Wilmingtonians laid aside political animosities to welcome former presidents James K. Polk and Millard Fillmore. The former appeared in 1849 immediately after leaving Washington, D.C. Arriving by train, Polk was greeted by the town commissioners at the Wilmington and Weldon depot, at which time a signal was given to fire salutes at the market dock, ring bells, and hoist flags in town and on ships in the harbor. A procession then formed, consisting of the chief marshal and his assistants, followed in order by the magistrate of police, town commissioners, officers of the army and navy, customhouse officers, a band, and citizens in double file, and escorted the former president to Mrs. Swann's Hotel. Afterward, Polk greeted visitors at the Masonic Hall. After a night's lodging, Polk left by steamer for Charleston amid the roar of cannons and shouts of hundreds who came by foot, horse, and carriage to witness the departure of a native North Carolinian. On the other hand, former president Millard Fillmore passed quietly through Wilmington in May 1854 on his way from South Carolina to Baltimore, tarrying only a few hours at Holmes Hotel before taking the train to the north.[29]

As with the presidency, Democratic voters in Wilmington usually outnumbered Whigs in elections for delegates to the House of Representatives from the Wilmington congressional district. Since the Wilmington district was so overwhelmingly Democratic, there was less incentive for Whigs (and Democrats) to go to the polls. As seen in Table 2, the Whig Party in the district on occasion failed to challenge the Democrats, particularly when the popular William S. Ashe from Rocky Point in New Hanover County was running for office. Still, the Whigs in Wilmington made the elections in 1845 and 1847 close. The only defeat suffered by the Democrats in Wilmington came in 1855 when the American Party peaked in popularity in the town. American candidate David Reid of Duplin County (a former Democrat and not to be confused with North Carolina governor and United States Senator David Settle Reid of Rockingham County) defeated Warren Winslow, 445 to 383. In the congressional district as a whole, however, Winslow, like James McKay and Ashe before him, easily defeated his opponent.

Expectedly, Democrats dominated gubernatorial elections in New Hanover County as decidedly as they did presidential contests. Only in Wilmington did Whigs offer more than token opposition. Edward B. Dudley, a resident of Wilmington, became North Carolina's first popularly elected governor, holding office between 1836 and 1841. As seen in Table 3, gubernatorial elections in Wilmington in 1840 and 1846 were reasonably close. And in 1856, Democrat Thomas Bragg narrowly defeated American John Gilmer. After the demise of the American Party and the reorganization of the Whigs, called the "Opposition" in 1860, John Pool, the Opposition candidate, dealt the Democrats their only gubernatorial defeat in Wilmington between 1840 and the Civil War.

New Hanover also sent solidly Democratic delegations—one senator and two commoners—to the state legislature during the last quarter of the antebellum era. Democrats relied upon Wilmington to enhance their majority in the county, and the town complied. Whigs rarely offered more than a token candidate for the senate, and their candidates for the house were overwhelmed. In 1858 an "independent Whig" candidate for the houses of commons polled 451 votes; the two Democrats, 1,212 and 1,188 votes. Finally, in 1860, the Whigs, or Opposition, in Wilmington managed a victory when their two house candidates, Oliver P. Meares and Frederick D. Poisson, polled 534 and 508 votes, respectively, and the Democrats, Samuel J. Person and Daniel Shaw, won 497 and 485 votes, respectively.[30]

Controversy engulfed the local scene in 1855 when the General Assembly passed legislation that required prospective voters for town commissioners to register and declare their residence at least one month before the municipal election. Further-

Edward B. Dudley (1789–1855), North Carolina's first popularly elected governor (1836) and first president of the Wilmington and Raleigh (Weldon) Railroad. Photograph courtesy of the New Hanover County Public Library, Wilmington.

The Dudley Mansion, built circa 1825, corner of South Front and Nun streets, home of Edward B. Dudley, who entertained Henry Clay (1844) and Daniel Webster (1847) at this residence. Photograph courtesy of the New Hanover County Public Library, Wilmington.

more, the legislation disbarred anyone from voting who had not paid municipal taxes the year prior to the election. Apparently the General Assembly hoped to prevent fraud in the electoral process (as well as to pressure delinquent taxpayers into meeting their obligations). Although the law was enacted in January, most paid little heed until late in the year. The town clerk only opened a registration book in mid–October, giving Wilmingtonians slightly more than a month to register. Wilmingtonians were hardly deterred, because they voted in record numbers in the election for town commissioners in 1855. Nevertheless, the law evoked a storm of protest that induced the legislature in 1856 to repeal the statute insofar as registration was concerned, though it retained a six-month residency requirement and the prescription for the payment of town taxes in order to qualify for the franchise.[31]

Politics also invaded the realm of the Board of Commissioners of Navigation and Pilotage for the Cape Fear River. Before 1847 the New Hanover County court selected the five-man board, but in that year the state legislature politicized the body by making its members subject to popular election. Immediately, advertisements proposed several slates of candidates. The Democrats won the initial contest in 1847, but thereafter

Democrats and Whigs (Americans) equally shared control of the board of commissioners through 1860. While some elections went uncontested and apathy reigned in others, the 1856 contest engendered the greatest interest, bringing a thousand voters to the polls and resulting in a mixed ticket—four Americans and one Democrat. Both parties held meetings in 1857 specifically to choose slates of candidates for the board of commissioners. The Democrats won that year and the following, but the Whigs triumphed in 1859 and 1860.[32]

The election of the commissioners of navigation and pilotage entailed more than a matter of party prestige, for the board exercised considerable patronage discretion. It appointed a port physician, a harbor master, fumigators, and a committee to examine and license pilots. A major flap over patronage occurred in 1845 when the county court still appointed the commissioners. A Democratic majority in that year replaced Whig Dr. Armand John DeRosset, Sr., who had served as health officer of the port for some thirty years, claiming negligence of duty. According to DeRosset's daughter, the action was "abominable," an indication that "the times are corrupt." Two years later Dr. William A. Berry was replaced by Dr. John L. Meares as health officer in an admittedly "political" move.[33]

Partisanship eventually permeated the elections for town commissioners of Wilmington. By the mid–1830s at least, electoral "tickets" of candidates began to appear, a practice that continued to the Civil War. Four tickets were offered for the election of 1853—the People's Ticket ("Old Board"), the Citizen's [sic] Ticket, the Poor Man's Ticket, and the People's Ticket (for a new Board). Interest waxed and waned over the years. In 1853, twenty-five men received votes. According to the *Herald*, it was well that "the people, are keeping a sharp lookout, and will hold ... [the commissioners] to a fearful responsibility, ... or else, by jingo, we'll turn'em out." Conversely, in 1859 there was little excitement when less than a third of the eligible electorate materialized to reelect the incumbents, whose performance the previous year seemed eminently acceptable.[34]

In a town divided fairly evenly between Democrats and Whigs (later Americans), elections often produced boards of commissioners containing members of both parties. When the American Party began an early preparation for the election in 1855, a correspondent to the *Daily Herald* decried the partisan politics and hoped that Wilmingtonians "of every political faith" would rise above party allegiances to seek the most qualified men for office. That proved illusory, for the two parties waged an exciting campaign, using political rallies, music, and processions to generate interest. As a result, 927 ballots were cast, "by far the largest vote ever polled" in Wilmington, in which the Americans barely carried the day. The Americans exulted in their victory, thronging the streets, burning tar barrels, and setting off rockets and fireworks. A procession, with music, torches, and transparencies, paraded through the streets to a "late hour." Enthusiasm over commissioner elections, and the American Party, dissipated quickly. In the ensuing years, turnout at the polls dropped precipitously, and the Democrats thereafter dominated commissioner elections.[35]

As Wilmingtonians went to the polls during the decade and a half prior to the Civil War, they were not unmindful of the international and national events surrounding them. After the United States declared war on Mexico in 1846, President James K. Polk asked for volunteers to supplement the United States Army. At a Wilmington town meeting a company was organized, consisting of approximately 50 volunteers. They were not needed immediately, however, but the following year the governor of the state called again for those willing to enlist in the cause against Mexico. New Hanover County at that time provided one of the state's ten military companies comprising North Carolina's regiment that went to the theater of the war.[36]

Company H, First North Carolina Regiment, which consisted mainly of New Hanover residents, along with some men from Wake and other counties, was captained by William J. Price. Although Company H and the rest of the regiment failed to see action, they suffered grievously in the war from disease. As the *Journal* declared, "They deserve the gratitude and thanks of the state just as much as if they had been in every battle." When the New Hanover men of Company H returned from Mexico, they were greeted by the booming of artillery at the wharf, escorted through town by the Clarendon Horse Guards, and treated to a public dinner. Wilmingtonians in 1857 again remembered the war with Mexico with a flag presentation to Company G, Twelfth Regiment, U.S. Infantry, in a ceremony at the Front Street Methodist Church. Company G of the regular army had embarked for Mexico in 1847 from Wilmington, and its commander returned to the town to acknowledge the favors that his men had received in the port.[37]

After the successful conclusion in 1848 of the war with Mexico, the United States immediately divided over the question of California statehood in 1849–1850. As Congress debated statehood and the concomitant compromise of 1850, Southerners worried about adequate protection for the institution of slavery, which came under fire from northern abolitionists. In bipartisan fashion, Wilmington Democrats and Whigs joined in a demand for the recognition of "Southern Rights," even to the point of contemplating Southern secession and the establishment of an exclusive southern trade with Europe to render the South independent of northern maritime commerce. County and district "Southern Rights" meetings, which involved Wilmingtonians, denounced northern attacks on slavery and prepared North Carolina for participation in the Nashville Convention, but the Compromise of 1850 patched up the breach in the Union for another decade.[38]

Throughout the 1850s the rift between North and South widened, exacerbated at the end of the decade by the publication of native North Carolinian Hinton Rowan Helper's *The Impending Crisis* in 1857, and John Brown's Raid in 1859. According to the *Daily Herald* in 1859, Helper should "be awaiting the doom that will consign his coworker in iniquity [Brown] into eternity.... He deserves, and, we hope, will receive a traitor's reward." Upon the notice of Brown's attack on the Harper's Ferry arsenal, the Wilmington Light Infantry militia company tendered its services to the governor of Virginia, who politely declined the offer. Unlike many in North Carolina, however, Wilmingtonians did not seem too perturbed about the Brown affair. Still, prominent merchant Platt K. Dickinson observed, "A few such [incidents as this], will, I fear, separate us as a people, and bring Father & Son into hostile conflict."[39]

The next fateful incident occurred in 1860 when Abraham Lincoln defeated John C. Breckinridge, Stephen Douglas, and John Bell for the presidency. As expected, Wilmington's Democrats and Whigs almost evenly divided. The former, by a slim majority, carried the election in town for Breckinridge, the southern candidate who represented secession to many. Whigs supported Bell, the Constitutional Union candidate, who represented caution and compromise. The ultimate election of Lincoln precipitated a battle of words between the party newspapers, the Democratic *Journal* and the Whig *Herald*. And the citizenry divided as well. A secessionist gathering met at the courthouse on November 19; a unionist meeting convened at Thalian Hall three days later. Subsequently, the volunteer military companies, the German Volunteers and the Wilmington Light Infantry paraded through the streets. A radical secessionist group called the "Minute Men," which organized at least as early as November 10, held meetings.[40]

As Wilmingtonians continued to debate the issue of North Carolina's place in the Union, the polls opened on December 20 for the election of town commissioners for the ensuing year. That election generated little excitement, but when news arrived of South Carolina's secession on the same day, a spirited reaction occurred. The Minute Men fired 100 guns in salute. The ship *Samuel W. Berry* added another salvo in honor of secessionist senator Louis T. Wigfall of Texas. The schooner *Alba* on the river answered gun for gun. During the early months of 1861 Unionist sentiment in Wilmington gradually waned, though North Carolina remained determined to avoid secession until the Confederacy's attack on Fort Sumter in Charleston in April and Lincoln's subsequent call for troops to suppress the rebellion in the South. At that juncture the state adopted the position held by most Wilmingtonians. Secession was preferable to war on sister southern states.[41]

Table 1
Voting for the President in Wilmington

	Democrat	Whig (American)
1840	265 (Van Buren)	277 (Harrison)
1844	354 (Polk)	333 (Clay)
1848	425 (Cass)	376 (Taylor)
1852	596 (Pierce)	296 (Scott)
1856	588 (Buchanan)	515 (Fillmore)
1860	593 (Breckinridge)	567 (Bell)[1]

[1] John Bell represented the Constitutional Union Party. Northern Democratic candidate Stephen Douglas received five votes in Wilmington in 1860.

Sources: *Chronicle*, November 18, 1840; *Journal*, November 8, 1844; November 10, 1848; November, 1852; November 7, 1856; November 8, 1860.

Table 2
Voting for the House of Representatives in Wilmington

	Democrat	Whig (American)
1845	244 (McKay)	212 (Meares)
1847	200 (McKay)	75 (Hall)[1]
1849	383 (Ashe)[2]	
1851	323 (Ashe)[3]	
1853	442 (Ashe)	165 (Leak)
1855	383 (Winslow)	445 (Reid)
1857	264 (Winslow)	152 (Meares)
1859	224 (Winslow)	43 (McDuffie)

[1] Sixty-seven votes were cast for an independent candidate, who appealed mainly to Whigs.

[2] William S. Ashe defeated another Democrat, David S. Reid, who received 31 votes in Wilmington.

[3] No organized opposition, though three votes were cast in Wilmington for one Winslow.

Sources: *Journal*, August 15, 1845; August 13, 1847; August 10, 1849; August 8, 1851; August 12, 1853; August 12, 1859; *Daily Herald*, August 3, 1855; August 13, 1857.

Table 3
Voting for the Governor in Wilmington

	Democrat	Whig (American)
1840	216 (Saunders)	199 (Morehead)
1842	270 (Henry)	180 (Morehead)
1844	355 (Hoke)	236 (Graham)
1846	241 (Shepard)	207 (Graham)
1848	319 (Reid)	233 (Manly)
1850	364 (Reid)	230 (Manly)
1852	476 (Reid)	282 (Kerr)
1854	393 (Bragg)	338 (Dockery)
1856	522 (Bragg)	466 (Gilmer)
1858	485 (Ellis)	331 (McRae)
1860	528 (Ellis)	539 (Pool)

Sources: *Chronicle*, Aug. 19, 1840; Aug. 10, 1842; *Journal*, November 8, 1844; August 14, 1846; November 10, 1848; August 9, 1850; August 13, 1852; August 11, 1854; August 13, 1858; *Daily Herald*, August 4, 1860.

Epilogue

As the Civil War loomed, Wilmington in 1860 constituted an anomaly in North Carolina—a significant urban area in an overwhelmingly rural, agrarian state. Though the town paled in comparison to Charleston, South Carolina, and cities to the north, Wilmington's population of 9,552 far outstripped that of New Bern, its nearest rival in North Carolina. A diverse populace shared the town, including free and enslaved blacks. While some white families were longstanding residents, others had gravitated to the port from North Carolina locales or had relocated from other parts of the United States. Because Wilmington was a major seaport, from its earliest years the town offered a home to many European nationals and their descendants, not only British but also continentals, particularly Germans. The latter provided the base of a growing Jewish community in Wilmington after the mid-nineteenth century. Moreover, Wilmington's population was decidedly transient and liberally augmented by numerous sailors of various nationalities, which gave a cosmopolitan atmosphere to the town and port.

African Americans represented a significant component of the residents of Wilmington. Their number continually rose during the antebellum era, though an increasing influx of whites gradually reduced the percentage of blacks in Wilmington. Still, African Americans accounted for 45 percent of the populace in 1860. Among them was a substantial number of free blacks, many of whom achieved prominence in the building trades. Others labored in obscurity, working on the docks, serving as draymen, and taking care of white households. Struggling within the confines of slavery and the rising discrimination against free blacks, African Americans fashioned life-styles for themselves which retained some elements of their ancestral ways but eventually represented an amalgam of African and European cultures. All the while, slaves at least appeared to enjoy a goodly degree of personal autonomy in their urban setting.

White Wilmingtonians emulated Americans throughout the country in their penchant for associative endeavors. In addition to establishing a rich religious tradition featuring Episcopalians, Presbyterians, Methodists, Baptists, Lutherans, Catholics, and Jews, townspeople organized a plethora of societies for the enjoyment of social companionship and charitable endeavor. The latter particularly concentrated upon destitute seamen, so prominent in the port, but did not overlook aged workingmen and poor women. The organization of bands that paraded on public occasions reflected a fondness for music in town; the appearance of militia companies showed the southern predilection for martial endeavors. Two of the most popular national fraternal organizations appeared in Wilmington—the Masons and the International Order of Odd Fellows. The antebellum temperance movement in the United States also gained limited support in the town.

Although Wilmingtonians did not refer to their town as the "Athens of North Carolina," the claim of New Bernians, residents of the port showed more than a passing interest in civic culture. Numerous schools for boys and girls, as well as for adults, offered a range of opportunities for learning, extending from the fundamentals of education to music in its many forms, dance, foreign languages, penmanship, and the martial arts. Wilmington supported an active press that usually consisted of two, and often more, newspapers that appeared tri-weekly, then daily, by the 1850s. The newspapers in turn spawned "reading rooms" and promoted a local library association. From the late eighteenth century onward, a local thalian organization betokened an ongoing theatrical presence before the Civil War. Ably supplementing the theater were various popular performances that both entertained and enlightened the townspeople.

While some Wilmingtonians enjoyed the amenities of urban life, the magistrate of police, later mayor, and commissioners entrusted with governing the community found their problems multiplying with the growth of the town. Particularly ominous was the threat of fire, which required the organization of a night guard and the maintenance of a fire department. Despite such precautions, conflagrations too often devastated parts of Wilmington. The commissioners also oversaw public structures, mainly the market house and town dock, and at the end of the antebellum era they assumed responsibility for Town Hall/Thalian Hall. Street construction and maintenance, regulation of traffic, animal control, and the protection of the public health added to the burdens of the town fathers. Various taxes and fees underwrote the expenses of governance, though growing civic responsibilities, including the bonded indebtedness to support the railroads, placed an ever greater strain on the finances of Wilmingtonians.

Ultimately, Wilmington owed its origin and eminence to the Cape Fear River and its consequent status as a port. Located on the only river in the state that flowed directly into the Atlantic Ocean, though some thirty miles from its mouth, Wilmington enjoyed an immense competitive advantage over other North Carolina ports. It monopolized the state's overseas commerce, in addition to conducting a substantial coastal and West Indian trade. Economic activity in the town, from stevedoring to shipbuilding to the mercantile trades, reflected the impact of shipping. Wilmington's commerce was oriented toward exports, mainly naval stores and wood products, though cotton showed promise during the decade prior to the war. Manufacturing in the town, mainly sawmills and turpentine distilleries, evidenced the emphasis on wood products and naval stores as Wilmingtonians converted natural resources into profitable exports.

The town and port stagnated in the early nineteenth century and began to realize its potential as a shipping center only with the advent of steam navigation and the internal improvements in North Carolina. Because overland transportation was so difficult and expensive, water constituted the key to internal transportation, particularly for bulky wood products and naval stores. Private and public efforts to improve the navigability of the Cape Fear River, especially the section from Fayetteville to Wilmington, combined with the increasing presence of steamboats to magnify water traffic to and from Wilmington. Most stimulating to the growth of the town was the appearance of the railroad. And the railroad not only energized the economy, contributing to a significant rise in population and wealth, it also more fully integrated Wilmington into state and national political and cultural affairs.

Politically, Wilmington resembled North Carolina generally during the antebellum era. Whigs and Democrats contested, sometimes hotly, elections for the presidency, governorship, county legislative representatives, town commissioners, and even commissioners of navigation and pilotage. The Democrats usually proved victorious, though even after the demise of the Whig Party in the early 1850s the opposition to the Democrats in Wilmington remained formidable. Predictably, Wilmingtonians divided over the results of the presidential election in 1860, won by Republican Abraham Lincoln. However, secessionists soon gained ascendancy and unionist sentiment waned in the early months of 1861. Nonetheless, North Carolina delayed joining the Confederate States of America until May 1861, after which Wilmington played a prominent role as a blockade-running port in the American Civil War.

Notes

1. THE EMERGENCE OF A TOWN

1. See Carl Bridenbaugh, *Cities in the Wilderness: Urban Life in America, 1625–1742* (New York, 1964, orig. 1938); *Cities in Revolt: Urban Life in America, 1743–1776* (New York, 1964, orig. 1955).

2. Daniel W. Fagg, Jr., "Sleeping Not with the King's Grant: A Rereading of Some Proprietary Documents 1663–1667," *North Carolina Historical Review*, 48 (1971): 171–185; Lawrence Lee, *The Lower Cape Fear in Colonial Days* (Chapel Hill, 1965), 41–53.

3. William L. Saunders, ed., *The Colonial Records of North Carolina*, 10 vols. (Raleigh, 1886–1890), 1:229, 231; Donald R. Lennon, "The Development of Town Government in Colonial North Carolina," in *Of Tar Heel Towns, Shipbuilders, Reconstructionists and Alliancemen. Papers in North Carolina History*, ed. by Joseph F. Steelman (Greenville, N.C., 1981), 2–3.

4. Herbert R. Paschal, Jr., *A History of Colonial Bath* (Raleigh, 1955); Alan D. Watson, *A History of New Bern and Craven County* (New Bern, N.C., 1987); Charles Paul, "Colonial Beaufort"; "Factors in the Economy of Colonial Beaufort"; "Beaufort, North Carolina: Its Development as a Colonial Town," *North Carolina Historical Review*, 42 (1965):139–152; 44 (1967):111–134; 47 (1970), 370–387; Thomas C. Parramore, *Cradle of the Colony: The History of Chowan County and Edenton* (Edenton: Edenton Chamber of Commerce, 1967).

5. Lee, *Lower Cape Fear*, 91–93.

6. Saunders, *Colonial Records*, 2:541, 562–563; 3:27–29, 138, 436, 526–527; Lee, *Lower Cape Fear*, 94–95.

7. *Ibid.*, 98–100.

8. *Ibid.*, 102.

9. *Ibid.*, 101–102; Alan D. Watson, "Cornelius Harnett," in Alan D. Watson, Dennis R. Lawson, and Donald R. Lennon, *Harnett, Hooper & Howe: Revolutionary Leders of the Lower Cape Fear* (Wilmington, 1979), 4.

10. Hugh Meredith, *An Account of the Cape Fear Country, 1731*, ed. by Earl Gregg Swem (Perth Amboy, N.J., 1912), 14–15; John Brickell, *The Natural History of North Carolina* (Raleigh, 1910; orig. 1737), 8–9; Lee, *Lower Cape Fear*, 109, 129–130.

11. Lee, *Lower Cape Fear*, 103–105; William S. Price, Jr., "A Strange Incident in George Burrington's Royal Governorship," *North Carolina Historical Review*, 51 (1974): 151–155.

12. Saunders, *Colonial Records*, 3:258, 261–262, 287, 296.

13. *Ibid.*, 3:1–3, 43, 48; Walter Clark, ed., *The State Records of North Carolina*, 16 vols., numbered 11–26 (Winston and Goldsboro, 1895–1906), 23: 133; Nina Moore Tiffany, ed., *Letters of James Murray, Loyalist* (Boston, 1901), 36.

14. William P. Cumming, *The Southeast in Early Maps* (Chapel Hill, 1962), plates 51–54, pages 36, 51, 83, 200–202, 280; William P. Cumming, "Wimble's Maps and the Colonial Cartography of the North Carolina Coast," *North Carolina Historical Review*, 46 (1969):157–170.

15. William P. Cumming, "The Turbulent Life of Captain James Wimble," *North Carolina Historical Review*, 46 (1969): 1–18.

16. New Hanover County Deed Book, AB, 126, 144–145, 146, 155, 156, 343 and passim, Office of Register of Deeds, New Hanover County Courthouse, Wilmington, N.C.; Saunders, *Colonial Records*, 4:43, 45, 48, 216; Clark, *State Records*, 25:218.

17. Lee, *Lower Cape Fear*, 120–121; Donald R. Lennon and Ida B. Kellam, eds., *The Wilmington Town Book*, 1743–1778 (Raleigh, 1973), 8–10.

18. Peter DuBois to Samuel Johnston, Jr., Feb. 8, 1757, Hayes Collection, Southern Historical Collection, Chapel Hill, N.C.; Lee, *Lower Cape Fear*, 121.

19. "A New Voyage to Georgia. By a Young Gentleman. London. 1737," in *Collections of the Georgia Historical Society*, 2:58; New Hanover County Deed Book AB, 48, 63, 76, 139, 148, and passim; Minutes of the New Hanover County Court of Pleas and Quarter Sessions, March 1737/38; March 1738/39, State Archives, Raleigh, N.C.

20. Saunders, *Colonial Records*, 4:43, 235–239, 241.

21. Clark, *State Records*, 23:215–219; Saunders, *Colonial Records*, 4:40, 44–45, 186–187, 205, 216, 271, 277, 328, 333, 335, 342, 372, 441.

22. Tiffany, *Letters of James Murray*, 28–29, 38. See also Lennon and Kellam, *Wilmington Town Book*, xxiii n. 23.

23. Tiffany, *Letters of James Murray*, 51–52; Saunders, *Colonial Records*, 4: 465–466.

24. Alan D. Watson, "Wilmington: A Town Born of Conflict, Confusion, and Collusion, part 2," *Lower Cape Fear Historical Society Bulletin*, 30 (May 1988): 3; Tiffany, *Letters of James Murray*, 54–55.

25. Saunders, *Colonial Records*, 4:337, 408; Clark, *State Records*, 23:127.

26. Clark, *State Records*, 23:234–237; New Hanover County Court Minutes, December 1739; Lee, *Lower Cape Fear*, 124.

27. Saunders, *Colonial Records*, 4:509.

28. *Ibid.*, 4:510–513.

29. Tiffany, *Letters of James Murray*, 54; Saunders, *Colonial Records*, 4:448–452.

30. Saunders, *Colonial Records*, 4:480–481; Clark, *State Records*, 23:131.

31. Clark, *State Records*, 23:133–135; Saunders, *Colonial Records*, 4:482–487, 534.

32. "Spencer Compton," *Dictionary of National Biography*, 4:906–907.

33. Saunders, *Colonial Records*, 4:424, 515; Clark, *State Records*, 23:131–135; New Hanover County Court Minutes, June 1740.

34. Saunders, *Colonial Records*, 4:418.

35. *Ibid.*, 4:448–453.

36. *Ibid.*, 4:455–460, 462–470.

37. Clark, *State Records*, 23:146–149.

38. Alan D. Watson, "The Town Fathers of Early Wilmington, 1743–1778," *Lower Cape Fear Historical Society Bulletin*, 24 (October 1980).

39. Clark, *State Records*, 23:234–237; 25:262.

40. Clark, *State Records*, 23:147, 234, 461; 25:262.

41. For this and subsequent paragraphs see Watson, "Town Fathers of Early Wilm-

ington." For biographical data, see Lennon and Kellam, *Wilmington Town Book*; New Hanover County Court Minutes, 1759–1775; Saunders, *Colonial Records*, vols. 4–10.

42. J. Bryan Grimes, comp., *North Carolina Wills and Inventories* (Raleigh, 1912), 164.

43. Lennon and Kellam, *Wilmington Town Book*, 212–213; New Hanover County Court Minutes, October 1774.

44. Lennon, "Development of Town Government," 6–9.

45. Lennon and Kellam, *Wilmington Town Book*, 127–134, 139–144.

46. *Ibid.*, 134–137, 144–176.

47. Petition to Governor Josiah Martin, December 7, 1773, CO 5/303, Part 2, fs. 256–258, Public Record Office, London, microfilm, North Carolina Collection, Chapel Hill, N. C.

48. Saunders, *Colonial Records*, 4:186–187; Clark, *State Records*, 23:135; New Hanover County Court Minutes, September 1741; September 1764; December 1765; March 1766; April 1768.

49. New Hanover County Court Minutes, September 1741; September 1764; October 1768; October 1772; October 1774; July 1779; Clark, *State Records*, 23:928–929; 24: 137–138, 393–394; *The Wilmington Centinel*, June 18, 1788.

50. Lennon and Kellam, *Wilmington Town Book*, xxxii; *Wilmington Centinel*, Feb. 12, 1789.

51. Clark, *State Records*, 23:259; 24: 620–621; Lennon and Kellam, *Wilmington Town Book*, xxxii, 57, 72, 76, 79, 88, 99, 107, 109, 116, 180, 181, 207, 237.

52. Janet Schaw, *Journal of a Lady of Quality* ... , ed. by Evangeline W. Andrews and Charles M. Andrews (New Haven, 1923), 284; Clark, *State Records*, 24:725–726; Lennon and Kellam, *Wilmington Town Book*, 200–203; Lee, *Lower Cape Fear*, 133.

53. Schaw, *Journal of a Lady of Quality*, 154; Clark, *State Records*, 23:236, 458–459, 867; 25:259; Lennon and Kellam, *Wilmington Town Book*, xxxiii, 66, 190–191.

54. New Hanover County Deed Books, C, 211; Lennon and Kellam, *Wilmington Town Book*, 217, 218, 229, 230, 231, 236, 237, 239.

55. Clark, *State Records*, 25:259; Lennon and Kellam, *Wilmington Town Book*, 14, 44–45, 146, 164.

56. Lennon and Kellam, *Wilmington Town Book*, 222, 223, 226, 227, 229, 230–231, 232; New Hanover County Court Minutes, October 1774.

57. Lennon and Kellam, *Wilmington Town Book*, 56, 161–162, 199, 210, 214, 232–233, 236–237, 238; Alan D. Watson, *Society in Colonial North Carolina*, rev. ed. (Raleigh, 1996), 122.

58. *South-Carolina Gazette* (Charleston), November 20, 1740; Lennon and Kellam, *Wilmington Town Book*, 89; *Virginia Gazette*, Rind (Williamsburg), February 21, 1771; Louis B. Wright and Marion R. Tinling, eds., *Quebec to Carolina in 1785–1786. Being the Travel Diary and Observations of Robert Hunter, Jr., A Young Merchant of London* (San Marino, Calif., 1943), 286–287.

59. Lennon and Kellam, *Wilmington Town Book*, 32, 46, 54, 73, 85, 94, 123, 135, 177–178, 197–198, 214–215, 228, 234; Clark, *State Records*, 25:260.

60. Lennon and Kellam, *Wilmington Town Book*, 34, 42–43, 66–67, 76, 156, 187–188, 197, 233.

61. Clark, *State Records*, 23:236; 25:260, 512; Lennon and Kellam, *Wilmington Town Book*, 51, 60, 63, 77-78, 79, 80, 81, 83, 87, 90, 160, 181, 207–208; *Wilmington Centinel*, February 19, 1789; Bridenbaugh, *Cities in Revolt*, 293–294. Although the legislature permitted the town to establish a fire company, apparently the commissioners simply relied on citizens who were willing to help extinguish a fire. Clark, *State Records*, 24:621; 25:513.

62. Clark, *State Records*, 23:460, 458, 868; Lennon and Kellam, *Wilmington Town Book*, 89, 225.
63. Clark, *State Records*, 24:619; 25:261; Lennon and Kellam, *Wilmington Town Book*, 34, 61, 196; Lee, *Lower Cape Fear*, 127.
64. Lennon, "Development of Town Government," 24–25.

2. Early American Life

1. Donald R. Lennon and Ida B. Kellam, eds., *The Wilmington Town Book, 1743–1778* (Raleigh, 1973), xxxv; H. Roy Merrens, *Colonial North Carolina in the Eighteenth Century: A Study in Historical Geography* (Chapel Hill, 1964), 64–65; Philip M. Hamer et al., *The Papers of Henry Laurens*, projected multivolume series (Columbia, 1968-), 1:120.
2. Don Higginbotham, ed., *The Papers of James Iredell*, 2 vols. (Raleigh, 1976), 2: 56; New Hanover Will Book B, 71, Office of the Clerk of Superior Court, New Hanover County Courthouse, Wilmington, N.C.; Mark A. De Wolfe Howe, ed., "Journal of Josiah Quincy, Junior, 1773," Massachusetts Historical Society *Proceedings*, 49 (1916):462. See also Janet Schaw, *Journal of a Lady of Quality* ... , ed. by Evangeline W. Andrews and Charles M. Andrews (New Haven, 1923), 154.
3. Alan D. Watson, *Society in Colonial North Carolina*, rev. ed. (Raleigh, 1996), 23; Francisco de Miranda, *The New Democracy in America. Travels of Francisco de Miranda in the United States, 1783–84*, trans. by Judson P. Wood and ed. by John S. Ezell (Norman, Okla., 1963), 5–6; New Hanover County Court Minutes, April 1775, State Archives, Raleigh, N.C.; *Wilmington Centinel*, November 19, 1788.
4. Lennon and Kellam, *Wilmington Town Book*, 77–78; Petition to Josiah Martin, December 7, 1773, CO 5/303, Part 2, stamped folios 256–258, Public Record Office, London, microfilm, North Carolina Collection, Chapel Hill, N.C.; Schaw, *Journal of a Lady of Quality*, 155; Vernon O. Stumpf, "The Radical Ladies of Wilmington and Their Tea Party," Lower Cape Fear Historical Society *Bulletin*, 16 (February 1973).
5. Lennon and Kellam, *Wilmington Town Book*, 35, 46, n.65, 49, 92, 110, 121 ns. 119, 120, 122; New Hanover County Court Minutes, February, May 1759; 1759–1775 passim, State Archives, Raleigh, N.C.; Schaw, *Journal of a Lady of Quality*, 178–179.
6. *Cape-Fear Mercury* (Wilmington), January 13, September 22, December 29, 1773; James H. Blackmore, "Herrall Blackmore: An Unknown Hero of American Independence," Lower Cape Fear Historical Society *Bulletin*, 19 (May, October 1976).
7. *Cape-Fear Mercury* (Wilmington), December 29, 1773; May 18, 1774; Marvin L. Michael Kay and Lorin Lee Cary, *Slavery in North Carolina, 1748–1775* (Chapel Hill, 1995), 19–22.
8. Kay and Cary, *Slavery in North Carolina*, 221, 227, 229; William S. Powell, ed., *The Correspondence of William Tryon and Other Selected Papers*, 2 vols. (Raleigh, 1980, 1981), 1:138.
9. Walter Clark, ed., *The State Records of North Carolina*, 16 vols. numbered 11–26 (Winston and Goldsboro, 1895–1906), 23:62–66, 191–204, 458; 24:621.
10. Lennon and Kellam, *Wilmington Town Book*, 168–169, 187, 205, 214, 234.
11. *Ibid.*, 148, 166, 167, 204, 233, 235.
12. *Ibid.*, 165, 204, 209–210, 211, 212–213, 214, 220, 221, 226–227, 233, 234, 235, 236, 238; *Cape-Fear Mercury*, September 22, 1773.
13. Clark, *State Records*, 24: 726–729.
14. Howe, "Journal of Josiah Quincy, Junior," 463; Elkanah Watson, *Men and Times of the Revolution; or, Memoirs of Elkanah Watson*, ed. by Winslow C. Watson (New York, 1857), 58; Johann David Schoepf, *Travels in the Confederation, 1783–1784*, 2 vols., ed. and trans. by Alfred J. Morrison (Philadelphia, 1911), 2:149.

15. New Hanover County Court Minutes, June 1767; Clark, *State Records*, 23: 106-107.
16. *The North Carolina Gazette* (Wilmington), July 10, 1765; *Wilmington Centinel*, June 18, 1788; New Hanover County Court Minutes, September 1767.
17. Alan D. Watson, "Impulse Toward Independence: Resistance and Rebellion Among North Carolina Slaves, 1750-1775," *Journal of Negro History*, 63 (1978):323-324; New Hanover County Court Minutes, March, September 1766.
18. Leora H. McEachern and Isabel M. Williams, eds., *Wilmington-New Hanover Safety Committee Minutes, 1774-1776* (Wilmington, 1974), 30, 43, 45, 47; Schaw, *Journal of a Lady of Quality*, 199-200; Watson, "Impulse Toward Independence," 324-325.
19. Higginbotham, *Papers of James Iredell*, 2: 329; Jeffrey J. Crow, *The Black Experience in Revolutionary North Carolina* (Raleigh, 1983), 72-77. See also the saga of Thomas Peters of the Lower Cape Fear, a sergeant in the Guides and Pioneers, a black provincial corps, who eventually went to Nova Scotia and then to Sierra Leone. Carole Watterson Troxler, *The Loyalist Experience in North Carolina* (Raleigh, 1976), 51-52.
20. *Wilmington Centinel*, July 2, August 13, 1788.
21. Lennon and Kellam, *Wilmington Town Book*, 125, 123, 183, 186, 191, 225; Clark, *State Records*, 24: 727-728; Crow, *Black Experience in Revolutionary North Carolina*, 29; *Heads of Families at the First Census of the United States Taken in the Year 1790* (Baltimore, 1966, orig. 1908), 10.
22. Clark, *State Records*, 23:462; 24:624; 25:263; *Wilmington Centinel*, Feb. 12, 1789; *State Gazette of North Carolina* (Edenton), March 26, 1789.
23. Donna J. Spindel, "Law and Disorder: The North Carolina Stamp Act Crisis," *North Carolina Historical Review*, 57 (1980):8; Schaw, *Journal of a Lady of Quality*, 170; Clark, *State Records*, 23:462; New Hanover County Court Minutes, April 1768.
24. William Logan, "William Logan's Journal of a Journey to Georgia, 1745," *Pennsylvania Magazine of History and Biography*, 36 (1912):13; Hugh B. Johnston, ed., "The Journal of Ebenezer Hazard in North Carolina, 1777 and 1778," *North Carolina Historical Review*, 36 (1959):379; Louis B. Wright and Marion Tinling, eds., *Quebec to Carolina in 1785-1786: Being the Travel Diary and Observations of Robert Hunter, Jr., a Young Merchant of London* (San Marino, Calif., 1943), 286-287.
25. Schaw, *Journal of a Lady of Quality*, 155-156, 284-285; Lennon and Kellam, *Wilmington Town Book*, 77-78, 83-84; Merrens, *Colonial North Carolina*, 195-198; Schoepf, *Travels in the Confederation*, 2:145.
26. William L. Saunders, ed., *The Colonial Records of North Carolina*, 10 vols. (Raleigh, 1886-1890), 4:43, 235; Peter DuBois to Samuel Johnston, Jr., February 8, 1757, Hayes Collection, Southern Historical Collection, Chapel Hill, N.C.; Schaw, *Journal of a Lady of Quality*, 156; Miranda, *New Democracy*, 14.
27. Nina Moore Tiffany, ed., *Letters of James Murray, Loyalist* (Boston, 1901), 63; William P. Cumming, "The Turbulent Life of Captain James Wimble," *North Carolina Historical Review*, 46 (1969):12.
28. Tony P. Wrenn, *Wilmington, North Carolina: An Architectural and Historical Portrait* (Charlottesville, Va., 1984), 201-203, 234-235; Catherine W. Bishir, *North Carolina Architecture* (Chapel Hill, 1990), 26.
29. *Dictionary of North Carolina Biography*, s.v. "Burgwin, John."
30. Howe, "Journal of Josiah Quincy, Junior," 462; William K. Boyd, ed., *Some Eighteenth Century Tracts Concerning North Carolina* (Raleigh, 1927), 443; Miranda, *New Democracy*, 14.
31. Peter DuBois to Samuel Johnston, Jr., February 8, March 5, 1757, Hayes Collection; Boyd, *Some Eighteenth Century Tracts*, 443.
32. Schaw, *Journal of a Lady of Quality*, 154; McEachern and Williams, *Wilming-*

ton–*New Hanover Safety Committee Minutes*, 14, 18, 20; Higginbotham, *Papers of James Iredell*, 2:417.

33. *Wilmington Centinel*, December 3, 1788; February 12, 1789. Actually, Washington was born on February 11, 1732, but the later British substitution of the Gregorian calendar for the Julian calendar resulted in changing the birth date to February 22.

34. Watson, *Society in Colonial North Carolina*, 15.

35. McEachern and Williams, *Wilmington–New Hanover Safety Committee Minutes*, 3–4.

36. Clark, *State Records*, 23:535–536; 25:391–392; *Wilmington Centinel*, January 29, 1789; Alan D. Watson, "The Lottery in Early North Carolina," *North Carolina Historical Review*, 69 (1992): 366–373.

37. Archibald Henderson, *North Carolina: The Old North State and the New*, 5 vols. (Chicago, 1941), 1:636; D. Anthony Rivenbark, "History of Theater in Wilmington and the Lower Cape Fear Region," in *Time, Talent, Tradition. Five Essays on the Cultural History of the Lower Cape Fear Region*, ed. by Janet K. Seapker (Wilmington, 1995), 57. For speculation that theatrical performances may have appeared early and in number in Wilmington, see Nancy Regan Ping, "Music in Antebellum Wilmington and the Lower Cape Fear," Ph.D. dissertation, University of Colorado, 1979, 469–475.

38. Rivenbark, "History of Theater," 57; Stephen Cymbalsky, "Literature of the Lower Cape Fear," in *Time, Talent, Tradition*, 34; Sherill V. Martin, "Music and Dance in the Lower Cape Fear," in *Time, Talent, Tradition*, 42. For Godfrey, see Ping, "Music in Antebellum Wilmington and the Lower Cape Fear," 475–483.

39. Henderson, *North Carolina*, I:637–639; Henry Steele Commager, ed., *Documents of American History*, 2 vols., 7th ed. (New York, 1963), 1:86; James H. Dormon, Jr., *Theater in the Ante Bellum South, 1815–1861* (Chapel Hill, 1967), 19; Ping, "Music in Antebellum Wilmington and the Lower Cape Fear," 472.

40. *The State Gazette of North Carolina* (New Bern), November 29, 1787; Henderson, *North Carolina*, 1:639–640, 646.

41. *Wilmington Centinel*, October 26, December 10, 1788; February 26, 1789.

42. Clark, *State Records*, 23:236–237, 461–462; 25:262; Alan D. Watson, "Ordinaries in Colonial Eastern North Carolina," *North Carolina Historical Review*, 45 (1968):67–83.

43. *Wilmington Centinel*, Feb. 5, 1789; E. Milton Wheeler, "Development and Organization of the North Carolina Militia," *North Carolina Historical Review*, 41 (1964):307–323.

44. Lennon and Kellam, *Wilmington Town Book*, 95; *Wilmington Centinel*, December 25, 1788; January 8, 1789; Thomas C. Parramore, *Launching the Craft: The First Half-Century of Freemasonry in North Carolina* (Raleigh, 1975), 2–6.

45. Lawrence Lee, *The Lower Cape Fear in Colonial Days* (Chapel Hill: University of North Carolina Press, 1965), 209–211.

46. *Ibid.*, 215–216.

47. Saunders, *Colonial Records*, 5:158; 7:104, 284; Clark, *State Records*, 23:535–537, 803, 25:348–349, 391–392; *North Carolina Gazette* (Wilmington), July 10, 1765; Lennon and Kellam, *Wilmington Town Book*, 123.

48. Saunders, *Colonial Records*, 4:605, 1209–1212; 6:58–59; New Hanover County Deed Books, AB, 344, Office of the Register of Deeds, New Hanover County Courthouse; Fredrick E. Maser and Howard T. Maag, eds., *The Journal of Joseph Pilmore, Methodist Itinerant* (Philadelphia, 1969), 175–176, 189–190; Alan D. Watson, "Cornelius Harnett," in Watson, Dennis R. Lawson, and Donald R. Lennon, *Harnett, Hooper & Howe: Revolutionary Leader of the Lower Cape Fear* (Wilmington, 1979), 20.

49. Lennon and Kellam, *Wilmington Town Book*, 201, n.153; Griffith J. McRee, ed., *Life and Correspondence of James Iredell*, 2 vols. (New York, 1949, orig. 1857), 2:217, n.217; William Hooper to George Hooper, c.1776, William Hooper Papers, State Archives, Raleigh, N.C.

50. J. Bryan Grimes, comp., *Abstracts of North Carolina Wills* (Raleigh, 1910), 179; Clark, *State Records*, 24:511–513, 984–985; *Wilmington Centinel*, July 30, October 26, 1788.

51. *Cape-Fear Mercury*, September 22, 1773; Alan D. Watson, ed., *An Index to North Carolina Newspapers, 1784–1789* (Raleigh, 1992), ix.

52. *Wilmington Centinel*, October 26, 1788; McRee, *Life and Correspondence of James Iredell*, 2:241, 243; Watson, *Index to North Carolina Newspapers*, xii.

53. *Virginia Gazette* (Williamsburg), May 25, 1739; *South-Carolina Gazette* (Charleston), April 26, 1739; *Cape-Fear Mercury*, December 8, 1769; May 11, 1774; *Journal Kept by Hugh Finlay, Surveyor of the Post Roads on the Continent of North America, ...* (Brooklyn, 1867), 69.

54. Higginbotham, *Papers of James Iredell*, 2:136; Archibald Maclaine to George Hooper, April 9, 1783, Archibald Maclaine Papers, State Archives; *Wilmington Centinel*, July 2, December 18, 1788; February 5, 1789.

55. Clark, *State Records*, 17:148, 152; Watson, "Cornelius Harnett," 11; Watson, *Society in Colonial North Carolina*, 68.

56. Clark, *State Records*, 23:357; Adelaide L. Fries et al., *Records of the Moravians in North Carolina*, 12 vols. (Raleigh, 1922–2000), 1:335; Higginbotham, *Papers of James Iredell*, 2:411; New Hanover County Court Minutes, October 1768.

57. Archibald Maclaine to George Hooper, April, 5, 9, 1783, Archibald Maclaine Papers; Higginbotham, *Papers of James Iredell*, 2:444; Watson, *Society in Colonial North Carolina*, 68–69.

58. *North-Carolina Gazette*, July 10, 1765; *Wilmington Centinel*, September 3, 1788; Watson, *Society in Colonial North Carolina*, 70.

3. A Developing Economy

1. Joseph A. Ernst and H. Roy Merrens, "'Camden's turrets pierce the skies': The Urban Process in the Southern Colonies during the Eighteenth Century," *William and Mary Quarterly*, 3rd Series, 30 (October 1975):549–574; Jacob M. Price, "Economic Function and the Growth of American Port Towns in the Eighteenth Century," *Perspectives in American History*, 8 (1974):123–186; John J. McCusker and Russell R. Menard, *The Economy of British America, 1607–1789* (Chapel Hill, 1985), 131–133.

2. H. Roy Merrens, *North Carolina in the Eighteenth Century: A Study in Historical Geography* (Chapel Hill, 1964), 142–166.

3. Lawrence Lee, *The Lower Cape Fear in Colonial Days* (Chapel Hill, 1965), 3–4.

4. *South-Carolina Gazette* (Charleston), October 17, 1761.

5. Lord Adam Gordon, "Journal of an Officer's Travels in America and the West Indies, 1764–1765," in *Travels in the American Colonies*, ed. by Newton D. Mereness (New York, 1916), 402; Janet Schaw, *Journal of a Lady of Quality ...* , ed. by Evangeline W. Andrews and Charles M. Andrews (New Haven, 1923), 145; Lee, *Lower Cape Fear*, 137–138, 164–165.

6. Alan D. Watson, "Port Brunswick in the Colonial Era," Lower Cape Fear Historical Society *Journal*, 31 (1989):23–32. See also Thomas C. Barrow, *Trade and*

Empire: The British Customs Service in Colonial America, 1660–1775 (Cambridge, Mass., 1967).

7. William L. Saunders, ed., *The Colonial Records of North Carolina*, 10 vols. (Raleigh, 1886–1890), 3:259; 4:6.

8. Lee, *Lower Cape Fear*, 166.

9. Charles C. Crittenden, *The Commerce of North Carolina, 1763–1789* (New Haven, 1936), 77–83; Lee, *Lower Cape Fear*, 162.

10. Saunders, *Colonial Records*, 6:969; Crittenden, *Commerce of North Carolina*, 80–81; Lee, *Lower Cape Fear*, 162–163.

11. Byron Eugene Logan, "An Historical Geographic Survey of North Carolina Ports," Ph.D. diss., University of North Carolina, 1956, 62; Crittenden, *Commerce of North Carolina*, 79, 79 n.5.

12. Crittenden, *Commerce of North Carolina*, 69–70; Lee, *Lower Cape Fear*, 164.

13. Merrens, *Colonial North Carolina*, 127; Crittenden, *Commerce of North Carolina*, 75–76, 84.

14. *South-Carolina & American General Gazette* (Charleston), August 5, 1768; Merrens, *Colonial North Carolina*, 131–132.

15. Lee, *Lower Cape Fear*, 155.

16. Merrens, *Colonial North Carolina*, 93–101.

17. *Ibid.*, 109.

18. *Ibid.*, 120–124; Saunders, *Colonial Records*, 9:539; Johann David Schoepf, *Travels in the Confederation, 1783–1784*, 2 vols., ed. and trans. by Alfred J. Morrison (Philadelphia, 1911), 2:129–130; Donald Jackson and Dorothy Twohig, eds., *The Diaries of George Washington*, 6 vols. (Charlottesville, Va.: 1976–1979), 6:119.

19. Hugh Meredith, *An Account of the Cape Fear Country, 1731*, ed. by Earl Gregg Swem (Perth Amboy, N. J., 1912), 20; Saunders, *Colonial Records*, 5:316; 6:1029; 9:270, 364; Nina Moore Tiffany, ed., *Letters of James Murray, Loyalist* (Boston, 1901), 78; Merrens, *Colonial North Carolina*, 125–128.

20. Tiffany, *Letters of James Murray*, 64; Schaw, *Journal of a Lady of Quality*, 177; Charles C. Crittenden, "Inland Navigation in North Carolina, 1763–1789," *North Carolina Historical Review*, 8 (1931):145–150.

21. Benjamin F. Hall Autobiography, Benjamin F. Hall Papers, State Archives, Raleigh, N.C.; Schaw, *Journal of a Lady of Quality*, 185.

22. Hall, Autobiography; Crittenden, "Inland Navigation," 151.

23. William K. Boyd, ed., *Some Eighteenth Tracts Concerning North Carolina* (Raleigh, 1927), 440; Hall, Autobiography; J. Bryan Grimes, comp., *North Carolina Wills and Inventories* (Raleigh, 1912), 153; James H. Brewer, "An Account of Negro Slavery in the Cape Fear Region Prior to 1860," Ph.D. diss., University of Pittsburgh, 1949, 126–127.

24. Watson, "Port Brunswick in the Colonial Era," 26.

25. *Ibid.*, 27.

26. Walter Clark, ed., *The State Records of North Carolina*, 16 vols. numbered 11-26 (Winston and Goldsboro, 1895–1906), 23:639, 790–801; 25:313–319, 378–387.

27. Saunders, *Colonial Records*, 4:5–6, 16; 8:186–189.

28. Saunders, *Colonial Records*, 4:6; 5:293, 316–317, 573–574, 714; 6:449, 1030; 8:38, 66; Clark, *State Records*, 23:613–614, 646, 649, 797–798; Schaw, *Journal of a Lady of Quality*, 195; Lee, *Lower Cape Fear*, 159–160.

29. Philip M. Hamer et al., eds., *The Papers of Henry Laurens*, projected multi-volume series (Columbia, S.C., 1968-), 3:95, 357, 374; 4:39–43, 208–209.

30. Lee, *Lower Cape Fear*, 172–180.

31. "A New Voyage to Georgia. By a Young Gentleman," [1737], in *Collections*

of the Georgia Historical Society, 2:54–56, 59; Hugh Finlay, *Journal Kept by Hugh Finlay, Surveyor of the Post Roads on the Continent of North America* (Brooklyn, 1867), 67; Schaw, *Journal of a Lady of Quality*, 202, 280.

32. Saunders, *Colonial Records*, 9:659; Clark, *State Records*, 23:753–754, 870–871, 908–909, 918–920.

33. Clark, *State Records*, 15:786; 23:791, 920–922, 974; 25:268–270, 786.

34. Saunders, *Colonial Records*, 4:449, 1030; Clark, *State Records*, 24:513–517; 25:470–472; Merrens, *Colonial North Carolina*, 157–160.

35. Boyd, *Some Eighteenth Century Tracts*, 448–449; Merrens, *Colonial North Carolina*, 159–161.

36. See Warran Boeschenstein, *Historic American Towns Along the Atlantic Coast* (Baltimore and London, 1999), 5–23.

37. Price, "Economic Function and the Growth of American Port Towns in the Eighteenth Century," 173.

38. Deed Book AB, Office of the Register of Deeds, New Hanover County Courthouse, Wilmington, N.C.; Donald R. Lennon and Ida Brooks Kellam, eds., *The Wilmington Town Book, 1743–1778* (Raleigh, 1973), 40, n.61; *North Carolina Gazette* (Wilmington), February 26, 1766; *Cape Fear Mercury* (Wilmington), September 22, 1773; May 18, 1774.

39. Schaw, *Journal of a Lady of Quality*, 155; Saunders, *Colonial Records*, 10:48; 236; Merrens, *Colonial North Carolina*, 152–153.

40. Schaw, *Journal of a Lady of Quality*, 323–325; Merrens, *Colonial North Carolina*, 153.

41. Robert Paul Thomas, "A Quantitative Approach to the Study of British Imperial Policy upon Colonial Welfare: Some Preliminary Findings," *Journal of Economic History*, 25 (1965):615–638; Roger Ransom, "British Policy and Colonial Growth: Some Implications of the Burden of the Navigation Acts," *Journal of Economic History*, 28 (1968):427–435.

42. Schaw, *Journal of a Lady of Quality*, 281; Joseph A. Ernst, *Money and Politics in America: A Study in the Currency Act of 1764 and the Political Economy of Revolution* (Chapel Hill, 1973), 203, 296; Boyd, *Some Eighteenth Century Tracts*, 448–449.

43. D. L. Corbitt, ed., "Historical Notes," *North Carolina Historical Review*, 5 (1928):329–330; Lee, *Lower Cape Fear*, 247–250.

44. Leora H. McEachern and Isabel M. Williams, eds., *Wilmington–New Hanover Safety Committee Minutes, 1774–1776* (Wilmington, 1974), 28.

45. Crittenden, *Commerce of North Carolina*, 125–126; Clark, *State Records*, 13:84–85.

46. William N. Still, *North Carolina's Revolutionary War Navy* (Raleigh, 1976), 3, 14; Lee, *Lower Cape Fear*, 275; Adelaide L. Fries et al, eds., *Records of the Moravians in North Carolina*, 12 vols. (Raleigh, 1922–2000), 3:1323.

47. Francisco de Miranda, *The New Democracy in America: Travels of Francisco de Miranda in the United States, 1783–1784*, trans. by Judson P. Wood, ed. by John S. Ezell (Norman, Okla., 1963), 14; Lawrence Lee, *The History of Brunswick County, North Carolina* (Charlotte, 1980), 86–87.

48. Crittenden, *Commerce of North Carolina*, 121; Clark, *State Records*, 24:686–688, 850–851.

49. Clark, *State Records*, 23:355–358, 381, 383.

50. *Ibid.*, 23:357; Fries, *Records of the Moravians*, 1:335; Minutes of the New Hanover County Court of Pleas and Quarter Sessions, October 1768, State Archives.

51. Clark, *State Records*, 23:650–652, 682–683.

52. *Ibid.*, 24:124–128, 167–168, 218–219.

53. Fries, *Records of Moravians*, 1:259; Clark, *State Records*, 24:218; McEachern and Williams, *Wilmington–New Hanover Safety Committee Minutes*, 70–72; Lee, *History of Brunswick County*, 47–48.

54. Clark, *State Records*, 24:502–508, 586–589.

55. *Ibid.*, 23:667, 682, 858; 24:502, 851.

56. *Ibid.*, 24:590–592; David Stick, *North Carolina Lighthouses* (Raleigh, 1981), 11–14.

57. Clark, *State Records*, 24:592; 25:57; *Laws and Resolutions of the State of North Carolina, 1802*, c. 46.

58. Griffith J. McRee, ed., *Life and Correspondence of James Iredell*, 2 vols. (New York, 1949, orig. 1857), 2:70, 115, 255; Clark, *State Records*, 14:553; 16:995; Crittenden, *Commerce of North Carolina*, 158.

59. Crittenden, *Commerce of North Carolina*, 158; *State Gazette of North Carolina* (Edenton), October 27, 1788.

60. Crittenden, *Commerce of North Carolina*, 160–161.

61. *Ibid.*, 161; Jackson and Twohig, *Diaries of George Washington*, 6:119.

62. Crittenden, *Commerce of North Carolina*, 162.

63. *Wilmington Centinel*, June 18, September 17, October 26, December 18, 1788; February 12, 1789.

64. McCusker and Menard, *Economy of British America*, 367, 373–375; Fries, *Records of the Moravians*, 4:1921.

4. Colonial Politics

1. Lawrence Lee, *The Lower Cape Fear in Colonial Days* (Chapel Hill, 1965), 229.

2. William J. Green, "Spanish Raids on the Coast of North Carolina, 1741–1748," *Tributaries*, 2 (1992):17–21.

3. Lee, *Lower Cape Fear*, 237–241.

4. Lawrence F. London, "The Representation Controversy in Colonial North Carolina," *North Carolina Historical Review*, 11 (1934):255–270; A. Roger Ekrich, *"Poor Carolina": Politics and Society in Colonial North Carolina, 1729–1776* (Chapel Hill, 1981), 86–109.

5. Mary Phlegar Smith, "Borough Representation in North Carolina," *North Carolina Historical Review*, 7 (1930):177–191; John L. Cheney, Jr., comp., *North Carolina Government, 1585–1979: A Narrative and Statistical History* (Raleigh, 1981), 1216.

6. Walter Clark, ed., *The State Records of North Carolina*, 16 vols. numbered 11–26 (Winston and Goldsboro, 1895–1906), 23:13, 146, 147; Donald R. Lennon and Ida B. Kellam, *The Wilmington Town Book, 1743–1778* (Raleigh, 1973), 3:n. 6, 40:n. 62; Cheney, *North Carolina Government*, 1216.

7. Alan D. Watson, "Cornelius Harnett," in Watson, Dennis R. Lawson, and Donald R. Lennon, *Harnett, Hooper & Howe: Revolutionary Leaders of the Lower Cape Fear* (Wilmington, 1979), 7; Jack P. Greene, *The Quest for Power. The Lower Houses of Assembly in the Southern Royal Colonies, 1689–1776* (Chapel Hill, 1963), 490.

8. Robert M. Weir, "North Carolina's Reaction to the Currency Act of 1764," *North Carolina Historical Review*, 40 (1963):183–199.

9. William L. Saunders, ed., *The Colonial Records of North Carolina*, 10 vols. (Raleigh, 1886–1980), 7:124; Lee, *Lower Cape Fear in Colonial Days*, 245.

10. Saunders, *Colonial Records*, 7:124–125, 131, 143; Donna J. Spindel, "Law and

Disorder: The North Carolina Stamp Act Crisis," *North Carolina Historical Review*, 56 (1981):8.

11. Saunders, *Colonial Records*, 7:127–128.

12. Samuel Johnston to ?, 1765, Hayes Collection, Southern Historical Collection, Chapel Hill, N.C.; *Maryland Gazette* (Annapolis), February 20, 1766.

13. Johnston to ?, 1765, Hayes Collection; *Maryland Gazette*, February 20, March 13, 1766.

14. William S. Powell, ed., *The Correspondence of William Tryon and Other Selected Papers*, 2 vols. (Raleigh, 1980, 1981), 1:261–262, 342–343.

15. Saunders, *Colonial Records*, 7:168d, 169–172, 174, 178–182; *Virginia Gazette* (Williamsburg), March 21, 1766; *North Carolina Gazette* (Wilmington), February 26, 1766; Lee, *Lower Cape Fear*, 249–251.

16. *South-Carolina Gazette* (Charleston), July 5, August 9, 13, 1770; Robert L. Ganyard, *The Emergence of North Carolina's Revolutionary State Government* (Raleigh, 1978), 20–21.

17. Powell, *Correspondence of William Tryon*, 2:657; William S. Powell, *The War of the Regulation and the Battle of Alamance, May 16, 1771* (Raleigh, 1949).

18. Powell, *Correspondence of William Tryon*, 2:659, 685, 694, 696, 747; *Pennsylvania Gazette* (Philadelphia), July 11, 1771; Janet Schaw, *Journal of a Lady of Quality ...* , ed. by Evangeline W. Andrews and Charles M. Andrews (New Haven, 1923), 319–321.

19. Mark A. DeWolfe Howe, ed., "Journal of Josiah Quincy, Junior, 1773," *Massachusetts Historical Society Proceedings*, 49 (1916), 460; Ganyard, *Emergence of North Carolina's Revolutionary State Government*, 25–26. For Howe see Charles E. Bennett and Donald R. Lennon, *A Quest for Glory. Major General Robert Howe and the American Revolution* (Chapel Hill and London, 1991).

20. Howe, "Journal of Josiah Quincy, Junior," 460; *Dictionary of North Carolina Biography*, r.v. "Hooper, William"; Lennon and Kellam, *Wilmington Town Book*, 174–175 n. 130; Cheney, *North Carolina Government*, 1216. For Hooper see Dennis R. Lawson, "William Hooper," in *Harnett, Hooper & Howe*, 35–67; Biographical sketch of William Hooper, ca. 1825, in the William Hooper Papers, State Archives, Raleigh, N.C.

21. Saunders, *Colonial Records*, 9:1016–1017; David T. Morgan and William J. Schmidt, *North Carolinians in the Continental Congress* (Winston-Salem, N.C., 1976), 3–25.

22. Lennon and Kellam, *Wilmington Town Book*, 77, 95, 125, n.124, 200, 218; Cheney, *North Carolina Government*, 153–159.

23. R. D. W. Connor, *Cornelius Harnett. An Essay in North Carolina History* (Raleigh, 1909), 112; Watson, "Cornelius Harnett," 11–16.

24. Alan D. Watson, "The Committees of Safety and the Coming of the Revolution in North Carolina, 1774–1776," *North Carolina Historical Review*, 73 (1996):132–133.

25. Leora H. McEachern and Isabel M. Williams, eds., *Wilmington–New Hanover Safety Committee Minutes, 1774–1776* (Wilmington, 1974), 1, 8, 21, 36–27, 45–46, 54, 62, 69.

26. *Ibid.*, 5–6, 13, 20, 24, 26, 51, 57, 58, 63.

27. Schaw, *Journal of a Lady of Quality*, 198; McEachern and Williams, *Wilmington–New Hanover Safety Committee Minutes*, 14–15, 27; Saunders, *Colonial Records*, 10:29–30.

28. McEachern and Williams, *Wilmington–New Hanover Safety Committee Minutes*, 18–19, 31–32; Saunders, *Colonial Records*, 9:1236–1238; 10:44, 61–62, 162–163;

Charles Grier Sellers, Jr., "Making a Revolution: The North Carolina Whigs, 1765–1775," in J. Carlyle Sitterson, ed., *Studies in Southern History in Memory of Albert Ray Newsome, 1894–1951* (Chapel Hill, 1957), 38.

29. Schaw, *Journal of a Lady of Quality*, 192–194, 198–199.

30. Mrs. Catherine Elizabeth DeRosset to John Burgwyn, August 25, September 10, 1775, in Kemp P. Battle, ed., *Letters and Documents Relating to the Early History of the Lower Cape Fear* (Chapel Hill, 1903), 22, 27; Schaw, *Journal of a Lady of Quality*, 180; Saunders, *Colonial Records*, 10:236.

31. McEachern and Williams, *Wilmington–New Hanover Safety Committee Minutes*, 73, 75, 77–79, 82.

32. Ibid., 9–10, 46, 52, 61–62, 68, 73–74.

33. Lindley S. Butler, *North Carolina and the Coming of the Revolution, 1763–1776*, (Raleigh, 1976), 58; Lee, *Lower Cape Fear*, 262–265; Vernon O. Stumpf, *Josiah Martin: The Last Royal Governor of North Carolina* (Durham, N.C., 1986), 114–116.

34. Robert Salter to Richard Caswell, June 3, 1775, Hayes Collection; McEachern and Williams, *Wilmington–New Hanover Safety Committee Minutes*, 44–47; Saunders, *Colonial Records*, 10:130–133; Lee, *Lower Cape Fear*, 265; Stumpf, *Josiah Martin*, 137–138.

35. McEachern and Williams, *Wilmington–New Hanover Safety Committee Minutes*, 49–50, 53–54, 61–62.

36. Ibid., 65, 68, 72–74. The committee also sought a house to serve as a hospital, and made arrangements to hire a nurse and equip the facility. Ibid., 70, 72–73.

37. Hugh F. Rankin, "The Moore's Creek Bridge Campaign," *North Carolina Historical Review*, 30 (1953):23–60.

38. Lee, *Lower Cape Fear*, 271–272.

39. Connor, *Cornelius Harnett*, 87; Watson, "Committees of Safety," 155.

40. William N. Still, Jr., *North Carolina's Revolutionary War Navy* (Raleigh, 1976), 4–6.

41. Clark, *State Records*, 11:674; 22:912; Still, *North Carolina's Revolutionary War Navy*, 14.

42. *North Carolina Gazette* (New Bern), December 26, 1777; Still, *North Carolina's Revolutionary War Navy*, 22–23.

43. Robert O. DeMond, *The Loyalists in North Carolina During the Revolution* (Durham, N.C., 1940); Carole W. Troxler, *The Loyalist Experience in North Carolina* (Raleigh, 1975); Wallace Brown, *The King's Friends: The Composition and Motives of the American Loyalist Claimants* (Providence, R.I., 1965), 195–210, 249–283.

44. Schaw, *Journal of a Lady of Quality*, 155; Lennon and Kellam, *Wilmington Town Book*, 180, n.141; Laura Page Frech, "The Wilmington Committee of Public Safety and the Loyalist Rising of February 1776," *North Carolina Historical Review*, 41 (1964): 31–32.

45. Clark, *State Records*, 11:546; Griffith J. McRee, ed., *Life and Correspondence of James Iredell*, 2 vols. (New York, 1949, orig. 1857), 1:405; Frech, "Wilmington Committee of Public Safety," 30–31.

46. Don Higginbotham, ed., *The Papers of James Iredell*, 2 vols. (Raleigh: 1976), 2:154, 161; Gregory De Van Massey, "The British Expedition to Wilmington, January–November 1781," *North Carolina Historical Review*, 66 (1989):388–389.

47. Massey, "British Expedition to Wilmington," 390, 392.

48. Undated deposition by Dr. A. J. DeRosset in the Charles Francis Jenkins Papers, State Archives; Lennon and Kellam, *Wilmington Town Book*, 209, n.158; Schaw, *Journal of a Lady of Quality*, 321; Massey, "British Expedition to Wilmington," 394.

49. Higginbotham, *Papers of James Iredell*, 2:327–329, 335–336; Massey, "British

Expedition in Wilmington," 394; Connor, *Cornelius Harnett*, 196–197. Remembering perhaps the indignity visited upon his wife by the British, and resettling his family with some difficulty in Wilmington, Adam Boyd beseeched Governor Thomas Burke in early 1782 to offer his services in hopes that he could "be employed so as to be of public use." Adam Boyd to Governor Burke, March 20, 1782, Adam Boyd Papers, State Archives.

50. Undated deposition by Dr. A. J. DeRosset, Charles Francis Jenkins Papers; Massey, "British Expedition to Wilmington," 396–297.

51. Massey, "British Expedition to Wilmington," 403–410; Hugh F. Rankin, *The North Carolina Continentals* (Chapel Hill, 1971), 367. For the loyalist exiles, see Troxler, *Loyalist Experience*, 37–55.

52. Alan D. Watson, "North Carolina: States' Rights and Agrarianism Ascendant," in *The Constitution and the States: The Role of the Original Thirteen in the Framing and Adoption of the Federal Constitution*, ed. by Patrick T. Conley and John P. Kaminski (Madison, Wis., 1988), 252.

53. Morgan and Schmidt, *North Carolinians in the Continental Congress*, 43–49; Watson, "North Carolina," 253.

54. Watson, "North Carolina," 255–258.

55. Higginbotham, *Papers of James Iredell*, 2:336, 444; McRee, *Life and Correspondence of James Iredell*, 2:178–179; Clark, *State Records*, 16:239–240; Cheney, *North Carolina Government*, 1218; Smith, "Borough Representation," 184.

56. Higginbotham, *Papers of James Iredell*, 2:337, n.3; Clark, *State Records*, 15:189–193; 16:31; 20:159–162; 21:73, 112; Smith, "Borough Representation," 184–185. For the election in 1788, see the *Wilmington Centinel*, July 16, August 13, 1788.

57. McRee, *Life and Correspondence of James Iredell*, 2:178.

58. Watson, "North Carolina," 260.

59. McRee, *Life and Correspondence of James Iredell*, 2:219, 221, 239–240; *Wilmington Centinel*, July 16, 1788.

60. Clark, *States Records*, 22:1–26; William C. Pool, "An Economic Interpretation of the Ratification of the Federal Constitution in North Carolina, Parts I and II," *North Carolina Historical Review*, 27 (1950):140–141, 303–304. See generally Louise I. Trenholme, *The Ratification of the Federal Constitution in North Carolina* (New York, 1931).

61. Jonathan Elliot, ed., T*he Debates in the Several State Conventions on the Adoption of the Federal Constitution*, 5 vols. (Philadelphia, 1836–1845), 4:10, 16, 26, 28–29, 34, 42, 46, 63–64, 69, 135–136, 139–140, 151–152, 161, 164, 175, 180–183, 188–190.

62. Watson, "North Carolina," 262.

63. Albert Ray Newsome, "North Carolina's Ratification of the Federal Constitution," *North Carolina Historical Review*, 17 (1940):287–301; J. Edwin Hendricks, "Joseph Winston: North Carolina Jeffersonian," *North Carolina Historical Review*, 45 (1968):290.

64. Clark, *State Records*, 22:36–53; William C. Pool, "An Economic Interpretation of the Federal Constitution in North Carolina, Part III," *North Carolina Historical Review*, 27 (1950):456–458.

65. Watson, "North Carolina," 262–263.

5. THE GROWTH OF A TOWN

1. Donald Jackson and Dorothy Twohig, eds., *Diaries of George Washington*, 6 vols. (Charlottesville, 1976–1979), 6:119; Alonzo Thomas Dill, Jr., "Eighteenth Century New Bern. A History of the Town and Craven County, 1700–1800." Part VIII. "New Bern at Century's End," *North Carolina Historical Review* 23 (1946):515–516; John L. Cheney, Jr., comp., *North Carolina Government, 1585–1979* (Raleigh, 1981), 1219.

2. *People's Press and Wilmington Advertiser*, February 4, April 18, October 9, 1835?; ? to John De Berniere Hooper, September 20, 1831, John De Berniere Hooper Papers, Southern Historical Collection, Chapel Hill, N.C.; Cheney, *North Carolina Government*, 1219.

3. *North State Whig* (Washington, N.C.), May 8, 1850; Guion G. Johnson, *Ante-Bellum North Carolina: A Social History* (Chapel Hill, 1937), 117; Cheney, *North Carolina Government*, 1219.

4. *Chronicle* (Wilmington), October 15, 1845; Nicholas W. Schenck Journal, 103, East Carolina Manuscript Collection, Greenville, N.C.; Testimony of Witnesses Before the Jury of Inquisition, November 22, 1839, Coroners' Inquests, County Records, New Hanover County, 1768–1866, State Archives, Raleigh, N.C.

5. Gotthardt D. Bernheim, *The First Twenty Years of St. Paul's Evangelical Lutheran Church* (Wilmington, 1879), 11–16; Bobbie Marcroft, "The Early Germans," Lower Cape Fear Historical Society *Bulletin*, 18 (February 1975).

6. *Wilmington Gazette*, December 4, 1800; December 2, 1806; March 3, 24, 1807; *Journal* (Wilmington), March 23, 1855; March 19, 1858; March 22, 1860; *Daily Herald* (Wilmington), March 17, 1856.

7. Kimberly Sims, "Wilmington Jewry:1800–1914," Honor's Thesis, University of North Carolina at Wilmington, 1999, 3–5; Jon Henry Gerdes, "The Early Jews of Wilmington," Lower Cape Fear Historical Society *Bulletin*, 28 (October 1984); *Commercial* (Wilmington), August 2, 1849.

8. Sims, "Wilmington Jewry," 10–11, 13, 20, 43.

9. Catherine W. Bishir, "Black Builders in Antebellum North Carolina," *North Carolina Historical Review*, 61 (1984):454, n.106; Stephen C. Worsley, "Catholicism in Antebellum North Carolina," *North Carolina Historical Review*, 60 (1983):406; Eighth Census of the United States, 1860, New Hanover County, North Carolina, Mortality Schedule—3, microfilm, State Archives.

10. Edward F. Turberg, "Architecture in the Lower Cape Fear," in Janet Seapker, ed., *Time, Talent, Tradition: Five Essays on the Cultural History of the Lower Cape Fear Region, North Carolina* (Wilmington, 1995), 20, 24; Janet K. Seapker, "James F. Post, Builder-Architect: The Legend and the Ledger," Lower Cape Fear Historical Society *Bulletin*, 30 (May 1987).

11. James Sprunt, *Chronicles of the Cape Fear River, 1660–1916*, 2d ed. (Wilmington, 1916), 229; *Wilmington Advertiser*, February 17, 1837; February 4, 1841; *Daily Herald*, October 31, November 1, 2, 1855; *Journal*, November 2, 1855.

12. Artemus Boies to "Dear Brother," April 7, 1819, Miscellaneous Letters, Southern Historical Collection; M. H. Walker to "My Dear Brother," June 28, 1856, Levin Lane Papers, Southern Historical Collection; Platt K. Dickinson to "My Dear Sister," July 2, 1857, July 27, 1859, Platt K. Dickinson Papers, Southern Historical Collection; *Chronicle*, October 15, 1845; *Herald* (Wilmington), September 10, 1857.

13. Phila Cohen Lazarus Calder to Gershon Lazarus, November 20, 1846, in "Lazarus-Cohen Correspondence, 1842–1871," Lower Cape Fear Historical Society *Bulletin*, 27 (October 1983); James W. Patton, "Glimpses of North Carolina in the Writings of Northern and Foreign Travelers, 1783–1860," *North Carolina Historical Review*, 46 (1968):321.

14. Journal of Susan D. Nye, May 7, 1815, Susan Davis Nye Hutchinson Papers, State Archives; Mortimer DeMott, "Sojourn in Wilmington and the Lower Cape Fear, 1837," Lower Cape Fear Historical Society *Bulletin*, 22 (May 1979); John A. Scott, ed., *Journal of a Residence on a Georgian Plantation in 1838–1839, by Frances Anne Kemble* (New York, 1961), 35.

15. Journal of Susan D. Nye, May 7, 1815; DeMott, "Sojourn in Wilmington and the Lower Cape Fear."

16. Scott, *Journal of a Residence on a Georgia Plantation*, 34–35.

17. Frederick Law Olmsted, *A Journey in the Seaboard Slave States, with Remarks on Their Economy* (New York, 1969, orig., 1856), 374; *Commercial* (Wilmington), May 28, 1852; *Herald*, February 21, June 2, 1852; *Daily Herald*, November 3, 1859; *Laws and Resolutions of the State of North Carolina, 1858–1859*, c. 257.

18. *Chronicle*, October 15, 1845; *Daily Herald*, January 16, 1857; *Laws, 1850–1851*, c. 212; Sprunt, *Chronicles of the Cape Fear River*, 163; Johnson, *Ante-Bellum North Carolina*, 233.

19. *Journal*, September 13, 1847; *People's Press and Wilmington Advertiser*, April 8, December 18, 1835; Sprunt, *Chronicles of the Cape Fear River*, 169.

20. Lydia Hall to "My Dear William," December 3, 1821, W. P. Hall Collection, State Archives; Phila Calder to Almira, May 23, 1850, in "Lazarus-Calder Correspondence."

21. *Daily Herald*, June 23, 1859. For washing machines, see *People's Press*, March 6, 1833; *Journal*, October 23, 1846; for sewing machines, see *Journal*, February 21, 1851; *Daily Herald*, January 1, 1857.

22. *True Republican* (Wilmington), April 18, 1809; *Wilmington Gazette*, October 15, 1805.

23. *Journal*, December 20, 1844; September 5, 1845; June 2, 24, 1859; 1851–1859 passim.

24. *North Carolina Journal* (Halifax), November 19, 1798; *Pennsylvania Gazette* (Philadelphia), May 16, 1798; *Raleigh Register*, November 12, 1819; "The Reverend Thomas Wright's Letters to Robert Scott," Lower Cape Fear Historical Society *Bulletin*, 23 (February 1980); *Fayetteville Observer*, January 24, 1828; *Laws, 1806*, c. 38; Sprunt, *Chronicles of the Cape Fear River*, 143.

25. Lydia Turrentine to "My very dear Aunt," January 18, 1840, Parrish Family Papers, Southern Historical Collection, Chapel Hill, N.C.; *Fayetteville Observer*, January 22, 1840; May 3, 10, 1843; November 11, 1845; *Chronicle* (Wilmington), November 5, 1845.

26. *Cape Fear Recorder*, July 1, 1829; *Fayetteville Observer*, March 4, 1830; *People's Press and Wilmington Advertiser*, July 9, August 13, 1834; *Journal* (Wilmington), January 9, November 20, 1846; September 7, 1849; *Daily Herald* (Wilmington), March 22, 1860; March 22, 1861.

27. *Wilmington Gazette*, July 28, 1807; *Raleigh Register*, November 19, 1819; *Carolina Observer* (Fayetteville), May 12, 1825; *Journal*, August 29, October 10, 1845; *Fayetteville Observer*, November 11, 1845; *Herald* (Wilmington), August 27, 1857.

28. *North Carolina Journal*, November 19, 1798; *Raleigh Register*, November 12, 1819; *Wilmington Chronicle*, May 10, 1843.

29. *Wilmington Gazette*, January 14, 1806; *Fayetteville Observer*, January 24, 1828; January 22, 1840; *Wilmington Advertiser*, March 25, 1836; *Herald*, August 27, 1857.

30. *Fayetteville Observer*, January 22, 1840; November 11, 1845; *Wilmington Chronicle*, May 17, 1843; *Journal*, November 7, 1845; February 20, 1852.

31. Dianne Cashman, *The Lonely Road: A History of the Physics and Physicians of the Lower Cape Fear, 1735–1976* (Wilmington, 1976), 18–19 (quotation); *Transactions of the Medical Society of the State of North Carolina, at Its Third Annual Meeting, ...* (Wilmington, 1852), 71.

32. *Wilmington Gazette*, April 1, 1802; April 6, 1816; *People's Press and Wilmington Advertiser*, October 30, December 11, 1835; *Journal* (Wilmington), February 2, April 17, 1846; January 31, 1851; Nancy Beeler and Rush Beeler, eds., *Wilmington Town Minutes, 1847–1855* (Wilmington, 1997), 42, 143; Alan D. Watson, *Wilmington: Port of North Carolina* (Columbia, S.C., 1992), 47.

33. *Transactions of the Medical Society of the State of North Carolina* (1852) 73–74; *Herald* (Wilmington), September 10, 1857.

34. *Transactions of the Medical Society of the State of North Carolina* (1852) 74–81; *Wilmington Chronicle*, July 19, 1843.

35. Eighth Census, 1860, Mortality Schedule—3, New Hanover County, North Carolina, microfilm, State Archives, *Journal*, January 21, 1859; January 2, 1860; *Daily Herald*, January 16, 1861.

36. DeRosset to "Darling Katie," July 6, 1847, DeRosset Family Papers, Southern Historical Collection, Chapel Hill, N.C.

37. *Wilmington Gazette*, April 23, 1805; *People's Press and Wilmington Advertiser*, October 29, 1834; Warner L. Wells, "Surgical Practice in North Carolina: An Historical Commentary," in Dorothy Long, ed., *Medicine in North Carolina: Essays in the History of Medical Science and Medical Service, 1524–1960*, 2 vols. (Raleigh, 1972), 2:634; *Journal*, May 8, 15, 1846; July 11, 1851; Sprunt, *Chronicles of the Cape Fear River*, 182–183.

38. "Progress Toward the Establishment of Medical Science in North Carolina, 1800–1850," in Long, *Medicine in North Carolina*, 1:54–55; "Organization of the North Carolina Medical Profession, 1799 and 1849," in *ibid.*, 1:74–75; Cashman, *Lonely Road*, 22.

39. *Transactions of the Medical Society of the State of North Carolina* (1852), 21–22; *Minutes of the Eleventh Annual Meeting of the Medical Society of the State of North Carolina*, ... (Wilmington, 1860), 17–26.

40. *Dictionary of North Carolina Biography*, s.v. "DeRosset, Armond John"; 6 vols. *Transactions of the Seventeenth Annual Meeting of the Medical Society of the State of North Carolina*, ... (Wilmington, 1870), 8–9.

41. *Daily Herald*, December 15, 1854; December 10, 11, 1860.

42. *Wilmington Gazette*, April 15, 1806; *Cape Fear Recorder*, May 27, 1816; *Wilmington Advertiser*, January 12, July 20, 1838.

43. Guion G. Johnson, *Ante-Bellum North Carolina: A Social History* (Chapel Hill, 1937), 749–751; *Chronicle*, July 19, 1843; *Daily Herald*, June 16, 1860.

44. *Wilmington Gazette*, May 12, 1812; *Cape Fear Recorder*, May 9, November 21, 1818; *People's Press and Wilmington Advertiser*, February 4, 1835; *Journal*, March 11, 1853; *Daily Herald*, September 7, October 17, 1860.

45. *Wilmington Gazette*, July 19, 1803; July 2, 1805; *People's Press*, February 13, 1833; *Wilmington Advertiser*, November 3, 1837; *Journal*, December 13, 1844.

46. *People's Press*, February 28, 1833; *Journal*, September 21, 1844; July 20, 1849; *Herald* (Wilmington), April 16, 1857; *Daily Herald*, September 7, October 3, 1860.

47. Samuel Jocelyn to Miss Elizabeth Jocelyn, August 24, 1800, Giles Family Papers, Southern Historical Collection; Nicholas W. Schenck Journal, 113; *People's Press and Wilmington Advertiser*, June 17, 1835; *Daily Herald*, May 16, 1859; Eighth Census, 1860, New Hanover County, Mortality Schedule—3, North Carolina.

48. M. H. Walker to "My Dear Brother," June 28, 1856, Levin Lane Papers; Sprunt, *Chronicles of the Cape Fear River*, 231–237.

49. *Laws, 1792*, c. 49; *1822*, c. 81; *People's Press and Wilmington Advertiser*, April 15, 1835; *Wilmington Advertiser*, November 27, 1835.

50. *Wilmington Gazette*, June 13, 1799; July 10, 1800; *Wilmington Advertiser*, February 5, 1836; *Journal*, January 5, 1860; Alan D. Watson, "The Lottery in Early North Carolina," *North Carolina Historical Review*, 69 (1992):365–387.

51. Hall's *Wilmington Gazette*, April 26, 1797; *Wilmington Gazette*, April 19, 1799; October 7, November 11, 1806; June 26, 1810; *Wilmington Advertiser*, February 9, 1838; February 1, 1839; *Journal*, April 11, 1845; January 31, 185; *Daily Herald*, December 9, 1854; November 23, 1857; December 8, 1859.

52. *Wilmington Gazette*, January 7, 1806; *Wilmington Advertiser*, November 3, 10, 1837; April 27, 1838; *Journal*, March 2, 1849; March 13, 1852; *Daily Herald*, March 3, October 22, 26, 1860; Nancy Regan Ping, "Music in Antebellum Wilmington and the Lower Cape Fear of North Carolina," Ph.D. dissertation, University of Colorado, 1979, 340–341.

53. Ping, "Music in Antebellum Wilmington," 156–158; Anna to Miss Ellen Mordecai, March 11, 1831, Pattie Mordecai Collection, State Archives; Deposition of Mary Pike, May 26, 1799, Coroner's Inquest, Coroners' Records, Records of New Hanover County.

54. Ada Amelia Costin Diary, December 15, 1860, Martin Smith Grant Collection, East Carolina Manuscript Collection; Willie to "My Dearest Sister," April 15, 1847; Kate to Mrs. A. J. DeRosset, October 3, 1850, DeRosset Family Papers; *Herald*, November 13, 1852; March 30, 1860; *Daily Journal*, June 22, 25, 1858. For boat races see *Herald*, July 21, 1852; *Daily Herald*, July 15, 1859; May 19, 1860.

55. *Wilmington Gazette*, October 29, 1801; October 25, 1803; December 15, 1807; *People's Press*, January 26, March 27, 1833; *Journal*, December 6, 27, 1844; January 1, 1859; *Daily Herald*, April 19, 27, 1860.

56. *Daily Herald*, January 1, 1856; January 1, 1857.

57. *Chronicle*, January 11, 1843; *Journal*, January 14, 1848; *Cape Fear Recorder*, January 14, 1829.

58. *Journal*, February 14, 1851; February 18, 1853; January 20, 1854; *Herald*, February 14, 1852; *Daily Herald*, February 15, 1855; February 14, 1860.

59. *Daily Herald*, February 14, 1857.

60. *Journal*, February 28, 1845; February 28, 1846; February 28, 1851; February 23, 1855; *Herald*, February 28, 1858; *Daily Herald*, February 22, 1860.

61. *Daily Herald*, January 7, February 13, 21, 25, 27, 28, March 2, 1857; *Journal*, March 6, 1857.

62. Ada Amelia Costin Diary, March 21, 1861; *Journal*, April 8, 1853; April 6, 1855.

63. *Wilmington Advertiser*, May 6, 1841; *Journal*, May 1, May 18, 1846; May 7, 1847; May 5, 1848; Mother to "Kate," May 21, 1856, DeRosset Family Papers.

64. *Wilmington Gazette*, July 2, 1801; July 5, 12, 1803; July 8, 1806; July 21, 1807; July 10, 1813.

65. *Wilmington Advertiser*, August 6, 1838; Beeler and Beeler, *Wilmington Town Minutes*, 27, 74, 166. For other, and varied, orders of processions see *Journal*, July 5, 1850; July 4, 1851; July 2, 1852; July 3, 1857.

66. *Wilmington Advertiser*, June 20, 1837; *Journal*, July 4, 11, 1845; July 7, 1848; June 29, 1849; July 2, 9, 1852; July 6, 1855; July 10, 1857; July 9, 1858; *Herald*, July 9, 1957; *Daily Herald*, July 5, 1859; July 2, 5, 1860. The Wilmington commissioners in 1855 restricted the firing of cannon in town due to accidents, except for the observation of the Fourth of July. Beeler and Beeler, *Wilmington Town Minutes*, 167.

67. *Daily Herald*, December 1, 1854; December 4, 1857; *Journal*, November 2, 1855; December 3, 1858; November 25, 1859; Ada Amelia Costin Diary, November 29, 1860.

68. *Journal*, January 3, 1845; December 22, 29, 1854; December 27, 1860; *Daily Herald*, December 15, 23, 1854.

6. The African American Experience

1. John L. Cheney, Jr., comp., *North Carolina Government, 1585–1979: A Narrative and Statistical History* (Raleigh, 1981), 1111, 1115, 1219, 1298.

2. *Population of the United States in 1860; ...* (Washington, D. C., 1864), 359;

John Hope Franklin, *The Free Negro in North Carolina 1790–1860* (Chapel Hill, 1943), 14–17; James Howard Brewer, "An Account of Negro Slavery in the Cape Fear Region Prior to 1860," Ph.D. diss., University of Pittsburgh, 1949, 30; Nancy Regan Ping, "Music in Antebellum Wilmington and the Lower Cape Fear of North Carolina," Ph.D., diss., University of Colorado, 1979, 22.

3. *Laws and Resolutions of the State of North Carolina, 1812*, c. 62; Elizabeth Francenia McKoy, *Early Wilmington Block by Block* (Wilmington, 1967), 72–73; Guion Griffis Johnson, *Ante-Bellum North Carolina: A Social History* (Chapel Hill, 1937), 592; Franklin, *The Free Negro in North Carolina*, 32–33.

4. Presentment, Summer Term, 1853, Superior Court (?), New Hanover County, Grand Jury Reports and Presentments, 1848–1871, New Hanover County, Miscellaneous Records, 1756–1945, State Archives, Raleigh, N.C.; *Laws,* 1818, c. 47; George P. Rawick, ed., *The American Slave: A Composite Biography. North Carolina Narratives* (Wesport, Conn., 1977), Vol. 15, Part 2:2; *Cape Fear Recorder* (Wilmington), December 7, 1816; *Journal* (Wilmington), February 27, 1852; Catherine W. Bishir, "Black Builders in Antebellum North Carolina," *North Carolina Historical Review*, 61 (1984):455; David S. Cecelski, "The Shores of Freedom: The Maritime Underground Railroad in North Carolina," *North Carolina Historical Review*, 71 (1994):195–197.

5. *Laws, 1795*, c. 37; *1827–1828*, c. 92; *1828–1829*, c. 112; *Wilmington Gazette*, February 3, 1807; *Journal*, December 13, 1847; James Howard Brewer, "Legislation Designed to Control Slavery in Wilmington and Fayetteville," *North Carolina Historical Review*, 30 (1953):157, 160.

6. Franklin, *The Free Negro in North Carolina*, 62–64.

7. *Ibid.*, 64–66; Brewer, "Account of Negro Slavery," 78–81.

8. Franklin, *The Free Negro in North Carolina*, 67–70; Nancy Beeler and Rush Beeler, eds., *Wilmington Town Minutes, 1847–1855* (Wilmington, 1997), 6–7.

9. *Ibid.*, 74; *Proceedings and Debates of the Convention of North-Carolina, Called to Amend the Constitution of the State,* ... (Raleigh, 1836), 72, 80–81, 354; Harold J. Counihan, "The North Carolina Constitutional Convention of 1835: A Study in Jacksonian Democracy," *North Carolina Historical Review*, 46 (1969):346–348. Actually, the vote in the convention was closer. Although the *Debates* give the numbers as 66 and 61, a count of the names reveals a vote of 64 to 62.

10. *Laws, 1824*, c. 78; *1826–1827*, c. 54; New Hanover County Court Minutes, June 1831, State Archives; Appointments of Patrollers, New Hanover County, December 1837, March 1844, March 1861, Slave Records, Patrols, 1819, 1830–1861, New Hanover County, Records of Slaves and Free Persons of Color, 1786–1888, State Archives.

11. *Aurora* (Wilmington) as reprinted in the *North Carolina Standard* (Raleigh), October 30, 1850.

12. *Hall's Wilmington Gazette*, April 29, 1797; *Cape Fear Recorder*, January 30, July 31, 1819; April 14, 1821; *Journal*, June 27, 1851.

13. *Wilmington Chronicle; And North Carolina Weekly Advertiser*, July 10, 1797; *Wilmington Gazette*, March 27, 1800; *Cape Fear Recorder*, April 14, 1821.

14. *Wilmington Gazette*, June 2, 1803; December 15, 1807; *True Republican* (Wilmington), April 18, 1809.

15. Cecelski, "Shores of Freedom," 174, 191–201. See also Brewer, "Account of Negro Slavery," 124.

16. *People's Press and Wilmington Advertiser*, May 1, 1833; May 20, 1835; *Daily Herald* (Wilmington), August 18, 1859. See also Beeler and Beeler, *Wilmington Town Minutes*, 52.

17. *Commercial* (Wilmington), January 10, 1850; Cecelski, "Shores of Freedom," 204–205.

18. Johnson, *Ante-Bellum North Carolina*, 577–578; *Journal*, October 19, 1849; "List of Vessels Searched and Fumigated, 1858–1862," and "Account of Records with Wm. J. Love," Board of Commissioners of Navigation and Pilotage for the Cape Fear River and Bar Papers, Rare Book, Manuscript, and Special Collections Department, Duke University Library, Durham, N.C.; Cecelski, "Shores of Freedom," 203.

19. Charles Edward Morris, "Panic and Reprisal: Reaction in North Carolina to the Nat Turner Insurrection, 1831," *North Carolina Historical Review*, 62 (1985):29–52; Brewer, "Account of Negro Slavery," 83–85.

20. Diary of Moses Ashley Curtis, September 21, 1831, Moses Ashley Curtis Collection, Southern Historical Collection, Chapel Hill, N.C.; Wilmington Town Commissioners to Montfort Stokes, September 14, 1831, Governors Papers, Stokes, State Archives.

21. Moses Ashley Curtis Diary, September 12, 13, 1831.

22. Moses Ashley Curtis Diary, September 13, October 4, 1831; *Fayetteville Observer*, September 12, 1831; *Raleigh Register*, September 29, 1831; ? to John De Berniere Hooper, September 20, 1831, John De Berniere Hooper Papers, Southern Historical Collection.

23. *Herald* (Wilmington), October 2, 1852; *Journal*, September 10, 1858; Franklin, *The Free Negro in North Carolina*, 238–246.

24. *People's Press and Wilmington Advertiser*, August 21, 28, September 4, 1835; *Wilmington Advertiser*, May 5, 1837; *Journal*, June 2, 1854.

25. John W. Owen to Benson S. Owen, December 20, 1860, A. G. Owen Collection, State Archives; *Journal*, December 27, 1860; *Daily Herald*, December 27, 1860.

26. *Journal*, June 4, December 31, 1847; *Daily Herald*, June 27, 1855; January 5, 1857.

27. Franklin, *The Free Negro in North Carolina*, 141.

28. Rawick, *American Slave*, Vol. 15, Part 2:2; Cecelski, "Shores of Freedom," 193; Bishir, "Black Builders in Antebellum North Carolina," 454–455.

29. Rawick, *American Slave*, Vol. 15, Part 2:2; John D. Bellamy, *Memoirs of an Octogenarian* (Charlotte, 1942), 8; *Chronicle* (Wilmington), July 1, 1846.

30. James B. Browning, "James D. Sampson," *Negro History Bulletin*, 3 (1940):56; Carter Evins to James Boon, January 30, 1848; William Jeffreys to ?, March 22, 1848, James Boon Papers, State Archives; Bishir, "Black Builders in Antebellum North Carolina," 453–454.

31. *Wilmington Gazette*, February 8, June 21, 1798; February 5, 1801.

32. *True Republican*, May 9, 1809; *People's Press*, January 23, 1833; *Daily Herald*, January 11, 1855.

33. *Journal*, July 31, August 7, 1857; *Herald*, August 6, 13, 1857.

34. *Journal*, July 31, August 7, 1857; *Herald*, August 6, 13, 1857.

35. *Journal*, July 31, August 7, 1857.

36. *Herald*, August 13, 1857; *Laws, 1835*, c. 127; *Daily Herald*, January 5, 11, 1855; Brewer, "Legislation Designed to Control Slavery in Wilmington and Fayetteville," 155–166.

37. Rawick, *American Slave*, Vol. 15, Part 2:3; Beeler and Beeler, *Wilmington Town Minutes*, 103; Brewer, "Legislation Designed to Control Slavery in Wilmington and Fayetteville," 160.

38. Ping, "Music in Antebellum Wilmington and the Lower Cape Fear," 165, 188, 326.

39. Andrew J. Howell, *The Book of Wilmington* (Wilmington, 1959), 102.

40. Ping, "Music in Antebellum Wilmington and the Lower Cape Fear," 327–328.

41. Elizabeth A. Fenn, "'A Perfect Equality Seemed to Reign': Slave Society and

Jonkonnu," *North Carolina Historical Review*, 65 (1988):127–153; Ira De A. Reid, "The John Canoe Festival: A New World Africanism," *Phylon*, 3 (1942):350–353; *Daily Journal* (Wilmington), December 23, 1851.

42. *Journal*, December 29, 1854; January 1, 1857; *Daily Journal*, December 24, 27, 28, 1859; December 26, 1860; Henry Bacon McKoy, *Wilmington, N.C.—Do You Remember?* (Greenville, S.C., 1957), 141, 143, 145; Louis T. Moore, *Stories Old and New of the Cape Fear Region* (Wilmington, 1968), 75–77.

43. *Daily Journal*, September 7, 1859; Ping, "Music in Antebellum Wilmington and the Lower Cape Fear," 547.

44. Grady L. E. Carroll, ed., *Francis Asbury in North Carolina. The North Carolina Portions of the Journal of Francis Asbury* (Nashville, Tenn., 1964), 184, 195, 204; *Daily Herald*, May 14, 1855; Ping, "Music in Antebellum Wilmington and the Lower Cape Fear," 398–399; Linda D. Addo and James H. McCallum, *To Be Faithful to Our Heritage: A History of Black United Methodism in North Carolina* (Winston-Salem, N.C., 1980), 14; Johnson, *Ante-Bellum North Carolina*, 344–345, 545.

45. Browning, "James D. Sampson," 56.

7. Fellowship, Fraternity, Association

1. Richard Rankin, ed., "'The Seat of Smiling Mirth': The Ninepenny Whist Club of Wilmington, North Carolina, 1801–ca.1807," *North Carolina Historical Review*, 68 (1991):38–57; Catherine DeRosset Meares, *Annals of the DeRosset Family: Huguenot Immigrants to the Province of North Carolina Early in the Eighteenth Century* (N. p., 1906?), 66.

2. *Wilmington Chronicle; and North-Carolina Weekly Advertiser*, July 31, 1795; *Commercial* (Wilmington), August 2, 1849.

3. *Daily Journal* (Wilmington), December 26, 1855; June 26, 1858; December 24, 1860; *Daily Herald* (Wilmington), December 26, 1855; March 5, July 5, 1856. See also *Journal* (Wilmington), January 1, 1857, for a reference to the "H. B. C. C," apparently an obscure organization.

4. Thomas C. Parramore, *Launching the Craft: The First Half-Century of Freemasonry in North Carolina* (Raleigh, 1975), 109, 143, 150–151; *Laws and Resolutions of the State of North Carolina, 1796*, c. 58; *1805*, c. 98.

5. *Wilmington Gazette*, June 19, 1804; January 2, 1810; *Cape Fear Recorder* (Wilmington), January 2, 1819; *Journal*, January 3, 1845, January 2, 1846; *Herald* (Wilmington), June 12, 1852; *Daily Herald*, December 28, 1854.

6. *Chronicle* (Wilmington), May 17, 1843; *Journal*, May 16, 1845; May 4, 1849; May 14, 1852; May 13, 20, 1853; *Herald*, May 15, July 31, 1852; *Daily Herald*, November 29, 1855; *Laws, 1842-1843*, c. 15; James Sprunt, *Chronicles of the Cape Fear River, 1660–1916*, 2nd ed. (Wilmington, 1916), 170.

7. *Hall's Wilmington Gazette*, March 30, 1797; *People's Press and Wilmington Advertiser*, September 17, 1834; *Wilmington Advertiser*, September 8, 1837.

8. Petition of Robert Rankin, November 14, 1818, General Assembly Session Records, 1818, State Archives, Raleigh, N.C.; *Journal*, February 25, 1853; November 10, 1854; *Herald*, November 20, 1855.

9. *Wilmington Gazette*, December 9, 1806; December 15, 1807; June 9, 26, 1810; *Journal*, October 25, November 29, 1844; *People's Press*, February 20, 1833; *People's Press and Wilmington Advertiser*, November 12, 1834; Memorial of the Inhabitants of Wilmington [1818], Petitions, General Assembly Session Records, 1818; Sprunt, *Chronicles of the Cape Fear River*, 194.

10. *Journal*, February 25, July 8, November 18, 1853; December 4, 1857; *Daily Herald*, January 28, February 16, 1861.
11. *Daily Herald*, January 30, 1859; *Wilmington Advertiser*, November 16, 1838.
12. *Daily Herald*, May 22, 1855; May 22, 30, June 1, 1860; *Journal*, May 15, 1857; *Herald*, May 7, 14, 1857.
13. *Journal*, January 3, 1851; May 15, 1857; *Herald*, November 10, 1852; May 7, 21, June 4, 1857; February 28, 1858; Paul Wilstach, *Mount Vernon: Washington's Home and the Nation's Shrine* (Garden City and New York, 1916), 257–260.
14. *People's Press*, January 16, March 6, 1833; *People's Press and Wilmington Advertiser*, June 5, 1833; April 23, 30, 1834; *Wilmington Advertiser*, January 8, 1836.
15. *Journal*, January 17, July 18, September 5, 1845; Nicholas W. Schenck Journal, 19, East Carolina Manuscript Collection, Greenville, N.C.
16. *Journal*, January 17, September 5, 1845; July 10, 1864; May 5, 1848; April 25, December 19, 1851; *Herald*, May 19, 1852; *Daily Journal*, May 21, 1852; *Laws, 1848–1849*, c. 161.
17. *Journal*, June 12, October 23, 1846; December 15, 22, 1848; December 19, 1851; October 28, 1853; April 21, June 16, 1854; *Herald*, June 16, 1852; *Daily Herald*, June 5, 1855.
18. *Chronicle*, October 4, 1848; *Daily Journal*, April 12, 1860; Nancy Regan Ping, "Music in Antebellum Wilmington and the Lower Cape Fear of North Carolina," Ph.D. diss., University of Colorado, 1979, 258–261.
19. *Wilmington Advertiser*, June 14, 1839; *Journal*, February 25, March 25, June 10, October 14, 1853; *Daily Herald*, May 10, November 15, 1855; Nancy Beeler and Rush Beeler, eds., *Wilmington Town Minutes, 1847–1855* (Wilmington, 1997), 65, 107–108. Wilmington commissioners on occasion conferred with the Chamber of Commerce when setting rates of drayage in town. Beeler and Beeler, *Wilmington Town Minutes*, 118, 125.
20. *Wilmington Gazette*, November 8, 1808; *Journal*, July 31, August 7, 1857; *Herald*, August 6, 13, 1857; *Laws, 1802*, c. 40; Guion Griffis Johnson, *Ante-Bellum North Carolina: A Social History* (Chapel Hill, 1937), 174.
21. *Laws, 1813*, c. 98; *Wilmington Gazette*, January 13, 1816; Cornelius O. Cathey, *Agriculture in North Carolina Before the Civil War* (Raleigh, 1966), 23.
22. *Journal*, October 17, 1854; July 12, 1860; *Daily Herald*, December 11, 1854; July 11, June 21, 23, 1860.
23. *Wilmington Gazette*, November 15, 1808; *People's Press and Wilmington Advertiser*, August 20, 1834; Ping, "Music in Antebellum Wilmington," 346–347.
24. *Cape Fear Recorder*, May 9, 1818; *Wilmington Advertiser*, May 13, 1836; Ping, "Music in Antebellum Wilmington," 400–405; Johnson, *Ante-Bellum North Carolina*, 371–396.
25. *Journal*, March 26, 1858; *Herald*, March 31, 1858; *Kelley's Wilmington Directory, ... for 1860–61* (Wilmington, 1860), 111; Walter W. Conser, Jr., *Sacred Spaces: Architecture and Religion in Historic Wilmington* (Wilmington, 1999), 18.
26. *Cape Fear Recorder*, April 24, 1819; *Wilmington Advertiser*, January 4, 1839; *Laws, 1796*, c. 42; *1812*, c. 121; Jas. G. Burr, *Sketch of St. James Parish* (New York, 1874), 21; Conser, *Sacred Spaces*, 15.
27. *Herald*, February 7, 1852; *Journal*, November 23, 1853; Conser, *Sacred Spaces*, 19.
28. *Cape Fear Recorder*, May 15, 1819; *Daily Herald*, April 29, 1861; *Laws, 1820*, c. 79; "Mother" to Kate, November 8, 1859, DeRosset Family Papers, Southern Historical Collection, Chapel Hill, N.C.; Ping, "Music in Antebellum Wilmington," 362, 370; Conser, *Sacred Spaces*, 19.

29. *Daily Journal*, September 7, 1859; *Daily Herald*, March 7, 1860; Johnson, *Ante-Bellum North Carolina*, 361; Conser, *Sacred Spaces*, 20.

30. *Wilmington Advertiser*, June 1, 1838; *Journal*, August 22, 1851; March 14, 1860; Ping, "Music in Antebellum Wilmington," 372; Conser, *Sacred Spaces*, 19-20.

31. Ping, "Music in Antebellum Wilmington," 387-389; Johnson, *Ante-Bellum North Carolina*, 344, 430.

32. *Journal*, February 14, 1845; Nicholas W. Schenck Journal, 118; *Kelley's Wilmington Directory*, 111; Rev. D. H. Tuttle and W. C. Merrett, *Directory of Fifth St. M. E. Church, South, Wilmington, N.C.* (Wilmington, 1888), 3-4. A number of African American members of the Front Street Methodist Church, perhaps dissatisfied with white leadership, may have left the Front Street church in the 1830s and organized their own congregation, whose average attendance may have totaled 300. See Ping, "Music in Antebellum Wilmington," 398-399; Johnson, *Ante-Bellum North Carolina*, 547; Linda D. Addo and James H. McCallum, *To Be Faithful to Our Heritage: A History of Black United Methodism in North Carolina* (Winston-Salem, N.C., 1980), 14.

33. *Journal*, July 23, 1847; Stephen C. Worsley, "Catholicism in Antebellum North Carolina," *North Carolina Historical Review*, 60 (1983):402, 409, 426-427; Johnson, *Ante-Bellum North Carolina*, 308.

34. Kimberly Sims, "Wilmington's Jewry: 1800-1914," Honor's thesis, University of North Carolina at Wilmington, 1999, 8-9, 23-29; Jon Henry Gerdes, "The Early Jews of Wilmington," Lower Cape Fear Historical Society *Bulletin*, 29 (October 1984).

35. Eighth Census, 1860, New Hanover County, North Carolina, Social Statistics, Schedule 6, microfilm, State Archives; Johnson, *Ante-Bellum North Carolina*, 683-693.

36. *Hall's Wilmington Gazette*, March 2, April 6, 1797; *Cape Fear Recorder*, April 4, 1827; Report of the Grand Jury, September Term, 1851, New Hanover County Miscellaneous Records, 1756-1945, State Archives; Johnson, *Ante-Bellum North Carolina*, 694-697.

37. *Laws, 1817*, c. 25; Johnson, *Ante-Bellum North Carolina*, 163.

38. *Laws, 1833*, c. 68; *Journal*, December 27, 1844; *Daily Herald*, January 20, February 7, 1857; December 6, 1858; May 12, 1859.

39. *Laws, 1852*, c. 174; *Journal*, April 13, 1849; April 5, 1850; April 11, 1851; April 10, 1852.

40. *Daily Herald*, February 28, April 18, 1855; March 4, 1857; *Journal*, April 12, 1860; *Morning Star* (Wilmington), March 4, 2000.

41. *Daily Herald*, March 3, 1855; January 24, 1857; *Journal*, April 12, 1860.

42. *Laws, 1795*, c. 25; *1815*, c. 68; *1824*, c. 129; *Cape Fear Recorder*, December 7, 1816.

43. "The Memorial of the Subscribers[,] Merchants and Inhabitants of the Town of Wilmington, December 16, 1817," Petitions, General Assembly Session Records, 1817.

44. Ibid.; *Laws, 1817*, c. 96.

45. *Journal*, February 13, 1846.

46. See Alan D. Watson, "Sailors, Wilmington, and the First Hospital in North Carolina," *Tributaries*, 7 (1997):41-42.

47. *Laws, 1792*, c. 12; *1794*, c. 50.

48. See Watson, "Sailors, Wilmington, and the First Hospital in North Carolina," 42-43, for this and the following five paragraphs. A marine hospital for seamen opened, at least briefly, in Smithville in 1816. *Cape Fear Recorder*, November 4, 1815.

49. The former hospital or hospital buildings were used, however, in 1851 to house an African American child who had contracted smallpox. *Journal*, January 24, 31, 1851.

50. *Daily Herald*, March 12, April 10, 1855, January 3, 27, February 17, 20, April 16, June 25, 1857; March 6, June 30, 1860; *Laws, 1856–1857*, c. 31; *1858–1859*, c. 59. Wilmington town commissioners declined to support the construction of the pest house, deeming it a federal responsibility. Beeler and Beeler, *Wilmington Town Minutes*, 133–134.

51. *People's Press and Wilmington Advertiser*, December 23, 1835; *Journal*, February 11, 18, October 21, 1853; *Daily Herald*, January 5, 1855; *Kelley's Wilmington Directory*, 108.

52. *Daily Herald*, November 21, 1859; June 30, 1860; *Journal*, November 25, 1859; August 23, 1860.

53. *Journal*, June 12, 1854; June 18, 1860; *Daily Herald*, June 30, 1860.

8. EDUCATION, ENLIGHTENMENT, AND CULTURE

1. *Wilmington Chronicle; and North-Carolina Weekly Advertiser*, August 4, 1796; *Wilmington Gazette*, April 10, 1800; March 24, 1807; *People's Press and Wilmington Advertiser*, October 23, 1833; *Wilmington Advertiser*, May 20, 1836; January 18, October 11, 1839.

2. *Wilmington Advertiser*, October 26, 1838; James Sprunt, *Chronicles of the Cape Fear River, 1660–1916*, 2nd ed. (Raleigh, 1916), 165, 170, 192.

3. *Daily Herald* (Wilmington), October 3, 1854; February 10, September 20, 1855; September 27, 1859, October 3, 1960.

4. *Laws and Resolutions of the State of North Carolina, 1803*, c. 34; *Wilmington Gazette*, May 7, 1805. References to the "Innes" academy and trustees cease after 1805. The depiction of an academy on the J. J. Belanger Map of 1810 refers simply to the "Academy."

5. *Laws, 1800*, c. 44; *1803*, c. 37; *1810*, c. 71; *1813*, c. 86; *Wilmington Gazette*, April 28, May 5, 1803; June 19, 1810; May 12, 1812. The theater may well have opened earlier.

6. *Cape Fear Recorder* (Wilmington), November 9, 1816; January 30, 1819; *People's Press and Wilmington Advertiser*, July 10, November 13, 1833; May 28, 1834.

7. *Chronicle* (Wilmington), June 10, 1843; Sprunt, *Chronicles of the Cape Fear River*, 172; Isabel M. Williams, "Thalian Hall," 4, Reports, Research Division, microfilm Division of Archives and History, Raleigh, N.C.

8. *Journal* (Wilmington), October 4, 1844; February 7, 1845; February 6, October 23, 1846; J. B. Newby to Horace Mann, October 1, 1846, J. B. Newby Letter, State Archives, Raleigh, N.C.; Sprunt, *Chronicles of the Cape Fear River*, 170–171.

9. *Journal*, February 6, 1846; May 28, 1847; Lossie to "Dear Sister," May 29, 1847; Alice to "Dear Sister," June 5, 1847; July 27, 1849, DeRosset Family Papers, Southern Historical Collection, Chapel Hill, N.C.; Sprunt, *Chronicles of the Cape Fear*, 171–172.

10. *Journal*, September 30, 1853; *Daily Herald* (Wilmington), October 31, 1854; June 18, 1859; May 24, June 28, October 3, 1860.

11. *People's Press* (Wilmington), May 8, 15, 1833; *People's Press and Wilmington Advertiser*, January 1, 1834; June 10, December 4, 1835; June 14, 1839; *Wilmington Chronicle*, September 21, 1842; Elizabeth Francenia McKoy, *Early Wilmington Block by Block* (Wilmington, 1967), 139–140.

12. *Daily Herald*, February 13, 1860; *Journal*, February 26, 1860; Nancy Regan Ping, "Music in Antebellum Wilmington and the Lower Cape Fear of North Carolina," Ph.D. diss., University of Colorado at Boulder, 1979, 72.

13. *Wilmington Advertiser*, August 16, September 20, 1839; March 11, 1841; *Journal*, October 14, 1859.

14. *Chronicle*, March 29, 1843; Report of the School Committee for District No. 2, July 1847, New Hanover County School Records, 1841–1913, State Archives; Guion Griffis Johnson, *Ante-Bellum North Carolina: A Social History* (Chapel Hill, 1937), 277.

15. *Wilmington Gazette*, November 20, 1804; *True Republican* (Wilmington), November 7, 1809; *People's Press*, March 6, 13, 1833.

16. *Chronicle*, November 10, 1841; March 23, 1842; *Daily Herald*, February 24, September 12, 20, 1855; January 4, September 15, 1860.

17. *Daily Herald*, January 19, 1855; January 4, 23, February 2, 1856; Ping, "Music in Antebellum Wilmington and the Lower Cape Fear," 80–81.

18. *Hall's Wilmington Gazette*, April 12, 1797; *Wilmington Gazette*, January 13, 1816; *Wilmington Advertiser*, September 15, 1837; *Journal*, December 10, 1847; *Herald*, October 16, 1852.

19. *Journal*, December 10, 1847; December 17, 1851; *Daily Herald*, December 28, 1854; March 29, 1855; *Herald*, April 8, 1858.

20. *True Republican*, June 6, 1809; *People's Press and Wilmington Advertiser*, October 23, 1833; *Wilmington Advertiser*, February 9, 1838; *Herald*, October 16, 1852; *Daily Herald*, February 17, 1855.

21. *Wilmington Gazette*, March 20, 1800; January 15, 1805; *People's Press and Wilmington Advertiser*, October 23, 1833; March 4, 1836; *Daily Herald*, February 6, 1860; Johnson, *Ante-Bellum North Carolina*, 289.

22. *Wilmington Chronicle; and North-Carolina Weekly Advertiser*, July 3, 1795; *Wilmington Gazette*, May 6, 1806; October 11, 1808; *Cape Fear Herald* (Wilmington), November 2, 1803; *True Republican*, January 1, 1809; *Cape Fear Recorder*, November 30, 1816; *The Dictionary of North Carolina Biography*, s.v. "Hall, Armond." 6 vols. (Chapel Hill, 1979–1996), 3:5–6.

23. *Carolina Observer* (Fayetteville), December 6, 1827; *The Liberalist, and Wilmington Reporter*, September 8, 1829; *Wilmington Advertiser, and Merchants' and Farmers' Gazette*, January 2, 1833; *People's Press*, January 9, 1833; *People's Press and Wilmington Advertiser*, May 22, 1833; *Wilmington Advertiser*, January 8, 1836; February 18, May 20, 1841; Sprunt, *Chronicles of the Cape Fear River*, 177–181.

24. *Chronicle*, April 15, 1840; *Herald*, May 10, 1851; *Journal*, September 2, 1844; *Daily Journal* (Wilmington), September 8, 1851.

25. *Commercial* (Wilmington), September 22, 1846; March 18, 1847; January 9, 1857; *Journal*, November 9, 1849; January 3, 1851; Johnson, *Ante-Bellum North Carolina*, 772–774. Another paper, the *Carolina Gazette*, whose editor and proprietor was William J. Yopp, began publication in December 1847, but it must have been a short-lived sheet. *Journal*, December 24, 1847.

26. *Wilmington Gazette*, November 15, 1798; January 3, 1804; *True Republican*, January 3, 1809.

27. *People's Press*, January 9, May 22, 1833; January 7, February 4, 1835; January 1, 8, 1836.

28. *Wilmington Advertiser*, December 7, 1838; *Journal*, September 27, 1844; Sprunt, *Chronicles of the Cape Fear River*, 178. Loring provided some balance, for his *Weekly Commercial* was "Whig in politics, but independently so," no doubt a reflection of his first principles, before he felt forced to champion the Democratic cause. Sprunt, *Chronicles of the Cape Fear*, 179.

29. *Wilmington Gazette*, May 1, 1804; June 2, 1807; *People's Press and Wilmington Advertiser*, October 22, 1835; *Journal*, October 25, 1860.

30. Statement of Thomas Loring, February 2, 1852, Cumberland County, Mis-

cellaneous Records, 1758–1965, State Archives; Johnson, *Ante-Bellum North Carolina*, 786–794.

31. *Wilmington Gazette*, November 13, 1798; *Cape Fear Recorder*, July 1, 1829; *People's Press and Wilmington Advertiser*, December 24, 1834; *Journal*, December 19, 1851; January 22, 1858.

32. *Herald*, October 31, 1854; August 6, 1859; Eighth Census, 1860, New Hanover County, North Carolina, Social Statistics, Schedule 6, microfilm, State Archives.

33. *Cape Fear Recorder*, March 20, 1819; February 2, 1822; *Wilmington Advertiser*, September 20, 1838; September 20, 1839; Johnson, *Ante-Bellum North Carolina*, 28, 30.

34. *Hall's Wilmington Gazette*, February 9, 1797; *Wilmington Advertiser*, October 20, 1837; December 21, 1838.

35. *Journal*, January 3, 10, 1845; January 28, 1853.

36. *Journal*, February 12, 1858; *Daily Herald*, October 15, 1859; March 3, 22, 1860.

37. *Laws, 1846–1847*, c. 55; *Journal*, April 7, 1848; October 25, 1860; *Commercial*, May 22, June 19, 1851.

38. *Wilmington Gazette*, November 22, 1808; *People's Press*, March 1833; *People's Press and Wilmington Advertiser*, December 11, 1833; January 1, 8, February 5, 1834; December 11, 1835; Johnson, *Ante-Bellum North Carolina*, 164; McKoy, *Early Wilmington Bock by Block*, 89–92.

39. *People's Press*, February 20, 1833; April 24, 1834; *Journal*, October 10, 1845; *Commercial*, September 22, 1846; *Daily Herald*, February 14, 1855.

40. *Daily Herald*, April 9, 10, June 20, October 9, November 22, 1855.

41. *Ibid.*, October 22, 24, November 4, 1859; January 18, February 10, March 20, April 3, 17, 19, September 20, 1860.

42. *People's Press*, February 13, March 6, 1833; *Wilmington Advertiser*, May 18, 1838; *Journal*, October 30, 1846; *Herald*, January 10, 1852; *Journal*, March 13, 1857; *Daily Herald*, November 15, 1859; February 13, 1860.

43. Stephen Cymbalsky, "Literature of the Lower Cape Fear," in Janet Seapker, ed., *Time, Talent, Tradition: Five Essays on the Cultural History of the Lower Cape Fear Region, North Carolina* (Wilmington, 1995), 34–35; *Journal*, October 22, 1858; Clyde Wilson, "Griffith John McRee: An Unromantic Historian of the Old South," *North Carolina Historical Review*, 47 (1970), 1–23; Powell, *Dictionary of North Carolina Biography*, s.v. "McRee, Griffith John."

44. Edward F. Turberg, "Architecture in the Lower Cape Fear," in Janet Seapker, ed., *Time, Talent, Tradition*, 20.

45. *Ibid.*, 21–26; Merle Chamberlain, "Connecticut Yankee in Wilmington," Lower Cape Fear Historical Society *Bulletin*, 42 (March 1998).

46. Turberg, "Architecture in the Lower Cape Fear," 26.

47. John Bivins, Jr., *Wilmington Furniture, 1720–1860* (Wilmington, 1989), 15; *Hall's Wilmington Gazette*, February 9, 1797; *Wilmington Gazette*, June 21, 1798; May 15, 1804, November 24, 1806. For upholstering, as well as curtains, carpet, and paper hanging, Wilmingtonians could call upon Garrit Heyer. *Cape Fear Recorder*, April 5, 1817.

48. Bivins, *Wilmington Furniture*, 21, 25; *Cape Fear Recorder*, November 4, 1816; *Wilmington Advertiser*, January 10, 1839.

49. John W. Myers, "Visual Arts," in Seapker, *Time, Talent, Tradition*, 71.

50. *Ibid.*, 72; *Wilmington Gazette*, October 20, 1807; *Journal*, April 18, 1851; January 27, 1854; August 20, 1858; *Daily Herald*, March 8, 1855.

51. *Journal*, April 6, 1849; June 7, 1850; *Daily Herald*, March 2, 3, 8, 1855; January 26, 1859; Myers, "Visual Arts," 73.

52. *Laws, 1848–1849*, c. 224; *Wilmington Gazette*, December 9, 1806; June 3, 17, 1816; *People's Press and Wilmington Advertiser*, February 12, 26, 1834; *Journal*, April 30, November 26, 1847; *Daily Herald*, April 20, 1855; June 30, 1859; Alfred M. Waddell, *A Colonial Officer and His Times* (Spartanburg, S.C., 1973, orig. 1885), 189; Ping, "Music in Antebellum Wilmington," 489.

53. Hall's *Wilmington Gazette*, February 9, 16, March 2, 1797; March 8, 1798; *Wilmington Advertiser*, May 20, 1841; *Journal*, April 4, 1845.

54. *Wilmington Gazette*, December 11, 1804; *Wilmington Advertiser*, May 14, 1840.

55. *Daily Herald*, April 10, 17, 18, 19, 24, 26, 1860; April 6, 11, 1861.

56. Hall's *Wilmington Gazette*, February 9, 1797; *Wilmington Gazette*, March 27, 1804; *Journal*, May 23, 1851; *Herald*, May 26, 1852; D. Anthony Rivenbark, "History of the Theater in Wilmington and the Cape Fear Region," in Seapker, *Time, Talent, Tradition*, 59.

57. Ping, "Music in Antebellum Wilmington," 423–242; *Chronicle*, May 28, 1845; *Journal*, March 20, 1846; January 16, 1848.

58. *Chronicle*, January 8, 1845; *Commercial*, January 20, 1855.

59. *Journal*, February 7, 1845; January 23, 1846; April 6, 1849; *Chronicle*, February 14, 1849.

60. *Chronicle*, December 18, 1850; January 1, 1851; Sprunt, *Chronicles of the Cape Fear River*, 265–267.

61. *Daily Herald*, January 16, 1857; Sherill V. Martin, "Music and Dance in the Lower Cape Fear," in Seapker, *Time, Talent, Tradition*, 57.

62. *Chronicle*, February 9, 1842; *Daily Herald*, February 29, December 12, 1860; Ping, "Music in Antebellum Wilmington," 520–529, 531.

63. *Daily Herald*, February 10, 1855; September 28, 1859; February 15, 20, 21, October 26, 30, November 1, 1860.

64. *Ibid.*, February 20, 1960.

65. *Chronicle*, August 10, 1842; *Daily Herald*, November 23, 1857; Rivenbark, "History of the Theater in Wilmington and the Cape Fear Region," 58.

66. James H. Dormon, Jr., *Theater in the Ante Bellum South, 1815–1861* (Chapel Hill, 1967), 151, n.110; *Daily Herald*, October 30, December 10, 28, 1855; *Journal*, October 15, 1858; Donald J. Rulfs, "The Professional Theater in Wilmington, 1858–1870," *North Carolina Historical Review*, 28 (1951):120–122; Rivenbark, "History of the Theater in Wilmington and the Cape Fear Region," in Seapker, *Time, Talent, Tradition*, 60–61.

9. URBAN GOVERNEMNT

1. John L. Cheney, Jr., comp., *North Carolina Government, 1858–1979* (Raleigh, 1981), 1219; *Laws and Resolutions of the State of North Carolina, 1848–1849*, c. 243; *1850–1851;* c. 313; *1854–1855*, c. 248; *Journal* (Wilmington), April 14, 1854; February 20, 1857; *Daily Herald* (Wilmington), March 21, 23, 1855; Nancy Beeler and Rush Beeler, eds., *Wilmington Town Minutes, 1847–1855* (Wilmington, 1997), 159, 175–176.

2. *Laws, 1794*, c. 74; *1795*, c. 37; *1799*, c. 103; *1842–1843*, c. 75; *Daily Herald*, February 24, 1855; Guion Griffis Johnson, *Ante-Bellum North Carolina: A Social History* (Chapel Hill, 1937), 124–125. For other objections to the law, see *Chronicle* (Wilmington), January 4, 1843.

3. *Laws, 1811*, c. 64; *1818*, c. 42; *1819*, c. 71; *1820*, c. 92; *1840–1841*, c. 36; *1848–1849*, c. 231; *Cape Fear Recorder* (Wilmington), May 15, 1819.

4. *Laws, 1852*, c. 221; *Daily Herald*, February 6, 7, September 12, 1855; February 3, 1857; *Journal*, February 9, 27, 1855.

Notes—Chapter 9

5. *Journal*, February 21, 1845; January 19, 1829; *Daily Herald*, February 23, 1861; Beeler and Beeler, *Wilmington Town Minutes*, 4–5.

6. *Wilmington Gazette*, April 8, 15, 1806; March 10, 24, June 23, 1807; July 12, 1808; *People's Press and Wilmington Advertiser*, September 4, 1833; *Daily Herald*, January 17, 1855; *Laws, 1792*, c. 59; *1811*, c. 64; Beeler and Beeler, *Wilmington Town Minutes*, 123, 137, 149, 150–151.

7. *Wilmington Gazette*, April 1, 1806; James Sprunt, *Chronicles of the Cape Fear River, 1660–1916*, 2d ed. (Raleigh, 1916), 174.

8. *Laws, 1804*, c. 58; *1811*, c. 64; *Wilmington Advertiser*, January 29, 1836; *Journal*, March 18, September 16, 30, 1853; March 24, 1854; March 12, 1858; Report of the Grand Jury, Spring Term, Superior Court, 1840, Reports, 1840–1871, New Hanover County, Miscellaneous Records, 1756–1945, State Archives, Raleigh, N.C.

9. *Journal*, August 8, 1847; Beeler and Beeler, *Wilmington Town Minutes*, 11; *Daily Herald*, February 22, 1860.

10. Beeler and Beeler, *Wilmington Town Minutes*, 30, 31–34, 147, 152.

11. *Laws, 1795*, c. 37; *1800*, c. 44; *Wilmington Gazette*, January 7, 1806; *Cape Fear Recorder*, November 4, 1820; *Journal*, July 20, 1855; *Herald* (Wilmington), January 28, 1858; *Daily Herald*, June 9, 1860; Beeler and Beeler, *Wilmington Town Minutes*, 118, 121–122, 167, 169, 171, 172, 173.

12. *Hall's Wilmington Gazette*, February 16, 1797; *Daily Herald*, February 24, 1855; January 10, 1857; Beeler and Beeler, *Wilmington Town Minutes*, 154.

13. Isabel M. Williams, "Thalian Hall, (unpublished research report)," n.d., microfilm, State Archives; *Daily Herald*, December 29, 1855; Beeler and Beeler, *Wilmington Town Minutes*, 138, 145, 171, 172, 180–183.

14. Williams, "Research Report;" *Daily Journal* (Wilmington), September 21, 1855; April 3, 6, 1858; *Daily Herald*, June 1, 1859.

15. *Daily Herald*, April 6, 1861; Committee to Supervise Construction of an Armory, March 1861, New Hanover County, Miscellaneous Records; *Laws, 1860–1861*, c. 180.

16. *Wilmington Advertiser*, February 2, 1838; February 22, 1839; *Chronicle*, June 4, 1845; *Daily Herald*, January 24, 1855; February 24, 1860; Beeler and Beeler, *Wilmington Town Minutes*, 7, 19, 24, 35, 53, 54, 114, 123, 124, 126, 130, 135, 153; Nicholas W. Schenck Journal, 114, East Carolina Manuscript Collection, Greenville, N.C.

17. *Wilmington Advertiser*, November 17, 1837; *Chronicle*, June 4, October 15, 1845; *Daily Herald*, January 11, 1855.

18. *Wilmington Gazette*, December 23, 1806; *True Republican* (Wilmington), November 7, 1809; *Journal*, May 2, 1851; *Chronicle*, January 6, 1841; Beeler and Beeler, *Wilmington Town Minutes*, 13, 72, 163.

19. *People's Press* (Wilmington), January 23, 1833; *People's Press and Wilmington Advertiser*, May 21, 1834; *Journal*, February 20, 1857; Beeler and Beeler, *Wilmington Town Minutes*, 131.

20. *Wilmington Gazette*, December 23, 1806; *Daily Herald*, January 16, 1857; *Laws, 1807*, c. 51; *1811*, c. 64; Beeler and Beeler, *Wilmington Town Minutes*, 94, 118, 126.

21. *Wilmington Gazette*, December 23, 1806; *Daily Herald*, March 23, June 6, 1855; Beeler and Beeler, *Wilmington Town Minutes*, 27, 160, 165.

22. *Laws, 1795*, c. 37; *1827*, c. 92; *1835*, c. 127; *Daily Herald*, January 11, 1855; Beeler and Beeler, *Wilmington Town Minutes*, 148.

23. *Wilmington Gazette*, December 23, 1806; *Wilmington Advertiser*, April 6, 1838; *Journal*, February 27, 1852.

24. *Laws, 1800*, c. 44; Petition of New Hanover residents to the General Assembly, December 16, 1844, Petitions, General Assembly Session Records, 1844–1845, State Archives.

276   Notes—Chapter 9

25. *Herald*, December 11, 1852; *Daily Herald*, February 24, 1855; Beeler and Beeler, *Wilmington Town Minutes*, 126, 129, 130, 137, 139, 153.

26. *Laws, 1791*, c. 60; *1806*, c. 37; *1820*, c. 45; *1858–1859*, c. 256; *Wilmington Gazette*, November 20, 1804; May 12, July 14, 1807; *Cape Fear Recorder*, November 4, 1816; April 14, 1821.

27. *Laws*, 1791, c. 60; *1820*; c. 45; *1829–1830*, c. 25; *1858–1859*, c. 256; *Carolina Observer* (Fayetteville), December 15, 1825; *People's Press*, September 4, 1833; *Chronicle*, November 5, 1845; *Journal*, November 7, 1845; January 8, 1858; *Daily Herald*, April 5, 1855.

28. *Cape Fear Recorder*, July 1, 1829; *Chronicle*, November 5, 1845; *Journal*, November 7, 1845; Johnson, *Ante-Bellum North Carolina*, 135.

29. *People's Press*, February 6, 1833; *Herald*, February 25, 1852; January 28, 1858; *Journal*, February 9, 1860; *Daily Herald*, February 4, 1861. The firemen may have been provided with uniforms in 1847. Beeler and Beeler, *Wilmington Town Minutes*, 3–4.

30. *Cape Fear Recorder*, April 14, 1821; *People's Press and Wilmington Advertiser*, July 9, 1834; *Wilmington Gazette*, March 6, 1800; *Commercial*, March 5, 1852; *Journal*, February 9, 1860.

31. *Laws, 1795*, c. 20; *1828*, c. 49; *Hall's Wilmington Gazette*, March 2, 1797; *Cape Fear Recorder* (Wilmington), June 17, 1816; *People's Press and Wilmington Advertiser*, July 7, 1833; Beeler and Beeler, *Wilmington Town Minutes*, 140–141, 168–169.

32. *Laws, 1821*, c. 53; *Wilmington Gazette*, September 6, 1803; June 19, 1810; *Daily Herald*, March 16, April 13, 1855; *Herald*, January 28, 1858.

33. *Journal*, October 3, 1845; May 7, 1847; *Herald*, March 31, 1852.

34. *Laws, 1852*, c. 175.

35. *Daily Herald*, February 16, 20, December 31, 1855; May 4, 1860; April 6, 1861; Beeler and Beeler, *Wilmington Town Minutes*, 170; *A Tribute to Oakdale, 1852–1991* (Wilmington, 1991). The commissioners apparently made an abortive attempt to obtain land for a pauper's cemetery. Beeler and Beeler, *Wilmington Town Minutes*, 92, 94–95, 160.

36. *Chronicle*, October 17, 1847; *Tri-Weekly Commercial* (Wilmington), July 21, 1853; *Journal*, January 14, 1860; *Morning Star* (Wilmington), May 6, 2000; William S. Reaves, *"Strength Through Struggle": The Chronological and Historical Record of the African-American Community in Wilmington, North Carolina, 1865–1950* (Wilmington, 1998), 176–178.

37. *People's Press and Wilmington Advertiser*, June 25, 1834; *Daily Herald*, February 24, 1855; Beeler and Beeler, *Wilmington Town Minutes*, 154.

38. *Wilmington Gazette*, December 23, 1806; *Daily Herald*, June 24, 1853; December 13, 1854; March 5, July 21, 1855; Beeler and Beeler, *Wilmington Town Minutes*, 155.

39. *Laws, 1804*, c. 50; *1805*, c. 37; *1848–1849*, c. 243; *Journal*, March 21, 1851; *Daily Herald*, December 11, 1855; January 6, 1857.

40. *People's Press and Wilmington Advertiser*, April 23, 1834; July 15, 1835; *Journal*, April 10, 1846; March 21, 1851; September 3, December 24, 1852; *Daily Herald*, March 31, December 17, 1855; Beeler and Beeler, *Wilmington Town Minutes*, 22, 24; Memorial of the Inhabitants of the Town of Wilmington [to the House of Commons], December 6, 1819, Petitions, General Assembly Session Records, 1819.

41. *Journal*, February 21, 1851; February 20, 1857; *Daily Herald*, December 29, 1855; February 3, 1860; *Laws, 1860-1861*, c. 180. See also *Laws, 1858–1859*, c. 198.

10. AN EXPANDING ECONOMY

1. *Wilmington Gazette*, March 14, 1809; Sarah McCulloh Lemmon, *Frustrated Patriots: North Carolina and the War of 1812* (Chapel Hill, 1973), 154–156.

2. "The Reverend Thomas Wright's Letters to Robert Scott, 1818–1832," Lower Cape Fear Historical Society *Bulletin*, 23 (February 1980); *Wilmington Advertiser*, May 26, 1837; February 11, l841.

3. *Daily Herald* (Wilmington), January 6, April 11, June 15, 1855; *Journal* (Wilmington), September 16, 1857; *Herald* (Wilmington), October 22, 1857; Roger B. Starling, "The Plank Road Movement in North Carolina, Parts I and II," *North Carolina Historical Review*, 16 (1939):169.

4. Joseph R. Blossom to ?, February 6, 1859, Francis M. Manning Collection, East Carolina Manuscript Collection, Greenville, N.C.; *Journal*, February 11, 1859; Alan D. Watson, ed., "Wilmington Commerce, 1816: A Document," Lower Cape Fear Historical Society *Bulletin*, 39 (April 1995).

5. Mother to Kate, September 19, 1859, DeRosset Family Papers, Southern Historical Collection, Chapel Hill, N.C.; *Wilmington Advertiser*, September 20, 1839; *Journal*, September 28, 1855. Much of the stock going to Wilmington was forwarded to Fayetteville and the interior of the state. *Wilmington Advertiser*, November 16, 1838.

6. *Cape Fear Recorder* (Wilmington), April 13, 1825; *Journal*, April 1, l853; *Daily Herald*, January 2, 1860.

7. *Journal*, January 1, l847; *Daily Herald*, September 20, 1854.

8. *Wilmington Chronicle; and North Carolina Advertiser*, August 4, 1796; *Cape Fear Recorder*, December 8, 1821; *Journal*, February 20, 1846; Mortimer DeMott, "Sojourn in Wilmington and the Lower Cape Fear, 1837," Lower Cape Fear Historical Society *Bulletin*, 22 (May 1979).

9. *Wilmington Gazette*, December 25, 1804; *Cape Fear Recorder*, December 8, 1821; *Wilmington Advertiser*, 1837–1839 passim; *Journal*, October 31, 1845; June 16, 1854; *Daily Herald*, April 12, 1855.

10. *Journal*, May 15, 1852; November 5, 1858; April 1, 1859; *Commercial* (Wilmington), May 28, 1852; *Herald*, June 2, 1852; *Daily Herald*, May 18, July 9, 1859; *Laws and Resolutions of the State of North Carolina, 1858–1859*, c. 257; *Kelley's Wilmington Directory, to Which Is Added a Business Directory for l860–6l*, comp. by T. Tuther, Jr. (Wilmington, 1860), 99.

11. Seventh Census of the United States, 1850, Industry, Schedule 5, North Carolina, Alamance-Yancey, 427, microfilm, State Archives, Raleigh, N.C.; *Wilmington Gazette*, May 12, 1812; *Wilmington Advertiser*, December 22, 1837; *Daily Herald*, April 5, 1855; *Kelley's Wilmington Directory*, 99.

12. *Wilmington Gazette*, March 11, 1806; *Journal*, January 24, 1851.

13. *Journal*, April 18, November 21, 1845; September 24, 1847; September 22, 1848; *Daily Herald*, May 3, 1860.

14. *People's Press* (Wilmington), January 16, 1833; *Journal*, January 24, 1845; *Chronicle* (Wilmington), August 20, September 3, 1845.

15. *Journal*, May 7, 1852; *Daily Herald*, March 10, 1855; May 12, 1859; Alan D. Watson, *Wilmington: Port of North Carolina* (Columbia, S.C., 1992), 68–69.

16. *Raleigh Register*, February 14, 1811; *Cape Fear Recorder*, April 11, 1827; Records of the 1820 Census of Manufactures, New Hanover County, microfilm, New Hanover County Library, Wilmington, N.C.; Seventh Census, 1850, Industry Schedule 5, North Carolina, Wilmington, microfilm, State Archives.

17. *Laws, 1807*, c. 73; *1818*, c. 47; *1821*, c. 70; *1838–1839*, c. 30; *1844–1845*, c. 49;

1852, c. 134; *Journal*, March 15, 1860; James H. Broussard, *The Southern Federalists, 1800–1816* (Baton Rouge and London, 1978), 341–344.

18. *Laws, 1854–1855*, c. 20; *1856–1857*, c. 47; *1860–1861*, c. 194; *Daily Herald*, February 24, March 5, 1855; Nancy Beeler and Rush Beeler, eds., *Wilmington Town Minutes, 1847–1855* (Wilmington, 1997), 154, 155–157, 158.

19. *Laws, 1804*, c. 21; *Wilmington Gazette*, February 5, 1805. For the Bank of the Cape Fear, see Robert S. Neale, *The Bank of the Cape Fear of Wilmington, North Carolina* (Wilmington, 1999).

20. *Laws, 1810*, c. 5; *1814*, c. 6; William K. Boyd, *History of North Carolina, Vol. 2: The Federal Period, 1783–1860* (Spartanburg, S.C., 1973, orig. 1919), 111, 125, 135; Alan D. Watson, *A History of New Bern and Craven County* (New Bern, 1987), 135, 137–138.

21. *Laws, 1833–1834*, cc. 1, 3; *1846–1847*, c. 4; *1850–1851*, c. 9; *1854–1855*, c. 81; *Daily Herald*, November 7, 1854; June 7, July 10, 1855; *Kelley's Wilmington Directory*, 110; Boyd, *History of North Carolina*, 135. The charter of the Bank of Cape Fear was renewed in 1855, at which time the capitalization of the bank was enlarged by an additional $500,000. *Journal*, March 9, 1855.

22. *Laws, 1854–1855*, c. 79; *1856–1857*, c. 85; *Journal*, March 2, May 11, 1855; *Daily Herald*, November 20, 1855; March 3, 1857.

23. Watson, *Wilmington*, 44–45, 65.

24. Frederick Law Olmsted, *A Journey in the Seaboard Slave States, with Remarks on Their Economy* (New York, 1969, orig. 1856), 374; *Wilmington Advertiser*, July 7, 28, 1837; F. Roy Johnson, *Riverboating in Lower Carolina* (Murfreesboro, N.C., 1977), 16–17.

25. *Fayetteville Observer*, as reported in the *Journal*, October 17, 1845; *Journal*, December 19, 1845. See also Olmsted, *Journey in the Seaboard Slave States*, 368; *Wilmington Advertiser*, August 9, 1839.

26. Joshua Potts, "On the Trade of Wilmington, N.C., May 1st, 1815," *Our Living and Our Dead*, 1 (Sept. 1874–Feb. 1875):51; Robert W. Brown, "On the Trade of Wilmington, N.C., August 1st, 1843," *ibid.*, 56; Watson, "Wilmington Commerce, 1816."

27. Watson, *Wilmington*, 66, 68–69.

28. Watson, "Wilmington Commerce, 1816"; Charles Livingston to William C. Lord, September 28, 1822, Livingston Papers, Rare Book, Manuscript, and Special Collections Library, Duke University, Durham, N.C.; *People's Press and Wilmington Advertiser*, May 28, 1834; *Wilmington Advertiser*, October 4, 1839; *Chronicle*, October 15, November 5, 1845; *Journal*, April 10, 1846; April 2, 1849; Percival Perry, "The Naval Stores Industry in the Ante-Bellum South, 1789–1861," Ph.D. dissertation, Duke University, 1947.

29. *Fayetteville Observer*, July 27, 1842; *Journal*, January 11, 1850; List of Vessels arriving at the Port of Wilmington for the Year Ending 1st of May, 1851, F. L. Bond Papers, East Carolina Manuscript Collection; Watson, *Wilmington*, 68–69.

30. Cecil Kenneth Brown, *The State Highway System of North Carolina* (Chapel Hill, 1931), 9; *North Carolina Standard* (Raleigh), December 6, 1848.

31. J. A. Holmes and Wm. Cain, *Road Materials and Road Construction in North Carolina*, 2nd ed. (Raleigh, 1893), 13.

32. Roger B. Starling, "The Plank Road Movement in North Carolina," *North Carolina Historical Review*, 16 (January/April 1939):1–22, 147–173;

33. *Laws, 1848–1849*, cc. 89, 213, 214.

34. *Laws, 1850–1851*, c. 138; *1854–1855*, c. 197; *Journal*, November 26, 1852; April 15, 1853; June 9, 1857; January 1, 1858; July 5, 1860; *Herald*, May 18, August 25, 1852; Beeler and Beeler, *Wilmington Town Minutes*, 98.

35. *Laws, 1808*, c. 45; *People's Press and Wilmington Advertiser*, March 13, May 8, 1833; February 26, 1834; *Wilmington Advertiser*, March 16, 1838; *Journal*, February 23, 1855; *Daily Herald*, February 23, 1855; Gordon P. Watts, Jr., and Wesley K. Hall, *An Investigation of Blossom's Ferry on the Northeast Cape Fear River* (Greenville, N.C., 1986), 10–11.

36. *Laws, 1805*, c. 23; *1811*, c. 29; *1815*, c. 15.

37. *Laws, 1816*, c. 36; *Cape Fear Recorder*, May 15, 1819.

38. *Laws, 1844–1845*, c. 29; *1846–1847*, cc. 15, 17, 18; *Fayetteville Observer*, June 22, 29, July 6, August 17, 1847; *Carolina Watchman* (Salisbury), July 9, 22, September 16, 1847.

39. *Laws, 1792*, c. 22; *1796*, c. 21; *1811*, c. 24; Ronald B. Hartzger, *To Great and Useful Purpose: A History of the Wilmington District U. S. Army Corps of Engineers* (N. p., n. d.), 11; Elsie Faye Russ, "The Cape Fear and Deep River Navigation Company, 1849–1873," M.A. thesis, Wake Forest University, 1980, 3–4.

40. *Laws, 1815*, c. 14; *Raleigh Register*, March 29, October 4, 1816; August 14, September 4, October 2, 1818; June 24, 1822; April 10, May 21, 1824.

41. *Laws, 1823*, c. 16; The Memorial of the President and Directors of the Cape Fear Navigation Company, December 19, 1825, Petitions, General Assembly Sessions Records, 1825; Treasurer's Report in *Laws, 1833–1834*.

42. Memorial of the President and Directors of the Cape Fear Navigation Company, December 19, 1825; *Annual Report of the Board of Internal Improvements, 1839* (Raleigh, 1839), 22, 24, 26–27.

43. Alan D. Watson, "North Carolina and Internal Improvements, 1783–1861: The Case of Inland Navigation," *North Carolina Historical Review*, 74 (1997):65.

44. *Ibid.*, 65–66.

45. *Fayetteville Observer*, October 29, 1829; June 10, September 16, 1830; June 5, 1844; November 18, 1845; December 7, 1852; A petition to charter a company for improving and making navigable New Hope Creek ... , November 17, 1830, Petitions, General Assembly Sessions Records, 1830–1831.

46. Watson, "North Carolina and Internal Improvements," 59–62.

47. *Journal*, March 12, 1852; February 11, March 11, April 1, 1853; Report of the Chief Topographical Engineer, Accompanying the Report of the Secretary of War, 1857, copy in Samuel A'Court Ashe Papers, State Archives.

48. *Journal*, April 8, May 13, April 14, May 26, June 2, July 28, 1854.

49. Hartzger, *To Great and Useful Purpose*, 19.

50. Watson, *Wilmington*, 65. In 1840 the Wilmington and Raleigh (Weldon) Railroad Company placed buoys and lights along the river to assist its steamships which ran from Wilmington to Charleston, South Carolina. *Wilmington Advertiser*, July 9, 1840.

51. Alan D. Watson, "Sailing Under Steam: The Advent of Steam Navigation in North Carolina to the Civil War," *North Carolina Historical Review*, 75 (1998):29–33.

52. *Ibid.*, 33, 35.

53. *Laws, 1827–1828*, cc. 50, 52; Petition of Merchants and Traders of the town of Fayetteville, November 1827; Petition of Merchants and Traders of the town of Wilmington (ca. 1827), Petitions, General Assembly Sessions Records, 1827–1828; *Carolina Observer*, August 18, 1825; April 11, May 10, July 5, October 18, 1826; June 7, 1827.

54. *Carolina Observer*, December 7, 1831; *Fayetteville Observer*, January 29, 1833; January 14, 1834; October 20, 1835; June 16, 1836; February 2, 9, 1837; January 31, 1838; *People's Press and Wilmington Advertiser*, November 6, 1833; January 22, December 3, 1834; July 29, 1835; *Wilmington Advertiser*, September 8, November 3, 10, December 29, 1837; January 25, 1839; Johnson, *Riverboating in North Carolina*, 43.

55. *Fayetteville Observer*, February 9, December 21, 1842; January 24, 1844; May 14, October 15, December 30, 1845; December 29, 1846; April 18, 1848; January 9, September 18, 1849; *Carolina Watchman*, February 5, 1947; *Laws, 1846–1847*, cc. 124, 125; 1848–1849, c. 223; Johnson, *Riverboating in North Carolina*, 45. From April 19 through April 22, 1852, steamers accounted for 6 of 9 arrivals and 10 of 13 clearances from the port of Wilmington. *Journal*, April 23, 1852.

56. *Journal*, December 5, 1851; September 18, October 23, 1857.

57. *Laws, 1854–1855*, c. 177; *Journal*, November 13, 1857; January 19, 1860.

58. *Wilmington Advertiser*, April 14, 28, 1837; September 21, 28, 1838; *Journal*, April 22, 1853; May 26, November 10, 1854; October 30, 1857; *Laws, 1854–1855*, c. 176. During its brief stay in the Lower Cape Fear, the *E. D. McNair* also ran on the Northeast Cape Fear River from Wilmington to South Washington in Pender County. *Wilmington Advertiser*, February 9, 1838.

59. *American Recorder* (Washington, N.C.), January 11, 1822; *Carolina Observer*, August 9, 1826; *Wilmington Advertiser*, August 11, September 1, 1837; John C. Emmerson, Jr., comp., *Steam Navigation in Virginia and Northeastern North Carolina Waters, 1826–1836* (Portsmouth, Va., 1949), 267–268, 293.

60. *Laws, 1835*, c. 30; *Wilmington Advertiser*, January 4, May 5, 12, June 9, September 29, October 20, November 3, December 8, 15, 1837; June 8, 1838; September 27, 1839; *Journal*, March 21, 1845. The railroad steamers also proved useful for rescue purposes. The *Boston* brought passengers from the wreck of the *Home* to Wilmington in 1837; the *C. Vanderbilt* towed the disabled brig *Leonara* to port in 1844. *Wilmington Advertiser*, October 27, 1837; *Journal*, October 25, 1844.

61. *Wilmington Advertiser*, August 24, November 30, 1838; January 4, September 27, 1839; *Journal*, April 21, 1854; James Sprunt, *Chronicles of the Cape Fear River, 1660–1916*, 2nd ed. (Raleigh, 1916), 195. The steamer *Huntress* briefly replaced the *North Carolina*, followed permanently by the *Gladiator*. Sprunt, *Chronicles of the Cape Fear River*, 195.

62. *Journal*, February 7, 1845; March 7, May 5, 26, June 2, 1854; July 17, December 25, 1857; July 26, December 27, 1860.

63. *Ibid.*, December 15, 22, 1854; March 22, May 3, June 14, 21, 28, July 5, 12, 19, August 2, 9, 16, 23, 30, September 6, 20, 27, October 4, 18, November 15, 29, December 20, 27, 1860; *Newbern Weekly Progress*, June 12, October 9, 1860; *Laws, 1858–1859*, c. 154.

64. *Laws, 1831–1832*, cc. 50, 51; *Fayetteville Observer*, May 14, 1832; *People's Press*, May 1, June 5, 12, 1833; *Carolina Watchman*, August 4, 18, 1832.

65. *Laws, 1835*, c. 30; *1836–1837*, c. 22; *North Carolina Standard*, February 25, 1836; *Wilmington Advertiser*, May 5, 1837.

66. *Fayetteville Observer*, December 27, 1837; *Wilmington Advertiser*, August 24, 1838; John A. Scott, ed., *Journal of a Residence on a Georgia Plantation in 1838–1839 by Frances Anne Kemble* (New York, 1961), 22, 23, 28.

67. *Laws, 1854–1855*, c. 235; *Newbern Weekly Progress*, October 9, 1860.

68. *Laws, 1846–1847*, c. 82; *Journal*, May 22, June 12, l846.

69. *Journal*, August 6, 1847; May 12, December 15, l848; January 4, 1850; February 21, 1851; *Herald*, December 3, 1857; Beeler and Beeler, *Wilmington Town Minutes*, 26, 29, 57, 66–67; *Laws, 1850–185l*, c. 26; Undated "Memorial of the undersigned citizens and tax payers of the town of Wilmington" to the General Assembly, Miscellaneous Papers, 1760–1923, C. B. Hellier Collection, State Archives. L. H. Marsteller, Wilmington town commissioner, lodged a spirited protest against the town subscription to railroad stock, claiming that the town commissioners could only expend public funds for "Municipal purposes." Beeler and Beeler, *Wilmington Town Minutes*, 58–59.

70. *Journal*, November 19, 1858; *Daily Herald*, August 19, 1859.
71. *Laws, 1854–1855*, cc. 225, 226; *Journal*, May 26, June 2, 1854.
72. *Laws, 1856–1857*, c. 67; *1858–1859*, c. 168; *Journal*, July 20, August 29, October 12, 1855; February 20, 1857; *Daily Herald*, May 17, July 20, 1859; January 9, 1861; Beeler and Beeler, *Wilmington Town Minutes*, 162, 164, 171, 174–175; John Wilkes to "My dear Father," February 27, 1859, Charles Wilkes Collection, Rare Book, Manuscript, and Special Collections Library, Duke University.

11. ANTEBELLUM POLITICS

1. James H. Broussard, "The North Carolina Federalists, 1800–1816," *North Carolina Historical Review*, 55 (1978):20.
2. Alan D. Watson, *Richard Dobbs Spaight* (New Bern, N.C., 1987), 15–17; "A Statement of Facts Relative to the Sloop Providence L'Aimee Marguerite," Treasurer's and Comptroller's Papers, Ports, Box 11, State Archives, Raleigh, N.C.
3. Broussard, "North Carolina Federalists," 19.
4. John L. Cheney, Jr., comp., *North Carolina Government, 1585–1979: A Narrative and Statistical History* (Raleigh, 1981), 1218–1219.
5. *Wilmington Gazette*, February 14, 1804.
6. Donald Jackson and Dorothy Twohig, eds., *The Diaries of George Washington*, 6 vols. (Charlottesville, Va., 1976–1979), 6:119–120 and notes.
7. *Ibid.*, 120–121 and notes.
8. *Raleigh Register*, July 20, 1802; *Wilmington Gazette*, March 14, 1809.
9. *Wilmington Gazette*, July 14, 21, 1807.
10. Elizabeth Gregory McPherson, ed., "Unpublished Letters from North Carolinians to Jefferson," *North Carolina Historical Review*, 12 (1935):355–356; *Wilmington Gazette*, June 28, 1808; March 14, June 6, 1809.
11. Sarah M. Lemmon, *Frustrated Patriots. North Carolina and the War of 1812* (Chapel Hill, 1973), 41–42; Petition of Jacob Hartman to the General Assembly, October 26, 1818, Petitions (Miscellaneous), 1818, General Assembly Session Records, State Archives.
12. Lemmon, *Frustrated Patriots*, 135.
13. *Ibid.*, 130; *Raleigh Register*, June 3, 1814.
14. Lemmon, *Frustrated Patriots*, 154–155.
15. *Ibid.*, 155, 156, n. 23; *Raleigh Register*, July 15, 1814.
16. Artemus Boies to "Dear Brother," April 7, 1819, Miscellaneous Letters, Southern Historical Collection; *Raleigh Register*, April 23, 1819; Sprunt, *Chronicles of the Cape Fear River*, 209–211.
17. Albert Ray Newsome, *The Presidential Election of 1824 in North Carolina. The James Sprunt Studies in History and Political Science*. Volume 23 (Chapel Hill, 1939), 156.
18. *Journal* (Wilmington), November 8, 1844.
19. Cheney, *North Carolina Government*, 1218–1819. Upon his departure from the General Assembly, friends of Joshua G. Wright arranged a formal dinner in his honor in Wilmington. *True Republican* (Wilmington), January 10, 1809.
20. Cheney, *North Carolina Government*, 1219; Mary Phlegar Smith, "Borough Representation in North Carolina," *North Carolina Historical Review*, 7 (1930):186–187.
21. *People's Press* (Wilmington), March 20, 1833; *People's Press and Wilmington Advertiser*, July 24, August 21, 1833; August 20, 1834; August 14, 1835.
22. *People's Press and Wilmington Advertiser*, May 21, 1835; Cheney, *North Carolina*, 1217–1218.

23. *Proceedings and Debates of the Convention of North-Carolina, Called to Amend the Constitution of the State* ... . (Raleigh, 1836), 32–35, 37–39; Harold J. Counihan, "The North Carolina Constitutional Convention of 1835: A Study in Jacksonian Democracy," *North Carolina Historical Review*, (1969):343.

24. *Proceedings and Debates of the Convention*, 32–59; Counihan, "North Carolina Constitutional Convention," 344–345.

25. *Proceedings and Debates of the Convention*, 49. See also *ibid.*, 202.

26. *Ibid.*, 212; *People's Press and Wilmington Advertiser*, July 1, 1835.

27. *Chronicle* (Wilmington), November [October] 7, November 11, 18, 1840; Nicholas W. Schenck Journal, 107, 109, East Carolina Manuscript Collection, Greenville, N.C.; James Sprunt, *Chronicles of the Cape Fear River, 1660–1916*, 2nd ed. (Raleigh, 1916), 175–177.

28. *Journal*, May 6, 1853.

29. *Journal*, March 2, 9, 1845; Sprunt, *Chronicles of the Cape Fear River*, 213.

30. *Ibid.*, August 14, 1846; August 13, 1858; August 9, 1860. The Democrats also elected the county sheriff, usually with little or no opposition, but see the election of 1856 for the exception.

31. *Journal*, October 5, 19, 1855; *Daily Herald* (Wilmington), October 12, 18, 22, 1855; *Laws and Resolutions of the State of North Carolina, 1854–1855*, c. 248; *1856–1857*, c. 106.

32. *Laws, 1846–1847*, c. 39; *Journal*, May 8, 1857; May 7, 1858; May 6, 1859; May 10, 1860.

33. *Journal*, April 9, 16, 1845; June 4, 1847; May 15, 1857; ? to Mrs. C. D. DeRosset, April 16, 1845, DeRosset Family Papers, Southern Historical Collection, Chapel Hill, N.C.

34. *People's Press and Wilmington Advertiser*, December 31, 1834; *Journal*, December 17, 1852; December 22, 1859; *Herald* (Wilmington), December 11, 1852.

35. *Daily Herald*, October 29, December 4, 21, 22, 1855; *Journal*, December 21, 1855.

36. *Journal*, June 5, 1846; William S. Hoffman, *North Carolina in the Mexican War, 1846–1848* (Raleigh, 1963), 14–17.

37. *Journal*, March 12, 1847; August 11, 1848; *Daily Herald*, February 24, 1857; Hoffman, *North Carolina in the Mexican War*, 30.

38. *Journal*, February 1, March 15, November 1, 1850.

39. *Daily Herald*, November 26, 1859; *Journal*, November 25, December 15, 1859; P. K. Dickinson to "My Dear Sister," November 12, 1859, Platt K. Dickinson Papers, Southern Historical Collection; Victor B. Howard, "John Brown's Raid at Harpers Ferry and the Sectional Crisis in North Carolina," *North Carolina Historical Review*, 55 (1978):396–420.

40. Richard Everett Wood, "Port Town at War: Wilmington, North Carolina, 1860–1865," Ph.D. diss., Florida State University, 1976, 32–39.

41. *Daily Journal* (Wilmington), December 20, 21, 1860; *Journal*, December 27, 1860; Wood, "Port Town at War," 47–54.

Bibliography

Primary

Manuscripts

North Carolina State Archives, Raleigh, North Carolina

Samuel A'Court Ashe Papers
James Boon Papers
Adam Boyd Papers
Benjamin F. Hall Papers
W. P. Hall Collection

C. B. Hellier Collection
William Hooper Papers
Archibald Maclaine Papers
Pattie Mordecai Collection
A. G. Owen Collection

Southern Historical Collection, University of North Carolina at Chapel Hill, Chapel Hill, North Carolina

Moseley Ashley Curtis Collection
DeRosset Family Papers
Platt K. Dickinson Papers
Giles Family Papers
Hayes Collection

John Berniere Hooper Papers
Levin Lane Papers
Miscellaneous Letters [Collection]
Parrish Family Papers

Rare Books, Manuscript, and Special Collections Department, Duke University, Durham, North Carolina

Board of Commissioners of Navigation and Pilotage for the Cape Fear River and Bar Papers

Livingston Papers
Charles Wilkes Papers

East Carolina Manuscript Collection, East Carolina University, Greenville, North Carolina

F. L. Bond Papers
Martin Smith Grant Collection

Francis M. Manning Collection
Nicholas W. Schenck Journal

Newspapers

American Recorder (Washington, N.C.)
Cape Fear Mercury (Wilmington)
Cape Fear Recorder (Wilmington)
Carolina Observer (Fayetteville)
Carolina Watchman (Salisbury)
Chronicle (Wilmington)
Commercial (Wilmington)
Daily Herald (Wilmington)
Daily Journal (Wilmington)
Fayetteville Observer
Hall's Wilmington Gazette
Herald (Wilmington)
Journal (Wilmington)
Maryland Gazette (Annapolis)
Newbern Weekly Progress
North Carolina Gazette (New Bern)
North Carolina Gazette (Wilmington)
North Carolina Journal (Halifax)
North State Whig (Washington, N.C.)
Pennsylvania Gazette (Philadelphia)
People's Press (Wilmington)
People's Press and Wilmington Advertiser
Raleigh Register
State Gazette of North Carolina (Edenton)
State Gazette of North Carolina (New Bern)
South-Carolina Gazette (Charleston)
South-Carolina & American General Gazette (Charleston)
Tri-Weekly Commercial (Wilmington)
True Republican (Wilmington)
Wilmington Advertiser
Wilmington Advertiser and Merchants' and Farmers' Gazette
Wilmington Centinel
Wilmington Chronicle; and North-Carolina Weekly Advertiser
Wilmington Gazette
Virginia Gazette (Williamsburg)

Unpublished Public and Official Records

New Hanover County Courthouse, Wilmington, N.C.

New Hanover County Deeds   New Hanover County Wills

New Hanover County Library, Wilmington, N.C.

Records of the 1820 Census of Manufactures, New Hanover County

North Carolina Collection, University of North Carolina at Chapel Hill, Chapel Hill, N.C.

Colonial Office Papers 5/303, Public Record Office, London, microfilm

North Carolina State Archives, Raleigh, N.C.

Coroners Inquests, County Records, New Hanover County
Eighth Census, 1860: North Carolina, New Hanover County
General Assembly Session Records
Governors Papers
Minutes of the New Hanover County Court of Pleas and Quarter Sessions
Miscellaneous Records, Cumberland County
Miscellaneous Records, New Hanover County
New Hanover School Records
Records of Slaves and Free Persons of Color, New Hanover County
Seventh Census, 1850, Industry Schedule 5, North Carolina

Published Letters, Memoirs, Travel Accounts, and Other Miscellaneous Sources

Annual Report of the Board of Internal Improvements, 1839. Raleigh, 1839.
Battle, Kemp P., ed. *Letters and Documents Relating to the Early History of the Lower Cape Fear.* Chapel Hill, 1903.
Beeler, Nancy, and Rush Beeler, eds. *Wilmington Town Minutes, 1847–1855.* Wilmington, 1997.
Bellamy, John D. *Memoirs of an Octogenarian.* Charlotte, 1942.
Boyd, William K., ed. *Some Eighteenth Century Tracts Concerning North Carolina.* Raleigh, 1927.
Brickell, John. *The Natural History of North Carolina.* Raleigh, 1910.
Brown, Robert W. "On the Trade of Wilmington, N.C. August 1st, 1843." *Our Living and Our Dead*, I (September 1874-February 1875):56–59.
Carroll, Grady, ed. *Francis Asbury in North Carolina. The North Carolina Portions of His Journal.* Nashville, Tenn., 1964.
Cheney, John L., Jr., comp. *North Carolina Government, 1585–1979. A Narrative and Statistical History.* Raleigh, 1981.
Clark, Walter, ed. *The State Records of North Carolina.* 16 vols. Winston and Goldsboro, 1895–1906.
Commager, Henry Steele, ed. *Documents of American History.* 2 vols. New York, 1963.
Corbitt, D. L., ed. "Historical Notes." *North Carolina Historical Review*, 5 (1928):329–330.
Demott, Mortimer. "Sojourn in Wilmington and the Lower Cape Fear, 1837." *Lower Cape Fear Historical Society Bulletin*, 22 (May 1979).
Elliot, Jonathan, ed. *The Debates in the Several State Conventions on the Adoption of the Federal Constitution.* 5 vols. Philadelphia, 1836–1845.
Emmerson, John C., comp. *Steam Navigation in Virginia and Northeastern North Carolina Waters, 1826–1836.* Portsmouth, Va., 1949.
Finlay, Hugh. *Journal Kept by Hugh Finlay, Surveyor of the Post Roads on the Continent of North America.* Brooklyn, 1867.
Fries, Adelaide, et al., eds. *Records of the Moravians in North Carolina.* 12 vols. Raleigh, 1922–2000.
Gordon, Lord Adam. "Journal of an Officer's Travels in America and the West Indies, 1764–1765," 367–453. *Travels in the American Colonies.* Ed. by Newton D. Mereness. New York, 1916.
Grimes, J. Bryan, comp. *Abstracts of North Carolina Wills.* Raleigh, 1910.
____, comp. *North Carolina Wills and Inventories.* Raleigh, 1912.
Hamer, Philip, et al., eds. *The Papers of Henry Laurens.* Projected multi-volume series. Columbia, S.C., 1968–.
Heads of Families at the First Census of the United States Taken in 1790. Baltimore, 1966.
Higginbotham, Don, ed. *The Papers of James Iredell.* 2 vols. Raleigh, 1976.
Howe, Mark A. DeWolfe, ed. "Journal of Josiah Quincy, Junior, 1773." *Massachusetts Historical Society Proceedings.* 49 (1916):424–481.
Jackson, Donald, and Dorothy Twohig, eds. *The Diaries of George Washington.* 6 vols. Charlottesville, Va., 1976–1979.
Johnston, Hugh B., ed. "The Journal of Ebenezer Hazard in North Carolina, 1777 and 1778." *North Carolina Historical Review*, 36 (1959):358–381.
Kelley's Wilmington Directory, to Which Is Added a Business Directory for 1860–61. Comp. by T. Tuther. Wilmington, 1860.

Laws and Resolutions of the State of North Carolina.
"Lazarus-Cohen Correspondence, 1842–1871." Lower Cape Fear Historical Society *Bulletin*, 27 (October 1983).
Lennon, Donald R., and Ida B. Kellam, eds. *The Wilmington Town Book, 1743–1778.* Raleigh, 1973.
Logan, William. "William Logan's Journal of a Journey to Georgia, 1745." *Pennsylvania Magazine of History and Biography*, 36 (1912):1–16.
McEachern, Leora H., and Isabel M. Williams, eds. *Wilmington–New Hanover Safety Committee Minutes, 1774–1776.* Wilmington, 1974.
McPherson, Elizabeth Gregory, ed., "Unpublished Letters from North Carolinians to Jefferson." North *Carolina Historical Review*, 12 (1935):252–283, 354–380.
McRee, Griffith J., ed. *Life and Correspondence of James Iredell.* 2 vols. New York, 1949.
Maser, Frederick E., and Howard T. Maag, eds. *The Journal of Joseph Pilmore, Methodist Itinerant.* Philadelphia, 1969.
Meredith, Hugh. *An Account of the Cape Fear Country, 1731.* Ed. by Earl Gregg Swem. Perth Amboy, N.J., 1912.
Minutes of the Eleventh Annual Meeting of the Medical Society of the State of North Carolina. Wilmington, 1860.
Miranda, Francisco de. *The New Democracy in America. Travels of Francisco de Miranda in the United States, 1783–1784.* Trans. by Judson P. Wood, and ed. by John S. Ezell. Norman, Okla., 1963.
"New Voyage to Georgia by a Young Gentleman, [1737]." Collections of the Georgia Historical Society, 9 vols. (Savannah, 1840–1916), 2:37–66.
Olmsted, Frederick Law. *A Journey in the Seaboard Slave States, with Remarks on Their Economy.* New York, 1969.
Population of the United States, 1860. Washington, D.C., 1864.
Potts, Joshua. "On the Trade of Wilmington, N.C., May 1st, 1815." *Our Living and Our Dead*, I (September 1874-February 1875):51–56.
Powell, William S., ed. *The Correspondence of William Tryon and Other Selected Papers.* 2 vols. Raleigh, 1980, 1981.
Proceedings and Debates of the Convention of North Carolina, Called to Amend the Constitution of the State. Raleigh, 1836.
Rawick, George, ed. *The American Slave. A Composite Biography. North Carolina Narratives.* Vol. 15. Westport, Conn., 1977.
"The Reverend Thomas Wright's Letters to Robert Scott." Lower Cape Fear Historical Society *Bulletin*, 23 (February 1980).
Saunders, William L., ed. *The Colonial Records of North Carolina.* 10 vols. Raleigh, 1886–1890.
Schaw, Janet. *Journal of a Lady of Quality... .* Ed. by Evangeline W. Andrews and Charles M. Andrews. New Haven, 1923.
Schoepf, Johann David. *Travels in the Confederation, 1783–1784.* 2 vols. Trans. and ed. by Alfred J. Morrison. Philadelphia, 1911.
Scott, John A., ed. *Journal of a Residence on a Georgian Plantation in 1838–1839 by Frances Anne Kemble.* New York, 1961.
Tiffany, Nina Moore, ed. *Letters of James Murray, Loyalist.* Boston, 1901.
Transactions of the Medical Society of the State of North Carolina at Its Third Annual Meeting. Wilmington, 1852.
Transactions of the Seventeenth Annual Meeting of the Medical Society of the State of North Carolina. Wilmington, 1870.
Tuttle, Rev. D. H., and W. C. Merrett. *Directory of Fifth St. M. E. Church, South, Wilmington, N.C.* Wilmington, 1888.

Waddell, Alfred M. *A Colonial Officer and His Times.* Spartanburg, S.C., 1973.
Watson, Alan D., ed. *An Index to North Carolina Newspapers, 1784–1789.* Raleigh, 1992.
____, ed. "Wilmington Commerce, 1816: A Document." Lower Cape Fear Historical Society *Bulletin,* 39 (April 1995).
Watson, Elkanah. *Men and Times of the Revolution; or, Memoirs of Elkanah Watson.* 2nd ed. Ed. by Winslow C. Watson. New York, 1857.
Wright, Louis B. and Marion R. Tinling, eds. *Quebec to Carolina in 1785–1786. Being the Travel Diary and Observations of Robert Hunter, a Young Merchant of London.* San Marino, Calif., 1943.

SECONDARY

Articles and Essays

Bishir, Catherine W. "Black Builders in Antebellum North Carolina." *North Carolina Historical Review,* 61 (1984):423–461.
Brewer, James Howard. "Legislation Designed to Control Slavery in Wilmington and Fayetteville." *North Carolina Historical Review,* 30 (l953):155–166.
Broussard, James. "The North Carolina Federalists, 1800–1816." *North Carolina Historical Review,* 55 (1978):18–39.
Browning, James B. "James D. Sampson." *Negro History Bulletin,* 3 (1940):56.
Cecelski, David. "The Shores of Freedom: The Maritime Underground Railroad in North Carolina." *North Carolina Historical Review,* 71 (l994):174–206.
Chamberlain, Merle. "Connecticut Yankee in Wilmington." Lower Cape Fear Historical Society *Bulletin,* 42 (March 1998).
Counihan, Harold J. "The North Carolina Constitutional Convention of 1835: A Study in Jacksonian Democracy." *North Carolina Historical Review,* 46 (l969):335–364.
Crittenden, Charles C. "Inland Navigation in North Carolina, 1763–1789." *North Carolina Historical Review,* (1931):145–154.
Cumming, William P. "The Turbulent Life of Captain James Wimble." *North Carolina Historical Review,* 46 (1969):1–18.
_____. "Wimble's Maps and the Colonial Cartography of North Carolina." *North Carolina Historical Review,* 46 (1969):157–170.
Cymbalsky, Stephen. "Literature of the Lower Cape Fear," 33–39. *Time, Talent, Tradition. Five Essays on the Cultural History of the Lower Cape Fear Region, North Carolina.* Ed. by Janet K. Seapker. Wilmington, 1995.
Dill, Alonzo Thomas, Jr. "Eighteenth Century New Bern. A History of the Town and Craven County, 1700–1800." Part VIII. "New Bern at Century's End." *North Carolina Historical Review,* 23 (1946):495–535.
Ernst, Joseph A., and H. Roy Merrens. "'Camden's Turrets Pierce the Skies': The Urban Process in the Southern Colonies During the Eighteenth Century." *William and Mary Quarterly,* 3rd Series, 30 (1975):549–574.
Fenn, Elizabeth A. "'A Perfect Equality Seemed to Reign': Slavery, Society, and Jonkonnu." *North Carolina Historical Review,* 65 (1988):117–153.
Frech, Laura Page. "The Wilmington Committee of Public Safety and the Loyalist Rising of February 1776." *North Carolina Historical Review,* 41 (1964):21–33.
Gerdes, Jon Henry. "The Early Jews of North Carolina at Wilmington." Lower Cape Fear Historical Society *Bulletin,* 28 (October 1984).
Green, William J. "Spanish Raids on the Coast of North Carolina, 1741–1748." *Tributaries,* 2 (1992):17–21.

Hendricks, J. Edwin. "Joseph Winston: North Carolina Jeffersonian." *North Carolina Historical Review*, 45 (1968):284–297.

Lawson, Dennis R. "William Hooper," 35–67. Alan D. Watson, Dennis R. Lawson, Donald R. Lennon, *Harnett, Hooper & Howe: Revolutionary Leaders of the Lower Cape Fear*. Wilmington, 1979.

Lennon, Donald R. "The Development of Town Government in Colonial North Carolina," 1-25. *Of Tar Heel Towns, Shipbuilders, Reconstructionists and Alliancemen. Papers in North Carolina History*. Ed. by Joseph F. Steelman. Greenville, N.C., 1981.

London, Lawrence F. "The Representation Controversy in Colonial North Carolina." *North Carolina Historical Review*, 11 (l934):255–270.

Marcroft, Bobbie. "The Early Germans." Lower Cape Fear Historical Society *Bulletin*, 18 (February 1975).

Martin, Sherill V. "Music and Dance in the Lower Cape Fear," 41-55. *Time, Talent, Tradition: Five Essays on the Cultural History of the Lower Cape Fear Region, North Carolina*. Ed. by Janet K. Seapker. Wilmington, 1995.

Massey, Gregory De Van. "The British Expedition to Wilmington, January-November 1781." *North Carolina Historical Review*, 66 (1989):387–411.

Morris, Charles Edward. "Panic and Reprisal: Reaction in North Carolina to the Nat Turner Insurrection, 1831." *North Carolina Historical Review*, 62 (1985):29–52.

Myers, John W. "Visual Arts," 71–83. *Time, Talent, Tradition: Five Essays on the Cultural History of the Lower Cape Fear Region, North Carolina*. Ed. by Janet K. Seapker. Wilmington, 1995.

Newsome, Albert Ray. "North Carolina's Ratification of the Federal Constitution." *North Carolina Historical Review*, 17 (1940):287–301.

"Organization of the North Carolina Medical Professions, 1799 and 1849," 1:69–96. Dorothy Long, ed., *Medicine in North Carolina: Essays in the History of Medical Science and Medical Service, 1524–1960*. 2 vols. Raleigh, 1972.

Patton, James W. "Glimpses of North Carolina in the Writings of Northern and Foreign Travelers, 1783–1860." *North Carolina Historical Review*, 46 (l968):298–324.

Paul, Charles. "Beaufort, North Carolina: Its Development as a Colonial Town." *North Carolina Historical Review*, 47 (1970):370–387.

_____. "Colonial Beaufort." *North Carolina Historical Review*, 42 (1965):139–152.

_____. "Factors in the Economy of Colonial Beaufort." *North Carolina Historical Review*, 44 (1967):111–134.

Pool, William C. "An Economic Interpretation of the Ratification of the Federal Constitution in North Carolina. Parts I, II, and III." *North Carolina Historical Review*, 27 (1950):119–141, 289–313, 437–461.

Price, Jacob M. "Economic Function and the Growth of American Port Towns in the Eighteenth Century." *Perspectives in American History*, 8 (1974):123–186.

Price, William S., Jr. "A Strange Incident in George Burrington's Royal Governorship." *North Carolina Historical Review*, 51 (1974):149–158.

"Progress Toward the Establishment of Medical Science in North Carolina. 1800–1850," 1:53–68. Dorothy Long, ed., *Medicine in North Carolina: Essays in the History of Medical Science and Medical Service, 1524–1960*. Raleigh, 1972.

Rankin, Hugh F. "The Moore's Creek Bridge Campaign." *North Carolina Historical Review*, 30 (1953):33–60.

Rankin, Richard D. "'The Seat of Smiling Mirth': The Ninepenny Whist Club of Wilmington, North Carolina, 1801-ca. 1807." *North Carolina Historical Review*, 68 (1991): 38–57.

Ransom, Roger. "British Policy and Colonial Growth: Some Implications of the Burden of the Navigation Acts." *Journal of Economic History*, 28 (1968):427–435.

Reid, Ira De A. "The John Canoe Festival: A New World Africanism." *Phylon*, 3 (1942):350–353.
Rivenbark, D. Anthony. "History and Theater in Wilmington and the Lower Cape Fear Region, 57–68." *Time, Talent, Tradition: Five Essays on the Cultural History of the Lower Cape Fear Region, North Carolina*. Ed. by Janet K. Seapker. Wilmington, 1995.
Rulfs, Donald J. "The Professional Theater in Wilmington, 1858–1870." *North Carolina Historical Review*, 28 (1951).
Seapker, Janet. "James F. Post, Builder-Architect: The Legend and the Ledger." Lower Cape Fear Historical Society *Bulletin*, 30 (May 1987).
Sellers, Charles Grier, Jr., "Making a Revolution: The North Carolina Whigs, 1765–1775," 23–46. *Studies in Southern History in Memory of Albert Ray Newsome, 1894–1951*. Ed. by J. Carlyle Sitterson. Chapel Hill, 1957.
Smith, Mary Phlegar. "Borough Representation in North Carolina." *North Carolina Historical Review*, 7 (1930):177–190.
Spindel, Donna J. "Law and Disorder: The North Carolina Stamp Act Crisis." *North Carolina Historical Review*, 57 (1980):1–16.
Starling, Roger B. "The Plank Road Movement in North Carolina." Parts I and II. *North Carolina Historical Review*, 16 (1939):1–22, 147–173.
Stumpf, Vernon O. "The Radical Ladies of Wilmington and Their Tea Party." Lower Cape Fear Historical Society *Bulletin*, 16 (February 1773).
Thomas, Robert Paul. "A Quantitative Approach to the Study of British Imperial Policy Upon Colonial Welfare." *Journal of Economic History*, 25 (1965):615–638.
Turberg, Edward F. "Architecture in the Lower Cape Fear," 17–31. *Time, Talent, Tradition: Five Essays on the Cultural History of the Lower Cape Fear Region, North Carolina*. Ed. by Janet K. Seapker. Wilmington, 1995.
Watson, Alan D. "The Committees of Safety and the Coming of the Revolution in North Carolina, 1774–1776." *North Carolina Historical Review*, 73 (1996):131–155.
_____. "Cornelius Harnett," 3–31. Alan D. Watson, Dennis R. Lawson, and Donald R. Lennon, *Harnett, Hooper, & Howe: Revolutionary Leaders of the Lower Cape Fear*. Wilmington, 1979.
_____. "Impulse Toward Independence: Resistance and Rebellion Among North Carolina Slaves, 1750–1775." *Journal of Negro History*, 63 (1978):317–328.
_____. "The Lottery in Early North Carolina." *North Carolina Historical Review*, 69 (1992):365–387.
_____. "North Carolina and Internal Improvements, 1783–1861: The Case of Inland Navigation." *North Carolina Historical Review*, 74 (1997):37–73.
_____. "North Carolina: States' Rights and Agrarianism Ascendant," 251–268. *The Constitution and the States: The Role of the Original Thirteen in the Framing and Adoption of the Federal Constitution*. Ed. by Patrick T. Conley and John P. Kaminski. Madison, Wis., 1988.
_____. "Ordinaries in Colonial Eastern North Carolina." *North Carolina Historical Review*, 45 (1968):67–83.
_____. "Port Brunswick in the Colonial Era." Lower Cape Fear Historical Society *Journal*, 31 (1989):23–32.
_____. "Sailing Under Steam: The Advent of Steam Navigation in North Carolina to the Civil War." *North Carolina Historical Review*, 75 (1998):29–68.
_____. "Sailors, Wilmington, and the First Hospital in North Carolina." *Tributaries*, 7 (1997):41–44.
_____. "The Town Fathers of Early Wilmington, 1743–1778." Lower Cape Fear Historical Society *Bulletin*, 24 (October 1980).

_____. "Wilmington: A Town Born in Conflict, Confusion, and Collusion." Lower Cape Fear Historical Society *Bulletin*, 30 (February, May 1988).
Weir, Robert M. "North Carolina's Reaction to the Currency Act of 1764." *North Carolina Historical Review*, 40 (1963):183–199.
Wells, Warren L. "Surgical Practice in North Carolina: A Historical Commentary," 2:632–643. Dorothy Long, ed., *Medicine in North Carolina: Essays in the History of Medical Science and Medical Service, 1524–1960.* 2 vols. Raleigh, 1972.
Wheeler, E. Merton. "Development and Organization of the North Carolina Militia." *North Carolina Historical Review*, 41 (1964):307–323.
Wilson, Clyde. "Griffith John McRee: An Unromantic Historian of the Old South." *North Carolina Historical Review*, 47 (1970):1–23.
Worsley, Stephen C. "Catholicism in Antebellum North Carolina." *North Carolina Historical Review*, 60 (1983):399–430.

Monographs and Compilations

Addo, Linda D., and James H. McCallum. *To Be Faithful to Our Heritage. A History of Black United Methodism in North Carolina.* Winston-Salem, N.C., 1980.
Barrow, Thomas C. *Trade and Empire: The British Customs Service in Colonial America, 1660–1775.* Cambridge, Mass., 1967.
Bennett, Charles E., and Donald R. Lennon. *A Quest for Glory. Major General Robert Howe and the American Revolution.* Chapel Hill and London, 1991.
Bernheim, Gotthart. *The First Twenty Years of St. Paul's Evangelical Lutheran Church.* Wilmington, 1879.
Bishir, Catherine W. *North Carolina Architecture.* Chapel Hill, 1990.
Bivins, John, Jr. *Wilmington Furniture, 1760–1820.* Wilmington, 1989.
Boeschenstein, Warren. *Historic American Towns Along the Atlantic Coast.* Baltimore and London, 1999.
Boyd, William K. *History of North Carolina.* Vol. 2. *The Federal Period, 1783–1860.* Spartanburg, S.C., 1973.
Bridenbaugh, Carl. *Cities in Revolt. Urban Life in America, 1743–1776.* New York, 1955.
_____. *Cities in the Wilderness. Urban Life in America, 1625–1742.* New York, 1964.
Broussard, James H. *The Southern Federalists, 1800–1816.* Baton Rouge and London, 1978.
Burr, Jas. G. *Sketch of St. James Parish.* New York, 1874.
Butler, Lindley S. *North Carolina and the Coming of the Revolution, 1763–1776.* Raleigh, 1976.
Cashman. *The Lonely Road: A History of the Physicks and Physicians of the Lower Cape Fear, 1735–1976.* Wilmington, 1976.
Cathey, Cornelius O. *Agriculture in North Carolina Before the Civil War.* Raleigh, 1966.
Connor, R. D. W. *Cornelius Harnett. An Essay in North Carolina History.* Raleigh, 1909.
Conser, Walter W., Jr. *Sacred Spaces: Architecture and Religion in Historic Wilmington.* Wilmington, 1999.
Crittenden, Charles C. *The Commerce of North Carolina, 1763–1789.* New Haven, 1936.
Crow, Jeffrey J. *The Black Experience in Revolutionary North Carolina.* Raleigh, 1983.
Cumming, William P. *The Southeast in Early Maps.* Chapel Hill, 1962.
DeMond, Robert O. *The Loyalists in North Carolina During the Revolution.* Durham, N.C. 1940.
Dictionary of National Biography.
Dormon, James H., Jr. *Theater in the Ante Bellum South, 1815–1861.* Chapel Hill, 1967.
Ekirch, A. Roger. *"Poor Carolina": Politics and Society in Colonial North Carolina, 1729–1776.* Chapel Hill, 1981.

Ernst, Joseph A. *Money and Politics in America: A Study in the Currency Act of 1764 and the Political Economy of the Revolution.* Chapel Hill, 1973.
Franklin, John Hope. *The Free Negro in North Carolina, 1790–1860.* Chapel Hill, 1943.
Ganyard, Robert L. *The Emergence of North Carolina's Revolutionary State Government.* Raleigh, 1980.
Greene, Jack P. *The Quest for Power. The Lower Houses of Assembly in the Southern Royal Colonies, 1689–1776.* Chapel Hill, 1963.
Hartzger, Ronald B. *To Great and Useful Purpose: A History of the Wilmington District U.S. Army Corps of Engineers.* N. p., n. d.
Henderson, Archibald. North Carolina: *The Old North State and New.* 5 vols. Chicago, 1941.
Hoffman, William S. *North Carolina in the Mexican War, 1846–1848.* Raleigh, 1963.
Holmes, J. A., and Wm. Cain. *Road Materials and Road Construction in North Carolina.* 2nd ed. Raleigh, 1893.
Howell, Andrew J. *The Book of Wilmington.* Wilmington, 1959.
Johnson, F. Roy. *Riverboating in Lower Carolina.* Murfreesboro, N.C., 1977.
Johnson, Guion G. *Ante-Bellum North Carolina: A Social History.* Chapel Hill, 1937.
Kay, Marvin L. Michael, and Lorin Lee Cary, *Slavery in North Carolina, 1748–1775.* Chapel Hill, 1995.
Long, Dorothy, ed. *Medicine in North Carolina: Essays in the History of Medical Science and Medical Service, 1524–1960.* 2 vols. Raleigh, 1972.
Lee, Lawrence. *The History of Brunswick County, North Carolina.* Charlotte, 1980.
_____. *The Lower Cape Fear in Colonial Days.* Chapel Hill, 1965.
Lemmon, Sarah McCulloh. *Frustrated Patriots: North Carolina and the War of 1812.* Chapel Hill, 1973.
McCusker, John J., and Russell R. Menard. *The Economy of British America, 1607–1789.* Chapel Hill, 1985.
McKoy, Elizabeth Francenia. *Early Wilmington Block by Block.* Wilmington, 1967.
McKoy. Henry Bacon. *Wilmington, N.C.—Do You Remember?* Greenville, S.C., 1957.
Meares, Catherine DeRosset. *Annals of the DeRosset Family: Huguenot Immigrants to the Province of North Carolina Early in the Eighteenth Century.* N. p., 1906?
Merrens, H. Roy. *North Carolina in the Eighteenth Century. A Study in Historical Geography.* Chapel Hill, 1964.
Moore, Louis T. *Stories Old and New of the Cape Fear Region.* Wilmington, 1968.
Morgan, David T., and William J. Schmidt. *North Carolinians in the Continental Congress.* Winston-Salem, N.C., 1976.
Neale, Robert S. *The Bank of the Cape Fear of Wilmington, North Carolina.* Wilmington, 1999.
Newsome, Albert Ray. *The Presidential Election of 1824 in North Carolina.* The James Sprunt Studies in History and Political Science. Vol. 23. Chapel Hill, 1939.
Parramore, Thomas C. *Cradle of the Colony. The History of Chowan County and Edenton.* Edenton, 1967.
_____. *Launching the Craft: The First Half-Century of Freemasonry in North Carolina.* Raleigh, 1975.
Paschal, Herbert R., Jr. *A History of Colonial Bath.* Raleigh, 1955.
Powell, William S., ed. *Dictionary of North Carolina Biography.* 6 vols. Chapel Hill, 1979–1996.
Rankin, Hugh F. *The North Carolina Continentals.* Chapel Hill, 1971.
Reaves, William S. *"Strength Through Struggle": The Chronological and Historical Record of the African-American Community in Wilmington, North Carolina 1865-1950.* Wilmington, 1998.

Seapker, Janet K., ed. *Time, Talent, Tradition. Five Essays on the Cultural History of the Lower Cape Fear Region, North Carolina*. Wilmington, 1995.
Stick, David. *North Carolina Lighthouses*. Raleigh, 1991.
Still, William N., Jr. *North Carolina's Revolutionary War Navy*. Raleigh, 1976.
Sprunt, James. *Chronicles of the Cape Fear River, 1660–1916*. 2nd ed. Wilmington, 1916.
Stumpf, Vernon O. *Josiah Martin: The Last Royal Governor of North Carolina*. Durham, N.C., 1986.
Trenholme, Louis I. *The Ratification of the Federal Constitution in North Carolina*. New York, 1931.
A Tribute to Oakdale Cemetery. Wilmington, 1991.
Troxler, Carole Watterson. *The Loyalist Experience in North Carolina*. Raleigh, 1976.
Watson, Alan D. *A History of New Bern and Craven County*. New Bern, N.C., 1987.
____. *Richard Dobbs Spaight*. New Bern, N.C., 1987.
____. *Society in Colonial North Carolina*. Raleigh, 1996.
____. *Wilmington: Port of North Carolina*. Columbia, S.C., 1992.
Watts, Gordon P., and Wesley K. Wall. *An Investigation of Blossom's Ferry on the Northeast Cape Fear River*. Greenville, N.C., 1986.
Wilstach, Paul. *Mount Vernon: Washington's Home and the Nation's Shrine*. Garden City and New York, 1916.
Wrenn, Tony P. *Wilmington, North Carolina: An Architectural and Historical Portrait*. Charlottesville, Va., 1984.

Theses, Dissertations, and Reports

Brewer, James H. "An Account of Negro Slavery in the Cape Fear Region Prior to 1860." Ph.D. dissertation. University of Pittsburgh, 1949.
Logan, Byron Eugene. "An Historical Geographic Survey of North Carolina Ports." Ph.D. dissertation. University of North Carolina, 1956.
Perry, Percival. "The Naval Stores Industry in the Ante-Bellum South, 1789–1861." Ph.D. dissertation. Duke University, 1947.
Ping, Nancy Regan. "Music in Antebellum Wilmington and the Lower Cape Fear." Ph.D. dissertation. University of Colorado, 1973.
Russ, Elsie Faye. "The Cape Fear and Deep River Navigation Company, 1849–1873." M.A. thesis. Wake Forest University, 1980.
Sims, Kimberly. "Wilmington Jewry: 1800–1914." Honor's thesis. University of North Carolina at Wilmington, 1999.
Williams, Isabel M. "Thalian Hall." N. d. Reports. Research Division, Archives and History, Raleigh, N.C.
Wood, Richard Everett. "Port Town at War: Wilmington, North Carolina, 1860–1865." Ph.D. dissertation, Florida State University, 1976.

Index

Abolitionist movement 128, 134, 135
Academies 46, 163–166
Accidents 118, 123
Addington, R. D. 117
African American artisans 126
African Americans: become musicians 139–140, 148; cemeteries for 196–197; and religion 140,141; respective percentages of population of, in Wilmington, during antebellum period 125; typical occupations of 136; work in maritime trades 131, 132, 136
Agricultural societies 148–149
Alba (schooner) 241
Albemarle region 5, 7; older counties in, retain disproportionate political representation 72
Aldermen 20
Alexander Hostler & Co. 31
Alexander Wise (brig) 218
Allen, Eleazar 7, 13, 16
Allen's Barber Shop 139
Allen's Rosebud Brass Band 139, 148
Amateur Brass Band 148
American Colonization Society 134
American Company of Comedians 43
American Medical Association 115
American Party 232, 236, 237, 239, 240
American Revolution 34, 44, 64, 65; disrupts trade on which Wilmington depended 63, 65, 70; divides patriots on constitutional matters 93
The American Singing-Book 47
Ancrum, John 19
Anglican Church (sect) 45, 150

Anglican church (Wilmington) 19, 46, 154
Anglican ministers 45
Animal control 191
Antifederalist Party 95, 96, 97–98, 227
Apothecaries 115
Arches (substitutes for bridges) 23
Architects 104–105
Architectural styles (in Wilmington) 177
Arlow, Bridget 29
Arlow, James 25, 29
Arrington, B. F. 118
Arson 110
Articles of Confederation 94, 95, 97
Artillery Company (volunteer uniformed militia company) 145
Artis family 137
Artisans 19, 126, 156; *see also* Craftsmen
Arts 42
Asbury, Francis 141, 149, 152
Ashe, John 90
Ashe, John Baptista 7, 8
Ashe, William S. 236, 237
Ashkenazic Jews 104, 154
Associations (written statements of principle employed by patriots) 84–85
Atkinson, Thomas 150, 176
Aurora (Wilmington) 170
Authors *see* Writers
Auxiliary Washington Society (temperance organization) 147

Bache, A. D. 215
Backcountry trade 59, 60, 61, 62
Backgammon 118–119

293

Index

Bailey Varieties (traveling theatrical group) 181
Bald Head Island 68
Bald Head Lighthouse 68, 215
Balfour, Nisbet 90
Balls 41
Bancroft, George 177
Bands (musical) 148
Bank of Cape Fear 205, 206
Bank of Newbern 205
Bank of the State of North Carolina 205, 206
Bank of Wilmington 206
Banks and banking 200, 205–206
Baptist church (Wilmington) 134
Baptists 141, 152
Barclay, John: newspaper advertisement for return of runaway slave of, quoted 131
Barker, Dr. (lecturer) 176
Barnes, Captain (commander of ship bound for Jamaica) 34
Barnes, George 30
Barnum, P. T. 181
Bath, N.C. 51
Bath Town 6
Battle of Alamance (May 1771) 79–80
Battle of Guilford Court House 92
Battle of Moores Creek Bridge 87, 89; commemoration of 122
Battle of Rockfish Creek 93
Battle of Tippecanoe 229
Bauer, William Henry 169
Bazadier, Philip 139
Beacons (at Federal Point) 215
Beard, Neil, Sr. 109
Beaufort, N.C. 6, 51
Belanger, J. J. 179
Bell, John 241
Bellamy, John Dillard 115, 149, 178
Bellamy Mansion 105, 108, 136, 178
Bellew, John 169
Bellfont (home of Gov. William Tryon) 75, 78
Benj. Blossom & Son (commission merchants) 200
Benning, Arthur 93
Berry, William A. 239
Bethelly, Mrs. (ferry operator) 29
Beze, Miss (music teacher) 167
Biddle, Mr. (candidate for constable) 186
Bilious fever 112, 113
Billiards 118–119
Biltz, Signor (ventriloquist) 119
Bishir, Catherine W.: quoted, concerning importance of African Americans in building trades 136
Blackmore, Harold 30
Blackmore, Lettice 36
Blacks *see* African Americans
Blake, Madam (dance instructor) 168
"Blank patents" (land grants issued by Richard Everard) 8
Blanks, John 210
Bloodworth, Timothy 227, 229
Bloodworth, Tom 94
Blossom, Joseph R. 200
Board of Commissioners of Navigation and Pilotage for the Cape Fear River 238–239; powers of 239; *see also* Commissioners of navigation and pilotage for the Cape Fear River
Board of Internal Improvements 212
Boardinghouses 106, 201; operated by women 202
Boards (wooden; as exports) 56, 69
Bode, Maurice (music teacher) 167
Boies, Artemus 105
Bonaparte, Napoleon 229
Boon, James 137
Borough government (Wilmington) 20
Borough representation (in lower house of colonial legislature) 73, 94, 233, 233–234, 234–235
Boston (oceangoing steamship) 219
Boston (slave of George Parker) 34
Bowden, Jesse 131
Bowen, Mr. (proprietor of newspaper) 47, 96
Boyd, Adam 29, 47, 91
Boyd, Mary 91
Braddock, Captain 120
Bragg, Thomas 237
Breckinridge, John C. 241
Brethren of the Unitas Fratrum *see* Moravians
Brice, Rigdon 93
Brickell, John: quoted, concerning future prospects for Brunswick Town 8
Bridges 23, 60, 210
Brigs (ships) 58, 208
Brison, Mr. (representative of national government) 48
British sympathizers *see* Loyalists
British troops: arrive in Lower Cape Fear region 87; attempt to extend British military control into N.C. 90; fight to

standoff in Lower Cape Fear 93; presence of, in Wilmington, alters course of Revolutionary War in southeastern N.C. 91
Brown, Asa A. 170, 171; announces support for Whig principles 171
Brown, John: raid 135, 241
Brown, Robert: newspaper advertisement for return of runaway slave of, quoted 131
Brown and Anderson, store of 156
Browne, W. G. 180
Brunswick County safety committee 87
Brunswick Town 6, 8, 51, 52, 60, 62, 87; briefly occupied by Spanish 71; demise of 66; described 8; designated as seat of New Hanover Precinct 8; overshadowed by town of Wilmington 52, 71; provides Wilmington with bulk of exportable products 206–207; in rivalry with Newton for supremacy in New Hanover Precinct 11, 12, 13, 14, 15, 16
Buchanan, Thomas 134
Buckley's Minstrels 182
Building trades 136–137
Bull, Ole 182
Bulwer-Lytton, Edward: play by 181
Burgwin, John 18, 22, 70, 129; brief biographical sketch of 39–40; family of, travels to escape summer heat 48; house of, described 39; portrait of, reproduced 39
Burgwin, John F. 200; quoted, concerning advisability of giving notice before shipping cargoes to Wilmington 207
Burgwin & Co. (commission merchants) 200
Burgwin-Wright House (Wilmington) 39, 92
Burnett, Lucinda 109
Burns, Otway 216
Burr, Talcott, Jr. 170, 179
Burrington, George 9, 53; instrumental in permanent settlement of Lower Cape Fear region 6, 7; issues patents for land in Cape Fear region 7; quarrels with "Family" over land granted under "blank patents" 8; quoted, concerning his efforts to encourage settlement of Lower Cape Fear 7; recommends establishment of a town along Cape Fear River 8; seeks to expand trade, enhance prosperity of his colony in Lower Cape Fear 6

Businesses (in Wilmington) 201
Butler (schooner) 132

C. D. McNair (steamboat) 218
C. Vanderbilt (oceangoing steamship) 219
Cabinetmakers 137
Calder, Phila Cohen Lazarus: quoted, concerning her pleasure at returning to Wilmington 105–106
Caldwell, Andrew 164
Caleb Nichols (sailing packet) 217
Calhoun (oceangoing steamship) 220
Calhoun (steamboat) 144
Camden and Gadsden Railroad (S.C.) 223
Camp meetings 149
Campbell, Montesquieu W. 186, 233
Campbell, Samuel 63, 91
Campbell, William 18, 30, 45, 196
Campbell Square 196
Campbell Square Cemetery 196
Campbellton 62
Canals 210–211
Cape Fear Agricultural Society 149
Cape Fear and Deep River Navigation Company (Works) 213, 214
Cape Fear and Western Steam Boat Company 217
Cape Fear and Yadkin Valley Railroad 221
Cape Fear Canal Company 211
Cape Fear Company 212
Cape Fear Herald (Wilmington) 169, 228
Cape Fear Lodge 124
Cape Fear Lodge, No. 2, International Order of Odd Fellows 144
Cape Fear Marine Total Abstinence Society 160
Cape-Fear Mercury (Wilmington) 47
Cape Fear Navigation Company 212–213, 214
Cape Fear Ocean Steamship Navigation Company 110, 220
Cape Fear Recorder (Wilmington) 170, 177
Cape Fear Riflemen (volunteer uniformed militia company) 145
Cape Fear River 6, 8, 51–52, 62, 88, 211; attempts to improve navigation of 68, 102, 107, 212–215; and canals 211; claims lives in accidents 118; commerce on, halted by inability of British to distribute tax stamps 64, 77; ferries over

60; improvements at mouth of 214; interrupted by British naval vessels, privateers, during Revolutionary War 65; pilotage system on 66, 67–68; proves of strategic value during American Revolution 86; shoals in 11; steam navigation on 216–221; trade on, expands rapidly after Revolutionary War 69; water levels of 207
Cape Fear Steam Boat Company (1822) 216
Cape Fear Steam Boat Company (1848) 218
Cape Fear Steam Saw Mill 110
Captive Israelites (traveling art exhibition) 180
Captured vessels: in Revolutionary War 65
Carey, James 169
Carolina (oceangoing steamship) 219, 220
Carolina (sailing packet) 217
Carolina Hotel 201, 202
Carolina Yacht Club 120, 123, 204
Carr, James: advertisement of, quoted 201
Carr, Thomas B. 117
Cartagena (Spanish fortress): English attack on 71
Carter, Mr. (magician) 119
Cassidey, James 104, 177, 195, 203, 204
Cassidey, Jesse J. 204
Cassidey House (1828) 177
Castle Hayne: ferry at 60
Castle Haynes Plantation 39, 40
Cazaux, Dominique 119, 201
Cazaux, John M. 102–103
Cemeteries 154, 179, 195–196; for African Americans 196–197
Chair makers 179
Chamber of commerce 148
Chapman, Mr. (writing instructor) 169
Charity schools *see* Free schools
Charles (slave of Dr. James Geekie) 34
Charles II 5
Charles Town (along Cape Fear River): site of first English attempt to settle Lower Cape Fear region 5–6
Charles Town (Charleston), S.C.: provides nucleus for settlement of South Carolina 6
Charleston, S.C. 42, 51, 54–55, 59, 70, 90
Charleston Theater Company 180
Charlotte, N.C. 51, 224; produce from, shipped to Cross Creek 62

Cherry Street Mariners' Church (New York) 160
Chesapeake (American naval frigate) 230
Chevra Kadisha (Jewish organization) 154
Children: and disease 113, 114
Chimneys: regulation of 25
Chinese Temple (plantation) 29
The Chorister's Companion (songbook) 47
Church of England *see* Anglican Church
Circe (British vessel) 231
Circuses 119–120
Cisterns 197
City Hotel (Wilmington) 107, 202
Civil disturbances 36
"Clampsus Vitus" (social group) 143
Clarendon (harbor steamer, 1850s) 224
Clarendon (steamboat, 1830s) 149, 217
Clarendon Company 217
Clarendon Horse Guards (volunteer uniformed militia cavalry company) 145, 240
Clarendon House (hotel) 201
Clarendon Lodge, No. 45, International Order of Odd Fellows 144
Clarendon Race Track 121
Clark, Samuel A. 171
Clark, Thomas 15
Clark's Island 230
Classical schools *see* Academies
Clay, Henry 232
Clay, Margaret 29
Claypoole, Dr. (physician) 49
Clinton, Sir Henry 87
Clothing business: women in 202–203
Coastal trade 208
Cobham, Thomas 80, 91
Cochran, Thomas 231
Cockfights 41
Coercive Acts *see* Intolerable Acts
Cohen, Dr. (physician) 115
Col. John McRae (barque) 218
Coleman, Richard 168
Collins, Mr. (comedian and vocalist) 181
Comedy *see* Theatrical entertainment
Commerce 51, 52–53, 53–54, 58, 59, 60, 63, 77, 156; central to Wilmington economy 200; rapid growth of 206, 208; resumes at end of Revolutionary War 66, 69, 70; *see also* Exports
Commerce (oceangoing steamship) 219
Commercial (Wilmington) 170, 172; attempts to provide news without use of telegraph 175

Index

Commercial Bank of Wilmington 205, 206
Commercial Hotel (Wilmington) 160, 201
Commercial vessels 56–57, 58
Commission houses 57
Commission merchants 200
Commissioners *see* Town commissioners
Commissioners of navigation and pilotage for the Cape Fear River 112, 132, 159, 195, 230, 239; *see also* Board of Commissioners of Navigation and Pilotage for the Cape Fear River
Committee of Thirteen 215
Committees of correspondence 80
Committees of safety 65, 90; demise of 87–88; enforce non-importation and non-exportation of British goods 83–84; engage in military preparedness 86, 87; key role of, in effecting American Revolution 88; resort to intimidation to secure support for Revolution 84–86
Common council 20
Common schools *see* Public schools
Company G, Twelfth Regiment, U.S. Infantry (Mexican War) 240
Company H, First Regiment (Mexican War) 240
Compromise of 1850 241
Compton, Spencer 14; pictured 15
Concerts 181–182
Concord Chapter, No. 6 (Masonic Order) 143
Congress: funds improvements to Cape Fear River 214, 215
Connor, R. D. W.: quoted, concerning Cornelius Harnett as first chief executive of N.C. 82
"Conservatives" (post–Revolutionary period) 93
Constables 26, 27, 186
Constitution (model ship) 235
Constitution of the United States 95; debate on ratification of 96–97, 97–98
Constitutional Convention of 1835 (N.C.) 128, 233–234, 234
Constitutional Union Party 241
Consumption 113
Contagious diseases *see* Epidemics
Continental Association 65, 83
Continental Congresses 65, 81, 83, 93
Cooke, Sarah Ann 167
Cooper English Opera Troupe 182

Cornwallis, Charles 87, 92; quoted, concerning importance of dispatching military expedition into Cape Fear region 90; seeks to establish military post in Wilmington 90
Costin, Ada Amelia 120
Costin, Miles 153
Cotton 59, 205, 207
Cotton Plant (steamboat) 216, 217, 218
Cotton Plant Steam Boat Company 216, 218
Council of Safety 82, 88
Cowan, Mrs.: house of, sustains fire 110
Cowan, Thomas 129, 229
Craftsmen 19, 30, 104; and development of Wilmington 63; *see also* Artisans
Craig, James Henry 90, 91, 92–93, 93; quoted, concerning need to reassure resident loyalists by sustained military presence 93
Crane, C. P. 116
Crime 109
Cromwell, Mr. (proprietor of traveling theatrical group) 181
Cronly, M. 135
Cross Creek (Fayetteville) 51, 61–62, 63
Cruizer (British warship) 82, 86, 87
Cultural activities 42–43
Cumbo, Solomon (free black) 36
Cunningham, Ann Pamela 146
Cunningham, Thomas 19
Cupid (runaway slave of Robert Brown) 131
Curfews 31, 36, 127, 192
Currency Act (1764) 64, 74
Curtis, Moses Ashley: quoted, concerning hysteria in Wilmington resulting from rumor of slave revolt 133
Cushing, Mrs. (music teacher) 167
Customs districts (British) 53
Cutlar, Andrew 142

Daguerreotypists 180
Dailey, Miss (music teacher) 167
Daily Herald (Wilmington) 173; see also *Wilmington Herald*
Daily Journal (Wilmington) 170, 173
Dan (free black) 133
Dancing 40, 41, 120
Dancing schools 168
Danseuse Viennoise (entertainers) 181
Davie, William R. 96, 143
Davis, Ansley 135
Davis, George W. 132, 146, 176

Davis, Jehu 7, 13
Dawson, John 202
Dayton, Henry 70
Debating societies 176
DeBois, John 57
De Chanla, Mr. (language instructor) 168
Declaration of Independence 81
"Declaration of Rights and Grievances" 75
Deems, C. F. 146, 176
Deep and Haw River Company 212
Deep River 51
Deism 46
de Miranda, Francisco: characterizes residents of Wilmington 40; quoted, concerning condition of houses in Wilmington 37-38
Democratic Party 171, 172, 235, 236, 237, 239, 240, 241
DeMott, Mortimer: criticizes Wilmington, its citizens, its lodgings 106
DeNeale, Mrs. (seller of food items) 202
Dentistry 117-118
Deportation (of free blacks, liberated slaves) 134
DeRosset, Armand J., Jr. 108, 115, 129, 177, 195
DeRosset, Armand John, Sr. 19, 29, 49, 115, 239
DeRosset, Catherine (Kate) Douglass (Mrs. Armand J. DeRosset, Jr.) 108; quoted, concerning care of sick children 113, concerning economic conditions in Wilmington 200
DeRosset, Elizabeth Catherine Bridgen 29
DeRosset, Lewis Henry 18, 19, 73
DeRosset, Mary 29
DeRosset, Moses John 19, 49; quoted, in mitigating Wilmington's opposition to Stamp Act 78
DeRosset and Brown (mercantile firm) 220
DeRosset House (1841) 177
DeVries, Madame Rosa (opera singer) 182
Il Diavolo Antonio (entertainer) 119
Dibble and Brother 218
Dick, William 201
Dickinson, Platt K. 105, 195; quoted, concerning implications of John Brown's Raid 241
Dick's Hotel 103, 201
Dickson, James H. 112, 115, 134, 176

Diligence (British sloop) 77, 78
Disloyalty (to American cause) 85
Dismal Swamp Canal 211
Divorce 31
Dix, Dorothea: quoted, concerning condition of New Hanover County poorhouse 155
Dobbs, Arthur 20, 59, 71, 73, 77; cited 53, 54
Dr. Laroque & Son 116
Dogs: control of 191-192
Dolphin (oceangoing steamship) 219
Domestic life *see* Family life
Don Quixote Invincibles (social group) 143
Donnetti, Sig. (entertainer) 119
Dorsey, Lawrence 44
Dorsey, Mrs.: tavern of 103
Dorsey's Tavern and Coffee House 41, 44, 142
Dougal, Captain (owner of steamboat) 217
Douglas, Stephen 241
Douglass, David 43
Drainage 23
Drama *see* Theatrical entertainment
Drays and draymen 190, 191
Drownings 118
Dry, N. 118
Dry, William 13
Dry-goods merchants 200-201
DuBois, Peter: quoted, concerning appearance of houses in Wilmington 37, concerning lack of social amenities in Wilmington 40
Dudley, Edward B. 105, 158, 233, 237; pictured 237
Dudley Mansion (ca. 1825): pictured 238
Dueling 118
Dunbibin, Daniel 18
Duncan, Alexander: will of, quoted 19
Duncan McRae (steamboat) 217
Dunmore, Lord (governor of Virginia) 35
Duplin Road 60
Duprez and Green's Minstrels 182

Eagles, Richard 15
Eagles Island 20, 60; causeway leading through, shown on detail of map 61; ferry operated to and from, pictured 61
Ecce Homo (painting) 45
Economic recessions 200

Edenton, N.C. 6, 37, 51, 53
Edward (black steward aboard brig *Fisher*) 132
Ehrhardt, ____ (German immigrant to Wilmington) 103
Elde, Mrs. (proprietor of boarding establishment) 202
Electoral "tickets" 239
Elizabethtown, N.C. 60
Ellenwood, H. S. 170, 171
Elliot, Mr. (Quaker): aids runaway slaves 131–132
Ellis, Charles D.: cited 161
Embargo of 1807 199, 230
Embezzlement 27
Emigration from N.C. 101
Empie, Adam 134
England *see* Great Britain
England, John 154
Entertainments *see* Public entertainments
Epidemics 49, 67, 109, 112–113
Episcopalians 141, 150
"Era of Good Feelings" 232
Estabrook, Mr. (lecturer) 176
Ethiopian Serenaders (minstrel group) 182
Etiwan (oceangoing steamship) 220
Evans, Allen 139
Evans, Nathaniel 42–43
Everard, Richard: makes land grants in Cape Fear region 7
Everett, Edward 146
Evergreen (light-draft vessel) 218
Every Man His Own Doctor; or, the Poor Planter's Physician (medical manual) 49
Excelsior Opera Troupe 182
Exports 206; expand rapidly after Revolutionary War 69; inspection system for 58, 204–205; from province of N.C. 55; from Port Brunswick 54–55; *see also* Commerce
Express (oceangoing steamship) 220

Factors 200
Fairchild, Mrs. (milliner) 202
Fallon, James 85
"Family" (men related by blood or marriage who received questionable grants of land in Cape Fear) 7, 8, 9, 12, 13
Family life 108–109
Fanning, P. W. 170; advertises houses for sale 107–108
Faris, William 15, 19, 45, 73

Faris & Lindsay (mercantile firm) 73
Fayetteville (steam tugboat) 218
Fayetteville (steamboat) 218
Fayetteville and Western Plank Road Company 209
Fayetteville Cadets (militia company) 146
Fayetteville Convention 97
Fayetteville Gazette 47
Fayetteville Independent Company (militia company) 146
Fayetteville, N.C. 37, 51, 62, 70, 73, 101, 102, 209, 210; percentages of African American population of, during antebellum period 125; percentages of free black population of, during antebellum period 126; in rivalry with Wilmington for trade and commerce 221
Fayetteville Observer 171, 172
Federal gunboat Number 9, 230
Federal-style architecture: Wilmington examples of 177
Federalist Party 95, 96, 97–98, 171, 205, 227, 228, 229, 230, 231
Fees 197, 198
Female Benevolent Society 155
Fennell, Owen 129
Ferguson, Wattie 181
Ferries 8, 10, 29, 60, 210; between Eagles Island and Wilmington, pictured 61
Fillmore, Millard: visits Wilmington 236
Fines 27, 197
Finian (summer residence of William Hooper) 80
Finlay, Hugh 48; detail of map by, reproduced 61; quoted, concerning condition of Wilmington 37
Finney, Thomas 18
Fire companies 122, 193
Fire engines 26, 193, 194
Fire insurance 111
Fire wardens 193, 194
Fireproof buildings 111
Fires 24–25, 39, 109–111, 194, 198; prevention of 193; protection from 20, 25–26, 111, 193
First Baptist Church 141, 152, 177; drawing of, reproduced 153
First North Carolina Regiment (Mexican War) 240
First Presbyterian Church 151, 177; drawing of, reproduced 151
Fisher (brig) 132
Flanner, Joseph H. 118
Flatboats (flats) 57, 206–207

"Flats" (shoals in Cape Fear River) 11, 52, 70
Flavell, William: will of, quoted 45
Flax 59
Fleming's Company (traveling theatrical group) 181
Flora MacDonald (steamboat) 122, 146
Florance, Z. 117
Florence (brigantine) 132
Flour (as export) 69, 207; regulations concerning inspection of, quoted 204
Foodstuffs (as export) 56, 59, 207
Forage (as export) 204, 205
Forster, John 88
Fort Cumberland (Md.) 72
Fort Johnston 49, 66, 66–67, 71; destroyed by militia assault 86
Fort Sumter: attack on 242
Fortuna (Spanish warship) 72
Fourth of July 123, 229
France: engages in war with Great Britain 71, 72
Frank (runaway slave owned by John Burgwin) 129
Frank (runaway slave owned by David Greer) 131
Frank Johnson's Band 139, 148
Franklin, John Hope: cited 127
Free blacks 35–38, 125–126; restrictions placed on activities of 127–128, 128–129, 129; work in building trades 137
Free Masons Hall 143
"Free Negro Code" 127, 128
Free schools 155, 166
Freeman, John H. 118
Freemasonry *see* Masonic Order
French and Indian War 67, 72, 74
French Opera Comique 182
Frensley, J. L. 168
Frensley's Dancing School 189
Front Street 62, 190
Front Street Baptist Church 150
Front Street Methodist Church 141, 152
Frost and Co. (equestrians) 119
Frying Pan Shoals 52, 68
Fugitive Slave Act 135
Fuller Mr. (Quaker): aids runaway slaves 131–132
Fulton, David 170; quoted, concerning utility of reading rooms 175
Funeral Procession in Charleston of John C. Calhoun (traveling art exhibition) 180
Funerary sculptures 179
Furniture 178–179

G. F. Marchant's Company (traveling stock company) 184
Gambling 42, 118–119; *see also* Wagering
Gas lights 107
Gaspee (British revenue cutter) 80
Gaston, William 234
Gause, Thomas F. 192
Gautier, Thomas N. 230
Geekie, James 34, 36, 49
General Assembly: addresses need to care for ailing seamen 157–158, 159, 160; approves quitrent legislation 12; attempts to curb gambling, excessive drinking, in ordinaries 44, to improve navigation of Cape Fear River 68, to lure backcountry trade to east coast 60, to regulate free blacks 36, 127–128, 128–129, to regulate slaves 126–127; authorizes new street in Wilmington 22; authorizes town commissioners to assess ground rents 22; confers power to tax upon Wilmington town commissioners 26; curbs disproportionate political representation of Albemarle region 73; declares existence of town (Brunswick) along Cape Fear River 8; directs Wilmington town commissioners to repair fire engine 26; enacts legislation restricting freedom of slaves in Wilmington 33; erects New Hanover Precinct (County), designates its seat 8; establishes Anglican Church in N.C. 45; establishes public school system 166; evidences deeper interest in creation of roads after War of 1812 209; institutes slave patrol system 34; names Newton as site of sessions of new court 12; officially confirms incorporation of Newton as town of Wilmington 16; orders construction of coastal forts 71; and pilotage system 66, 67; places restrictions on eligibility for voting in Wilmington municipal elections 237–238; quoted, concerning absence of prison in Wilmington 36; responds to petition in favor of erecting Newton as town of Wilmington and seat of New Hanover County 13–14; underwrites, requests federal funding for improvements at mouth of Cape Fear River 214

Gen. Clinch (oceangoing steamship) 220
General Washington (brig) 88, 89
George (brig) 36
George II 14
Geo. Christy's Minstrels 182
George Harris (schooner) 132
George L. Champion (harbor steamer) 224
German Brass Band 143
German immigrants (to Wilmington) 103, 152
German Volunteers (militia company) 103, 123, 145, 241
Gibbs, M. M. (Miss) 182
Gillott, Benjamin 179
Gilmer, John 237
Gladiator (oceangoing steamship) 219
Glasgow (runaway slave of Taylor & Williams): newspaper advertisement for return of, reproduced 130
Glee club 147
Godfrey, Thomas, Jr. 42
Gothic Revival architecture: Wilmington examples of 177
Gov. Dudley (oceangoing steamship) 219, 220
Gov. Graham (steamboat) 218
Graffenried, Christoph von 6
Graham, William A.: quoted, concerning maintenance of highways 209
Grainger, Joshua, Sr. 9
Grand Encampment of Odd Fellows in North Carolina 144
Grand Lodge of North Carolina, International Order of Odd Fellows 124
Grand Royal Arch Chapter of North Carolina (Masonic Order) 144
Grange, John 7
Gravestones: carving of 179
Gray, William 9, 10
Great Britain: attempts to strengthen control over American colonies in wake of victory in French and Indian War 74; engages in war with Spain and France 71; forcefully regulates commerce of its empire 52–53, 63–65; trade with 53, 54, 55, 66, 69, 70
Great Moguls (social group) 143
"Great Northern and Southern Mail" (coastal mail route) 174
Great Revival 149
Greek Revival architecture: Wilmington examples of 177

Green, Rebecca 49
Green, Samuel 19, 49
Greene, Jack P.: cited 74
Greene, Nathanael 90, 92
Greer, David 131
Gregory, Mrs.: hotel of 121
Grigg, Fredrick 17
Griswold, Mr. (singing instructor) 168
Gubernatorial elections 232, 237
Gunn, I. C. C. 201

Hale, Edward J. 172
Halifax, N.C. 51
Hall, Allmand 169, 171, 172
Hall, Clarinda L. 163
Hall, Lydia: quoted, in chastisement of her son 108
Hall, William 108
Hall's Wilmington Gazette 169
Halsey, Henry: "New House" of 183
Halton, Robert 13, 16
Hamilton, Alexander 227
Hamilton, Elizabeth 118
Hamilton, Thomas D. 162
Hanover Hotel 201
"Hanover Lodge" (Masonic Order) 44
Hanover Sons of Temperance 147
Harbor master (for Wilmington) 68, 69
Harbor steamers 224
Harmonic Society (musical group) 147
Harnett, Cornelius 17, 18, 28, 29, 44, 48, 63, 73, 74, 78, 80, 81, 84; becomes Wilmington's most active patriot 82–83; captured by British 92; epitaph of, quoted 46; quoted, concerning Articles of Confederation 94, concerning consistency of local resistance to British tariffs 79
Harnett, Cornelius (the elder) 7–8
Harnett, Mary 29–30
Harris, William J. 115
Harris and Springs (Wilmington blacksmiths) 129
Harrison, Mr. (daguerreotypist) 180
Harrison, William Henry 235
Harriss, George 220
Hartford Fire Insurance Company 111
Hart's Free School 166
Harvey, John 74
Hasell, William S. 169, 171, 175
Hathaway, John 200
Haw River 51
Hawkins, Mr. (candidate for constable) 186

Haynes, Margaret 39
Hazard, Ebenezer 48; quoted, concerning appearance of Wilmington 37
Headstones: carving of 179
Health *see* Public health
Hebrew Cemetery 154
Hector (ship) 58
Hellier, Richard 18, 23
Helper, Hinton Rowan 241
Hemp 59
Henrietta (steamboat) 216, 217, 218
Henrietta Steam Boat Company 216, 217–218
Hermitage plantation 40
Heron, Benjamin 26
Heron, Mary 28
Heron's Bridge 210
Hewes, Joseph 81
Higginbotham, Matthew 10
Higgins, Michael 9, 45
Highland Scots 86, 87, 89; *see also* Scots
Highways *see* Roads
Hill, Frederick C. 170
Hill, John: quoted, concerning unhealthy geographic characteristics of Wilmington 111–112
Hill, Joseph A. 233, 234
Hill, William 49
Hill, William H. 97
Hillsborough Convention 96
Hillsborough, N.C. 51, 63, 79; produce from, shipped to Cross Creek 62
Hilton Bridge 210
Hiram (schooner) 230
Hirsh, S. 179
Hogg, James 63
Hogg, Robert 63, 80, 89
Hogg and Campbell (merchants) 63
Holden, Thomas 109
Holiday observances 121–124, 140
Holmes, L. 163
Holmes, Owen 128, 234, 235; quoted, in opposition to borough representation 234–235
Holmes Hotel 236
Hook and Ladder Company Company No. 1 194
Hooper, Johnson Jones 177
Hooper, Mrs. William 35
Hooper, Thomas 28
Hooper, Tom 46
Hooper, William 33, 80, 81, 95; becomes leading opponent of British policies in Wilmington 80; elected Wilmington borough representative in General Assembly 94; portrait of, reproduced 81; quoted, concerning activities of loyalists in Wilmington 90, concerning fate of letter to friend 48; concerning his son's future 46, concerning institution of marriage 28, concerning loyalty of slave during Revolutionary War 35, concerning treatment of women during British occupation of Wilmington 91–92; signs Declaration of Independence 81
Horse Artillery (volunteer uniformed militia company) 145
Horse racing 41, 120–121
Hort, William P. 115
Hospital Fund (federal; for sick or disabled American seamen) 157, 161
Hospitality (of province of N.C. and Wilmington) 40
Hostler, James (liberated slave) 126
Hotels 106, 107, 108, 201–202
House of Commons (lower house of colonial N.C. legislature): considers legislation to establish a town named Wilmington 10–11; quickly approves bill to incorporate Newton as town of Wilmington 13
Houses 37–39
Houston, William 36; quoted, concerning reaction to his appointment as Stamp Receiver 75
Howard, Caleb D. 47, 96
Howard, Henry B. 194
Howard Fire Company 122, 194
Howe, Robert 80; leads assault on Fort Johnston 86
Howe family (African Americans) 137
Hunt, Thomas P. 146
Hunter, Robert 116
Hunt's Free School 166
Huske, John 44, 91, 95, 96, 97, 228
Hyrne, Edward 7

Illegitimate children 28
Immigration (to Wilmington) 28, 102–105
The Impending Crisis 241
Imports 53, 54, 70, 207–208
Incorporated Master Mechanics 148
Indentured servants 30
Independent Artillery Company (volunteer uniformed militia company) 145
Indigo 59; as export 56

Index

Infant mortality 114
Infidelity 28
Innes, James 46, 71, 72; will of, quoted 46
Innes Academy 46, 163
International Order of Odd Fellows 111, 124, 144, 164
Interstate packets *see* Packets
Interstate steam navigation 219–221; *see also* Steam navigation
Intolerable Acts (1774) 65, 81
Iredell, James 96; quoted, concerning grand ball in Wilmington 41
Irish 103
Italianate architecture: Wilmington examples of 177

J. Insco Williams's Bible Panorama (traveling exhibit) 180
J. L. Cassidey (flatboat) 207
J. Morris's Concert and Olio Company (minstrel group) 182
J. W. Blodgett (barque) 218
Jack (runaway slave of Samuel Noble) 131
Jackson, Andrew 121, 171
Jackson, William C. 175
Jacksonian Democrats 232
Jacobs Spring 197
James, Thomas 19
Jarman, Harvey 57
Jasper (oceangoing steamship) 220
Jefferson, Joseph: quoted, concerning condition of theater in Innes Academy 184, concerning variety of dramatic fare offered in nineteenth century 181
Jeffersonian Republicans 171, 205, 227, 228, 229, 230, 231, 232
Jeffreys, William 137
Jenner, Edward 112
Jewett, George W. 165
Jews 103–104, 154
Jocelin, Henry 178
Jocelyn, Amaziah 70
Jocelyn, Betsy 118
Jocelyn, Clara 118
Jocelyn, F. J. 179
Jocelyn, Samuel: quoted, concerning death of his daughter 118
John (otherwise unidentified native of Portugal) 103
John (slave) 132
John (slave of William Hooper) 35
John (slave, possibly an apprentice of cabinetmaker John Nutt) 137

John Brown's raid 135, 241
John C. Calhoun (pilot boat) 204
John Kuner (John Kooner, Jonkonnu, John Canoe; Christmastime entertainment) 140, 143
John Ravel (ship) 218
John Walker (steamboat) 217
Johnson, A. L. D. 109
Johnson, Matthew 29
Johnson, Prisillla 29
Johnston, Gabriel 8, 13, 59, 71; challenges supremacy of Brunswick Town by acquiring land near forks of Cape Fear River 9; counters opposition to bill incorporating Newton as town of Wilmington 13–14; instrumental in transforming Newton into town of Wilmington 12, 13–14, 15; justifies incorporation of Wilmington as county seat of New Hanover 15; quoted, concerning goal of having all public business transferred from Brunswick Town to Wilmington 15; seeks to curb disproportionate political representation of Albemarle region 72–73; shows favoritism of Newton over Brunswick Town 11
Johnston, Samuel 96
Jones, Ann 22–23
Jones, Carter 169
Jones, Edward 142; elected Wilmington borough representative in General Assembly 94
Jones, John D. 233
Jones, Thomas 7
Jones, William W. 233
Jonkonnu *see* John Kuner
A Journal of a Tour in Texas; with Observations on the Laws, Government, State of Society, etc., etc. 101
Julien's Minstrels and Burlesque Opera Troupe (minstrel group) 182
Juvenile Female Working Society 155
Juvenile Poems on Various Subjects with The Prince of Parthia (volume of poetry by Thomas Godfrey Jr.) 43

Kate McLaurin (steamboat) 110
Kelly, Mary (indentured servant) 30
Kemble, Frances Anne (Fanny): quoted, concerning trip by railroad from Weldon to Wilmington 222–223, concerning Wilmington, its lodgings 106

Kemmerer, Mr. D. (singing instructor) 168
Kendall plantation 80
Kenna Company of Comedians 43
Kennedy, B. A. 117
Kennedy, Catherine G. 155
Kenon, Mrs. (teacher) 162
Kernington (brig) 58
Kilmiste, Eliza 181
Kilmiste, Emma 181
King George's War 71, 72
King Tammany (brig) 88
King's Highway 48
Kiple, Mr.: convicted of theft 109
Kitty (runaway slave of Jesse Bowden) 131
Know-Nothing Party 232–233
Kunke's Nightingale Opera Troupe (minstrel group) 182

Labazdier, Papen 169
Lacedemonian (British warship) 231
Ladies Benevolent Society 155–156
Ladies Working Society of St. James Episcopal Church 155, 166
The Lady of Lyons (play by Edward Bulwer-Lytton) 181
LaFayette Hotel 201
Lafayette Light Infantry (Fayetteville militia company) 146
L'Aimee Marguerite (French privateer) 228
Lamont, Alexander 186
Land grants: source of political divisiveness in Lower Cape Fear region 7, 8, 9
Langdon, William J. 161
Langdon, William S. 115
Language instruction 168–169
Lapierre, John: quoted, concerning settlement along Lower Cape Fear River 8
Larkins, Solon 135
Latimer, Zebulon 104; house of (1852) 108, 177
Laurens, Henry 59
Law enforcement 26, 186
Lawyers 19
Lazarus, Aaron 103–104, 154, 174, 177
Lazarus House (1819) 177; pictured 178
Lectures 119, 176
"Lectures on Hearts" (by a Mrs. Robinson) 43
Lee, Lawrence: cited 53
Legislative elections 228, 233, 234, 237
Leopard (British man-of-war) 230

Le Tellier, John 117
Levy, Jacob 104, 142, 154
Liberalist (Wilmington) 170
Libraries 175–176
Life and Correspondence of James Iredell 177
Lighthouses 68, 215
Lincoln, Abraham 135, 241, 242
Lind, Jenny 181, 182, 184
Lindsay, Robert 165
Liquor *see* Spirituous liquors
Livestock 210; as export 59, 207; regulation of 20, 24
Livingston, Duncan 119
Lobb, Jacob 78
Lockwoods Folly (Brunswick Town) 66, 211
Lodgings *see* Public accommodations
Logan, William 36
Long, J. S. 176
Lord, Eliza 166
Lords Proprietors 5, 6; desire establishment of towns in their overseas holdings 6
Loring, Thomas 117, 169–170, 170, 171, 172, 173, 176; elected special magistrate 186; opens reading room 175; quoted, concerning previous disagreement with fellow editor 172, concerning undesirability of political neutrality 171
Lotteries 42, 45, 119
Love, Mr. (entertainer) 119
Lovely Lass (privateer) 199, 231
Lower Cape Fear Historical Society 177
Lower Cape Fear region: avoids threat of invasion during Seven Years War 72; and backcountry trade 59, 60, 61, 62; center of opposition to Stamp Act 75–78; commerce of 58; control of, elusive to loyalists and British military 93; first English attempt to settle 5–6; harbors inordinately high numbers of slaves 31; major supplier of naval stores 55; permanently settled 7; plantations in, depicted on map 32; proves strategically important during American Revolution 86; resembles Lowcountry South Carolina 30; and runaway slaves 131; supplied with goods from northern coastal ports 208; unable to attract backcountry trade 59
Loyal Militia 91
Loyalist Claims Commission 89
Loyalists: characteristics of 89; heavily

Index

represented among merchants of Wilmington 89; persistence of 89–90
Lucy (runaway slave of John M. Van Cleef): newspaper advertisement for return of, reproduced 130
Lumber (as export) 56, 69, 207
Lumber River 211
Lumber River Canal Company 211
Lutherans 103, 152
Lyon, John 17, 63

Mackay, John 93
MacKenzie's Vaudeville Troupe 124
Maclaine, Archibald 19, 49, 80, 81–82, 94, 96; elected Wilmington borough representative in General Assembly 94; quoted, concerning excessive campaign tactics in municipal elections 94–95, on opinions of U.S. Constitution held within N.C. 95; supports proposed Constitution at Hillsborough Convention 96
Maclaine, Thomas 35, 91
Madame Rosa DeVries (opera singer) 182
Madison, James 230
Magee, Miss (teacher) 163
Magill, Captain (of sloop *Ranger*) 84
Magistrate of police (town office) 185, 186, 190
Mail *see* Postal service
Mail contracts 74, 219, 220
Mail routes 174
Malaria 48
Mann, Horace 164
Manufactured goods (as imports) 53–54
Manufacturing 203–204
Marek, John 167
Marine Hospital Service 157
Marine hospitals 157–160
Marine Hotel 202
Mariner (steam tugboat) 218
Mariners 36–37, 44, 156–157; health and welfare of 157–161
Marital infidelity 28
Marital separations 29
Market Street 62, 190
Marsden, Rufus 18
Marshall, Frederick William: quoted, concerning negative effects of American Revolution 70
Marsteller, Lewis H. 128, 234, 235
Martin, Catherine 47
Martin, Josiah 21, 34–35, 82, 86, 87, 90;
quoted, concerning efficacy of measures requiring mandatory militia service 85, concerning power exercised by committees of safety 88, concerning widespread indebtedness 64
Mason, Caleb 19, 23
"Masonborough's Grove" (poem by Thomas Godfrey, Jr.) 42
Masonic Hall 144, 184
Masonic Order 44, 119, 143
Massalong, Mr. (itinerant artist) 179
Mathews (member of outlawed group of runaway slaves) 131
Maxwell, William 24
McAden, Hugh 46
McDonald, Mrs. (proprietor of hotel) 202
McDowell, John 45
McKay, James 237
McLauchlin, Robert 164
McLorinan, Catherine 29
McLorinan, Charles 29
McMaster, William 109
McRae, Archibald 109, 175
McRae, Duncan 217
McRee, Griffith John 146, 149, 176; author of work on James Iredell 177
McRee, James F. 115, 116, 134
Meares, Gaston 108
Meares, John L. 115, 239
Meares, Kate DeRosset 120
Meares, Oliver P. 237
Mechanical Society 156
Mechanics 148, 156
Mechanics' Benevolent Society of Wilmington 156
Mechanics' Hotel 202
Medicines and medical practices 49–50, 116–117
Medway, A. 115
Medway, Miss (music teacher) 167
Meginney, Levin 164, 165
Mengart, Mrs. B. M. 203
Merchants 18, 31, 40, 148; and development of Wilmington 63; exhibit tendencies toward loyalism 89; in post-Revolutionary War period 70; selfishly profit from military contracts during War of 1812 231
Merchants' Coffee House 201
Merchants' Steam Boat Company 218
Meredith, William 152
Merrill, Walter A. 167
Messenger (Wilmington) 170, 172

Methodist church (Wilmington) 134
Methodist Meetinghouse 152
Methodists 46, 141, 152–153
Mexican War 240
Militia: in War of 1812 231; see also Patriot militia
Militia companies 103, 121, 122, 144, 241; see also Volunteer militia companies
Militia musters 44, 193–194, 230
Militia service 85, 193
Miller, Alexander C. 167
Milliners 203–204
Mindel, A. E. 103
Mineral springs 105
Minerva Wright (schooner) 132
Minstrel shows 182
"Minute Men" (radical secessionist group) 241
Miriam the Prophetess (traveling art exhibition) 180
Miss Eveline (dancer) 181
Mr. Edgar (traveling entertainer) 181
Mitchell, William 108
Moir, James 45; cited 46
Monroe, James 216, 232; visits Wilmington 231–232
Montgomery, John 13
Moore, George 22
Moore, Harriet 163
Moore, James: quoted, concerning his inability to hold under guard a man accused of disloyalty 85
Moore, Maurice: earliest known resident of Lower Cape Fear region 7; instrumental in permanent settlement of Lower Cape Fear 6, 7
Moore, Roger 7, 11, 12, 13, 16
Moore, Verina S. 163
Moravians 46, 59; trade with 60
Morris, Antone 103
Morris, James T.: advertisement for sale of slaves, quoted 135
Morse, Samuel F. B. 175
Mortality 118; by age 113–114; from disease 113; by months of year 114
Mortimer, James 19
Mortimer, John 49
Moseley, Edward 7, 8, 13, 16; map drawn by (1733) 9
Moses (runaway slave of John Barclay) 131
Mt. Tirza: hospital at 112, 159, 160
Mount Vernon Ladies' Association of the Union 146

Mozart Club 103, 148
Mozart Hall 168, 184
Mrs. Swann's Hotel 236
Mulattoes 28, 35
Mulock, Jesse 162–163
Municipal elections (Wilmington) 94–95
Murphey, Archibald D. 211
Murphy, Thomas 154
Murray, James 15, 16, 18, 28; appointed member of council 14; describes his dwelling 38; pictured 12; quoted, concerning necessities for doing business in Lower Cape Fear region 56, concerning prospects for town of Newton 11, on refusing to go to Brunswick Town to clear a vessel 12
Music schools 167
Musicians 143, 148
Myers, John W.: quoted, concerning importance of visual arts to cultural life in Lower Cape Fear 179
"Myrover House" 108

Napoleonic Wars 199, 206
Nash, Abner: quoted, concerning probable effects of British military occupation of Wilmington 90–91
Nash, Solomon 137
Nashville Convention 241
Nat Turner Insurrection 101, 133
National Republicans 232
Naval stores 55, 58–59, 59, 69, 204, 207, 220
Navigation Acts 52, 64
Navy (created by N.C. Provincial Congress to protect sounds, Cape Fear River) 88
Ned (runaway slave belonging to John Burgwin) 129
Neuse region 6
New Bern, N.C. 6, 37, 38, 51, 78, 79, 101, 102; percentages of African American population of, during antebellum period 125; percentages of free black population of, during antebellum period 126
"New Carthage town": shown on map drawn by James Wimble 9
New England: trade with 70
New Exeter 60
New Hanover Agricultural Society 149
New Hanover and Brunswick Agricultural Society 149

Index

New Hanover County court 13, 15, 19, 21, 26, 34, 129, 131
New Hanover County Courthouses 21, 187; location of, shown on map 38
New Hanover County jail 21; location of, shown on map 38; responsibility for upkeep of 187
New Hanover County militia 144–145
New Hanover County poorhouse 155
New Hanover County: population of 101; public buildings of, in Wilmington 21–22
New Hanover Horse Guards (volunteer uniformed militia company) 145
New Hanover Precinct (County) 8
New-Hanover School 163
New Hanover Troop of Light Horse (volunteer uniformed militia company) 145
New Inlet 52, 215
New Light Baptists 46
"New Liverpool" (early name for Wilmington) 9, 10
New Orleans Opera Troupe (minstrel group) 182
"New Town" (early name for Wilmington) 9, 21
Newbern Steam Boat Company 216
Newspaper publishing 172–173, 175
Newspapers 47, 169–173; important role of, in politics 171–172
"Newton" (early name for Wilmington) 9–10, 37; early growth of 10; favored by politicians over Brunswick Town 11, 12; initial dimensions of 10; named as site of sessions of new court 12; proposed for incorporation as "Wilmington" 11; residents of, seek to build courthouse 13
Newton, Thomas 19
Ninepenny Whist Club 142
Nixon's Royal Circus 120
Noble, Samuel 131
Non-exportation (of British goods) 83, 84
Non-importation (of British goods) 78–79, 83–84
Norcem, J. T. 168
Norfolk (steamboat) 216
North Carolina (colony): ruralism of 5
North Carolina (interstate packet intended to connect Wilmington and Philadelphia) 220
North Carolina (oceangoing steamship connecting Wilmington and Charleston) 219, 220
North Carolina (steamboat) 216, 217
North Carolina Baptist State Conference 152
North Carolina Confiscation Act (1779) 89
North-Carolina Gazette (Wilmington), page from, reproduced 76
North-Carolina Gazette and Weekly Post Boy (Wilmington) 47
North Carolina Grand Lodge (Masonic Order) 143
North Carolina Hotel 201
North Carolina Medical Society 115
North Carolina Militia 144
North Carolina Mutual Insurance Company 111
Northeast (branch) Cape Fear River 9, 52, 56, 57, 60, 62, 206, 210; ferries over 60
Northwest (branch) Cape Fear River 9, 51, 56, 61, 62, 206, 210
Nowland, Maurice: cited 56
Nutt, Henry 195
Nutt, John 178; advertisement for sale of slave of, quoted 137
Nye, Susan D.: comments on lodgings in Wilmington 106; criticizes Wilmington 106

Oak City Guards (Raleigh militia company) 146
Oakdale Cemetery 154, 179, 196, 197
Oceangoing steam navigation *see* Interstate steam navigation
Odd Felllows (fraternal organization) *see* International Order of Odd Fellows
Odd Fellows Academy 122, 189
Odd Fellows Hall 144
Odd Fellows School 164–165
O'Hanlon, Doyle 216, 218
"Old Drury" (theater) 184
"Old '76 Coffee House" 182
Oldfield, Captain: store of, catches fire 24
Olmsted, Frederick Law: quoted, concerning public accommodations in Wilmington 107
O'Neill, Glasgow (runaway slave of Taylor & Williams): newspaper advertisement for return of, reproduced 130
"Opera House" (Town Hall/Thalian Hall) 184
Opera troupes 182

Ophean Family (musical performers) 181
"Opposition" (reorganized Whigs) 237
Ordinances *see* Town ordinances
Ordinaries *see* Taverns
Otis, James 80
Outdoor activities *see* Social activities
Overland transportation 209–210
Owen, John 128

Packets (coastwise sailing vessels) 208, 217, 220
Painters 179
Pamlico region 6
Panic of 1819 101, 198, 199, 205
Panic of 1837 101, 199, 200
Panic of 1857 150
Panorama of the Mississippi River (traveling art exhibition) 180
Parker, Elizabeth 91
Parker, George 34
Parkersburg (interstate packet) 220
Parmele, Samuel 179
Parsley, Oscar G. 195, 202
Parties *see* Social activities
Party system 171
Patent medicines *see* Medicines
Patriot militia 84, 85, 86, 87, 90
Paupers *see* Poor relief
Peacock (British warship) 231
Peanuts (as export) 207
Pearl ash 59
Pee Dee Ethiopian Opera Troupe (minstrel group) 182
Peggy (runaway slave belonging to Jonathan Stanly): newspaper advertisement for return of, quoted 129
Peirson, Mrs. V. R. 202
Pelot, William M. 169
Penn, William 81
Pennsylvania: trade with 55, 59
Pennsylvania Farmer (brig) 88
People's Press (Wilmington) 170, 171
People's Press and Wilmington Advertiser 170, 171, 172
Person, Samuel J. 237
Peter (runaway slave found guilty of stealing) 35
Peter (runaway slave of Samuel Noble) 131
Peter (slave of Wilmington merchant): aids runaway slaves 131–132
Peter (slave who piloted ships in Wilmington harbor) 126
Petersburg, Va.: trade with 59

Petteway, S. 186
Philanthropist (proposed temperance newspaper, Wilmington) 147
Philanthropy 155
Phipps, Constantine 77
Phoenix Insurance Company 111
Physicians 19, 49, 114–116
Pierce, Franklin 236
Pilmore, Joseph 46
Pilot House (hotel) 202
Pilotage system 66, 67–68
Pilots (on Cape Fear River) 67, 68
Pine Forest Cemetery 197
Pitch *see* Naval stores
"A Plan of the Town of Wilmington" (map by C. J. Sauthier, 1769) 38
Plank roads 209–210
Plantations (along lower Cape Fear River): map of, reproduced 32
Plantations Melodists (minstrel group) 182
Player, Richard 18
Pleasants, Dr. (dentist) 117
Poisson, Frederick D. 237
Poisson, Louis J. 111, 115
Police officers 186
Polk, James K. 240; visits Wilmington 236
Pomarede, ____ (proprietor of traveling art exhibitions) 180
Pool, John 237
Poor relief 154–156
Poorhouses 154–155
Population statistics (Wilmington) 37, 101
Port Bath 53, 54
Port Beaufort 53, 54
Port Brunswick 11, 18, 52, 58, 66, 69; exports from 54–55, 56; imports through 53–54
Port Currituck 53, 54
Port Roanoke 53, 54, 69
Port Wilmington 66, 69
Porter, John 7, 8, 15
Portrait painters 179
Ports: regulation of, following Revolutionary War 66
Post, James F. 104, 178
Post offices (in N.C.) 174
Postal service 47–48, 173–174
Potash 59
Potter, Gilbert 160
Potts 94, 95
Prenuptial agreements 29

Presbyterian church (Wilmington) 134
Presbyterians 46, 150–151, 155, 166
Presidential elections 231–232, 235–236
Price, Alfred J. 170
Price, William J. 240
Primitive Physick, or an Easy and Natural Method of Curing Most Diseases (medical manual) 49
The Prince of Parthia (tragedy by Thomas Godfrey Jr.) 42, 43
Printens, I. A. 169
Printers 47
Privateering (off N.C. coast) 65, 231
Prizes of war *see* Captured vessels
Professional men 19
Prohibitory Act (1775) 65
Prometheus (steamboat) 216, 218, 232; drawing of, reproduced 217
Propeller (oceangoing steamship) 220
Prosser, Gabriel: insurrectionist plot of 133
Provincial congresses (N.C.) 81–82, 83, 88
Provincial Council 82
Provisions (as exports) 69, 204, 205
Public accommodations 106–108, 201–202
Public charity 111
Public dock: regulation of 22; responsibility for 187, 188–189
Public entertainments 119–120
Public health 48, 111–115, 195; and mariners 157–158
Public houses *see* Taverns
Public lectures *see* Lectures
Public market *see* Town market
Public schools: beginnings of 166–167
Purnell, Robert F. 116

Qua (slave) 35
Quakers 46, 132
Quamino (slave) 34
Quarantine regulations 66, 67, 195
Quince, Ann 228
Quince, John 58
Quincy, Josiah, Jr.: characterizes William Hooper 81; quoted, concerning efficacy of committees of correspondence 80, concerning hospitality encountered in province of N.C. 40, concerning treatment of slaves in province of N.C. 33

R. G. Musicians (musical group) 143
Rabies 24

"Radicals" (post–Revolutionary period) 93, 94, 95
Rafts 57, 206
Railroad excursions 120, 123
Railroads: contribute to economic growth, prosperity, of Wilmington 221–225; mail contracts of 74, 219, 220; speed arrival of news to newspaper publishers 174
Raleigh, N.C. 101, 102; percentages of African American population of, in antebellum period 125; percentages of free black population of, during antebellum period 126
Raleigh and Gaston Railroad 174, 223
Ranger (British sloop) 84
Rankin, Laura 147
Rankin, Robert: cited, quoted, concerning problems encountered by militia system 144
Rannie, Mr. (entertainer) 119
Read, Colonel (opponent of ratification of U.S. Constitution) 95, 97
Reading rooms (in libraries) 175, 176
Recessions *see* Economic recessions
Recorder (town official) 20
"Red Men" (association) 143
Regulator Movement 44, 79–80
Reid, David (of Duplin County) 236
Reid, David S. (of Rockingham County) 215
Reliance (oceangoing steamship) 220
Religion 45–46, 149–154; practiced by slaves 140–141
Republican Society of Wilmington 228
Republicans *see* Jeffersonian Republicans
Respiratory diseases 113
Restraining (Fisheries) Acts (1775) 65
Resurrection (traveling art exhibition) 180
Retail merchants 201
The Return of the Dove to the Ark (traveling art exhibition) 180
Revenue Act of 1764 64
Revenues (Wilmington) 197–198
Revival of 1858 149–150
Revolutionary War: and privateering 65; and slavery 35
Rice (as export) 56, 69, 205, 207
Rice, Nathaniel 13, 16
Rice mills 204
Richardson, Miss (teacher) 164
Rifle Cadets (volunteer uniformed militia company) 145

Index

Ritter, Hannah 109
Ritter, Moses: quoted, concerning pledge to support wife 109
River pilots *see* Pilots
Rivermen 57
Roads: construction, maintenance of 209; described 60; in eastern province of N.C. 60; state interest in, increases 209
Robinson, Mrs. (lecturer) 43
Robinson, R. 201
Robinson and Eldred Circus 119–120
Robinson and Lakes Great Southern Menagerie and Circus 120
Rock Spring Hotel 201, 202
Rock Spring Restaurant 201
Rock Spring Tent, No. 180, International Order of Rechabites (Wilmington temperance organization) 147
Roger (brig) 30
Roman Catholics 154
Rosin 55, 57, 207
Ross, Alexander 19
Rossiter, Mr.: traveling art exhibit of 180
Rowan (steamboat) 218
Rowan, Matthew 13, 16
Royal, Anne: praises Wilmington 106
Runaway slaves 34, 35, 129–131; newspaper advertisements for return of, reproduced 130
Rush, Benjamin 49
Russell, Mary E. 163
Rutherford, Griffith 93
Rutherfurd, John 18

Safety committees *see* Committees of safety
Sailors *see* Mariners
St. Andrew's Day 41, 103
St. Andrew's Presbyterian Church 151
St. David's Day 103
St. James Episcopal Church (Anglican prior to American Revolution) 19, 42, 45, 46, 140, 150, 154, 177, 179; cemetery of 195, 196; location of, shown on map 38
St. James Parish 16, 19, 45, 46, 150
St. John's Day 45, 143
St. John's Episcopal Church 150
St. John's (Masonic) Lodge (chartered as "St. John's No. 1," 1796) 44, 45, 143, 179
St. Mary's (oceangoing steamship) 220
St. Patrick's Day 103
St. Paul's (Episcopal) Church 141, 150
St. Paul's Evangelical Lutheran Church 103, 141, 152, 177
St. Philips Parish 45
St. Tammany's Lodge, No. 30 (Masonic Order) 143
St. Thomas Church (Roman Catholic) 154, 177
St. Thomas Parish (Roman Catholic) 154
Salem, N.C. 51, 60; produce from, shipped to Cross Creek 62
Salisbury, N.C. 51; produce from, shipped to Cross Creek 62
Sally Ann (schooner) 132
Sampson, James 137, 141
Sampson, Jessie B. 162
Samuel Beery and Sons: shipyards of 203, 204; steam sawmill of, destroyed by fire 110
Samuel W. Berry (ship) 241
Sarah (runaway slave): newspaper advertisement for return of, quoted 130
Saunders, Elizabeth 36
Sauthier, Joseph: map by 37, reproduced 38
Savannah, Ga. 90
Sawmills 56, 110, 204
Scantling (as export) 56, 69
Schaw, Alexander: quoted, concerning lack of hard money 64
Schaw, Janet: quoted, concerning ball in Wilmington 41, concerning houses in Wilmington 37, concerning intimidation of citizens to sign associations 84–85
Schaw, Robert 18, 80
Schenck, Nicholas W. 147
Schoepf, Johann David: quoted, concerning auction of slave father and son 34; estimates number of houses in Wilmington 37
Schools 162–167; abound in Wilmington in 1850s 163; for boys 162–163; initially fostered by religious sects 46
Schooners 58, 203, 206, 208
Scotch-Irish 46, 63, 89, 150
Scotland: trade with 54
Scots 41, 46, 63, 103, 150; *see also* Highland Scots
Scott, Andrew 116
Scott, Isaac 133
Scott, Robert 68
Scott, W. R. 117
Seamen *see* Mariners

Seamen's Bethel (church) 150, 160
Seamen's Friend Society 160–161; drawing of headquarters of, reproduced 161
Seamen's Home (Wilmington) 155, 160; drawing of, reproduced 161
Seawell, James 216
Secessionists 241
Second Bank of the United States 205
Second party system 232
Second Presbyterian Church 151
Separations (marital) 29
Sephardic Jews 103, 104, 154
Seven Years' War 72
Shaw, Daniel 237
Shaw, Mrs. (milliner) 202, 202–203
Shays Rebellion 94
Sheetz, Mr. (proprietor of singing school) 168
Sherwood, Daniel 233
Shingles *see* Wood products
Shipbuilding 203–204
Shipping *see* Commerce
Shriver, A. J. 118
Sidewalks 190
Silbey, John 47
Silk 59
Simmons, Samuel 109
Singing schools 168
Single women 29; *see also* Widows; Women
Slater, Dr. (lecturer) 176
Slave artisans 136, 137; competition from, resisted by white artisans 138–139, 148
Slave code 31
Slave insurrections 133; fear of 34–35, 133–134, 135; possible insurrection, prevented by militia 44; rumors of 133–134
Slave labor: town oversight of 192
Slave patrols 34, 35, 129
Slave trade 31, 54
Slavery 30, 240; associated to wealth of Lower Cape Fear region 31; generally defended in wake of antislavery efforts by abolitionists 134–135; in N.C. 125
Slaves (African) 30; diversions of 139–140; effect their escape from Wilmington aboard ships 131–132; enjoy relative freedom within towns 31–33; enjoy relative freedom within Wilmington 126; legislation governing, largely unenforced in Wilmington 137, 139; liberation of 35, 126; living conditions of 33–34; punishment of 34; regulation of 20, 33, 31–33, 35, 192; and religion 140–141; represent threat to white society after American Revolution 35; respond to bondage 34; restrictions placed on activities of 33, 126–127, 192; theft by 126; unusually large numbers of, reside in Lower Cape Fear region, Wilmington 31; work in building trades 136
Sloops 57, 58, 203, 206
Smallpox 49, 67, 112, 157, 195
Smallwood, James 18
Smith, Benjamin 68
Smith, Edward 7
Smith, John 231
Smith, Michael 45
Smith, Mrs.: boardinghouse of 110
Smith, William 13, 14, 16
Smith, William Russell 180
Smith-Anderson House (Wilmington) 39
Smith's Creek 210
Smithville 105, 219; steamship route to and from Wilmington 218–219
Smithville Canal Company (Brunswick County) 211
Snead, Thomas 230
Social activities 40–42, 120
Society Hall 187
Society of Friends: members of 46, 132
"Solomon's Lodge" (Masonic Order) 44
Sons of Liberty 75, 78, 79
"Sound Serenaders" (minstrel group) 182
South Washington (Watha) 60
"Southern Rights" 240–241
Spaight, Richard Dobbs 96
Spain: engages in war with Great Britain 71, 72
Spaulding, Philip 70
Spencer, Mr. (lecturer) 176
Spirituous liquors: sale, regulation of 193
Spray (steamboat) 122, 219
Sprunt, James: quoted, concerning Edward B. Dudley 105
Stamp Act (1765) 36, 64, 65, 74–78; local opposition to, noted in newspaper 76
Stamp Act Congress 75
Standard of Temperance (proposed Wilmington newspaper) 147
Stanly, Jonathan 129
Star (Raleigh): comments on reading rooms 175

Index

State Bank of North Carolina 205
Staves *see* Wood products
Steam navigation 215–219; *see also* Interstate steam navigation
Steam tugboats 218
Steamboat excursions 120, 123, 124, 140, 144, 146, 147
Steamboat traffic 107, 174, 207
Steamboats (on Cape Fear River): constitute fire hazard 110
Steuart, Andrew 47, 49
Stewart, Rev. Mr. (prospective schoolmaster) 47
Stokes, Montfort 133
Stores (in Wilmington) 201
Streets (in Wilmington) 23, 190
Sugar Act (1764) 74
Suggs, Simon (fictional creation of Johnson Jones Hooper) 177
Sun (steamboat) 110
Sutton, Lucy Ann 103
Swann, John 7
Swann, Mrs.: hotel of 236
Swann, Samuel 7, 8
Swiss Bell Ringers (musical performers) 181

Taggart, Sarah Jane 202
Tamar (liberated slave) 126
Tanneries 63
Tar *see* Naval stores
Tarboro, N.C. 51
Tariffs (imposed by British) 78
Tate, James 46
Tate, Robert 162
Tatum, Joel 180
Tavern keepers 29, 30, 36
Taverns 41, 43–44, 156, 193
Taxation 26–27, 197–198
Taylor, John A. 195
Taylor, John Louis 143
Tea Act (1773) 65, 81
Telegraph 172, 174–175
Telfair, James 142
Temperance newspapers: proposed for Wilmington 147
Temperance Sentinel (proposed Wilmington newspaper) 147
Temperance societies 146–147
Temple of Israel 154
Templeton, Mr. (vocalist) 181
"Test" *see* Associations
Thalbert, Sigismund 182
Thalian Association 43, 123, 124, 163, 180, 182, 184, 189, 210
Thalian Hall 180, 181, 182; *see also* Town Hall/Thalian Hall
Thally, David: advertisement of, quoted 201
The "Theatre" 184
Theatrical entertainment 42, 43, 180–181
Thetia (English brig) 218
Thomas (free black) 36
Thomas, George (indentured servant) 30
Thomas Smith & Co.: announcement of closing its mill, quoted 200
Thompson, Dugald 31
Thompson, Duncan 216
Thresal, Robert 31
Thumb, "General" Tom 119
"Tickets" (electoral) 239
Timber products 59, 207
Tobacco (as export) 56, 69, 207
Toole, Henry I. 170
Toomer, Henry 18, 24
Toomer, Joshua 19, 28; will of, quoted 44
Toomer, Magdalin Mary 126
Toomer's Alley 164
Topsail Tent (temperance organization) 147
Tories *see* Loyalists
Torrie, Dominque 102
Tousley, Mr. (bookkeeping instructor) 169
Town bell 197
Town clock 197
Town commissioners: actions by 17–20, 22, 23–24, 24–25, 46, 110, 111, 112, 127, 133, 137, 157, 185, 189, 190, 192, 193; and party politics 239–240; resolutions by (1847), affecting slaves, enumerated 127; specific responsibilities of 187, 188
Town Creek 11
Town governance (in province of N.C.) 20
Town Hall/Thalian Hall 105, 136, 175, 178, 184; construction of 189; drawing of, reproduced 183; *see also* Thalian Hall
Town market (Wilmington): regulation of 20, 22, 23–24, 187–188
Town ordinances: enforcement of 186; not obeyed by town commissioners 19; subjects of 20
Town revenues 197–198
Town watch 186–187, 198
Town wharf *see* Public dock

Towns: appear in province of N.C. 6; development of, in province of N.C. 60; in post–Revolutionary N.C. 101
Townshend tariffs (1767) 65, 78, 79
Trade *see* Commerce
Trade, Serena 109
Tradesmen: early examples of, in Wilmington 63
Tragedy *see* Theatrical entertainment
Transportation: advancements in 208–226
Trash: control of 24
Traveling art exhibitions 180
Treadwell, David: advertises sale of house 108
Trimble, James M. 178
True Republican (Wilmington) 169, 171, 228
Tryon, William 43, 44, 59, 60, 71; accepts apology for resistance of people of Wilmington to Stamp Act 78; attempts to placate opposition to Stamp Act 75–77; confronts Regulators at Hillsborough 79; moves seat of government to New Bern 78; quoted, concerning competency of his militia forces to quell uprising by Regulators 80, concerning need to accept provisions of Stamp Act 77, concerning support of people of Cape Fear region for action against Regulators 79, concerning value of slaves as dowry 31; reacts to armed resistance to provisions of Stamp Act 78
Tryon Palace (New Bern) 78
Turberg, Edward F.: quoted, concerning Bellamy Mansion 178
Turnpikes 209
Turpentine 55, 57, 63, 69, 207
Turpentine distilleries 110; drawing of distillery, reproduced 203
Tuscarora Indians 7
Tuscarora War 6, 72
Twelfth Regiment, U.S. Infantry (Mexican War) 240

Underground Railroad 131
Union Free School 166, 167
Unionists 241, 242
U.S. Army Corps of Engineers 214, 215
U.S. Public Health Service 157
Upper House (of colonial legislature): members of, express opposition to bill to incorporate Newton as town of Wilmington 13; membership of, altered by Gabriel Johnston as ploy to secure passage of bill erecting Wilmington as seat of New Hanover 14
Urbanism: in English America 5; in province of N.C. 60
Usher, James: newspaper advertisement for return of runaway slave of, quoted 130–131
Utley, John 186

Vail, Jeremiah 22
Vail, Mosely 7
Van Bokkelin, A. H. 219
Van Buren, Martin 235
Vann, W. T. J. 186
Vesey, Denmark: insurrectionist plot of 133
Virginia (oceangoing steamship) 219
Virginia Company of Comedians 43
Virginia ports 55
Visual arts 179–180
Volunteer militia companies 144, 145–146; *see also* militia companies
Vosburgh & Childs (chair makers) 179

"Waccamaw Tribe" (association) 143
Wachovia 59
Wagering *see* Gambling
Walker, David 128
Walker, John 15; quoted, concerning a political opponent 95; runs for Wilmington borough representative in General Assembly 94
Walker's Appeal in Four Articles (1829) 128
Wallace, S. D. 167
Walpole, Robert 14
Walter, Thomas U. 150
War of 1812 199, 206, 228, 230–231
War of Jenkins' Ear 71
War of the Regulation *see* Regulator Movement
Wardens of the poor 154, 158
Ware, William 117
Washington, George 97, 122, 228; cited 56; visits Wilmington 228–229
Washington and New Orleans Magnetic Telegraph Company 174–175
Washington House (hotel) 202
Washington Temperance Society 147
Water Street 62, 190
Watermen 57

Index

Watha, N.C. 60
"Watson" (town shown on map drawn by Edward Moseley) 9
Watson, Elkanah: quoted, concerning separation of a slave woman and her child 33–34
Watson, John 9
Watters, John W. 115
Waxworks 43, 47, 119
Weekly Herald (Wilmington) 173; see also *Wilmington Herald*
Wells 26
Wells, Robert 19
Welsh 103
Wessel, Jacob 103
West, S. M.: advertisement of, quoted 201
West, William M. 120–121
West Indies: trade with 53, 54, 56, 59, 66, 69, 70, 208
Westley, John 49
Whig Party 171, 172, 232, 233, 235, 235–236, 237, 239, 240, 241
Whigs (Revolutionary patriots) 84
Whitaker, Mrs. (music teacher) 167
Whitaker, S. W. 121
Whitney, John H. 167
Whooping cough 113
Widows 29; *see also* Single women; Women
Wigfall, Louis T. 241
"Wild Goose Club" (association) 143
Wiley, Calvin H. 176
Wilkins, M. R: store of 50
Wilkins, William C. 118
Wilkinson, Mrs. (milliner and mantua maker) 203
Wilkinson, William 18, 19, 63
William B. Meares (steamboat) 218
William Neff and Son: wharf of 220
Williams, D. Brown (lecturer) 176
Williams, G. W. 160
Williams, L. M. 186
Williams, Mr.: convicted of theft 109
"Williams' Long Room" 183
Williamsburg, Va. 42
Wilmington (oceangoing steamship) 219
Wilmington (steamboat) 147, 217
Wilmington, N.C.: accounts for large share of state's exports 206; advantages of life in 50; and American Revolution 63–65; architectural styles of homes, buildings in 177–178; attracts diverse population 28, 102–105; authorizes lotteries 42; avoids threat of invasion by British troops 87; borough charters of 20, 21; brief biography of namesake of 14; British occupation of 90–93; civil disturbances in 36; commissioners of 17–20; condition of streets in 23; crime in 109; cultural pursuits in 42–43; designated seat of New Hanover County 15; early governance of 16–18, 20–21, 22–27; early names for 9–10; early names for streets in 10; early surveys of 22; economic growth of 102, 206; emerges as cultural center 162, as incipient town 9; engraving of port of, reproduced 102; establishment of, enmeshed in political controversy 11; fires in 24–25, 39, 109–111, 194, 198; focal point for opposition to British 74, 75; initial major streets in 62; lack of public accommodations in 106–108, 201–202; legislators representing 73; maintenance of streets in 23; map of, at time of British occupation, reproduced 92; municipal elections in 94–95; occupations of early residents of 63; officially confirmed as seat of New Hanover County by General Assembly 16; opinions of early visitors to 37; population of 37, 101, 102, 105; public buildings in 22; public health of 48, 111–115; rapid growth of 185; regarded as hotbed of loyalism 89; residents of, take defensive measures against British, loyalists 87; in rivalry with Fayetteville for trade and commerce 221; shipping activity in, increases 208; social activities in 40–42; stagnates economically until 1840 199; stores in 201; streets, sidewalks in 190; taverns in 44; as transshipment point 62; undergoes boom period during late antebellum era 107; visitors' reactions to 106
Wilmington Academy 163, 164, 183, 184; drawing of, reproduced 165
Wilmington Advertiser 170, 171; quoted, concerning problems with delivery of mail 173
Wilmington Advertiser, and Merchants' and Farmers' Gazette 170
Wilmington and Charlotte Railroad 224
Wilmington and Manchester Railroad 174, 198, 220, 224
Wilmington and Masonboro Plank Road Company 209, 210

Wilmington and Raleigh Railroad 174, 221–222, 223; steamship line of 219–220
Wilmington and Raleigh (Weldon) Railroad Company 218
Wilmington and Smithville Steamboat Company 219
Wilmington and Top Sail Sound Plank Road Company 210
Wilmington and Walker's Ferry Plank Road Company 209, 210
Wilmington and Weldon Railroad 102, 105, 107, 122, 174, 203, 220–221, 222–223, 223, 224
Wilmington and Weldon Railroad Bridge 190
Wilmington Band 148
Wilmington Cemetery Company 195
Wilmington Centinel 95
Wilmington Centinel, and General Advertiser 47, 48, 169
Wilmington, Charlotte and Rutherford Railroad 198, 225
Wilmington Chronicle; and North Carolina Weekly Advertiser 169
Wilmington Cornet Band 148
Wilmington Empire Restaurant 201
Wilmington Fire-Company 193
Wilmington Fire department 194
Wilmington Gas Light Company 107
Wilmington Gazette 169, 171, 172, 228
Wilmington Herald 170, 172, 173, 175; *see also Weekly Herald* (Wilmington)
Wilmington Hotel 201
Wilmington Hotel Company 107, 202
Wilmington Institute 165
Wilmington Jockey Club 120
Wilmington Journal 170, 172, 173, 175
Wilmington Library Association 175, 176
Wilmington Light Infantry Armory 184
Wilmington Light Infantry Company (volunteer uniformed militia company) 145–146, 241
Wilmington Male and Female Seminary 165
Wilmington Marine Hospital Association 159
Wilmington-New Hanover Committee of Safety 65, 67, 83
"Wilmington Night Watch" 187
Wilmington Reporter 170
Wilmington safety committee 35, 41, 86;

advises against practice of horse racing 41–42; makes extensive preparations for war 87; quoted, concerning prohibition of exports 84; requires mandatory service in militia, signatures for associations 85
Wilmington St. Andrew's Society 103
Wilmington Savings Bank 206
Wilmington Steam Tug Company 218
Wilmington Temperance Society 146
"Wilmington Theatre" 184
Wilmington Total Abstinence Society (temperance organization) 147
Wilmington Volunteer Corps of Light Infantry (volunteer uniformed militia company) 145
Wilmington Volunteers (volunteer uniformed militia company) 145
Wilmington Weekly Chronicle 170, 171, 172
Wilmington Whistling Society 142
Wimble, Captain James (son of James Wimble) 39
Wimble, James 9; house of, appears on early maps 38, 39
"Wimbleton's Castle" (home of James Wimble) 38
Winslow, Warren 236, 237
Women: and home life 108–109; occupations of 202–203; and personal freedom 29; punishment of 26; *see also* Single women; Widows
Wood, Col. (entertainer) 119
Wood products 55, 56, 59, 69, 207
Woodward, Samuel 15
Word, J. (dance instructor) 168
Wright, Joshua Grainger 228, 233
Wright, Thomas: quoted, concerning economic conditions in Wilmington 199–200
Writers 177
Wye, Prof. (magician) 119

Yadkin and Cape Fear Canal Company 211
Yadkin River 211
Yates, Thomas Hall 126
Yellow fever 49, 109, 112, 157, 195
YMCA, Wilmington chapter 150
"The Young Men's Lyceum and Mercantile Library Association" 175

www.ingramcontent.com/pod-product-compliance
Ingram Content Group UK Ltd.
Pitfield, Milton Keynes, MK11 3LW, UK
UKHW041924140426
5217IPUK00014B/302